THE OUTBOARD BOATER'S HANDBOOK

THE OUTBOARD BOATER'S HANDBOOK

Advanced Seamanship and Practical Skills

Edited by
David R. Getchell, Sr.

International Marine
Camden, Maine

Published by International Marine®

10   9   8   7   6   5   4   3

Copyright © 1994 International Marine, a division of McGraw-Hill, Inc.

Library of Congress Cataloging-in-Publication Data
Getchell David R.
　　The outboard boater's handbook : advanced seamanship and practical skills / David R. Getchell, Sr.
　　　　p.　　cm.
　　Includes bibliographical references and index.
　　ISBN 0-87742-409-8 (alk. paper)
　　1. Outboard motorboats.　2. Seamanship.　I. Title.
VM348.G37　1994
623.88'2313-dc20　　　　　　　　　　　　93-48642
　　　　　　　　　　　　　　　　　　　　　CIP

Questions regarding the content of this book should be addressed to:
International Marine
P.O. Box 220
Camden, ME 04843

Questions regarding the ordering of this book should be addressed to:
McGraw-Hill, Inc.
Customer Service Department
P.O. Box 547
Blacklick, OH 43004
Retail customers: 1-800-822-8158
Bookstores: 1-800-722-4726

The Outboard Boater's Handbook is printed on acid-free paper.

Unless otherwise noted, all photographs and illustrations are by David R. Getchell, Sr.

Printed by Malloy Litho, Ann Arbor, MI

Design by John Reinhardt

Production by Dan Kirchoff

Edited by Jonathan Eaton, Pamela Benner, and Dorathy Chocensky

CONTENTS

ACKNOWLEDGMENTS

A BOOK AS LARGE AND BROAD in its coverage as this one draws on the expertise of many persons. It would not have been possible to create it, in fact, were it not for two main groups of contributors: the writers whose work appeared over the years in *Small Boat Journal* and its successors, who readily agreed to having their articles reprinted here, and the writers of many of the books published by International Marine, who let us reprint excerpts from these books that were directly applicable to small outboard-motor boats.

Represented in these pages from *Small Boat Journal* (now *Boating World*) are William C. Blizzard, the highly talented team of Paul and Marya Butler (whose work comes both from *Small Boat Journal* and International Marine books), Gary Diamond, Ray Hendrickson, Art Mosca, Charles Neuschafer, Graeme Paxton, Dag Pike, Nick Rukavina, Randy Scott, Bob Stearns, the late Norm Strung (represented here by his wife, Sil Strung, whose photos appear with Norm's article on electric outboards), Charles Summers, Ken Textor, Kevin Vanacore, Bob Whittier, and John Page Williams. Another important contributor is veteran outdoor writer Art Michaels.

International Marine writers include Captain Bob Armstrong, Jim Anderson, Nigel Calder, Don Casey, Leonard Eyges, Steve Henkel, Richard Thiel, and Allan H. Vaitses.

Deserving special mention for his knowledgeable writings and also for his welcome technical comments on the manuscript—to say nothing of his unflagging patience and cooperation in answering my interminable questions—is *Boating World* editor Richard Lebovitz. In the same expert league is Pamela Benner, International Marine's associate managing editor, who always kept things moving no matter what the complications.

And then there were old friends with whom I have shared untold hours in work and play and who have given unstintingly of their wisdom over the years. These are mentor John Gardner, whose inspiration and expertise have fueled my love for small boats for some 35 years; Chris Cornell, longtime fishing and boating companion and presently editor of *Professional BoatBuilder* magazine; Steve Spencer, a passionate lover of small boats and wild islands; and Jim Fullilove, who took over my old job as editor of *National Fisherman* and has capably filled that seat for nearly a dozen years.

Finally, this book would not exist without the direct help and loving encouragement and support of my wife, Dorrie.

—David R. Getchell, Sr.

INTRODUCTION

THE SMALL OUTBOARD-MOTOR BOAT is the ultimate magic carpet. With it you can visit thousands of places where yachts can never go, and yet you can go nearly everywhere the larger pleasure boats do. Unlike heavier craft, your little boat can be driven over land as easily as over water, and though your boat may not yet be flown, it can be used to realize your dreams of adventure like nothing else, carrying you on journeys of seeking and of self to the point where you are pushing the limits of boat and master. Strangely enough, few people, including thousands of small-boat owners, are aware of the real potential resident in that 16 feet or so of fiberglass, aluminum, or wood sitting on a trailer in their backyard.

The purpose of this book is to show you how to turn that potential into reality. To do so requires a lot of how-to information, and there is plenty of good stuff here to help you get off on the right course. But equally important is lots of you-can encouragement, urging you to open your mind and talents to the almost limitless possibilities inherent in small boats and not be intimidated by Conventional Wisdom (CW) or Certified Experts (CE). CW is composed mainly of the great American public which, as a body, knows virtually nothing about small boats. As for the many experts, some are and some are not—expert, that is. In this book, we share the expertise of a few real CE's, ones who have become so by studying their craft, learning from others, and, significantly, by doing. We also get good advice from other doers, ordinary people who have "been there," whether their "there" is building a boat, modifying one to meet their specific needs, cruising to some distant shore, or just making an insightful comment, such as the following by John Page Williams on what was and is a good hull: "It is too bad they don't make a nice, round-sided planing hull like the old MFG anymore. It is so good for some needs." We will revisit the theme of his lament more than once in these pages and show how what was good with the old can be had once again.

In order to take full advantage of a boat, one needs to know what can be expected of it and what cannot. This requires knowledge of hull shapes, how they behave in various stages of water, what the addition of power does to the equation, the effects of the presence or absence of seamanship, and a whole raft of other bits and pieces of information, both obvious and arcane. The idea for this book came because such a compilation of knowledge for the operation of small motorboats did not exist.

The immediate response to this last statement, of course, is that such a book does exist in *Chapman's Piloting, Seamanship & Small Boat Handling,* and we would be the last to deny that this impressive, long-lived tome holds a wealth of excellent advice and knowledge for small-boat skippers whose boats measure over 20 feet in length. However, in the 652 pages of *Chapman,* only 32 pages are devoted exclusively to smaller outboard boats, and while it is solid stuff, as is most of the material in the book, it is of limited use to the owner of a small outboard boat who is looking for short, practical answers to the care and handling of his boat.

We are in no way disparaging *Chapman,* which has stood the test of time and has been the primary means of educating thousands of skippers of powerboats and sailboats. But what surprised us when we went looking for specific information in *Chapman* was how much was not there when it came to boats of our special interest, namely small motorboats under 20 feet in length. We keep returning to that 20-foot size because it seems to be a definite dividing line between what we call *big* small boats and *small* small boats. And the differences are great, in some ways more so than the differences between *Chapman's* "small boats"—mainly yacht-size craft—and big commercial vessels.

The factor dividing "small," as we define it, from big boats is weight. As boats get longer, their size and weight increase dramatically. This can be seen in a comparison between two wooden rowboats. One is 12 feet long and 4 feet wide and weighs 150 pounds. The second boat is 15 feet long and 5 feet wide—the length and beam each increased 25 percent over the 12-footer. But the weight of the larger boat, all else being equal, will be between 250 and 300 pounds, a doubling of this critical factor. Here is the reason that horsepower requirements shoot up as planing boat size increases; by the time you are in the high teens in length, many planing hulls need 100 h.p. or more to perform well. Yet, to move that heavy hull *through* the water (its so-called displacement or hull speed) rather than *over* it (in its planing mode) calls for only a few of those 100 horses—10 should be plenty in most cases. That is why the majority of sailboats, which cannot plane with their rounded hulls, have such low-horsepower auxiliary engines. That's all they need. Strange things happen when you move from land to water.

Weight also figures prominently in the way a boat handles, a point a small-boat skipper ignores to his peril. The survivability of any vessel rests in its buoyancy, a truism more and more apparent the smaller a boat gets. A 9-foot dinghy with a single person rowing is light and quick to respond. With three aboard it lies deep in the water, and handling is slow and logy. Add just a couple of gallons of free water in the bilge and that little boat is in imminent danger of capsizing. Put a larger load in any larger small boat, and the results will be the same. And now what we call the 20-foot factor again becomes prominent. Winds of 10 to 20 m.p.h. are common on most lakes and in coastal areas. Such breezes create waves in the 1- to 3-foot range that are no great challenge to boats over 20 feet but can give all sorts of grief to smaller craft. To contend safely, if not always comfortably, with the waves, the small-boat skipper should use the buoyancy and quick response of his "scat-back" boat, working his way around and over this rough water rather than bucking straight into it. If his boat is loaded to its maximum or more, much of this advantage of light weight and fast response will be lost.

To this point we have generalized a good deal in order to emphasize what we mean by "small boats." While the truisms we have discussed are common to all boats, nowhere do changes in form, function, and power produce more dramatic differences in the end result than in small boats. This sensitivity is the source of tremendous pleasure and, at times, frustration. This fact brings to the fore another benefit of small boats—their relatively low cost lets us have more than one so that we can have the right boat for the job at hand. This writer's personal fleet, for instance, includes two canoes, a kayak, a low-powered canoe-type motorboat, and an 18-foot, outboard-powered aluminum skiff. To one just getting into boating, five boats may seem excessive, but this collection is the accumulation of many years—the survivors, so to speak, of more than a dozen boats that have come and gone. All of the five are still used for the purposes to which they have been found especially well suited, three of them

being powered on occasion by one of the four outboard motors that have also been added to the collection.

Were this entire fleet, including motors, to be bought new, the cost would still be thousands less than one new 22-foot center-console outboard.

So, if our magic carpets are not much more than throw rugs when it comes to size, they are full size in pure potential. And while some of us may bemoan the fact that today's outboard market is totally dominated by planing hulls, the truth is that with imagination and ingenuity even this lack can be overcome, as we will show.

Since the nature of this book requires such a broad range of skills and knowledge, we looked far and wide for sources of material we believe will be of practical use to small-motorboat owners. In the end, we found we were concentrating on three sources. One of these was back issues of *Small Boat Journal* (now *Boating World*), which, since its founding in 1979, has become a treasure chest of information on the subject. One of the greatest pleasures in gathering material for this book was reading through old *SBJ's,* the only real problem being the distraction of wanting to read articles not directly related to the subject at hand. The material we have selected only skims the surface of the vast lore stored in those hundreds of pages.

A second valuable source of material was the sizable library of books published by International Marine. The excerpts we present from writers here and abroad show the universal nature of small boats.

The final source is this writer's own experience, and here a disclaimer is in order. I lay no claim to being a boating expert (CE) in the traditional sense. But I have been involved with small boats over much of my working life, which spans more than four decades. For the past 15 years, my work has included thousands of hours on the water, all in boats under 20 feet in length, and the sheer "time in grade," as they say in the military, has meant a long, drawn-out education in the use and misuse of small boats. Needless to say, much of the education came the hard way, and at times it was more to the credit of the little boats and their inherent survivability than to my own skill that I got through some of the bad places. What I did garner was a lot of experience and bits of information that I have not seen elsewhere in print, and I pass much of it on in these pages, with the hope that it will help others in their attempts to understand and enjoy small boats. Some of this material I touched on in the "Gunkholing" columns I used to write for *SBJ*. There are also articles I wrote for *SBJ* and other publications that are reprinted here with little or no change. Finally, seeing gaps in some of the subjects covered, I have written new material to bridge them.

The reader will notice at times that parts of my commentary appear to be in disagreement with other writers in this book. There are good reasons for this, the most important being that there is often more than one way to do something. There may also be differences in our boating philosophy, especially with regard to gear and equipment, but occasionally in my approach to boating in general. I believe there is something to be gained by offering alternatives and letting the reader choose.

With regard to equipment, for example, I have never been an advocate of electronics on small boats that are being used on lakes or inshore coastal waters. My reasons are both practical and philosophical—practical, because in my own experience I have found little or no need for anything more than a weather radio aboard my small craft during almost a lifetime of boating, and thus have preferred to spend my money on more useful gear and gadgets; philosophical, because I use small boats to go one-on-one with whatever the day may bring and don't want to turn to others via radio to solve my problems. I love fishing, but I have seen how electronics have helped bring the commercial fisheries to the edge of disaster and how the same thing is happening in the sport fisheries with the increasing use of "fish finders" of one ingenious sort or another. My personal preference is to go the other way, trimming my fishing gear to the basics, bending down the barbs on my hooks so most or all of the day's catch can be returned to the water unharmed, and trying to learn the ways of the fish in order to outwit them.

Many will say my arguments are silly, that electronics make boating safer and fishing easier and more rewarding. They are just as right as I am. But I am not making judgments, only saying there are choices.

Many have contributed to this book, and I have tried to remember them all in the Acknowledgments. Following each contribution, however, is the byline of its author. My own byline appears as DRG.

We would like to expand this book sometime in the future, since there is still much to be learned about this fascinating subject. Readers are encouraged to write to the editor about their experiences with these marvelously versatile little boats. Oh, and by the way, don't be bashful about letting us know where and how things may have gone wrong (if your experience is anything like mine, they probably will, sooner or later!). We will not tell the world your name, but your problem and its solution may well save another from similar grief.

Now *that* is progress!

CONTRIBUTORS

JIM ANDERSON

CAPTAIN BOB ARMSTRONG

WILLIAM C. BLIZZARD

MARYA BUTLER

PAUL BUTLER

NIGEL CALDER

DON CASEY

GARY DIAMOND

LEONARD EYGES

RAY HENDRICKSON

STEVE HENKEL

RICHARD LEBOVITZ

ART MICHAELS

ART MOSCA

CHARLES NEUSCHAFER

GRAEME PAXTON

DAG PIKE

NICK RUKAVINA

RANDY SCOTT

BOB STEARNS

NORMAN STRUNG

CHARLES SUMMERS

KEN TEXTOR

RICHARD THIEL

ALLAN H. VAITSES

KEVIN VANACORE

BOB WHITTIER

JOHN PAGE WILLIAMS

THE BOATS

Introduction

Boats are what make life on the water special, and in the process they do strange things to people. The natural human tendency is to always want a boat at least a little larger than the present one. Contributing to this desire may be the memory of the day you tried to cram a picnic party of eight into a 16-footer, or of a brisk day offshore when you and your boat took more of a pounding than either found beneficial. Soon you are looking in the magazines at boats you know you can't afford and are running all sorts of wild schemes through your head to see if there isn't *some* way you can pull off a deal for that 30-foot cruiser. Hide the mortgage, Mother, he has that look in his eye!

What goes unnoticed in this bigger-is-better progression is the eventual turn in the other direction by a considerable number of boatowners. The burden of buying, berthing, maintaining, and using a large boat can be onerous. The last point—using—may be underestimated until one is actually faced with choices. But if you have a $50,000 investment swinging on a mooring and have scrimped and saved to put it there,

there is a definite feeling of obligation to use it as often as possible. This is a welcome sort of "duty" if you are totally devoted to boating or if you have enough money to let your boat lie to her tether without worrying about the cost, but otherwise there is apt to be a constant nagging in the back of your mind that you *ought* to be doing something back on shore if you are on the water, or you *ought* to be out in your expensive boat if you are ashore. Nagging has a way of cooling one's ardor.

So you look back and remember the fun you had in those little boats during your early days of messing about with small stuff. The boat rested on a trailer in the backyard during the summer storms and you rested in your bed without concern for a yacht thrashing about at her mooring. If a weekend came when you wanted to picnic in the moun-

tains or visit Aunt Janie on the farm, you went with a clear conscience and no thought of the boat left behind. When you wanted to go upcountry lake fishing, your little boat went with you, and if catching a mess of mackerel in the bay was the choice, your boat was there too. Some of the most appreciative small-boat skippers are those who have gone the big-boat route.

No one has to be told the cost of boating always seems to be going one way—up. Sticker shock can be just as great in the showroom of a boat dealer as that of a car dealer, and the first-time boat buyer may decide that the sport is too rich for thin wallets. It well may be so if you have your mind set on something like that lovely red runabout in the showroom with its awesome 125-horse black outboard—you're looking at new-car prices here. But if getting on the water is more important than style, ask the dealer what he has in other "packages," those combinations of boat, motor, and trailer that may lack the gloss of the runabout but also may offer a lot more utility than the fancier model. For instance,

> *Our emphasis is not on today's most popular boats—although they are covered here, many in detail—but rather on alternatives.*

1

the runabout type is not the easiest boat to fish from with its high sides and seats that always seem to get in the way. And though it may be a first-rate boat for pulling a water-skier, it is an awkward thing, at best, if you want to go ashore over the bow. We watched a resourceful Maine guide nose his big white runabout up to the beach of a campsite, pick up a 6-foot stepladder from the cockpit, snap it open, and lower it over the bow, and then calmly unload the four sports he was guiding. If your boat is large enough to carry its own bow stepladder, maybe the runabout will do. Just remember, there may not always be a smooth beach to land on.

A decided advantage of the smaller rig, usually a 14- or 16-foot fiberglass or aluminum boat, is its usefulness as a place to learn the ropes. Without having to make a large financial investment, you can find out if boating is really *your* sport, and you also can learn a lot about boats and the water and how different they are from life on land. As time goes on, you may choose to move on to another boat (this is all part of the fun—and more the rule than the exception), and when you do, you will be in a far better position to decide

what you want in your new craft.

Rather than go into particular boat models in this section, the essays comment instead on the various aspects of boats, their hull shapes, the materials from which they are made, what to look for and perhaps avoid, and other information that will make your decision easier. Our emphasis is not on today's most popular boats—although they are covered here, many in detail—but rather on alternatives. Perhaps the popular

Some of the most appreciative small-boat skippers are those who have gone the big-boat route.

boats are just right for you, but you won't know until you have a chance to sample the field.

To many people, a boat is merely a means, a tool for carrying out a job or providing pleasure. But eventually, after you and your boat have been through a number of trials together, you'll find that you are developing a definite attitude toward your craft. There will be things about it that you like and things you do not, and one feeling may predominate to a degree you would not have believed possi-

ble and probably would not admit to, even among friends.

There also can be instant reaction to a boat one doesn't own. We remember with no fondness whatsoever the Dinghy from Hell, the tender of a small cruiser. She was nine feet of round-bottomed recalcitrance that was unanimously hated by all who used her. The Dinghy from Hell apparently sensed this universal animosity and got her jollies by regularly dumping even competent seamen.

By contrast, we have real affection for our big aluminum skiff that has been through all sorts of adventures with us for nearly 15 years. If this sounds silly or maudlin, consider a study made by the University of Rhode Island School of Fisheries several years back, in which commercial fishermen, whose pragmatism is exceeded only by their skepticism, were asked where their boats stood in their personal scheme of things. The rankings showed that many fishermen considered their vessel the most important thing in their lives, with their wives coming in second!

—DRG

It's All in the Hull

There are two types of hull shapes of general interest to the small-boat skipper. These are displacement hulls—those that go through the water—and planing hulls—those that go over the water. The differences between the two are basic to an understanding of small motorboats—and in selecting a boat that

will suit your requirements.

In still water, a boat displaces an amount of water equal to its weight. For example, if the boat weighs 1,000 pounds, it will displace 1,000 pounds of water, and since the total volume of the boat is much greater than the volume of the water it displaces, a lot of the boat shows above

the surface—it floats. By contrast, a rock weighing 1,000 pounds has less volume than the water—and sinks. Whenever the bulk or volume of an object is greater than the weight of water it displaces, it floats, which is why hulls built of steel, aluminum, fiberglass, and even cement float. But if water penetrates the hull—that is,

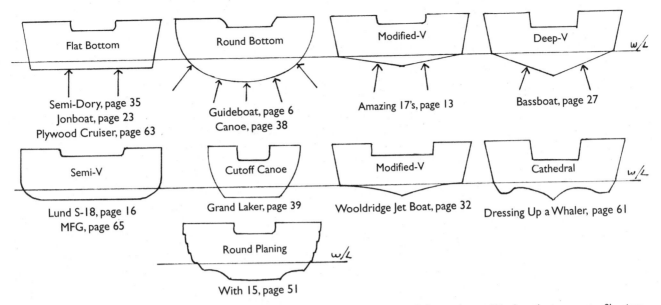

Four basic hull shapes of small motorboats are shown in top row, with variations in the column below each type. We show the transom profile, since the bottom shape at that point pretty much determines the boat's planing ability. Where boats or hull type are discussed in this book, the pages are noted beneath the type. The arrows indicate lifting pressure when power is applied, with vertical arrows providing the greatest lift and therefore requiring the least power. It is interesting to note that there really are only two shapes—flat and round. All others are variations of these two.

replaces much of the volume created by the hull (most of which is air)—then the steel, aluminum, fiberglass, or cement has nothing to hold it up except its own volume, which is less than water; thus the boat sinks.

A hull will move through water with relatively little effort (power) up to a speed equal to the square root of its waterline length. The late naval architect Weston Farmer called this the *natural speed* of a hull. Another term for this through-water mode is *displacement speed*. Beyond this point, rapidly increasing amounts of power are needed to push a hull through the water. A so-called *displacement hull* is designed to operate within or somewhat above this natural speed limit. There are a number of advantages to this: a very modest amount of power is needed to move the hull, weight is relatively unimportant, and the hull can be designed to be both eminently seaworthy and seakindly. A good displacement hull is well rounded so as to "give" with rough

seas from any quarter and often has at least a modest amount of rocker in its keel. Many of the best models are quite long and lean, about four times as long on the waterline as their beam. The most efficient of them are double-enders or have transoms that just brush the water. In brief, such boats almost flow through the water, creating little stir in their passage. The best of these may be pushed to

> *Nothing is perfect, however—especially in small boats—and the deep-V is no exception.*

twice or maybe two and one-half times their natural speed, but if forced much beyond that can literally founder in the bow wave they are pushing.

You can quickly figure the "natural," or "hull," speed of your boat (with a calculator, anyway!). If the waterline length of your 18-footer is 16 feet, you find the square root

of 16, which is 4. Since the last number is in knots, we convert to miles per hour by multiplying by 1.15. As a result, the "natural speed" of your boat is 4.6 m.p.h., or what would be an easy jogging speed on land. Next time you are out on the water, notice how little power is required to reach the natural speed of your boat even when it is loaded. This is why a backup or trolling motor needs so little horsepower compared to your regular motor; it is only expected to move your boat at this speed or less.

All hulls are in their "displacement mode" when at rest, and they remain displacement hulls until they are pushed beyond their natural hull speeds, at which time they become something else. This is the point where hull shape, power, and other factors begin to make a big difference. This is also the point where some boat terms make descriptions easier, so let's take a moment to look at the language.

Deadrise. The angle of the bottom from the horizontal.

Deep-V. A bottom with steep deadrise throughout the length of the boat, usually 20 degrees or more.

Modified-V. A bottom with steep deadrise in the bow that flattens to a shallow V of only a few degrees at the stern.

Cathedral. A varying, modified form of the deep-V. The name is a combination of catamaran and dihedral. Author Richard Henderson describes a common variation as "centrally veed in section but with a small underwater V-shaped sponson on each side . . . the sponsons afford good stability, and a certain amount of air-cushioning is provided in the tunnels between the sponsons and central hull." In some designs, the sponsons are almost as large as the central hull, giving the impression of three hulls joined together, or *tri-hull*, as they are often called.

Chine. The angle where the bottom meets the sides. If the angle is sharp, it is called a *hard chine*; if the angle is modest, it's a *soft chine*. There is a frequent confusion of terms here. For instance, if

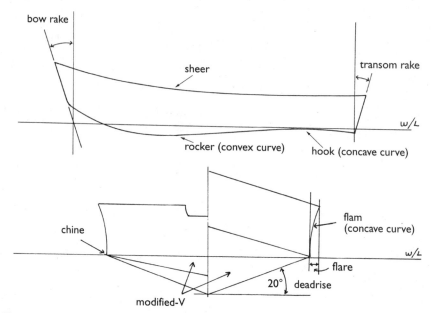

The various characteristics of an outboard motorboat. The two views are of different hulls.

the connection between the bottom and sides is rounded rather than angled, this may also be called a *soft chine,* which is technically incorrect though common usage.

Rocker. The fore-and-aft convex curve in the keel. Rocker is often built into true displacement hulls in order to make them more seakindly. Rocker works against planing by forcing the bow up and the stern down.

Rake. The fore or aft angle from the vertical of a stem, transom, etc.

Flare. The outward angle from the vertical of the bow and sides that helps provide lift when the hull dips into a wave. It may also cut down on spray coming aboard—but this is not guaranteed.

Flam. The sharp concave curve or "hollow" of the flare.

Hook. A concave turn of the bottom near the transom that may provide lift when a hull is planing.

Reserve buoyancy. The flaring or bulging of the hull above the waterline that increases the buoyancy of the boat as weight is added. The Banks dory, with its small, narrow bottom and sharply flaring sides, is a prime example, a relatively small dory able to carry a huge load.

In contrast to the displacement mode, the physics of which are quite passive, planing is a matter of dynamics. Simply put, if a planing hull is pushed beyond its hull speed, it will no longer be able to shove aside the water but rather, because of its shape, will ride up onto the surface and skate along the top. Once it exceeds its displacement speed and

The arrow points to a "soft chine," a relatively small angle between the deadrise of the bottom and the side of the boat.

National Fisherman

A flat-bottomed skiff on plane rides almost on the surface of the water. Such craft are often favored as workboats because they have a large capacity and working area but require modest power.

breaks loose of the water's grip, its speed is limited only by its weight and the amount of power being applied. Thus, Donald Campbell was able to get his 2¼-ton Bluebird K7, powered by a turbo-jet engine, up to 328 m.p.h. This was the highest speed ever achieved on water, although neither boat nor driver survived. On a more comprehensible scale, some outboard-powered racing boats can top 100 m.p.h.—which is quite a bit faster than their hull speed!

Effective planing usually requires a flat surface of some kind. The flat-bottomed skiff is the ultimate example here, needing only very modest power to jump up onto the surface of the water and skitter along with little strain. The garvey and the jonboat are not far behind. All three types are flat-water boats, though, and a bit of chop will begin to rattle the fastenings out of them. To counter this, boatbuilders put a sharp V in the forward half of a flat-bottomed boat and then let this "warp" into a flat planing surface aft, thus providing wave-cutting bow forward and easy planing aft. This model in many variations is most common in aluminum skiffs, but is popular right up to the big boats.

The problem is that the V-bowed, flat-bottomed boat lifts its bow out of the water as it comes up on plane, and the waves hit the bottom back

where it is flattening out. This leads to severe pounding, and forces a skipper to throttle back to a point where the sharp bow is again in the water doing its job. The deep-V hull bypasses this problem to a fair extent by carrying the sharp V of the bow all the way to the transom. This provides a wave-cutting ability to the hull even in rough water and permits the deep-V to proceed on plane long after a boat with only a V bow has quit the fast track. Nothing is perfect, however—especially in small boats—and the deep-V is no exception. The deep hull tracks well but turns hard, and it sometimes is predisposed to ride over on one of its two planing surfaces, a tendency (called *chine walking*) that necessitates the addition of running strakes and chine flats (see photo on page 50).

Some deep-Vs have a small flat section aft to assist in planing and steering, but a better answer in many cases is the modified-V, which sports a deep V in the bow warping to a lesser V aft. This is a worthwhile compromise for small boats, because they have to deal with such a great variety of wave conditions and because quick response is so important to safe handling.

In efforts to encompass the best qualities of more than one type of

boat, designers have produced a dazzling, if not baffling, array of hull shapes, many of which are touted as wonder boats at their unveiling but soon end up as backyard turkeys. In trying to pierce the "corporate veil," so to speak, or in plainer language, to figure out what the hell the designer had in mind when this whiz-bang took shape on his drawing board, you have to look behind the graphics, the metal flake, the voluptuous bulges and sleek indentations (you can make almost any shape in fiberglass) and try to determine what is being offered in the way of a boat. In most cases, you will see what we have been talking about—a deep-V, a modified-V, a V-bowed flat-bottom, or some variation of these such as a cathedral hull or even a catamaran.

What must be answered—as always—are these recurring questions: What do I want this hull to do? Are the design parameters logical? What will this boat be like in the water? Does the interior of the hull provide the room I need? Bear in mind that just about every new small motorboat you see will have a planing hull of some sort; but how will it work in the displacement speeds required in crowded harbors or rough seas? You can make a good guess based on what appear to be the apparent phys-

An aluminum boat with a modified-V hull. This shape requires more power than a flat-bottomed boat but less than a full deep-V.

A small guideboat type being tested by the author banks sharply in a turn even though the 8-h.p. motor is only half her rated horsepower. This dangerous tendency was attributed to the lack of bearing in the after planing surface. Below, the same boat slides gently upright through a "hard-over" turn under the full-power thrust of a 2-h.p. motor.

ics, but the only real and reliable answer will come when you try the hull in the water. Don't be surprised if you are surprised; ordinarily what looks good, is good, but there are exceptions.

We once tested what appeared to be a lovely little motorboat hull derived from a guideboat model. A fiberglass 15-footer, it was rated for a maximum of 15 h.p., but we were confident we could get a good idea of what the boat was like by using our 8-h.p. motor. We got an idea all right! The center thwart was so close to the after seat that two persons had to interlock their knees to face one another. The tiny bow seat was so far forward that the fine bow provided very little bearing, so if the second person moved there the boat would travel bow-down. The after end had rounded sides that pinched in to a small transom, and thus there was not enough bearing for the boat driver and motor. On a fast turn, the boat would drop into a steep inside bank because of this lack of buoyancy, and I felt certain that a 15-h.p. motor could easily overpower the boat in a turn and either flip it or cause the hull to go out of control (see photo above left). Even with half its rated horsepower, and that not wide open, the boat scared the daylights out of me. A 3- or 4-h.p. outboard would have been adequate for this easily driven hull, but how could a buyer be expected to go so conservatively when the boat was rated for almost four times that power? Here was proof positive that no rating system is perfect.

It is not difficult to see why shape is so important in your determination of a hull type for personal use. What suits your neighbor is important only to the extent that your requirements and attitudes are similar. Beyond that, it is worth taking the time and effort to run your own tests so you can be confident that the thousands of dollars you are about to invest will give you what you want.

—DRG

How to Test a Boat

If you have the opportunity to test a boat before you buy it—and we strongly recommend that you try to arrange it—there are many things you'll want to know about it other than how fast it will go. In fact, that particular feature should be well down your list, for reasons that will become clear in a moment.

Start your test before the boat goes in the water. This should include a close look at the hull and general condition, both inside and out. If it is a new boat, check the fastenings, finish, and the way things are put together. Note carefully the transom, motor mounts, and controls. Does styling interfere with vision, interior room, or safety?

Once the boat is in the water, step aboard and note its stability, and visibility from the controls. If you're testing a small boat, we recommend you wear a PFD—not because of any violent maneuvers you may be planning but rather as a precaution. An unknown boat is just that—unknown. It could hold some unpleasant surprises.

Start the motor and let it warm up before you cast off. Select an open area without traffic, if possible, and move ahead at slow speed, testing the controls and steering. Slowly increase the speed through the range from slow to half speed, noting how much the bow rises as well as the point at which water begins to break cleanly from the transom. Some boats respond and handle poorly in this important speed range.

Test the handling at half throttle by making easy turns right and left and, if satisfactory, tighten the radius of the turns. Try the same procedure at three-quarter throttle but not wide open.

Drop back to idling speed and check for clear water ahead, and then quickly open the throttle to full speed. Note how much the boat squats and how quickly it comes up on plane. If the boat feels solid as it comes up to speed, and if speed is what you are looking for and you are an experienced powerboater, this is a good time to "see what she'll do."

Don't try violent maneuvers at high speed any more than you would with a fast car; you are after a general feel for the boat. If the boat jumps up onto plane, she is probably well matched to her power. If she is hesitant or even logy getting up, she may be telling you she is overweight and likes to eat a lot.

Many things will become apparent as you go through this testing process. In smaller, lightweight boats, you may need weight forward for safe operation. A boat without good bearing aft may take a sharp and perhaps dangerous inward lean in turns. The boat may "porpoise" (a rhythmic bouncing) at planing speed, a warning sign of poor trim or an improperly set up motor. There may be a racing of the motor (called *cavitation*) in the sharper turns, a signal that there is a poor flow of water to the propeller because of the hull configuration or, again, a poorly set up motor.

Few boats are faultless under all circumstances, so we are not making judgments here, but careful testing, based on a gradual increase of power and tight handling, will reveal many strong and weak points of the boat. It is up to you to choose whether or not you can or want to live with the latter.

—DRG

Twenty Questions to Ask When Selecting a Boat

Let's make the process of boat selection simpler by encapsulating it in twenty questions you should ask yourself before or as you look. Write down the answers so you'll be sure not to overlook anything.

1. *How will I most often use the boat?* Be realistic. Don't talk yourself into an impractical boat simply because it has desirable features. Remember that your boat should make your favorite on-the-water activities easy. I might also add, fun. Look for the boat that will suit your intended uses, and don't settle for anything else. And remember, you can't find the boat best suited to your needs until you define your needs.

2. *Where will I use it?* The answer is going to influence many things about your boat: its size, power plant (remember, outboards and sterndrives are generally better for trailered boats), the amount of beef in its construction, the amount and type of shelter aboard, and more. Be realistic at the outset, and you'll be happier down the line.

3. *How much time do I have to use it?* It's easy to overestimate available time when you are excited about buying a boat. Time shrinks in the real world, and there's nothing worse than having a boat that needs more time and attention than you can give it.

All boats need attention, mostly in the form of simple routine maintenance, but some need more than others. Likewise, some boats need more attention before you leave the dock and when you get back. The less time you have, the more important it is to have a simple, no-frills boat. Do you think oiled teak covering boards are the saltiest-looking cosmetic treatment a boat can have? Get them, if you have time to keep them oiled. If your time is limited, you'd be better off with surfaces that only ask for washing.

Back before I got my priorities straight and decided it was better to work all the time on someone else's boat than to work five days ashore to get two on a boat of my own, I made it a rule never to accept an invitation that would keep me ashore on a weekend during the boating season. Friends often felt snubbed until they experienced one weekend of cruising themselves. Then, usually, they would envy me for spending every weekend on my boat. It worked for me, but I'm not so sure it would for everyone. Be serious in your estimates of available time and plan your boat accordingly.

4. *Where will I keep it when I'm not using it?* If you are new to boating, this question might seem irrelevant. But it won't be long before you realize that slip space is often as scarce as virgins in Times Square, and when you find space, you'll discover it can be as precious as platinum. Space is available, even if you have to suffer through a couple of years on a waiting list to get it. My point is, don't go out and buy a 40-foot cabin cruiser, even if it suits all your other needs perfectly, unless you have a place to park a 40-footer when you're not using it. If it's going to have to sit in your driveway, it's going to have to fit in your driveway (and be trailerable to boot).

5. Will it be my boat or a family boat? Since boating is a perfect sport for the whole family to enjoy together, maybe the question needn't be asked. But boating isn't always for everyone, and it just may be that what you need is the perfect boat for occasional use by you and some fishing buddies rather than a larger, more luxurious vessel your spouse and kids could enjoy on a regular basis. If you plan to include your family, however, make sure the boat is meant for a family. Comfort can be subjective; let your family help judge what is comfortable.

6. Is the answer to question 1 in line with the answer to question 5? Could be you've already covered this one. But it won't hurt to double-check. In listing needs by use, have you thought of everyone who will regularly be using the boat with you? Some compromise may be necessary here; the boat that best fills most of your criteria may not suit everyone in the family equally well. Better to consider all needs and compromise accordingly than to spoil the fun for other family members.

7. How much can I spend to buy it? A wag once described a boat as "a hole in the water surrounded by fiberglass into which one pours money." As with many jests, there's an element of truth in it. The purchase is just the beginning, so don't blow your budget up front. Like all

rules, this one can be bent slightly, but don't bend it too far or you'll break yourself rather than the rule.

8. How much can I spend on operation? Most operational expenses are directly related to the size and type of boat you buy. Marina and yard charges, for example, are usually based on overall length. While many costs are fixed—dockage, insurance, hauling, and winter storage if you are a seasonal boatman, for example—fuel and some maintenance costs will vary with use. Obviously, the more you use your boat, the more hours the fixed costs are spread over and the less the cost per hour. Still, your choice of boat will influence operational costs; a gas-guzzling twin-engine racer will burn more fuel per hour than a more economical, moderately powered runabout. This doesn't make the runabout better; it only

means that you have to face and plan for long-term expenses. Check with marinas and yards to determine current costs and figure accordingly. This may help you determine how large a boat you can afford. Find out about insurance—different types of boats carry different rates. In short, be sure to include a realistic appraisal of *all* operating costs when you make up your boating budget.

9. How much can I spend on maintenance? Maintenance costs depend to a degree on the size of the boat, but even more on its simplicity. The more fancy stuff you have aboard, the more time and money it will take to keep everything ship-shape and working properly. If you want to spend your time and money enjoying the boat rather than taking care of it, keep it simple.

One way to save on maintenance is to spend time instead of money—do the work yourself. And that brings up the next question.

10. Is do-it-yourself maintenance practical for you? If you resent the hours spent on maintenance, be prepared to pay others to work on your boat when you can't be there. But perhaps you'll find, as many have, that maintaining your boat can be a big part of the enjoyment. If this is the case, you may even discover that when other engagements prevent you from taking the whole day to go boating, you can still spend a morning or afternoon on needed maintenance.

The more work you do yourself, the better you'll know your boat and its systems and the less you'll be upset should something go awry underway. Of course, this presupposes that you have the requisite knowledge, but as your boating experience grows, there's no reason why your maintenance knowledge can't grow with it.

11. How big a boat do I need? Bigger is not necessarily better, but you do need a boat large enough to be comfortable for all concerned. A boat that's too small won't be fun. When you examine all the elements—purchase price, operational costs, and so forth, *plus* the needs of your family—you may decide that a larger simple boat will fit your needs better than a smaller fancy one at the same bottom line.

12. How big a boat can I handle? Generally speaking, the bigger the boat, the more knowledge and experience you need to handle it properly. The reason is simple: Larger boats react more slowly. That means more planning ahead on the part of the skipper. The less experience you have, the tougher it is to plan ahead.

The 80-foot boat I'm currently

> *If it's going to have to sit in your driveway, it's going to have to fit in your driveway.*

If you're trying to get into boating on a small budget, consider carefully the need for accessories. For instance, this neat little aluminum steering console could be duplicated in wood; better still, consider doing without it on an open 16-footer like this boat. The console takes up scarce room, adds complication to a simple layout (such boats handle more easily and respond more quickly from the stern seat), and may throw off the trim if the skipper is a heavyweight.

skippering takes about 30 to 40 seconds to react to a change of controls. Not only do I have to know what I want to happen, I have to decide what adjustment will achieve the desired result nearly a minute ahead of time so as to initiate the proper action at the proper time. I don't think I could do it if I hadn't been running big boats for a number of years. You can learn with the boat no matter what its size, but you'll have an easier time of it if you don't bite off too much too soon.

13. *What's the biggest boat that suits all of the above?* This is your upper limit. You don't have to get one that big, and you might find something smaller that meets all your needs best, but you do have to set limits. Decide what you can accept as your biggest boat *at this time,* then live with your decision no matter how appealing some larger boat might be.

14. *What's the smallest boat that suits all of the above?* Again, you may well buy something larger, but you have to define your limits in order to narrow your choices. Just as you might pass by the exciting two-seater sports car when you're really in the market for a station wagon, you have to bypass boats too small for your current purposes if you want to make your search realistic and practical.

15. *What features are most important?* Remember that every boat is a compromise; you have to know which features are least negotiable before you can begin making deals with yourself. The best way to handle this is simply to list everything you are looking for in a boat, and then arrange the items in order of descending importance.

16. *What features are least important?* This should be fairly easy; just don't be hasty. It is entirely possible that some of these least important features are attainable, but you can't count on it, so don't list anything that isn't truly expendable.

17. *What features are absolutely necessary?* This again is simply a matter of drawing a line—in this case between those things you really need

and those you only want very much. Though the principle of compromise is to give up what you want least to gain what you want most, sometimes in the real world you have to give up what you would want more to gain what you want most. Be very clear in your own mind as to which features are positively *not* negotiable.

18. *What features are absolutely unnecessary?* The point in even including these items (since they most likely won't be a part of your boat) is simply to help you get priorities completely straight in your mind. If it isn't on your list, you won't know where it fits into your priorities.

Here's a suggestion: After you have made your initial list of desirable features, assign each item to a category from 1 to 5. Use 5 for things you must have, 4 for those you would like very much, 3 for those that would be nice, 2 for those that are expendable, and 1 for those you can definitely do without. Then rearrange and start shopping with full confidence that you know exactly what you are looking for.

Again: Too many 5s on your list, and it just won't work. That's not to say the list must be perfectly balanced, but if everything on your list is a "must have" you leave yourself no room to compromise.

19. *Have I found the best dealer?* This question can be far more important than you might imagine. In fact, finding the right dealer can be more critical than finding the right boat.

Because nothing made by the hand of man is perfect, you have to face the truth that your wonderful new boat is going to give you some problems. It will when it's new; it will after you've owned it awhile. It will, period. The pleasures of owning a powerboat far outweigh the problems, however, and this is especially true if you have a cooperative and understanding dealer. A good dealer will do his utmost to minimize your problems and maximize your fun. But you must also be a good customer. The customer-dealer relationship is often a matter of chemistry, which means the right dealer for you is not necessarily the right dealer for your best friend.

There are some general guidelines, however. The best dealer will have a strong service department with the tools, parts, and knowledgeable mechanics it takes to get your service work done quickly and correctly, handling everything from warranty work to routine maintenance. But a good service department will be busy, so smart dealers pay attention to their own customers first—one good reason not to look only at the purchase bottom line. If you shop entirely by sticker price, expecting to get another dealer to do the service work, be prepared to stand in line behind the dealer's regular customers every time. For similar reasons, the best dealer will be close to your boating area, even if you can get a seemingly better deal farther down the road.

The best dealer will be more concerned with helping you find the right boat than merely with making a sale. He wants to sell you a lot of boats, not just one, because chances are that if you enjoy boating, you won't stop with one boat. After a few years you'll want something else—most likely something bigger. (That's why in question 13 I made the point about determining the biggest boat that suits you *at this time;* eventually you will answer the question differently.) Boatbuilders recognize the probability of this progression and keep adding to the top of their lines. In the late 1970s, for instance, the largest Sea Ray was a 36-footer, and the biggest factory Hatteras was 77 feet (though some dealers specialize in making customized stretch models that are longer than standard). By the late 1980s, Sea Ray had gotten up to 50 feet and Hatteras to 120!

A truly smart dealer knows that you won't want to move up to something bigger unless you like nearly everything about the boat you have now except its size. If he steers you wrong in the beginning, that first boat may be the only one you ever get. Some dealers are happy with that single sale. The good ones look ahead and cultivate long-term customer relationships.

20. *Have I found the best deal?* Unless the boat meets the criteria you have outlined for yourself, the answer to this question is "no"; no matter what incentives a dealer may offer, you don't have a good deal if the boat isn't right to begin with. But let us assume for the moment that the boat is essentially ideal and take a look at what makes a good deal better and

Finding the right dealer can be more critical than finding the right boat.

what you can do to make it best.

Shop around. Sure, I said the dealer with the lowest price is not necessarily the best place to buy your boat, and I will stand by that advice. But until you see what the marketplace has to offer, you can't begin to negotiate. And you should negotiate, provided you are realistic. The dealer with the great service department and in-depth parts inventory will probably have a higher overhead than the dealer who sells but doesn't service boats. Don't expect to get the same price from both. But by knowing what the lowest price may be, you will have a better idea of what an acceptable price should be from the dealer you would rather do business with. Even the best dealer will usually start out asking more than he expects, just so he has room to come down a bit. It's the nature of the business.

Consider the cost of money along with the cost of the boat. A boat is a major purchase, so you will probably be financing it with a consumer loan. Lenders appreciate boat buyers, who, for the most part, are good customers. Using the boat as collateral, you can borrow a large chunk of the purchase price.

Though pleasure boating has long since ceased to be the sole province of the very rich, it is still a luxury. If you have the discretionary income to be able to afford boating, you probably have the savvy to shop for your boat loan as carefully as you shop for the boat itself. So I will just add the reminder.

Popular production boats are much like automobiles in that they depreciate quickly when new. This has been aggravated in recent years by an excess of demand over supply of popular new boats (which keeps their prices up), coupled with excess supply in the used-boat market (which holds their value down). You should ensure if possible that you owe no more on your boat than you could get if you were to sell it tomorrow. A dealer may be reluctant to let you in on how much you are going to lose to initial depreciation, but you should try to ascertain it nevertheless. Otherwise, when you prepare to trade up to something bigger in a year or two, you will discover that not only does your boat not have any trade-in value, you might actually have to add *cash* just to pay off the note and satisfy the lien—particularly if you made little or no downpayment to begin with.

—Captain Bob Armstrong
(*Getting Started in Powerboating,*
International Marine, 1990)

The Matter of Speed

The American obsession with speed is expressed on land with fast cars. All too frequently this obsession is carried over to the water but with some unexpected and perhaps unsettling results. In the small-motorboat market, fast boats predominate, but they often come up short in bringing our boat dreams to reality.

Speed has its place on the water; our mistake is that we too often put it ahead of more important things, and, in so doing, compromise the latter's value. Before elaborating on this premise, though, let's see where speed does make sense.

Get-up-and-go is an asset in commuter boats, exemplified by the many variations of the runabout, that cover the same stretch of water day after day. Speed is also needed for water-skiing boats and certain types of sportfishing craft. And of course there is no denying that it is fun to go flying like the wind over quiet waters.

But the fast lane exacts its price, financially and otherwise. A boat does not have to be very large before the cost in design, engine, and fuel becomes sizable. A 12-foot skiff and outboard capable of going 25 m.p.h. can be bought for less than $2,000. Increase the length by just 6 feet and add some amenities, and the same speed can cost $10,000. Add 6 feet more plus the capability of 40 m.p.h. and you can soon be in the high-end luxury-car class.

If money were the only factor, speed might be worth it. But things are more complicated than mere price. Fast cars are designed for smooth roads, for instance, but water rarely is as smooth as the ads would have you believe. Weight is needed to soften out bumpy water or your boat will literally take off. Weight, though, is expensive to build, and

> *If money were the only factor, speed might be worth it.*

hull design that will withstand the pounding is costly. Finally, plenty of power is required to force the boat up onto and over the surface of the water. Given these considerations, we begin to see why even small fast boats cost so much to buy and run.

There are some obvious detrimental effects caused by this search for speed. Having all those horses in one's hands fosters a thrilling sense of power, but not everyone can handle it. In a word, it can be dangerous, if not to the skipper then perhaps to others. More than one sea kayaker and small-boat owner has told me of the cold fear he felt as he watched the swift approach of a sharp bow with a bone in its teeth. "I never know if the guy at the wheel can see over that high prow," one said, "and even if he can, he may not see me because he is going so fast." An open expanse of water can also hide its fangs in the form of a sodden log just breaking the surface or rocks lying just beneath it. Where a slower-moving boat would give the operator more time to see such hazards, a go-fast boat would be on them in an instant. High speed demands a high

Bayliner Marine Corp.

Speed plays an important role in the purchase of most outboard motorboats, and for good reason. But the exhilaration of going fast on water is limited to nice weather conditions and certain needs. The rest of the time, it's less important, and the fast boat may not do the other things you want to do as well as other boat types might.

sense of responsibility and a corresponding degree of skill.

With power to burn, skippers come to depend on speed to get them out of trouble. A common rationalization for a fast boat is the need for speed "to run from bad weather." Anyone who spends a lot of time on the water will know this argument is mostly baloney. Bad weather is almost never that sudden, and an alert skipper should have ample warning of the pending change to head for port in time. If he has waited so long he has to run for it, chances are it already is so rough he won't be able to use all the power he has at hand. Better to hone your skills of observation and cautiousness than to rely on speed to offset faulty judgment.

More subtle detriments should also be considered.

Sometimes a person hurrying over the water does not realize how irritating and even intimidating his or her boat can be to those in self-propelled boats, or to other boatowners operating more sedately in a busy waterway. Just as a speeding car is unwelcome in a suburban neighborhood, so is a speeding boat unwelcome close to shore on a quiet lake or pond.

Speed can also be just plain boring. A lake 5 miles long is a respectable piece of water, but at 30 m.p.h. you can be up and down it in 20 minutes, having seen a lot of waves but not much else. You are left with three choices: (1) Haul your boat and go home; (2) go over the same water again; or (3) slow down and enjoy the scenery. The last seems the best choice, but now the hull features that enhance speed may begin to work against you.

If the displacement pace of your boat, say 6 or 7 m.p.h., is fast enough to suit you, you're in good shape, but anything in the 10-m.p.h. range is going to be less than satisfactory, creating a steep fore-and-aft angle of attack and a very big wake as the

motor tries to push the boat up on plane. This steep squatting attitude is common to heavy high-speed hulls and makes it difficult for the boat driver to see ahead. If you need to slow down because of rough going, this same squat leaves you staring at a huge stern wave ever threatening to come crashing aboard if you suddenly stop.

To their credit, small-boat designers have done wonders in offsetting many problems inherent with speed. There are deep-V and modified-V hulls, a whole bevy of scow types and tri-hulls, along with many catamaran designs. Good as they may be, especially with their ability to carry a lot of power, they are still compromises, each with its own set of drawbacks.

There are alternatives to fast motorboats that may suit your needs better and more cheaply while still providing a fair turn of speed. These are basically traditional hulls with V-bows to cut the waves and flat planing surfaces aft to lift the boat easily with modest power. The better models usually have a length-to-beam ratio of approximately 3:1. That master of wooden-boat builders, the late Pete Culler, was an advocate of long, narrow outboard boats of close to 4:1

ratio, and his Blonde Bombshells were light, comfortable, and reasonably fast with impressively small motors for their length. Small-boat expert Bob Whittier designed and built a 21-by-6-foot fiberglass boat he called the Seamaster that made so little fuss going through the water at any speed that it earned some popularity with college sculling coaches, who could run alongside their crews without swamping the low-sided

The late Pete Culler in one of his handsome wood outboard boats. These long and narrow boats are fast and comfortable, and require very modest power by today's standards. The post just forward of the skipper was called a "chicken post" by the builder and is used for a steadying grip while standing, a most comfortable position in small boats.

Long and lean, Bob Whittier's Seamaster creates little fuss in the water, whether idling along or planing.

sculls. He once showed that the boat would plane with a 9.9-h.p. outboard, although its usual power was a 40- to 50-horse kicker, still conservative for a 21-footer.

As an aside, the Seamaster model never caught on with boatbuilders or the boating public. As for Culler's pretty and practical Blonde Bombshells, they were little more than an attractive oddity—made out of wood, for cripe's sakes!—in an endless passing parade of fiberglass beasts and beauties. Did Culler and Whittier, two extremely knowledgeable small-boat designers *and* users, know something most of the experts did not?

My own workboat, which I use to range over a 300-mile stretch of coastal waters, is nothing more than an 18-foot open skiff with exactly a 3:1 length-to-beam ratio. Its 25-h.p. outboard is less than half the rated horsepower, but after a dozen years and many thousands of river, lake, and ocean miles, I see little need for more. My average day's run is from 50 to 75 miles, which is quite a lot more than most outboard boats used for pleasure, and although the motor will give a flat-out speed in the mid-20s, I almost always cruise at ¾ throttle or less, for an average of 15 to 20 m.p.h. The lightweight, aluminum, semi-V hull with its small motor is almost too buoyant and consequently something less than comfortable in a chop, but I've never had to worry about being overcome by the sea.

My work also requires a great deal of cruising in my boat's semidisplacement speed range (8 to 15 m.p.h.)—the squatting range—but the squat is greatly mitigated by the light motor and relatively long, narrow hull. Still, the boat is adequately fast for the usual conditions found in broad reaches of water. Sure, there are times when I would like to have more power to go faster, but it has been a pleasant discovery to find that this desire is of a very occasional nature.

Many hours at the tiller have convinced me that speed is merely one of many objectives a buyer should seek in selecting a boat. And, as often as not, it should not be the most important one.

—DRG

The Amazing 17s—
and Others of a Rugged Breed

One of the most versatile classes of boats in the 20-foot-and-under range is a group of open fiberglass 17- and 18-footers with long-distance capabilities and seaworthiness that imbue them with exciting possibilities in the hands of experienced skippers.

Names associated with this class are familiar to almost everyone with any interest in small powerboats: Boston Whaler Montauk, Mako 17, Aquasport 17, Pro-Line 17, to name just a few that have been around for 20 years or more. That the same model should remain in a company's stable of offerings for so long implies that these boats must be something special. And they are.

First of all, they have in good measure the attributes so necessary in an ideal small boat. They are rugged, seaworthy, fast, trailerable, and eco-nomical to operate when compared with their "larger" brethren in the mid-20-foot range. We put "larger" in quotes because the entire breed of center-console fishing boats is small in actual size when seen beside the traditional 40-foot offshore sportfisherman.

Offshore fishing in a 17-footer is not for everyone, but it is not a stunt. It is done, especially in warmer climates where ocean fish can be found within a few miles of shore. This brand of fishing is not always easy, and misjudgments of the weather can result in an unmerciful beating, but in the right hands these little sluggers can handle a lot of water. In brief, if you have the required seamanship skills and want to push the limits of small motorboats, these are the ones to do it in. A look at the features of

Two of the earlier 17-foot center-console boats that are still going strong are the Mako 17 and the Boston Whaler Montauk 17.

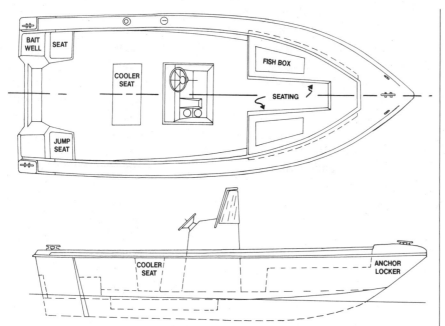

Answer's 17-foot Fishing Machine is a good example of the breed, with lots of space (as 17-footers go), built-in 32-gallon gas tank, bait well, fish box, and self-bailing cockpit. An 18-footer has the same layout.

the type will show why this is so.

A key factor is weight, with 1,200 pounds being a fair average. All are molded in fiberglass, and the better builders don't stint on materials, be it cloth, resin, or internal stiffening. They know how the boats will be used, and they don't want them brought back for warranty work. Too, in these boats weight is to be desired, for it ensures a good grip on the water and a smoothing out of the small waves that can jiggle your ears off in lightweight craft. The bottom is either deep-V or modified-V (shallow-V), with most of those mentioned above having shallow-V hulls. One shape or the other is almost a necessity if you are going to drive a small boat over big water. The cockpit is open, with most of the limited seating being built around a center console where all of the controls are located (when it is choppy, you almost certainly will want to stand, not sit). As a rule, these boats will shed water from the cockpit in a hurry, usually by self-bailing scuppers.

Power for the 17s is in the so-called midrange of outboard motors, with choices ranging all the way from 50 to 120 h.p. or more. Some owners opt for twin outboard installations, although knowledgeable skippers like the economy and simplicity of a single motor backed up by a low-horsepower outboard. The motors are bolted to the transom, with a splash well to handle slop over the cutout in the stern. Built-in fuel tanks are available in several models, a useful—if sometimes controver-

sial—feature because of the relatively high fuel requirements for long-distance travel (for more on fuel tanks, see page 99).

If not exactly common, it still is not unusual to see a full complement of electronics mounted in one of these boats. Virtually standard are magnetic compass, VHF radio, Loran, and LCD (liquid crystal display) depthsounder and fish finder. If room can be found, some skippers will add a depth recorder and even radar and a GPS (global positioning system) receiving unit. Throw in a broad selection of fishing gear, and costs of these fishing machines can boil upward well into five figures. However, if you can contain your "must-have" list to a few basic needs, a boat, motor, and trailer package might come in under $15,000.

The small center-console type makes a fine fishing boat for two or three persons, but numbers above a threesome quickly degenerate into a crowd, even though the hulls can

Privateer

Tashmoo

Wahoo!

Three hull types are represented in this class of boats with the modified-V Privateer, the traditional launch-type Tashmoo 18, and the cathedral-hulled Wahoo! 17.

This 15-year-old-plus Tripp Angler 18 carries her years well despite steady use by owner John J. Gould. Notice the high angle of the wheel—most of these boats are operated from a standing position.

Somewhat more elaborate in seating and console design, this Aquasport 17 leaves lots of room for fighting fish.

safely carry a half-dozen or more. We noted the shortage of seating space, but equally important is the need for room to move around when casting or handling a fish. We've fished aboard a 23-footer with six aboard, and it was just too crowded for relaxing comfort. In addition, people-weight adds up a lot more quickly aboard a 17-footer than in a 22-footer; the heft of five or six persons is going to affect fuel consumption, speed, and maneuverability, all critical factors in any long-distance fishing trip.

Given a reasonable crew size, though, these boats offer a lot for a little. They are big enough to carry a good selection of rods, tackle, and bait, and if a bit on the small size for outriggers, there is no denying they are close to the water when it comes time to land a fish. Their weight and low fuel consumption make them good, "long-legged" trollers, and once a big fish is hooked, their maneuverability can be used to advantage. They will also lie in the water reasonably well without blowing off downwind. Their speed is another advantage if you are sight-fishing for surfacing schools of gamefish. Their powerful hulls can be driven into snorting afternoon sea breezes without fear that they will disintegrate under the pounding. In fact, the pas-

sengers will probably fall apart first!

Many of the attributes of these center-console boats are attractive for uses other than fishing. The sturdy hulls and powerful motors provide the acceleration and course-holding ability that skiers like, so the 17s make good if not spectacular water-skiing boats. A basic model without all the fishing features and electronics is also a safe and roomy family boat that will serve well in coastal areas and on big lakes.

Some of the center-console boats would be good cruisers, too, depend-

ing on the location and size of the console itself, since these two factors pretty much determine the remaining space. As these are fairly small boats, most have raised platforms forward in order to best use the space over the V of the bow. The step-down space between the platform and console might be made more useful with a built-in filler "floor," which, in concert with a canvas dodger, would be adequate for a small sleeping area for two. However, a runabout version of the same hull would make a better cruiser because of the comfortable

Rigged for comfort in the cockpit, a Mako 17 sports a sprayhood to protect passengers in the forward console seat. The boat is really too small for sleeping aboard, one of the limitations of the center-consoles in this size class.

seats that quickly convert to usable, if narrow, bunks.

Nearly all the boats of this type have hull liners, an inner skin that adds stiffness, reduces maintenance, and cuts noise. Since storage space is at a real premium, it is a good idea to get your boat with a cooler/seat option (or build one yourself) that adds a large, relatively dry place to put things out of the way. Another option that helps make the boats a little drier is the use of readily available custom-fitted dodgers, a first big step toward making your little boat a cruiser.

Despite the many attractive features of the 17s, we would suggest that you think twice before buying one as a *first* boat. They were conceived as fishing boats, and their layout reflects this fact. The center-console configuration might prove uncomfortable or inadequate if your main reason for buying one of these boats were for uses other than fishing. Also, these rigs are not cheap, and by the time you have bought boat, motor(s), trailer, and gear your cost may be in the middle to upper teens, the same price as a new mid-size automobile. Since few people stay with their first boat purchase very long, you could end up losing a fair piece of change in moving to another type, even though the center-consoles hold their value better than many other recreational boats.

Having stated our opinion, it is only fair to present an equally valid opposite argument, namely one *for* one of these as a first boat. A good

> *Offshore fishing in a 17-footer is not for everyone, but it is not a stunt.*

friend who has had more experience than the writer with this particular breed of outboard boats says the simplicity of the 17s is a plus for first-timers. It means less maintenance for new buyers, he claims, "and they have the chance to think about ideal seating and storage in the next boat." Since his brother owns an old SeaCraft 20 ("Arguably the best boat of its type ever built," says my friend), and he himself is in the process of ordering a Parker 18, another fine example of the breed, you can use his argument to convince your spouse that this is the way to go.

We mentioned above that these boats cost about the same as a new car, and speaking of cars, you might be shocked to discover that your present auto is not up to towing one of these rigs, which can top the one-ton mark in some cases when the total weight of the boat, motor, trailer, and gear are computed. Towing a trailer and cargo this heavy is enough to wreck many car warranties—to say nothing of the cars. And if the only answer to having this boat of your dreams is to buy another automobile or even a truck, your cost of boating may be far beyond what you had planned.

All this aside, experienced skippers looking for truly capable boats will find a wide and exciting choice in the center-console field. But if you plan to save money by looking for a used 17, you may have to do a lot of scratching. Those who have 'em, love 'em and keep 'em.

—DRG

The Tin Skiff: America's Favorite Fishing Boat

Ice could still be seen among the trees on the shore of Moosehead Lake, Maine, as I trolled for salmon near Sugar Island in my 14-foot Starcraft Seafarer outboard skiff. The wind was piping out of the south, rolling great graybeards before it, and the rugged little aluminum boat was coming off some of the tops with a gear-rattling crash. But I was dry, comfortable, and catching fish, confident the boat was up to the day's demands.

It was several years after that and some 1,500 miles north when a friend and I dragged our big 18-foot Lund aluminum boat up a gravel beach in northern Labrador to leave it while we went mountain climbing. We had just traveled 450 miles up that wild and barren coast from the Strait of Belle Isle and would begin our return the same way in a couple of days.

Today, the Starcraft is gone and missed—sold for more than I paid for her after a dozen years of hard use. She was replaced by the Lund, my first new aluminum boat, which has carried me thousands of miles in the 14 years I've had her. As can be deduced from the record of these two boats, well-made aluminum skiffs given reasonable care will last a long time.

Tin boats? I love 'em! And I'm not alone in my passion. Millions of aluminum boats ply the waters of North America, and thousands more are sold each year. Some serve as first or backup boats for people who go on to larger craft or yachts; for others, this is all the boat they will ever need or want. Innumerable other aluminum boats go to work each day, carrying commercial fishermen, game wardens, rescue teams, and construction workers to a thousand different tasks.

The key to the pervasive popularity of aluminum boats is their utility. For those going on the water for recreational activities, for work, or for just getting from one place to another quickly and cheaply, the boats have a lot going for them. Better still, it's hard to get a real dunker today because pleasure boats have to meet certain safety standards of the U.S. Coast Guard, and a lot of them are built to American Boat and Yacht Council voluntary standards as well.

Though the Coast Guard sets flotation and powering standards, the designer and builder decide how the boat will be built. Thus, there are mediocre boats, good ones, and a few excellent ones, and since all of them cost a fair bundle of money, it's nice to have some idea as to how you can find the best boat for your money.

USE AND PERFORMANCE

As always, when choosing any boat, one should first list the jobs the craft will be expected to do. Pond fishing calls for one kind of boat, water-skiing another, coastal cruising something else, and ocean fishing still another. Almost every boat is a compromise, so it's good idea to list what these will be so your ski-loving family isn't shocked when you show up with a river-floating jonboat.

Deciding in advance how the boat will be used is important, but you can still make mistakes. I recall watching an experienced Canadian guide proudly leave the dock in his new sharp-nosed aluminum skiff with a pair of hefty sports sitting side by side a bit forward of amidships. A moderate chop was coming down the lake, pushed by a breeze that was just right for fishing, but his clients were quickly soaked as the sleek boat plunged into every wave, throwing spray and occasional dollops of solid water over the sides. Since his livelihood depended on his boat, the guide soon unloaded his streamlined beauty for a more practical apple-bowed model that would lift to the seas and stay dry.

If you go cold into the business of boat shopping, you can easily be lost in the maze of claims. It helps to talk with other boatowners first, especially those with boats you like; they may go so far as to take you for a ride and direct you to a reliable dealer. Ask questions that concentrate on subjective as well as objective features. For instance, how is the boat in rough water? Is it wet or dry? Noisy? Hard riding? Has it stood up to use? How long have you had it?

Of course, you have to consider the "owner factor" in evaluating the answers. No one likes to say his boat is piece of junk, but the tenor of his replies can tell you a lot. If he has had the boat for several years, chances are his comments will be closer to the actual truth.

A good dealer will sound out your needs and show his wares, pointing out the strong points of his boat line. His advice will be helpful, depending on his own knowledge of small

One of the most popular and versatile of all small boats, the 14-foot aluminum skiff may well be the most used boat in America. This solidly built Sea Nymph 14M is one of the better models and, in experienced hands, is quite able to go on lake, river, or ocean.

The floor frames (called floors) in this 16-footer indicate that the cockpit will have a deck and the spaces between floors will be filled with foam. Note the two transom knees.

boats, but you should also take the time to examine the boats by yourself to look for the things that separate the good from the not so good.

If you are a first-time buyer, your best bet is to heed this venerable truism: You probably won't be satisfied with your first boat very long. Experience invariably changes one's conceptions, and usually one's desires. So a conservative choice will serve you best, whether you choose to keep your first pride for use as a second boat, or to sell or trade it toward another.

With this simple caveat in mind, the next thing to do is to look right past the graphics, the shiny paint, and the gleaming accessories to concentrate on the boat itself. In aluminum skiffs, almost everything is right there to look at, warts and all. Because no mass-produced small boat is perfect, weigh the pros and cons fairly by deciding what you can and cannot live with. In an aluminum boat, the finished product is supposed to be a carefully planned fusion of the parts: Seats serve as supporting

frames to the hull, knees stiffen against twisting and bending, gunwales keep the sides from flapping, the plywood chunk on the transom absorbs the thrust of the motor.

QUALITY OF CONSTRUCTION

It's easy to spot the signs of quality workmanship. Aluminum hulls are either welded or riveted, and when done properly either method will result in a strong, leak-free hull. Welding allows for smoother expanses of metal; rivets give an impression of strength. Smooth welds without a lot of irregular or crusty-looking lumps in the bead indicate skill in the process (Crestliner and Fisher boats are good examples). Rivets should line up evenly and be spaced far enough apart for a good bite of metal but close enough so that the plates are held flat against one another. Double lines of rivets at high-stress points, such as the joining of side and bottom plates and the transom and sides, are sometimes used on larger skiffs.

The aluminum itself should be of the 5000 series of high-magnesium-

content marine alloys. Just about all aluminum boats are built with these alloys today, but if you are buying new, it won't hurt to ask. Plate thickness is fairly consistent among builders, ranging from .050 inch in the 12-footers up to .072 inch in some of the 16-footers. Some builders often use a heavier sheet in the bottom and lighter sheets on the sides. Most of the well-built boats carry 10-year hull warranties for pleasure use, a good indication of their expected durability.

Another sign of quality is how the various parts fit. Gaps in riveted joints, uneven or ragged cuts in plates, poorly fitting seats, flush cuts on floor frames instead of tapered or rounded stampings show hurried or poorly trained workmanship and money-saving shortcuts. Any sharp edges or corners should be filed or rolled. No matter how nice everything seems, it is worth the time to go over the entire boat with a file after you get it home to smooth out any prickle points the builder may have left. If not, someone is sure to find them with bare feet or thighs.

Exposed wood in the seats and lockers should be sanded smooth and have a durable finish. If it is peeling

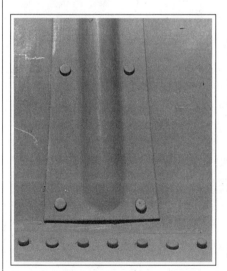
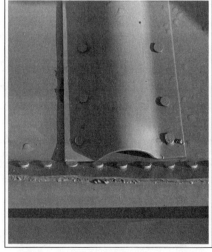

These two views look down inside at the floor of two skiffs. Notice how the floor frame of the one on the left is rounded and fits smoothly, while the one on the right was simply cut off. The latter could be hard on bare feet; it also warns of hurried, cost-cutting construction.

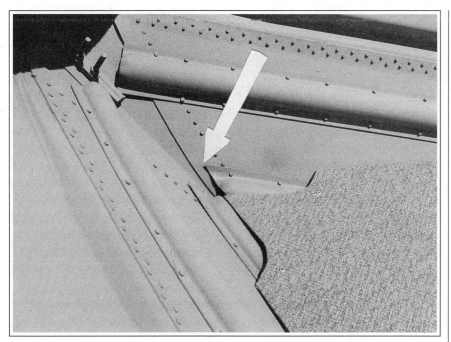

Looking down inside the bow of this skiff you can see solid construction. But the owner will want to take a hammer to bend down the two points of the frames (arrow). It is good practice for a new owner to go over the boat with file, hammer, and screwdriver at hand to make sure all is complete on these mass-produced boats.

or beginning to check while still at the dealer, imagine what it will look like after two months of sun and water.

If you look at a number of different boats, you will see two lines of thought on transom design. One school leaves the wood exposed with nothing more than a couple of coats of paint. The other school may go to great pains to encase wood in aluminum and even provide an additional metal plate for motor clamps. Even though the second, more expensive method may simply add more beef to an already rugged transom, there is no denying that it improves the looks (Sea Nymph does a particularly good job in this respect), especially a year or so down the road when the paint is peeling from the plywood, and motor clamps have gouged deep, ugly scars in the unprotected wood of the exposed transom.

Another place where you will find two different approaches to construction is the spray rails. Some manufacturers stamp them in the side plates; others rivet a separate rail to the side. The latter could be called overbuilding, since both

ways are strong enough to serve as side girders. Bottom skegs, once common on virtually all aluminum skiffs, are missing from many boats.

"If the omission of outside skegs is compensated for inside with additional floor frames, there is no apparent loss of strength," says Harvey Kowitz, vice president of production for Lund in New York Mills, Minnesota. "There is no question they help the flatter hulls to track, but the deeper-V hulls get along nicely without them."

A strong argument can be made for the skegs as bottom protection. My 18-footer has spent a decade of hard work on Maine's rockbound coast and granite-lined inland lakes. It has been grounded hundreds of times on sand, gravel, boulders, and ledges along with having "touched" occasionally while underway. The five skegs show nicks, cuts, and minor dents, but the bottom is virtually unmarked, thanks almost exclusively to the added protection.

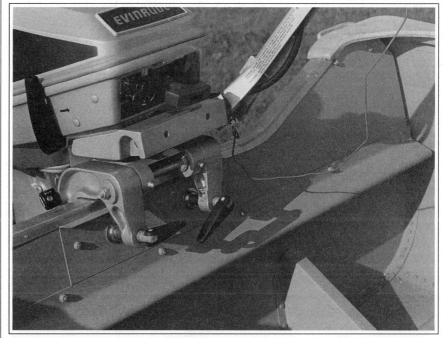

The well-designed transom on this 14-footer is thick plywood encased in aluminum. Note the lip just above the motor clamps, which would prevent the motor from jumping off should the clamps work loose.

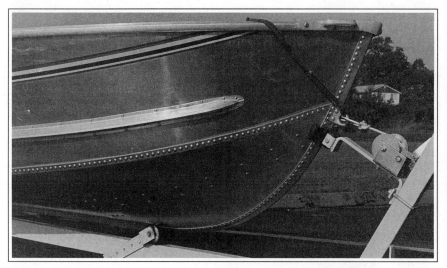
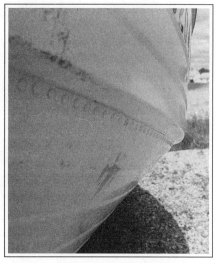

Two types of spray rails common in skiffs are an external one riveted to the hull (left), and one pressed into the metal (right). The effectiveness of the riveted rail can be seen in the photo on page 17. Spray rails are a necessity on virtually all small motorboats.

HANDLING EASE

Since small boats are manhandled a lot, it pays to try the various places where fingers will be in contact with metal. Most skiffs have a cast aluminum breasthook at the point of the bow, some with handholds built in, others with rounded inner edges. This is one of the most commonly grasped places on the boat, and it is important that the edge be comfortable and nick-free to the hand. The same holds true for the cast quarter knees at the corners of the transom. Even if additional handles are provided, the knees will be grabbed a lot and should be free of sharp edges.

Some of the castings are simply screwed on top of the gunwales and transom, so their strength is mainly that of their fastenings, which may be nothing more than small screws. The best castings are fitted to the curves in the gunwale and transom caps and contribute measurably to the strength of the boat (see bottom photo on page 19).

The gunwale cap or caprail is not only an important stiffening member for the sides, but it is also used a great deal as a hand grip. Make sure the rails are well fastened and offer a good grip on both sides.

Don't expect perfection in the paint job. Aluminum boats are spray-painted for aesthetic reasons and not preservation, and minor runs and spray overlaps can sometimes be found. However, look for rust dots on nuts, bolts, and washers, especially if you plan to use the boat in salt water. These indicate zinc-chromated or thinly galvanized steel fastenings that may eventually corrode through.

We mentioned earlier that just about all aluminum boats are now built of highly corrosion-resistant marine alloys. Problems may arise, though, if the aluminum is in direct contact with other metals in salt water. The electrolytic current flow between these dissimilar metals can lead to corrosion of the aluminum. "An obvious and often effective method" to prevent this, says Kaiser Aluminum in its informative soft-cover book, *Aluminum Boats*, "is to separate the aluminum surfaces from those of dissimilar metals by means of gaskets, washers, sleeves, and bushings of insulating materials such as Neoprene, Alumalastic, Fairprene, Presstite, and Micarta." An outboard motor might set up such a current, but motors usually have sacrificial zinc anodes that eliminate this possibility.

When you are eventually through studying rivets, welds, and carpet colors, and have kicked the trailer tires, get on the water in the boat before you buy. Some dealers keep demonstrators and are happy to give test rides to prospective customers. When testing, don't concentrate only on speed but try the hull from a crawl to about three-quarters throttle, the speed range in which you will probably be doing much of your boating. Notice particularly the point where the hull goes from displacement speed to planing. Some boats squat badly at this changeover point, resulting in poor visibility and handling at a speed that can be very useful other-

The quarter knees are an integral part of an aluminum skiff, and some have a lifting handle built in.

wise. If the boat will be used for a lot of trolling while fishing, low-speed characteristics of the hull will be important, as will be the fullness of the bow to lift easily over the waves. (For more on testing a boat, see "How to Test a Boat" on page 6.)

Aluminum boats are light, immensely tough, easy to care for, and modest in cost. Many of the more expensive models feature carpeted decks and seats and are as quiet as any other open boat. It comes down in the end to the old adage that beauty is in the eye of the beholder. After you have lived with your tin skiff for awhile, you will be surprised at how nice it looks.

—DRG

The Ever-Popular Runabout

Trying to determine when the first fiberglass runabout was built is a little like trying to determine when the yam entered the food chain. No one really knows for sure, and neither was accepted that quickly.

Fiberglass entered the boatbuilding industry through the slow process of technological evolution. As with any pioneering effort with a new material, many designs and construction methods were tried. Some worked, some did not.

For centuries prior to the advent of fiberglass, wood had been *the* boatbuilding material. But each boat required hundreds of man-hours by skilled craftsmen, and the high-quality materials necessary for long-lived boats were becoming increasingly scarce and expensive. In the 1940s, many U.S. companies were involved in the research and development of a new wonder material, fiber-reinforced plastic (FRP). The Owens-Corning Corporation emerged as the clear front-runner in the early 1950s with the creation of their trademark product, "Fiberglas." Their intensive promotion and marketing were largely responsible for introducing the new technology into the boating industry.

It was then up to the marine industry, anxious to meet expanding demand for recreational watercraft in the booming postwar years, to develop practical applications for the new product. One of their first attempts, in the early 1950s, involved covering conventional wooden hulls with a thin fiberglass shell. This took advantage of the watertight characteristics of fiberglass but mostly ignored its added strength and durability. More important, it did little to reduce the long and expensive hours of maintenance necessary to keep a wooden boat looking spiffy. It did accomplish one thing, though: It whetted the boat-buying public's appetite for sleeker, faster boats that required less maintenance.

Builders responded quickly, and by the mid-1950s the first solid fiberglass hulls and decks began to appear

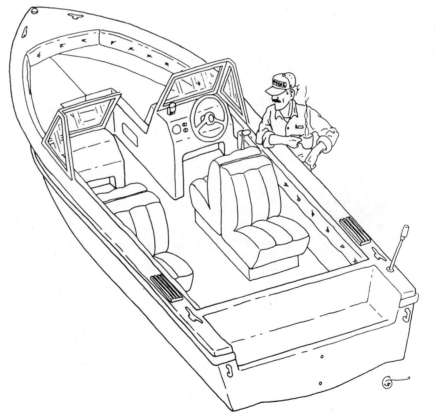

Rob Groves

Runabout layout has changed little over the years. Typical is the large slop well in the stern, with fore-and-aft seats on either side of a walk-through aisle that leads forward to the bow seating well. The starboard steering console may have a few or many controls, depending on the model.

Jim Anderson

A modified-V runabout is usually a good sea boat, but early models like this one didn't allow access forward.

Jim Anderson

This tri-hull (also called cathedral hull) runabout has access and seating forward, but the hull type might gain space inside at the cost of a rougher ride in choppy water.

faced monumental problems.

Despite the mistakes, these early designs led a revolution in the boating industry. Suddenly, boatbuilders had at their disposal a composite material that could be sprayed or molded into a boat by semiskilled labor in a fraction of the time required for a wooden boat to be laboriously constructed, piece by piece, by artisans. Molded fiberglass boats made possible the dream of an affordable, easily maintained, well-performing boat for Everyman.

DESIGNS

While builders were busy developing new construction methods from scratch, they were also faced with developing designs that appealed to an eager new market, much of which owed no allegiance to and had no love for traditional naval architecture.

The low freeboard and flat bottoms of the early models were quickly replaced by deeper V-hulls, which eliminated many of the handling problems. The V-hull also gave a quieter, safer, and more comfortable ride, which was substantially enhanced by the boat's weight. This was when American industry seemed to overbuild everything. Our automobiles were made of real steel and lots of it. That same more-is-better philosophy also applied to the fiberglass boats of the 1960s and early 1970s. The comparison between boats and automobiles didn't stop at weight, either. The car-like boats of the late 1950s and early 1960s were all but indistinguishable from the boat-like car: the steering wheels and dashboards were a near match; pleated upholstery was everywhere; and fins were in.

Although the V-hull was a vast improvement over the first flat-bottomed efforts and provided a sound basic design from which to ex-

in showrooms. One of the early successes was the Larson Boat Company and its popular Falls Flyer and Play-Boy models. Today the Falls Flyer is considered a classic; a nicely restored one may sell for $4,000 or more.

Although technology was advancing rapidly, early fiberglass boats were plagued with design and con-struction flaws. Boats of this era had little freeboard and flat bottoms, which made them exciting to say the least. The Falls Flyer, for example, has been known to roll over on short, fast turns. The fledgling industry, with few guidelines or regulations as to horsepower rating, flotation, or structural engineering, periment, its execution left much to be desired. Again, in an attempt to be as car-like as possible, a typical 16-foot boat might have nearly a third of its length covered by a long, hood-like deck—usually topped by an oversized windshield, which made it difficult to move forward when docking or beaching. The space under the deck was good only for storage and severely limited room for passengers.

To make use of this wasted space in the bow, designers in the late 1960s and early 1970s came up with the walk-through, or bow-rider, which had a seating area forward of the control console. Although I can't find anyone to confirm this, I suspect that, now that the boat's extreme bow could be occupied by passengers, designers felt it necessary to add stability forward by widening the bow. At any rate, simultaneous with the appearance of the walk-through came the tri-hull.

All the added interior space made the tri-hulls immediately popular, but then new design problems surfaced, most noticeably in the ride. Unlike the V-hulls, which cut through the waves, the tri-hulls tended to slap over them, resulting in a much rougher ride. The constant pounding at high speed also caused windshield hardware, electrical connections, seat hardware, etc., to work loose. The tri-hulls may have been stable in calm water, but when things got a little sloppy they proved difficult to handle. In heavy seas, some of the early models were downright unsafe.

Over the years many companies experimented with the basic tri-hull design, and it has been extensively modified in an attempt to minimize its drawbacks. However, except for a few notable exceptions, such as the Boston Whaler, tri-hulls have not stood the test of time, and today new boats with the traditional tri-hull are hard to find.

Today's showrooms are filled with a new generation of runabouts, often referred to as fish-and-skis, which combine the comfort, safety, and inherent stability of the V-hull with an open bow previously found only in tri-hulls. These boats are available with wide array of accessories—removable pedestal seats, live wells, extra power—and appeal to a wide variety of boaters.

—Jim Anderson
(*Runabout Renovation*,
International Marine, 1992)

The Handy Jonboat

Almost everyone knows what a jonboat is. For years now, aluminum ones have been a common sight in dealer showrooms, bait and tackle shops, department stores, discount houses, and other outlets, but few boating enthusiasts realize how versatile and practical these durable, inexpensive boats are.

Consider the dart-shaped airplanes that kids love to make—they are a production engineer's dream come true. Take a single sheet of material, make a few simple folds, and you have a finished product! An aluminum jonboat is, as far as manufacture is concerned, a floating version of the paper airplane.

The builder starts with a large sheet of aluminum, pressed to form V-shaped grooves that stiffen the sides and bottom as well as serving as rubrails and antiskid strips. Two deep, fairly narrow, V-shaped cuts are made at one end of the sheet so that the sides can be bent inward and the bottom bent upward. Seams, where these panels join, are welded

If you put too much power on, you will have a tiger that refuses to be held by the tail.

to form the jonboat's shovel bow, and the basic hull is complete. It is then a simple matter to rivet in place the transverse ribs (all of which are the same shape), the seats, and the gunwale trim strips. The finished jonboat doesn't need painting, because it is made from highly corrosion-resistant marine aluminum. To kill the glare, the entire hull is painted the same color, an unobtrusive green or beige. Fancier jonboats are, however, available in a variety of colors, and some include stripes and other graphics on the side.

Because these simple boats have no decks, shippers nest them like Banks dories and stack large numbers of them on tractor-trailer rigs for delivery to dealers all over the country. Simple, rapid construction and the economy of volume shipping have made the jonboat one of the best buys in boating. Many of the smallest, most basic boats, appropriate outboard motor included, sell for as little as $1,200.

The aluminum jonboat was, in the

Mercury Marine

Cheap, tough, and useful, today's aluminum jonboat is derived from the long, narrow riverboats of the Ozark country, which in turn are derived from unknown earlier boats—perhaps the punt?

beginning, a product of necessity, a way to keep existing facilities busy. During World War II, many companies installed sheet metal equipment to produce fuel tanks, shipping containers, aircraft components, and many other items for the armed forces. When the war ended, most of these companies rushed to return to civilian production. Grumman put its stretch presses to work making canoes. Meyers Aircraft switched from training planes to personal planes to aluminum boats. At the same time, metal fabricators in the Ozark region of Missouri and Arkansas, looking for likely products, saw how popular the wooden jonboat was on the rivers there and decided to make aluminum versions.

Lighter to haul out of the water and load onto trucks than the original wooden ones, aluminum jonboats could be stored dry and launched without worrying about leaks. The boats captured the fancy of Ozark boatmen. Manufacturers began to distribute these useful boats to outlets farther and farther away, and during the last 30 years jonboats have become common everywhere a need for simple, inexpensive boats exists.

Jonboats are available in sizes from 10 to 20 feet. The smaller ones have all but driven the once ubiquitous 8-foot plywood pram from the boating scene, and the larger ones have become as useful around the waterfront as pickup trucks are around the farm. V-bottomed versions that are more controllable and seakindly at planing speeds have

been designed, and from these, designers developed the freshwater bassboat (see page 27) that now can be seen on lakes and rivers across the country.

The jonboat's history is a lot clearer than the origin of its name. None of the manufacturers know, nor do any of the national, state, and local historical organizations. In fact, not even the august Smithsonian Institution knows from where the name *johnboat,* or more commonly, *jonboat,* came. Undaunted by one blind alley after another, I made use of the reader letters columns in newspapers in St. Louis, Little Rock, and New Orleans, asking persons in those areas to write if they had any information.

A gentleman from Missouri insisted that jonboats got their name from his father, whose name was John and who had built hundreds of them. A woman from St. Louis said that the boats were named in honor of their resemblance to the long, narrow, jonboat dish used for serving nuts and relishes. A man from Little Rock claimed that the name is a corruption of *cajun boat*. A correspondent from New Orleans vigorously rejected the cajun-boat theory by pointing out that nothing resembling the Ozark-style jonboat had ever been built in Louisiana. So we are left with a mystery. I had assumed that Ozark-style jonboats originated in the Ozarks. During my search for the name's origin, however, I discovered earlier references to jonboats that were made in other places. A paragraph about the term *johnboat* in a dictionary of American colloquialisms mentioned the appearance of the phrase "Missouri River johnboat" in a piece of literature dated 1905. The Smithsonian Institution sent a photocopy of a drawing of a 30-foot Cumberland River jonboat, and a notation on the drawing said that the lines had been taken off a derelict example of the type in 1938. A Currier & Ives print shows three gentlemen fishing on a pond from a boat that looks much like a jonboat. Currier & Ives prints were produced between 1860 and 1880, and it is reasonable to infer that craft of the jonboat type were being built in the eastern part of the country well before 1900. In a book describing the Howe Caverns, located several miles southwest of Schenectady, New York, two woodcuts made in the 1860s show cave exploration boats that appear to be identical in shape and construction to the later Ozark jonboats.

Settlers who trickled into the Ozarks during the nineteenth century existed primarily through farming, but they added variety to their diets with local fish and game. At first, men fished from riverbanks, but it wasn't long before they built crude boats—boxlike affairs that one might expect to see knocked together by farmers who were accustomed to making hog troughs and outhouses. Details of construction varied from boat to boat, depending on who built them. One characteristic, however, remained constant: these crude boats looked a great deal like the Eastern jonboats.

By the last decade of the nineteenth century, some Ozark men had become professional fishermen and plied the waters of the Piney, James, White, Gasconade, and Osage rivers. Originally, farmers after panfish were

> *Simple, rapid construction and the economy of volume shipping have made the jonboat one of the best buys in boating.*

content to use their own crude boats to paddle a few hundred yards up or down the river in search of deeper water. The commercial fishermen, on the other hand, began to cover more territory, using the current for power. They began to make boats up to 30 feet long and as little as two feet wide on the bottom. The narrow beam allowed the boats to slip through openings between river rocks and enabled a person to dip his paddle into the water first on one side, then on the other for maneuvering.

Typically, these boats were built with low sides made from long, 10- to 12-inch-wide boards, and with cross-planked bottoms made from 4- to 8-inch boards. Builders planked the bottoms leaving ⅛-inch gaps between the boards, which, they hoped, would close and seal when the wood swelled. Some builders chose to use three fore-and-aft planks on the bottom. Skegs covered the seams, sealed out water, and provided rubbing strips. Other builders used tongue-and-groove planking on the bottom, but those who wanted to simplify the building even more used paint-soaked strips of canvas or flannel. It was all self-taught, carpenter-style boat-building.

During the 1920s and on into the 1930s, sportsmen from Midwestern cities began discovering the excellent hunting and fishing the Ozarks provided, and float-fishing trips down the region's rivers grew into a thriving business. Guides became licensed, and entrepreneurs assembled fleets of jonboats and advertised for customers.

Builders began tailoring jonboats for this duty, and the length of the boats shrank to between 15 and 20 feet. As backyard builders gained skill, they introduced flare into the hull sides. Some had scowlike bows and sterns; others had flat bottoms amidships with some rocker built in toward the bow and stern to make for easier maneuvering. Seats were set right across the tops of the gunwales at a reasonably comfortable height for those low-sided boats. Sometimes old kitchen chairs or folding director's chairs were put aboard for the client's comfort. Occasionally a board would be set onto the stern and an outboard mounted to it.

A handful of handymen made a regular business out of providing jonboats to float-trip operators. Many built hundreds of boats; a few built as many as thousands, using whatever wood—usually pine, sometimes cypress—they could find locally. Construction details varied from man to man, but the boats were always on the rough-and-ready side. A loose knot in a board, for example, would be set in tar and left at that. There was no attempt at ostentation. These jonboats were built for fishing and camping, for utilitarian pleasure.

Ozark jonboats lived a rough life. They were scraped over rocks, hauled onto the shore, and loaded by the dozens onto railroad flatcars, later stake trucks, for shipment back to their owner's base of operations at the end of the float trips. Service seldom exceeded two or three years. If folks called these rigs *Ozark jonboats*, they did so more because a lot of them happened to be built and used there than for any notable refinement in design or construction.

Things changed fast after World War II. Highways were built, developers built summer cottages, rivers were damned and became artificial lakes, and aluminum jonboats appeared on the market. The artificial lakes got rough on blustery days; so the aluminum-smiths introduced wider, deeper models. Outboard power increased, and heavier construction was used to accommodate it. People may call these aluminum versions jonboats, but only in the squarish bow and flat bottom do they resemble the old float-fishing jonboats.

Modern jonboats are available in a range of sizes and types, including narrow ones up to about 16 or 17 feet long and around 32 to 34 inches across the bottom. These slim ones appeal to a lot of boaters because they will fit between the wheel wells of a station wagon or a pickup.

While most jonboats have oarlocks, they are not good rowboats. Because of the two upward folds made in the sheets of aluminum to form the sides, the chine line has to be dead straight from the end of the bow's upturn all the way back to the transom. They have no rocker at all. When being rowed, they drag water with their transoms and are as slug-gish as mortar beds. The rockerless bottom with skid *cum* reinforcing strips makes them hold a course like railroad cars, and at the same time makes them as maneuverable in tight spaces as a log in a swimming pool. If a decent rowboat is what you want, a jonboat isn't for you.

Because of the flat bottom, all planing lift acts directly upward. No power is wasted pushing a lot of water to port and starboard as with a deep-V hull. Jonboats need little power to get them on plane, and a small one, say 12 feet, will plane, with two kids aboard, on 3½ to 4 h.p. With two adults aboard, the same boat wants 7½ to 15 h.p.

One has to believe what the capacity plate on a jonboat says about the recommended load and power. The fairly narrow bottoms provide less hull volume than similar but beamier boats of the same length. The result is less initial buoyancy, and the low sides don't offer much reserve buoyancy. The narrow bottoms let jonboats bank into turns all right at speeds attainable with the recommended power, but if you put too much power on, you will have a tiger that refuses to be held by the tail.

The traditional jonboat has been gussied up with decks, carpeting, and swivel seats. As with many bassboats, it has been given a V-shaped bow and bottom and enough power to all but fly.

Devoid of floorboards, sidedecks, and fancy trim, a jonboat is a light craft. Under more power than it needs, it will get up on plane and scat like a cat on ice. Wind will get under the shovel-nosed bow and lift it, the boat will start to porpoise, and the steering will get hairy. The chine or the skid strips or both may bite water on the outside of a turn, and the centrifugal force will flip the works.

If you intend to do a lot of solo flying in a jonboat that has fairly decent power for its size and beam, get a tiller extension for your outboard motor. It will allow you to move forward one seat, and the shift in weight will, nine times out of ten, stop the porpoising. The tiller length will also provide a reduction gear effect, which requires broad movements at the extended handle to create the same effect that small movements did at the standard tiller.

It's not a good idea to stand up in the narrower jonboats, because they don't have enough lateral stability. On the other hand, their length-to-beam ratio gives them a lot of longitudinal stability. The upturned bows vary from make to make and model to model. Some lift over a chop all right; others have a quirk. Going into a chop, the low, flat bow may plow into one wave at the same time as the crest of another wave lifts hard on the afterbody of the boat. As the stern goes up, an equal and opposite reaction will hold the bow down. If the wave into which the craft is poking is big enough, you are likely to ship solid water in over the bow.

The wider jonboats, say 55 to 65 inches on a length of 16 feet, are designed for intermediate-size motors of 25 to 50 h.p. These *lake jonboats*, as one might call them, are higher in the sides and more heavily built than the narrow *river jonboats*. Moderately priced and durable, they make good utility boats for couples who love bay fishing, scalloping, and gunkholing. Some of the larger ones have been fitted with shelter cabins that are open on the after end.

With 35, 40, or 50 h.p. on the stern, a flat-bottomed jonboat will start to pound badly when the breeze builds up a chop, so makers offer V-bottomed models. This shape can take the sting out of a moderate chop, but one must remember that when any shovel-bowed boat meets a fairly heavy chop, the whole underbody forward will connect with the wave faces at once. A tremendous amount of lift is generated, and the boat behaves like a bucking bronco. If you expect to encounter that kind of water, forget about jonboats and look for some of the more burdensome, pointed-bow aluminum skiffs. Shovel bows do have some advantages. They allow the craft to be run up onto a riverbank or beach. The flatness of the bottom up forward will hold the bow steady, and the overhang will let you step onto dry ground.

Prices for jonboats run the gamut from the low hundreds to several thousand for some of the fancy bassboats. At a typical retail outlet, you will see only a few of the many brands and models available. If you want to see more, and you should, write to the manufacturers and ask for their advertising literature and whatever technical literature they are willing to send. Read the material carefully and make your choice.

—Bob Whittier
(*Small Boat Journal* #23)

> An aluminum jonboat is a floating version of the paper airplane.

The Booming, Zooming Bassboat

Simply by existing in great numbers in a wide variety of environments and exhibiting the predatory, pugnacious nature that has endeared it to generations of sportfishermen, the freshwater bass spawned a boat called, not surprisingly, a *bassboat*. In about 25 years, this craft has evolved from homely jonboat-style to sleek, high-tech performer.

In the Old South, the ubiquitous flat-bottomed jonboat (see previous piece), easily fashioned from rough-cut lumber and "corked" with remnants of discarded garments, was a universal, all-purpose waterway conveyance. Heavy oars propelled these small craft as late as the early years of the twentieth century, although they could also be paddled or sculled.

But as more leisure time and sophisticated tackle became available, anglers who enjoyed fishing for bass became more numerous and, inevitably, began to alter their boats to suit their avocation. Low-horsepower outboard motors appeared and began to replace sweat and muscle.

It would be a long time, however, before bass fishermen felt the need for a great deal more than a flat-bottomed, slow-moving craft that could work in the shallows of small streams and lakes. On such small water, the angler encountered ripples, not waves. Fishermen rarely paddled, rowed, or put-puttered far from home.

Safety features were ignored or little thought of. If your boat capsized, a rare event in placid water, you simply swam or waded to shore. You then righted your craft and continued fishing.

BASSBOAT ORIGINS

By the 1930s, Holmes A. Thurmond, a Shreveport, Louisiana, Evinrude dealer, had heard enough round-the-stove talk from bass fishermen to conclude that they would buy a lighter, faster, well-constructed boat that would let them fish more in a given time with less of that time tied up in slow travel. He also wanted such a boat for himself. Thus was born the first Skeeter.

It was constructed of ⅜-inch marine plywood with a somewhat beefier transom, fastened with marine nails and brass screws. Framing was at first oak and later mahogany.

Thurmond fished from his boat for a time and then put it on the market for $154. It was an instant hit. The light little boat with its pointed bow and partial deck looked good to anglers accustomed to craft modeled after the garbage-scow school of design. The Skeeter functioned well in the small streams and lakes it was designed for. It was fast and energy-efficient. For only two fishermen,

however, its narrow, 14-foot length was confining, and stability was not a strong point. Tall waves were seldom encountered in small local waters, but if confronted they could douse boat occupants and require bailing.

The role of Holmes Thurmond and his Skeeter in early bassboat evolution is undisputed. But it is universally conceded by chroniclers of piscatorial esoterica that the modern bassboat really began with Forrest Wood of Flippin, Arkansas, who set up shop behind a local filling station in 1967.

Wood had been a fishing guide for 14 years at Bull Shoals and other lakes in the Arkansas Ozarks. A tall,

At speeds of 40 m.p.h. or less, under most conditions, the bassboat handles like the family car and is dry and comfortable.

lanky man, he had spent much of his youth with chin on knees in the cramped, wooden jonboat of his region.

He experimented with wood and aluminum, but by 1968 was making a boat with a wooden frame and flat-bottomed fiberglass hull. In that year, he visited the second bass tournament sponsored by the fledgling B.A.S.S. (the Bass Anglers Sportsman Society), hauling his glorified jonboat with him. B.A.S.S. anglers liked his demonstration model, and he went home with several orders for custom versions geared to the needs of bass-tournament fishermen. This was an orientation that ultimately turned the former Arkansas farm boy into the owner of a multimillion-dollar business.

At the 1968 B.A.S.S. tournament, Wood also met Ray Scott, who had

founded the Bass Anglers Sportsman Society only the year before and who was struggling to make bass-tournament competition, a small-time Southern fun-and-games recreation, into a money-making enterprise.

In 25 years Scott's organization, on the crest of a national fad, has grown into a society of more than 560,000 members, with worldwide affiliations. Wood, in on the watery ground floor with his improved bassboat, has ridden that boat into fortune.

The boating needs of the bass-tournament angler in 1968 were many. Wood could not, by any means, fill all of them at once. Pros no longer sat down to fish; they stood up, usually in the bow, and they needed a good nonskid deck to stand on. They required a boat with shallow draft and the stability of a flat bottom, but at the same time one that would rise from the thrust of a powerful engine and take off at high speed to a new location or a far-away dock. Time, for the tournament angler, was literally money.

And boats had to have built-in flotation, for big East Texas lakes like Sam Rayburn posed threats to life not faced in small streams and lakes. Aerated livewells were also needed, for dead bass at weigh-in could cost anglers a small fortune.

Finally, the fundamental design of the bassboat needed change. Pro angler Rick Clunn points out that in the 1960s speed was not so important. His first boat was a 14-footer with a 25-horse Evinrude. "A 15-footer," says Rick, "was a big boat then. But when there were four-foot waves and that little pointed nose went through a couple of them, you said, 'Hey, either I quit fishing these big lakes or I get a boat that can get across this wide open area.'"

According to Rick, the narrow, pointed-nose boats with very low freeboard, built like the pioneer Skeeter, became submarines under such conditions. "One minute," he recalls, "you were running, and the next you were underwater."

Even though the bassboat is a popular general-purpose recreational vehicle, there is no way to separate the development of the bassboat from B.A.S.S. or from bass-tournament fishing. Rapid changes in boat design and equipment came about in the pressure-cooker of tournament competition because much was at stake. It is no longer uncommon for a tournament pro to compile yearly winnings of more than $250,000, not counting income from product endorsements.

BASSBOAT DESIGN

Forrest Wood's glorified jonboat did not in one magical leap become the sleek, efficient craft of today. It remained flat-bottomed for a time, but that quickly changed, for tournament fishermen needed speed and a V-hull to cut through waves. Powerful outboard motors had been developed and transoms had to be strengthened to accept increased stress.

In this connection, it should be noted that the tournament pro's principal interest in speed is not to outgun a competitor to a prized fishing spot, but to use as much of his allotted fishing time as possible in actual fishing. Some pros make as many as 15 casts a minute, or 6,000 in a long day. So, five minutes spent in casting

rather than running has often won a tournament. An improvement, popular for a time, was the sponson-type or cathedral hull—a V-hull with a "gull-wing" look when viewed head-on. The sponson was an attempt to solve the problem of boat stability at rest coupled with an ability to cope with 3- or 4-foot waves. In practice, it did not ride rough water as well as the plain-V that is standard today.

The old transoms were straight across, or nearly so. Today, Ranger sterns have concave corners. This configuration sets the transom-mounted motor back from the stern to give quicker lift and top speed.

The riding pad, simply a few square inches of flat surface to which the V-hull tapers, solved the problem of combining high-speed potential

Mercury Marine

Today's bassboats manage to meet a number of conflicting requirements: blazing speed, stability, and seaworthiness. Development has been spurred by professional fishing tournaments.

and stability in the same boat. In fact, the modern bassboat's stability is usually attained by a wide transom, with the greatest beam at the stern of the craft. A bassboat equipped with a pad and a high-performance outboard comes out of the at-rest "hole" in a hurry and speeds along with minimal contact with the water. Today's boats also have "upright and level" foam flotation, so no good bassboat is going to sink, even if it is full of water.

When involved in tournament fishing, the modern bassboat is designed to get there in a hurry, get bass into the livewell while there, and head back for the weighing podium like a speeding bullet.

Though some firms make excellent aluminum bassboats, Ranger used only fiberglass until recently, when they also introduced an aluminum model. Their most popular fiberglass models weigh, on average, about 1,200 pounds and are 17 or 18 feet long with 80- to 88-inch beams. The widest section of the boat is at the transom. There is little deadrise, and draft is only a few inches at rest. At high speed, only a tiny bit of pad touches the water.

Bass-fishing pros continue to insist upon their own boat modifications. For instance, bass pro Basil Bacon states flatly that "there is no such thing as a bassboat that doesn't need a jackplate." The jackplate's primary purpose is to set the motor away from the boat transom by 5¾ to 6½ inches. This arrangement provides additional leverage to lift the bow of the boat, getting it into action faster from a dead start. Once the boat is on plane, the operator can eke out more speed by raising the engine height to decrease lower unit drag. Bacon also uses the hydraulic jackplate to modify the boat handling with load increases or decreases. And in shallow water, the hydraulic jackplate can lift the motor straight

Not your Sunday-afternoon pond-basser, this Astro is a high-priced fiberglass tournament boat designed to get its fishermen back to the dock in minutes and back to the fishing grounds in even less time. (No, Mother, they aren't fishing out the lakes; the fish are weighed and thrown back, and dead fish usually count against your point total.) Note how the deep-V hull is riding on just its after few feet of length. Note also the running strakes, clearly visible on the underbody, which combat the chine-walking tendency of a deep-V hull.

up while underway, whereas the manual user has to tilt his engine to keep the prop off the bottom, slowing down in the process (see "Why Jack an Outboard?" on page 94).

Powerful outboards have made necessary far stronger transoms. For example, Ranger's new "pultruded" fiberglass transom is so hard that water-cooled, tungsten-carbide bits are needed to drill mounting holes.

Since the early days, the trolling motor has been an essential part of a bassboat, whether in a big-bucks tournament or on a family outing. The small, quiet, battery-driven motor pushes a 1,200-pound boat around efficiently and does not spook fish. In addition to increased power, their most significant change over the years has been to move from the stern of the boat to the bow.

For years the top bassboats have been built of fiberglass, but aluminum-boat builders like Fisher are now competing for a share of this lucrative market.

The real market is not the pros but the average motorboat owner. This Bayliner Cobra can be equipped for fishing, water-skiing, or just plain ramming around. Other manufacturers are doing the same.

FAMILY CRAFT

The modern bassboat is a marvel of efficiency in terms of both fuel use and performance. It combines eye-watering speed with incredible stability at rest. Console seats are comfortable, while pedestal seats on deck, handy for quick rest while fishing, may be removed. Storage space for fishing rods, clothing, food, cameras, TVs, whatever, is all over the boat, and that storage is dry.

Such features have caused the bassboat to evolve into a safe, enjoyable craft suitable for family fun. Although Ranger and other manufacturers still provide boats as specialized tools for a specialized outdoor activity, Cliff Shelby, advertising director for Ranger Boats, says about 40 percent of that firm's sales comes from dual-console family-recreation boats. "Bassboat," says Shelby, "is now a misnomer."

Many a "press angler," by the way, seated beside a tournament pro be-hind the console, has prayed for a bassboat improvement that has yet to arrive: a painless ride at high speed over rough water. Larry Nixon, a veteran of more than 20 years of bassboat tournaments, opines that "we need to come up with some kind of shock-seat or something."

But the owner of a recreational

> A gamefish has spawned a boat genus; has been responsible for the amassing of at least two fortunes; and has made a great deal of money for many good ole boys.

bassboat is under no compulsion to stress himself, his family, or his boat. At speeds of 40 m.p.h. or less, under most conditions, the bassboat handles like the family car and is dry and comfortable.

Hank Parker, another pro angler (now retired), says that comparing the regular pleasure or runabout boat to a bassboat is like comparing a Chevrolet to a Ferrari. "Its handling," he says, "is far superior to the big runabout. The hull design is superior. It is probably more seaworthy than 50 to 60 percent of the big runabouts of the same length."

Although some firms are building bass/motor combinations capable of 100-m.p.h. speeds, Forrest Wood has always built boats with safety and handling performance as primary virtues, with speed secondary. The Ranger bestseller today is a fish-and-ski configuration.

"A lot of people," says Cliff Shelby, "are boat camping. Storage areas in our boats are sealed and waterproof and can hold picnic gear, clothing, camping gear, tents, and other supplies. In lots of places you have to get a permit to camp, and camping areas are crowded; but, if you are on the water, miles and miles of shoreline are often open to camping. And in the big reservoirs and rivers, there are plenty of islands on which to camp and explore."

So, a gamefish—the freshwater bass—has spawned a boat genus; has been responsible for the amassing of at least two fortunes; has its fins firmly embedded in the affairs of many businesses from small locals to multinational corporations; and has made a great deal of money for many good ole boys in a manner no one would have believed possible two decades ago.

The end is by no means in sight, though it is probable that the bass itself would just as soon rest under a big lily pad awaiting the arrival of a tasty, absolutely nonartificial, hookless frog.

—William C. Blizzard
(*Small Boat Journal* #67)

Skinny-Water Boating in the Western Jet Boat

Most boaters avoid shallow water and rocky shoals like the plague—especially if they've had to repair bent shafts, broken propellers, or damaged hulls. Jet-powered aluminum boats, however, have all but eliminated those threats, and they have dramatically increased whitewater river access for outdoor sportsmen.

The Pacific Northwest has been at the center of the development of jet-powered aluminum boats, according to Glen Wooldridge of Wooldridge Aluminum Boats in Seattle, particularly with outboard jets. "Many people are now realizing the jet's capability throughout the U.S. and the world," Wooldridge says. "Northern California and Missouri are enthusiastic, and I am now shipping boats to Texas, Kentucky, Virginia, Penn-sylvania, and the Great Lakes. I've also got two boats in Chile, and I'm filling orders for impellers to Sweden."

My first chance to experience this increasingly popular type of boating came when Wooldridge offered a test ride on the Skykomish River, 30 miles north of Seattle. Not only did he prove the claim that his outboard jet pump–powered boats could do 40 m.p.h. in 4 inches of water, but he made me appreciate the unique challenge of navigating a shallow and rocky river.

The Skykomish is best known to fishermen for the prized runs of salmon and steelhead that return to spawn in the headwaters and small feeder creeks each year. The river's width and limited access along the bank require a boat to reach many of the best fishing spots, but the shallow, rock-strewn bottom is too risky for a conventional outboard. And drift boats are slow and can't go back upstream.

Similar circumstances in rivers throughout the mountainous Western states created a fertile testing ground for the jet pump technology first developed by the Hamilton company in New Zealand about 1955. Jet pumps were initially driven by inboard engines. A pump at the stern sucked water from beneath the boat and blew it astern with enough force to push the boat forward. By 1962, Dick Stallman of Specialty Manufacturing Co. in San Leandro, California, had introduced an outboard-powered version that could replace a standard lower unit.

Glen Wooldridge's grandfather and namesake, a legendary fishing guide, river runner, and boatbuilder on Oregon's Rogue River, was one of the first to combine the water jet with another new technology during the 1960s: welded aluminum boats. Today, the younger Wooldridge is president of the Seattle-based family business that specializes in riverboats 14 to 30 feet in length, most of which are powered by inboard or outboard jets.

"Part of the outboard jet boats' popularity is the novelty of just being able to run in shallow water," he says. "And part is for the fisherman who knows there are fish upriver, but who dings his prop or damages the hull every time he goes boating. So it is the pure functional ability of

Charles Summers

Is that spray or dust billowing behind this 17-foot Wooldridge aluminum riverboat, pushed by a big Evinrude jet outboard? You can't really appreciate a jet boat until you've streaked in but a few inches of water across a bar like this one.

The high bow and spacious cockpit indicate that the boat can carry a good cargo through the standing waves of mountain rivers.

being able to go places you couldn't reach before." Wooldridge says the inboard jet, by contrast, is typically a bigger, heavier, and more expensive boat.

The Wooldridge 14- to 20-foot Alaskan series was designed especially as "go-anywhere" boats, and the 17-foot windshield model with an 88-h.p. Evinrude jet was particularly well suited for our demonstration ride. The first features I noticed were the low, wide, flat bow and the recessed forward deck, both of which were covered with nonskid diamond plate. Mountain rivers do not have many docks or floats, so boats are typically beached on a bank or sandbar. Loading and unloading, therefore, are done over the bow, and I found the step up and into this boat to be very easy and stable.

Wooldridge's unique two-piece walk-through windshield also added to the convenience of walking aft to the cockpit. The port-side window swings open like a door and lies flat against the other side, leaving a wide, 28-inch passageway and only an 8-inch-high coaming to step over. Not

only does this allow better access for a fully equipped fisherman, but leaving it open while drifting or fishing at anchor makes the entire boat usable.

Although the 30-inch-high windshield may seem out of proportion, the use of two such large windows instead of the typical three-window walk-through design provides excellent visibility. As we got underway, Wooldridge noted, "You'll be able to see sitting down. Most small boats have windshields so low they aren't realistic. We mount the steering wheel nice and high, too."

I didn't realize how important these features would be until I saw the speed and skill with which Wooldridge had to read the water ahead of us and maneuver accordingly—picking his way through a minefield of rocks, uprooted trees, and other debris remaining from winter floods. I consider myself an experienced boatman and usually expect to take the wheel during a boat test, but I quickly decided that running this kind of river in a 40-m.p.h. jet boat should be left to an expert.

"The texture on the surface tells

you what's underneath," Wooldridge explained. "The moving ripples indicate shallow water, but if the white stuff on top is stationary, it's a rock. Also, if I run up the backside of a gravel bar, I have to make sure that I have a way out—I can run in very little water up on step, but I can't stop. Then, after you're all proud of yourself for getting up the river without a problem, it can be even harder to read going back down, because you're looking at it backward, plus you're going faster. If you don't remember how you got up, all of a sudden you're on top of something and it's too late."

Wooldridge admits he is not a fisherman, and some of his customers still wonder how he can build such great fishing boats. "There are certain features a boat needs to be a good fishing boat," he explains, "and I can learn those from my customers. But you don't learn what makes a good riverboat from fishing—that comes from running rivers, and I know how to do that."

He confirms his appreciation for the needs of fishermen with the arrangement of the Alaskan's after cockpit, designed with as much usable space as possible. Nonskid vinyl covers the solid aluminum flooring, swivel seats are mounted on aluminum storage boxes, and handy gear storage trays run along both sides. An optional aluminum fishbox can be built into the forward deck.

Underneath the removable floor, Wooldridge uses precut foam blocks for buoyancy. The foam lies on top of the framing approximately 1¼ inches above the bottom of the boat, which allows water and sand to drain without saturating the foam. Also, since the foam can be removed, there is easy access to repair dents or other damage.

The bottom of the Alaskan is a modified-V with 9 degrees of deadrise. But the wide bow often leads observers to lump it with the "jet sleds," a designation derived from the many aluminum riverboats with squared-off noses and flat bottoms like those of jonboats.

"The flat bottom has a terrible ride and poor cornering and handling," he says. "It's also prone to cavitation, because air comes straight back and gets in the jet. The semi-V improves the ride and cornering, and makes it less apt to cavitate because the air is pushed out to the sides so more solid, air-free water arrives at the stern to be picked up by the jet. The slight V also breaks the suction of a totally flat bottom, and is actually a little faster."

Compared to a deep-V hull, our ride through the 6- to 12-inch chop on the Skykomish seemed bumpy, so I had to take Wooldridge's word that a flat bottom would have been far worse. "You would be sore already," he assured me.

But his claim for cornering ability was clearly evident when he unexpectedly threw the Alaskan into a tight, high-speed turn. Instead of the jet pushing the stern into a slide and bringing the bow around in a wide arc, it was as if a corner of the transom had been staked down and the rest of the boat forced to whip around a stationary pivot point.

A major factor contributing to this ability was the surprisingly short and shallow dimensions of a tunnel at the stern—a patented design that has been very successful, according to Wooldridge. This small, approximately 2-inch-deep rectangular depression with a corresponding cutout in the transom serves to prevent the otherwise smooth bottom from slipping sideways, and to channel solid water back and into the jet-pump intake.

"It makes a dramatic difference," says Wooldridge. "The sides of the

The shallow draft of the Wooldridge riverboat is evident when she is on a trailer. Rugged cockpit railings and high windshield are welcome in rough going.

tunnel act like a little inverted skeg on a hard corner and bite into the water. They also act like a squeegee and collect water for my jet intake, so I don't have the typical problem of outboard jets grabbing air in aggressive corners."

The Alaskan's speed with three adults aboard was also impressive. The test results on the 17-foot

> *After you're all proud of yourself for getting up the river without a problem, it can be even harder to read going back down.*

Alaskan, using an 88-h.p. Evinrude, indicated a top speed of 40 m.p.h. with a 400-pound payload, which dropped only to 37 m.p.h. when an additional 700 pounds was added.

The acceleration was better than I expected, too. "It's not neck-snapping," says Wooldridge, "but it's powerful enough to pull a skier on two skis. With a jet, you have instant r.p.m. and full thrust immediately, whereas with a prop boat you have to build r.p.m. A jet is just pushing

water through a hole, and it doesn't know if it's tied to a dock or doing 50 m.p.h.—it has nothing to do with getting the momentum of the boat going."

Although a shallow-draft jet drive, sharp eyes, and good judgment are supposed to keep you off the rocks, quality construction is still important for the inevitable bumps and scrapes.

"We weld the sides and bottoms of our Xtra Plus models at the chine continuously inside and out," says Wooldridge. "Then we put an extrusion over the outside for additional protection of the weld. Also, we run the ribs on all the boats longitudinally, because you're more apt to have a hole right in front of a crossrib. With longitudinals you may end up with a long crease from going over a rock, but you won't have the dents where the rock hits the resistance of crossribs."

Unlike the heavier Wooldridge Xtra Plus models that have seamless, one-piece bottoms, the Alaskan is constructed with two precut ⅛-inch marine-grade aluminum sides, each with preformed chines and gunwales joined at the keel.

"The trick is to make an aluminum boat strong and light," says Wooldridge. "By spending money on the corrugations and chines, we add rigidity and strength without physical weight. By keeping the weight down, we can use a smaller motor and lighter trailer to reduce the package price."

To boaters like me who appreciate traditional glossy paint and varnished mahogany, or to those who prefer the sleek lines of today's fiberglass boats, Wooldridge's unpainted aluminum hulls with square bows and oversized windshields may seem ugly. The softer ride of a deep-V hull and the additional torque of a standard propeller may also be better in some boating applications. But for anyone who wants access to river fishing and wilderness areas formerly denied by shallow water, a jet-powered Alaskan appears to be the perfect boat.

—Charles Summers
(*Boating World* #82)

The Semi-Dory Lives On

All those that glitter are not the only boats on the market. In fact, a boat type whose origins reach far back in the shadows of time has been modified and adapted for outboard power, and its many forms continue to rate high with a small band of knowledgeable boatowners. The basic type is a simple, seaworthy open skiff with high bow, a nice turn of sheer, and straightforward construction that appeals to both the commercial and the backyard boatbuilder. In its many forms it is known as the Lowell skiff, the Chamberlain skiff, the North Carolina skiff, the Simmons Sea Skiff, the Oregon dory, the Alaskan skiff, and the Texas Dory, among other names. But the basic form is called simply the *semi-dory*.

At first glance the boat appears to be what its name implies, a round-sided Swampscott or traditional straight-sided Banks dory with its after end cut off and replaced with a transom. The boats are considerably more changed than that, though, with a widened flat or shallow-V bottom and a straight flat run replacing the narrow, rockered, flat bottom of the dories. In *The Dory Book* (available from Mystic Seaport Museum, Inc., 75 Greenmanville Avenue, Mystic, CT 06355-0990), John Gardner's excellent treatise on the traditional type, the author lists a bottom made of lengthwise boards as one of the identifying features of a true dory. Time and changing materials have muddied the picture somewhat with fiberglass and plywood, especially the latter, now common replacements for the long boards. In addition, designers, builders, and various amateur wood-butchers have instituted other changes in building materials, framing, lines, transoms, decks, washboards, and interior layouts, to name a few. It is a powerful tribute to the type that so many good boats have come from this watery fricassee.

Gardner considers the building of a semi-dory well within the capabilities of most amateurs reasonably well skilled in woodworking. His *Dory Book* tells in detail how to go about it, and several fine skiffs are described along with plans and a bill of materials. His 14-footer can be rigged as a motorboat, rowboat, and sailboat all in one, while the 16- and 19-foot models offer the builder a fine, rugged hull to rig as workboat, fishing boat, family dayboat, or small cruiser. As with most boats of this type, large-horsepower motors are unnecessary for the moderate planing speeds that seem to best suit these hulls.

While a few semi-dories of various designs are built commercially in glass or wood on the East Coast today, the center of popularity is North Carolina, where the late T. N. Simmons developed in the decades after World War II a handsome outboard-powered semi-dory for commercial fishing. It eventually became legendary as a seaboat. He turned out hundreds of his skiffs in lengths of 18 and 20 feet before retiring in 1972, and many are still in use. Writing in *Boating World*'s "Favorite Boat" column, retired Coast Guard Captain Bill Brogdon described these durable Simmons

> They played a bellwether role in establishing that outboard-powered boats could be suitable for offshore use as well as for protected waters.

Captain Jim Orrell

CAROLINA DORY/SKIFF

RI 9855 E

This "Carolina" skiff is a classic semi-dory. Building plans for 19- and 20-foot models are offered by Captain Jim Orrell. Most of the Carolina boats have inboard wells for the motor.

Nelson Silva

This handsome 20-foot Simmons Sea Skiff is built by Nelson Silva in Wilmington, North Carolina, and features a fiberglass bottom and wood sides. An 18-foot model is available in kit form.

David Roberts

A warped-V hull gives Nexus Marine's West Coast skiff a somewhat softer ride. Builder David Roberts added beam and higher sides to the conventional semi-dory. Most Western-built skiffs have the motor mounted on the transom.

skiffs as follows: "The boats are fast with modest power. A 20-foot Simmons loaded with two people, two tanks of fuel, and fishing gear gets nearly 30 knots when powered by a 40-h.p. engine. Acceleration is excellent, a great advantage when entering an inlet. But according to reliable reports, they don't respond well to excessive horsepower."

That last comment tells us a lot about the importance of weight—the 20-footer scales only about 400 pounds, a mere fraction of the weight of most fiberglass 20-footers that require two or three times the horsepower of the wood Simmons. Lightweight boats have a tendency to get frisky when overpowered.

"The Simmons Sea Skiff is the best small boat I've ever used around inlets and offshore," Captain Brogdon writes, summing up his favorite boat. "It is an excellent seaboat, pretty but not dainty, and the builder used innovative ideas to make the boat more useful. Perhaps most importantly, they played a bellwether role in establishing that outboard-powered boats could be suitable for offshore use as well as for protected waters."

Transplanted New Englander Nelson L. Silva set up shop at 7980 Market Street in Wilmington, North Carolina, a few years ago and began repairing old Simmons skiffs and building his own version. "I have significantly changed the way the boats are built," he writes, but "one aspect of the boat I have not changed is the shape. . . . Simmons, who built over 1,200 Sea Skiffs, had it right, so why mess with success?"

Silva's major innovation is a foam-filled molded fiberglass bottom to which the wood sides are fastened, and a fiberglass-covered plywood deck that makes the skiff self-bailing. These boats run a few hundred pounds heavier than the all-wood boats and thus will handle more powerful motors, the 18-footers being rated for 30 h.p. and the 20-footers from 50 to 70 h.p.

An interesting feature of the Simmons boats and the North Carolina semi-dories in general is the motorwell, which is built inboard of the high, steeply slanted transom. A cutout in the transom lets the propeller wash stream aft without interference, but it is not so large as to reduce the effectiveness of the big transom in deflecting following seas.

In addition to his production skiffs, Silva offers a kit for his 18-footer for those who want to save money by doing a lot of the building themselves. And if you want to start from scratch, plans for both the 18- and 20-foot models are available from the Cape Fear Museum, 814 Market Street, Wilmington, NC 28401. Prices for the plans in early 1993 were $30 for the 18-footer and $45 for the 20-footer. A similar skiff, although not the Simmons design, is the Carolina Dory Skiff, a semi-dory designed for Captain Jim Orrell, P.O. Box 720, Galveston, TX 77553-0720. A number of these boats have been built by well-satisfied owners. Orrell offers plans for 19- and 20-foot models in a "two-fer" package of only $20. By the way, the Carolina Dory Skiff is but one of many dory types for the backyard builder, the plans for which are offered by Captain Orrell.

On the West Coast, David Roberts of Nexus Marine took the 18-foot East Coast sea skiff version of the wood semi-dory and changed it still further. "Our version has a lot more twist in the bottom, the maximum for ½-inch hard plywood, which gives it 30 degrees of deadrise in the bow," he writes. "We also increased the beam and freeboard for open-water use. When the boat is on plane, you can leave the wheel, lean over the side, and trail your hands in the water without the boat changing course particularly."

Roberts says there is a difference between his skiffs and dories. "In our flat-bottomed boat line, we differentiate between our recreational and workboats by calling the former 'planing dories' and the latter 'skiffs.' Technically, I suppose they are all semi-dories, being planked longitudinally over transverse sawn frames without keels. What we mean to suggest by our terminology is that the 'dories' are narrower on the bottom than the 'skiffs.' Also, the 'skiff' out here has a definite connotation, among commercial fishermen, of a flat-bottomed boat that is used in

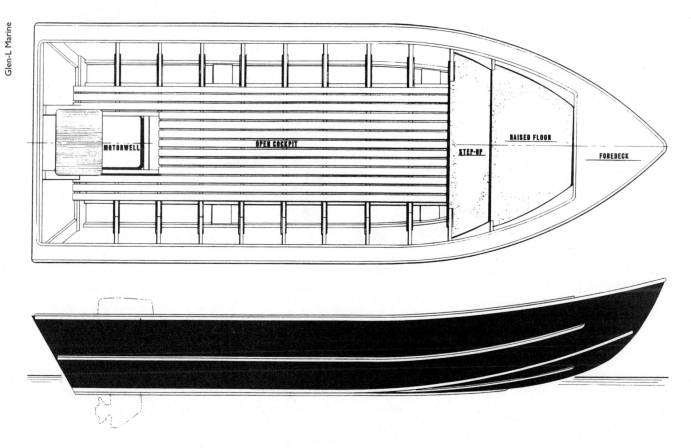

The straightforward wood construction of the West Coast–style semi-dory, this version with an inboard well. Glen-L Marine Designs offers a variety of semi-dory designs in plan and kit form.

the beach fisheries. The narrower-bottomed boats offer the big advantage of reduced pounding. The wider skiffs can carry unbelievable payloads."

The wide range of possibilities in the semi-dory hull is revealed in the offerings of Glen-L Marine Designs (9152 Rosecrans, Bellflower, CA 90706) with its Hunky Dory series of boat plans. These range from the 18-foot, 3-inch Little Hunk to the 22-foot, 10-inch Hunky Dory to the 26-foot, 7-inch Big Hunk. All would be described as "skiffs" in the commercial fishing lingo explained by Dave Roberts above, but their great attractiveness is to the amateur builder, who can build and power these big boats about as cheaply as one could hope for and still end up with a boat adapted for his or her particular needs. Glen-L also has plans for cabins and interiors for these boats.

Of course, there is no free lunch when it comes to boat design, and one choosing a semi-dory, particularly the flat-bottomed "skiffs" of the West Coast workboat type, must expect some or a lot of pounding in rough water, depending on the design and final weight. They must also accept the fact that their craft are from a workboat family and thus lack any traces of glamour on a sea of glamorous boats.

You can't have everything!

—DRG

Canoe Power

We were a good 10 miles up Moosehead Lake, Maine, from the landing when our little 2-horse outboard decided it was through for the day. There we were, two men and all our camping gear, looking at a slow trip home. We pulled up to a tiny gravel beach, readjusted our gear, broke out the spruce oars, and pointed our little Sport Boat, a derivation of Grumman's famous aluminum canoe, down the lake.

A canoe? With motor and oars? Whatever happened to paddles?

The answer is that while the Sport Boat shows her canoe heritage in a nicely turned bow, rounded hull lines, sweeping sheer, and a hearty curve of rocker in her bottom, the boat is really just that—a boat, a highly successful modification of the traditional double-ended canoe hull designed to accommodate an outboard motor. In many respects, the 15-foot Sport Boat is a modification of the larger Grand Laker, a transom-sterned canoe that in turn is a modification of a 20-foot guide's model canoe with a tiny transom built in to replace one of its pointed ends. This last model derives from a traditional double-ended canoe with a small outboard motor mounted on an outrigger.

What all this points to is the fact that canoes do not take well to power, and to make them safe and handy with an outboard requires changes

Still seeking better answers, canoe builders gave up trying to mount a V-8 in a go-cart.

sufficient to make a canoe no longer a canoe. Let's see why this is so.

MECHANICAL PADDLES

No sooner had the outboard motor been invented than it was being tried on just about every hull that it could conceivably drive. The only way a double-ender, whether boat or canoe, could mount a motor was on an outrigger attached just behind the stern seat. To say this made these canoes a bit tiddly, especially with the relatively heavy early outboards, is an understatement. But the determination of mankind to overturn the laws of physics is unquenchable, and the side motor-mount is still in use, a bit more successfully than in yesteryear because of today's lightweight motors.

Nevertheless, canoes with an off-center motor are cranky. They don't steer well, particularly if they lack a keel; the controls are unhandy to operate; they concentrate weight in a part of the canoe where there is little bearing in the water, thus necessitating offsetting weight elsewhere in the boat; and they detract from the canoe's greatest strengths: its lightness, its silence, and its maneuverability.

Our ancestral boat designers were not dummies, and they immediately began looking for ways to offset the incompatibility of canoes and outboard motors. An obvious first step was to cut a chunk off the stern, nail in a little transom, and mount the motor on that, thus doing away with

An Old Town canoe was modified by dropping the bow seat 4 inches to lower the center of gravity, and by extending the motor mount, since the usual motor mounting behind the rear seat was rejected in favor of the slightly wider forward seat (the hull is the same in either direction). A large plastic airtank is placed aft of the seat as extra flotation and is held in place by the motor mount.

the need for off-balance mounts and improving the steering. The results were some minor gains in utility, but all you have to do is try to run for several hours a motor that is directly behind you in the narrowest part of the boat, and you will know that it is not the final answer. If your arm muscles don't seize up, your bottom muscles will because of the constant need to counter the insecurity of the seating position. Yet, this design also remains among today's choices, but it is little improved over those first tentative chop-offs.

Still seeking better answers, canoe builders did what the double-ended guideboat builders did (we won't attempt to decide who did it first!) and gave up trying to mount a V-8 in a go-cart. Realizing there simply was not enough room aft for all that motor folderol, they abandoned the double-ended design, added some beam back where it was needed, widened the transom, and installed a seat wide enough to permit someone other than a contortionist to run the motor. The wider bottom permitted some flatness in the run, and suddenly they had the makings of a planing boat. The result might look like a canoe in its construction and forward profile, but they now had a true transom-sterned boat. Many builders produced one model or another of the type; Old Town built an unusually handsome one using conventional cedar-canvas construction with built-in sponsons along the low sides that made the boats unsinkable.

THE GRAND LAKER

The canoe builders of eastern Maine played a variation on the theme by widening the stern of their big guide canoes just a bit and adding a transom just large enough to take up to a 10-h.p. motor, and a seat one could live with, if not always enjoy. With construction centered on several canoe builders in the Grand Lake Stream area, these seaworthy craft came to be known as Grand Lake canoes, or Grand Lakers, and a few are still built each year in cedar and canvas or wood strips and glue. The Grumman Sport Boat might easily be mistaken for a miniature Grand Laker at a short distance.

What can one expect from a canoe under power? Certainly not speed. A traditional double-ended canoe with a small outboard on a side mount can be pushed up to her hull speed of roughly 5 m.p.h., but little more. Steering will be slow and uncertain, and, if any wind is blowing, may be next to impossible if the boat is light. A Grand Laker is considerably better in both handling and speed; a 6- to 10-h.p. motor will begin to push it up on top of the water into a semidisplacement mode, with a speed of 10 to 15 m.p.h. The Sport Boat will do even better, nearing 20 m.p.h. in ideal conditions with its maximum rated horsepower of 7.5. However, both the Grand Laker and the Sport Boat are much more at home in the

Don Kleiner

The Grand Laker, a modified canoe with a small transom for the motor, gains stability and partial planing capability, thanks to its length of 18 to 20 feet and its flat midsection. However, there is little bearing aft for the motor, and all of these boats have a tendency to squat when pushed hard.

The 15-foot Grumman Sport Boat is wider at the transom than most longer Grand Lakers, and a long spray rail helps reduce the inherent wetness of the type.

10-m.p.h. range. When pressed, both show the speed-killing qualities inherent in bottom rocker, rounded sides, and relatively narrow bottoms. Even with considerable weight forward, they love to go down the lake with their noses high in the air, like a dowager confident in the purity of her forebears. However, both types are good seaboats, although inclined to be wet if driven into a chop.

For those interested in power requirements, I find the Sport Boat goes quite well with a 2-h.p. outboard and will begin to plane with 4 to 6 h.p. I also have an 8-h.p., 80-pound motor I use for fishing because it is so quiet. On rare occasions I have run it wide open, but I would not recommend the practice on such a lightweight craft. My son tells of a Sport Boat used as a support boat in the Florida Keys; it was outfitted with a 10-h.p. Merc that drove it "like a scared rabbit." From my experience, I would guess the driver was just as scared as the bunny. And then there is the book about a feller's long-distance cruise in an early Sport Boat fitted with a 35-h.p. outboard motor. This tells us something about the good bearing aft in this little boat, but does not say much about anyone who would use a motor more than four times the maximum horsepower of the hull.

SAFETY CONSIDERATIONS

In powering any canoe type, it is a good idea to always wear a life jacket, especially if you plan to use a side mount on a small model. The phrase "tippy canoe" has more than a thread of truth in it, and an off-center motor is only going to add to the validity of the title. If it is flat-out speed you want, a 12-foot aluminum cartopper with an 8-h.p. outboard will do circles around a Sport Boat.

Having had a modicum of experience with all the types mentioned above, my advice to a prospective power canoeist is as follows: Don't bother with outfitting a traditional double-ender with an outboard motor unless you have strong reasons for doing so, as these pretty boats were designed for potato power and not smelly gasoline. If you do insist on saving your muscles for hoisting cool ones and pushing lawnmowers, outfit your double-ender with an electric outboard. The only real weight for these little mills is the drive motor down in the water and the storage battery on the floor of your canoe. That low-down weight will work to keep you upright. Today's electrics will more than replace paddle power. But why bother with power in the first place with these dainty craft?

Don't buy a canoe with a tiny motor transom until you have tried it with the motor you plan to use on it. If you feel you can live with its many limitations, more power to you. (Nope, that's not the right phrase—lotsa luck.)

A Grand Laker or another of its

The fiberglass Old Town Discovery Sport, like the Grumman Sport Boat, is widened aft to accept a small motor. Spray rails are molded into the hull. The electric outboard motor is a good choice for this small boat.

Old Town Canoe Co.

type might be a good choice if you can find one. We are not going to offer the names of builders, because they come and go and because they may or may not want to build a boat for you. If you are really interested, first check one out by heading for Grand Lake Stream, Maine; and if you live in Tacoma, Washington, it may take a while to get there. If it is open-water season, you can be sure of seeing a Grand Laker in action, and if you are still interested, you may be able to find a willing builder.

On the other hand, if the desire for utility is stronger than your taste for tradition, consider the Grumman Sport Boat. At about 120 pounds, it can be cartopped or trailered, is reasonably fast and seaworthy, is well built, rows surprisingly well but paddles poorly, and is a terrific boating buy at about $1,500.

—DRG

Gear for Your Boat

A boat intended for extensive use on salt water or other large bodies of water, such as the Great Lakes, requires a more elaborate outfit than the same boat used on smaller local waters. The reason is safety. When things go wrong at sea, there usually is no one around to help, and assistance, if obtainable, may be a long way off. Distances are great and small boats can be hard to find. The big difference in coastal boating, however, is that vast expanse of open water to seaward. You really don't want to go there in your small boat, so a significant amount of your basic gear is meant either to keep you from drifting off into that void if something goes wrong, or to keep you alive and healthy if you do.

Below we offer a list of items that should be aboard your boat *every* time you go out on big water. Some people will scoff that you don't need all that stuff when you are just going out for an afternoon of fishing. They are of the "look-I've-never-carried-it-and-I'm-still-around" school. That doesn't mean they are necessarily smarter than those who go prepared for problems. Fortunately, the suggested gear is neither of large quantity nor great expense, and most of it is not something you *might* use; rather, you'll find that it makes life easier and more comfortable all the time.

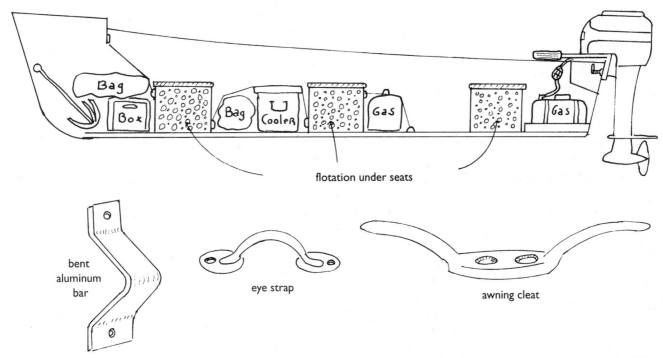

flotation under seats

bent aluminum bar

eye strap

awning cleat

By the time a small boat is loaded for a trip, it will be cluttered unless everything has its place and preferably is tied down. Lightweight gear should be stored forward; heavier gear amidships or slightly aft of the midpoint, depending on human cargo. If tied down, gear will serve as flotation in the event of a swamping. Tie-downs can be made from bent aluminum bar, regular eye straps, or small cleats.

Type III life jackets are comfortable, an important feature if they're to be worn at all times. The Mustang vest (left) has the added advantage of a collar lined with brushed nylon, sizable pockets with protective flaps, and handy (and welcome) hand-warmer pockets behind the larger pockets.

U.S. COAST GUARD–REQUIRED EQUIPMENT

There is some safety gear that most small boats—especially those that are powered—are required by law to carry. Be sure that you fit your boat according to the rules. The equipment is not very expensive and, at best, having it could save your life; at least, having it will save you an expensive summons if the Coast Guard or Marine Patrol stop you.

A PFD (personal flotation device) for every person aboard. We like the trim Type III vests rather than the cheaper but equally effective Type II "horse collars" because people are more receptive to wearing them (see page 197 for more detail on life jackets). Not surprisingly, the most expensive and safest of PFDs, the Type I, is often the least comfortable to wear, and such a life preserver, stored in the cuddy to protect it, is not going to preserve as many lives as a less buoyant one being worn by a passenger. It is a good idea to carry a few of these or some of the cheaper models for unexpected visi-

tors or as second PFDs if you ever have to abandon ship (they will be welcome!). Make sure each of your passengers is fitted with a jacket and knows how to put it on. PFDs should be kept handy, not stored in a locker.

A Class IV throwable cushion or lifering is required on boats 16 feet or more in length. A major change is in the works, however, with regard to throwables. To date, boats under 16 feet could get away with cushions as PFDs; beginning in May 1995 there must be a wearable PFD for every person aboard. Sailboards, personal watercraft, canoes, and kayaks will continue to be exempted from the federal rules, but states will be granted the right to make their own rules regarding these craft. States will also be able to set their own rules on children's life jackets.

Signaling equipment. This includes three aerial flares, a smoke signal, a dye marker, a horn or whistle, and a signaling flag. Most marine supply stores carry these items in a kit. We recommend carrying extra hand-held flares, aerial flares (legally, these have to be replaced periodically—

keep your old ones as spares), and a few pin-on lights for life jackets.

Fire extinguishers. Required only if enclosed machinery spaces can entrap inflammable gases or vapors.

RECOMMENDED BUT NOT REQUIRED

Some of this gear, particularly the first couple of items, we consider every bit as important as the Coast Guard–required things. There may be other equipment, such as a radio, that you rank up there with the necessities. In short, it will pay you to weigh your own needs and feelings when deciding what to carry aboard for safety reasons. You can readily spend a fortune on this stuff, though, so go easy until you have a feel for what is best for you.

Anchor and line. Don't try to save money by getting the smallest anchor recommended for your boat. Little anchors may hold well under ideal conditions, but the ocean bottom is rarely ideal. Weight helps an anchor get to the bottom quickly and dig in. A short length of galvanized chain (6 to 10 feet) shackled to the anchor and with the anchor line tied to the chain makes the hook even more effective. For most small boats, an anchor in the 10- to 15-pound range will hold under just about any conditions. Don't stint on line either; carrying one 50-foot coil and one of 100 feet will cover most of your requirements. A second 100-foot coil is not too much if you expect to be anchoring overnight. We suggest a minimum rope size of ⅜-inch nylon, not so much for its strength (it is more than strong enough) but rather for its ease of handling and wide safety margin. Extra line in various lengths and diameters is always useful; we carry several. (For more on anchoring, see page 156.)

Drinking water. This easily overlooked item should be near the top of your list. It is best to store it in more than one container in case of breakage or leakage. Two-liter soda bottles, wine bladders, or plastic 2-quart milk jugs work well.

Tool kit. Hammer, pliers, screwdriver, and adjustable wrench are basic; you may want other tools. Electrician's tape, duct tape, galvanized wire, rustproof nuts, bolts and screws, nylon twine, and a small hacksaw are also useful. A waterproof fishing-tackle box makes a good tool kit, but it is still necessary to keep all metal items in the kit well oiled because of the damp environment. You may want a smaller separate kit containing special tools, spark plugs, and the manual for your outboard motor. We carry a spare propeller and a change of spark plugs, but no other motor parts; we have a spare motor instead.

Compass and charts. Invaluable for safe navigation, these items may not be necessary in familiar waters, but there will come a time when you absolutely need them. Sailboats and powerboats require different types of compasses. A sailboat instrument must be mounted in gimbals so that it will adjust to the heeling of the boat, while a powerboat needs a compass with heavy dampening so that it will not spin when it is jarred as the boat pounds over waves. Some compasses are designed for both sail and power. An adequate instrument can be purchased in the range of about $40 to $100, depending on model and features. Since everything gets wet in a small boat, we suggest a clear plastic waterproof envelope for your charts.

Two-way CB or VHF radio. Well aware that we are treading on sacred ground, we will state that electronics are vulnerable on small open boats

On small boats, most problems are best solved by those aboard; the worst troubles are quick and catastrophic, and here a radio will make little difference.

and are not absolutely necessary, although a radio may be a comfort to you. In many years of saltwater boating under all kinds of conditions, we've never once felt the absolute need to call someone. Many will argue, sometimes adamantly, that a radio is a major safety device, which it is aboard larger vessels. But on small boats, most problems are best solved by those aboard; the worst troubles are quick and catastrophic, such as capsizing, fire, or collision, and here a radio will make little difference. If you disagree and will feel more secure with a VHF or CB at hand, by all means carry one. To some, a radio will be welcome as a means to call home, to contact other boats, to receive weather reports, and generally to keep in touch. But be fully prepared to do without it.

First-aid kit. This doesn't have to be elaborate, but it is needed.

Fog horn. One of the little handheld, gas-powered horns available at any marine store puts out a powerful blat. A brass or plastic traditional fog horn does, too, and only requires refilling from your lungs. The gaspowered horn is louder, though. The choice is yours, but you will need one or the other.

Pocket knife. The trusty Swiss Army type is tough to beat.

Pail. The 10-quart size is best; plastic doesn't rust, but metal doesn't melt. Take your pick. Uses are legion: bailing the boat, toilet, shellfish collecting, beachcombing, wastebasket, storage container, cooking pot, etc.

Riding lights. Any boat traveling at night is required to have a light, and all but the smallest must have red and green bow lights and a white stern light. *However, most boats in our class are required to have lights only if they are traveling at night.* Unless you have reason to use them, installed lights are a bother on a small boat since they are just one more thing to go wrong and are readily damaged. Low-priced snap-on lights are an alternative. These are powered by flashlight batteries and are designed to be removed and stored out of the way until needed. They used to be made of metal and as a result corroded quickly; now, allplastic models improve their durability to some extent. If you use lights that are attached with suction cups, we recommend that you also tie them to the boat with a piece of strong nylon cord, since suction cups are of questionable holding power if accidentally struck.

Flashlight. You may not plan to be out after dark, but you never know. In any event, the light will be welcome

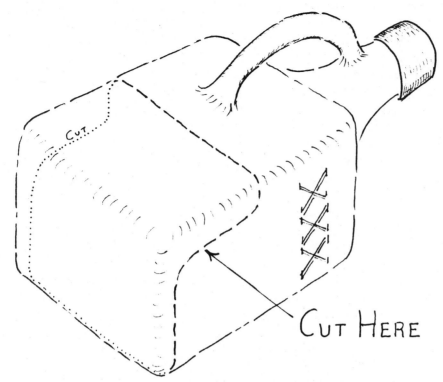

An accessory no small boat should be without is a good bailer. The best available, in our opinion, is free and is nothing more than a plastic jug cut to suit. The most useful size seems to be a gallon container, which can move a lot of water in a short time. If you have to get between floor boards or frames, the 2-quart size might be preferred. Bailer connoisseurs are divided on whether a round or a rectangular jug is better. A technical note: the bailer seems to work better if the upper side is cut back, as shown here.

in camp. The case should be rugged and waterproof. A spare set of batteries will ensure bright light for emergencies and signaling. A headlamp may prove handier than a straight flashlight; sea kayakers traveling at night find one indispensable.

Foul-weather gear and sea boots. Everyone aboard will need waterproof clothing; the boots are a welcome option. A spare set of gear is appreciated by those who come aboard unprepared.

Spare food. High-calorie, high-carbohydrate foods such as sweets, chocolate, dried fruits, cheese, and crackers are best. A strong, waterproof container will help keep your emergency rations edible. We eat this food before it gets too stale and replace it with fresh.

Sunglasses and protective skin cream. These are necessities on the water. A cap with a long visor will shade your eyes from the sun and keep the hood of your foul-weather gear off your face.

Bailer. A cutout plastic bottle makes a tool, the lip of which will conform to the curves in the bottom of the boat. The plastic is less apt to scar the finish than a metal bailer.

NICE-TO-HAVE ITEMS

Weather radio. Here is a cheap (about $25) and useful alternative to a VHF if your principal interest in having a radio is weather forecasts. This little box brings you daily NOAA weather reports, storm warnings, and up-to-date reports on noxious red tide, the latter info important for those who like to forage for mussels, clams, and other shellfish. The radio is a two-station receiver only and does not bring in commercial radio broadcasts.

Binoculars and camera. Uses are obvious. Water-resistant cases are needed for both, and care should be taken to keep them from being banged around in the boat or dropped in the bilge. With regard to the latter point, a good rule is to *always put the strap around your neck* before using camera or glasses.

Fenders. These clutter up smaller boats, but they are welcome—and appreciated by all sides—if you will be rafting to other boats.

Fishing tackle. A simple handline might save the day in an emergency. Beyond that, you are limited only by the capacity of your boat and your wallet as to what you want to carry.

Foraging book. Many islands and wild coasts are vegetable garden and meat factory in one. A copy of Euell Gibbons's classic foraging book, *Stalking the Blue-Eyed Scallop*, will open a new world to the inquisitive gourmand.

Camping stove and pot. These are handy for cooking what you forage. Be mighty careful if you use an open flame aboard a boat carrying gasoline, though. It is safer to do your cooking ashore. (For more on the subject, see page 219.)

Small waterproof tarp. This is a good item for protecting gear aboard the boat from spray and providing emergency shelter if stranded.

STORAGE BOX

Although the gear listed above does not take up a great deal of space, it can make a terrible clutter aboard a small boat if not contained. Fortunately, tough, waterproof plastic containers of all sizes are available from mail-order houses, hardware stores, and many department stores. These are useful not only for storage, but also to let you carry a lot of gear ashore, thus protecting it from theft—while providing an opportunity to dry out and reorganize stuff that may have been used.

Another relatively inexpensive container is a plastic cooler. A 48-quart box, for instance, will hold a fair amount of gear and make a good table or seat at the same time. In addition, the handles make it easy to shift about the boat, a small but welcome convenience when you are adjusting trim under less than favorable circumstances.

—DRG

Thieves Are Eyeing Your Boat

If a thief were eyeing your boat, motor, trailer, and other equipment right now, would the precautions you have taken prevent him from stealing your hard-earned rig and gear?

Probably not, considering the statistics on boat theft. According to the FBI's National Crime Information Center, the number of boats and outboard motors stolen nationwide during the last few years has increased dramatically. In 1987, some 27,934 boats were reported stolen. In 1988, the number was 28,209. In 1989, some 29,732 boats were reported ripped off. The most recent figures indicate that the numbers will rise even higher.

This increase suggests that boaters don't think they will become victims, so they don't take adequate protective measures. Maybe that is why boats, motors, trailers, electronics, fishing tackle and water-skiing gear are such popular targets.

The fact is, dissuading a professional thief from getting your gear is nearly impossible. But the greatest threat to your equipment is not the practiced pro but rather the casual thief.

A casual thief is an opportunist. He seeks to make quick money on the theft. Luckily, most strategies that put off a casual thief just require adopting safety-conscious habits. Many effective security measures can make a thief look elsewhere, and these safeguards cost little or nothing.

Effective security measures depend on three main factors to foil a thief: visibility, time, and noise. If a thief thinks he will be seen, he will likely look elsewhere. If a robber needs a lot of time to heist an item, he will probably pick another target. If a crook needs to make a lot of noise to rip you off, he's apt to decide not to risk it.

The following security measures use one or more of these factors to slow or stop a thief. Use these proven ideas to protect your valuable equipment.

COUPLERS

Lock your boat trailer coupler to the tow vehicle's hitch ball whenever your trailer is attached to the tow vehicle. Several locks are made specially for this purpose, and you can find them in marine supply stores, in catalogs, and at many boat dealerships. In a pinch, even a common padlock works. However, practiced thieves hatch elaborate plans to rip off trailers. For this reason, in addition to locking the coupler to the hitch ball, tack-weld the threads on

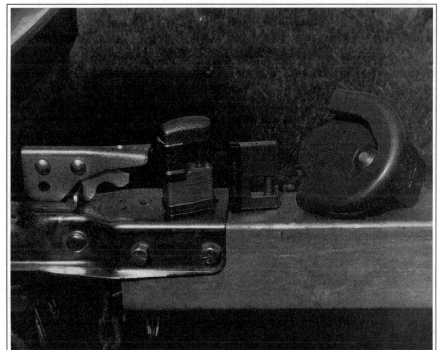

Coupler locks will help keep the trailer attached to the vehicle. The two padlocks at left will fit the hole in the hitch (arrow), while the one at right locks the trailer to the ball itself.

A long bicycle cable woven through the wheel cutout and around the trailer frame will discourage theft, although professional thieves may have heavy cable cutters with them.

the end of the hitch ball's bolt. This prevents a thief from removing the hitch ball and stealing your rig even with the hitch ball still locked to the coupler. A thief plans for this occurrence by rigging another coupler to accept a locked hitch ball.

In addition, tack-weld the threads of the bolts that hold the coupler assembly on your trailer tongue. This prevents a thief from removing the bolts that hold the coupler assembly to the trailer tongue. Thieves who use this method of operation may bring trailers and trunk contraptions just to cart off trailer rigs.

Another way to dissuade a thief is to disable the trailer. You can remove one wheel and prop up the wheel-less axle, or you can run cable through the wheel rims and around the axles and lock the two cable ends together.

These ideas are important because you risk having your trailer ripped off while you are on the water. If a thief steals your trailer as you motor away from the dock, you won't discover the theft for hours, maybe even all day, and in some locations you might not even be able to notify the police immediately when you do discover the theft.

Protecting your equipment while traveling is another challenge. The best strategy for keeping your rig safe is simple: Never leave your rig unattended on the road. And that really means NEVER, not even for the quickest coffee break or fuel stop in the most deserted place. The problem is that while you are on the road, a thief may steal an item and you will only discover the loss hours later and miles away.

When your trailer is not attached to your tow vehicle, use a lock that covers the coupler cavity completely. You will need a coupler cavity lock when you store the trailer, or if you detach it from the tow vehicle while on the road. This kind of lock deters someone from stealing your trailer by preventing the thief from locking the trailer onto a hitch ball in the usual manner. Coupler cavity locks are also available in marine supply stores, catalogs, and dealerships. However, practiced pros can defeat these particular devices, so the precaution discourages only casual thieves.

STORAGE STRATEGIES

When you are not using your boat, store it out of sight. Rent space in a commercial storage facility, or leave your boat in a locked garage. If you store your trailered boat in your backyard, let the trailer tongue face a wall, a group of trees, or a line of shrubs so that the trailer would have to be turned around to attach it to a tow vehicle. Park a vehicle in front of the trailer so that the path to move it is blocked. Light the rig well at night. You may also want to remove one or both wheels and prop up the trailer frame on cinder blocks.

Don't leave anything valuable in your boat while it is stored. Remove your electronics, batteries, fishing tackle, water-skiing gear, other boating items, and tools.

You may also want to consider a security system for your stored rig. Most systems are either wired or wireless, and may be do-it-yourself or professionally installed. Wireless security measures are generally easier to put in place than wired ones. Costs vary greatly, from a few hundred dollars to nearly $1,000 installed.

It's a good idea to apply alarm system decals to your rig whether or not you install a security system. Determining whether or not a rig is protected by a security system is difficult and takes time, even for professional thieves. So a decal might cause a thief to reconsider your rig as an easy mark.

Propellers are a common target of thieves, because most props are easy to steal and are often unprotected. A thief simply removes the bolt and cotter pin and lifts the prop quickly and quietly off the shaft.

The best defense is to use a prop lock that replaces the nut on the end of the prop shaft. The prop can't be removed without unlocking the device, but the motor still runs normally with the lock in place. You simply install it and keep the keys in a safe place. This idea should be seriously considered if you own a stainless steel prop, because stainless wheels are considerably more expensive than aluminum ones.

ACCESSORIES

If a thief can't see something to steal, he will likely look elsewhere for an easier target. For this reason, keep all your gear out of sight while on the road. Pack your equipment and electronics in your car trunk, or when someone stays with the rig during a stop, keep your gear in the boat's lockable storage compartments. If there are no such storage areas, consider building them.

Another practical idea is to inscribe your electronics and other equipment with your social security number or driver's license number. Precede the driver's license number with the two-letter abbreviation for your state and the letters "DL." For instance, if you live in Florida, you would inscribe "FLDL" and then your driver's license number.

The driver's license number inscription makes recovery of the equipment easier, because this number can be traced quickly to you. If a thief who has an item that contains your driver's license number is apprehended, there is strong evidence that he possesses stolen property.

Similarly, you might want to inscribe your boat's hull identification number (HIN) in several hidden places on the hull or on other items. Whether you use the HIN, social se-

curity number, or driver's license number, be sure to mark all your equipment.

Your boat's name on the transom or on both sides of the hull may discourage thieves, because the painted name makes your boat tougher to resell illegally.

We make a thief's job easy because we often can't produce the model number and serial numbers of stolen items. A list that contains all these vital statistics lets you report a theft promptly and accurately. (See the sample equipment inventory list below.) The list also gives you the best chance of identifying and therefore recovering your equipment.

List all model names and numbers, serial numbers, and other identifying marks. Include the tow vehicle's VIN, the trailer manufacturer's name, the trailer serial and model numbers, and your license plate numbers. Boat data should include the HIN, make and model numbers, and state registration number. Record the brand name and model and serial numbers of the motor along with similar information for your electronics, binoculars, and other gear. Keep one copy of this list with you at all times and a second copy at home in a safe place.

EASY PICKINGS

Thieves steal outboard motors of about 30 h.p. and less because these engines are light. They can be lifted easily by one person and placed unobtrusively in a waiting truck or van.

If you own a small outboard, a clamp bracket lock may or may not be in place to secure the engine. If not, a thief simply removes the long bolt that holds the motor to the transom bracket, stealing the engine and leaving the locked bracket in place. If you are unsure about whether a clamp bracket lock safeguards your engine, ask your dealer.

Protect your small outboard further by bolting it to your boat. If you store your boat in winter on your property, you may want to remove the engine from the boat and store it in a locked garage or in your basement.

It will require some extra effort, but it pays to take well-focused color photographs of your boat from several angles and keep them with your list of vital numbers.

A lock on screw clamps really works. The torn plastic on this lock shows where thieves tried unsuccessfully to break it. Vandals will also be slowed if the motor is bolted to the transom.

TOW VEHICLES

Thieves break into cars and vans because boaters often leave in their vehicles the boxes that equipment comes in. Thieves are tempted by reading box labels that suggest what might be inside. Camera bags and lens cases, which might indicate that they contain expensive photography equipment, are also tempting, as are bags and satchels in which boaters stash wallets, keys, cash, and credit cards. Showing that boxes and containers in your tow vehicle are empty can ward off an attempted heist and its related vandalism.

Similarly, even though you may have removed the electronics and other expensive items from the boat, don't invite vandalism by a thief who thinks there's something aboard to steal. Arrange things so that you don't suggest that you are trying to hide something. Radio connector wires should be left hanging in plain sight, for instance, and if storage compartments are visible but empty, leave them wide open.

Never leave ignition keys, including spare sets of keys, in your boat, either, because thieves know to look for them and are shrewd enough to find them.

Do you rent space in a marina? Get to know the security personnel. Make sure they know that only you are allowed to move or board your boat for any reason. Make sure they also know to call you immediately if someone claiming to be a relative or friend wants to board or move the boat. Write these instructions in a letter to the marina's management.

Make sure your boat, motor, trailer, and other gear are adequately insured; your homeowner's or renter's policy may not provide adequate coverage, and with some policies, it may not

Propellers are a common target of thieves.

even cover your boat and equipment. To better safeguard your investment, you will probably want to consider special boatowner's insurance.

If you become the victim of theft, contact the local law enforcement authorities first, as quickly as possible. These agencies can begin an investigation immediately, which may include entering descriptions and serial numbers of the stolen items into the National Crime Information Center's (NCIC) computer. If your boat is stolen, the second agency you should notify is your state boat registration authority.

Don't keep thinking that "the other boater" becomes the victim all the time and that you are safe from theft no matter what you do. If you believe that, sooner or later the thief who is eyeing your rig will leave you adrift without a boat to float in.

CHECK THE CHECK

Boat thieves also steal boats the easy way, with bum checks. A thief studies the newspaper classified advertisements for a likely boat. Then he contacts the seller and works out a price. The sales transaction takes place when banks are closed, usually weekends or evenings, and to cover himself, he may suggest that the seller hold the registration and sales transaction documents until the check is approved. The thief then makes off with the boat. The seller believes he is protected by this arrangement, but the thief's check is forged and the paperwork is also false.

If you are selling your boat, do not conduct business when a check cannot be authenticated.

—Art Michaels

Equipment Inventory

Cut or copy this page from the book. Make two copies of the completed inventory. Keep one copy at home in a safe place. Keep the other copy in your wallet.

BOAT

_____
Manufacturer, model name and number, description (color)

_____
Registration number

_____
HIN

OUTBOARD MOTOR

_____
Manufacturer, model name and number

_____
Serial number

BOAT TRAILER

_____
Manufacturer, model name and number, description (color)

_____
Serial number

TOW VEHICLE

_____
Manufacturer, model name and number, description (color)

_____
VIN

EQUIPMENT

Description of Item	Model Number	Cost	Serial Number

NOTES

UPGRADES AND CONVERSIONS

Introduction

Everyone loves a good bargain, and there are times when a used boat can be a real steal. If you are not careful, you can also be stolen blind. Most used boat transactions fall somewhere between these extremes.

The safest buy, in our opinion, is the open aluminum skiff, where the wear, tear, dings, and dangs are right there in plain sight, both inside and out. The trickiest for most of us are wooden boats, mainly because we are unfamiliar with wood as a boat-building material and because wood rots and fastenings corrode. Fiberglass boats may be just as difficult to examine as wood boats, especially if the hull laminations include a core material of balsa wood, sheet foam, or other material, or if large areas of the interior are hidden by foam, an inner lining, or carpeting. Because small boats rarely warrant the expense of a professional survey, trying to decide if a boat is a beaut or a bummer is left pretty much to one's self or friends. That is why this section begins with essays on surveying fiberglass and aluminum boats.

As the new owner of another's discard, you now have to weigh the consequences of your purchase. It is not uncommon to have found a boat, motor, and trailer that have hardly been used because the former owner (or the owner's spouse!) found that boating was not to his or her liking. If the rig is exactly what you were looking for and you get it at a bargain price, you are in Fat City.

More often, there will be changes you wish to make, perhaps with the idea of restoring the boat to its origi-

Art Michaels

In looking for the used boat of your dreams, you might find a real bargain and exactly what you want in a well equipped and cared-for boat like this Bayliner. More likely, you will be shopping first for the right hull, and considerable modifications will be necessary. Notice the running strakes and chine step on the bottom of this deep-V hull.

nal luster, but more likely to fix it up for some special purpose. Here again, the low cost of small boats lets you dabble in dreams without having to sell the farm to do so. There is only so much you can do to smaller small boats, but many in the 15- to 20-foot range can be modified or converted with exciting results.

Take one of the broad-beamed aluminum jonboats as an example. A 16-footer can easily accommodate a lightweight cabin for two with room to spare for a portable toilet and a small galley. Attach one of the modern, low-horsepower, quiet-running outboard motors and you have a dandy little river packet that will supply a great amount of pleasure for a low investment of time and money. Such a craft has the advantage of very shallow draft as well as compactness and maneuverability that let you explore creeks and oxbows where few boats ever venture.

Transfer this same concept to a more seaworthy hull, lower the height of the cabin to reduce windage, boost the horsepower to the point where the motor will plane your boat without undue effort, and you have a serious cruiser that will take you over long distances. One should keep in mind that, compared to the riverboat, the seagoing cruiser needs a stronger house structure—or, surprisingly, one made of fabric. The reason for this is that your hull will be working more in rough water, and a fixed structure must be kept from being bent out of shape by the flexing. It may also take some slamming from seas coming aboard, although our preference in this case is to be tucked into a quiet anchorage. A good fabric dodger, by the way, will absorb quite a slop of water without damage, while flexing of the hull will not affect it at all. It can also be rolled out of the way in good weather to provide welcome moving-around

The rounded bottom of the With 400 (a 15-foot fiberglass skiff) shows here the secrets of her easy planing ability. The upper arrow points to the slight hook, or reverse curve, in the bottom where it meets the transom. This provides lift, as does the raised strake (lower arrow) that flattens into a planing surface. This rather sophisticated design permits the use of modest power in what is a fairly heavy boat at about 400 pounds.

room aboard a small boat.

Weight rapidly mounts aboard any cruising boat, as we note in detail in the section on cruising. So in modifying your boat, we would caution you to think twice or thrice before installing integral fuel tanks to extend your range. Such tanks take valuable space, are prone to leaking, may interfere with trim, and, in all but the rarest cases with small boats, are unnecessary. (See also "The Ticking Fuel-Tank Bomb," page 99.) A couple of 6-gallon plastic tanks will carry you from one refueling port to another almost everywhere today, so we suggest carrying as *little* fuel, not as *much*, as you can.

We mentioned earlier that the motorboat market is heavy on planing and power, and light on alternatives.

One will be hard pressed to find a comfortable, round-sided small boat hull designed specifically for outboard power. We had high hopes for the Norwegian-built "With" hull introduced in this country back in the early eighties. Using very sophisticated design, the Norwegians managed to build a round-sided hull that planed nicely with low power—a combination many boat people would say was impossible (see photo). We had the opportunity to test a 15-foot model of this boat over a season and were tremendously impressed with both performance and potential. Unfortunately, the U.S. marketplace was not ready for such a boat, and we have heard nothing about it in recent years.

Given the limited choices (there

A wreck? No—neglected. We spotted this aluminum runabout in the corner of a boat dealer's yard. Under the mess, the metal appeared in fine condition and little worn, and the interior floor paint was hardly scratched. A boat like this lends itself to a host of uses and interior layouts.

This husky 15-foot aluminum boat had been stripped to the metal and all but abandoned. It was purchased for $100, and a winter's work in a home shop gave new life to the boat and great pleasure to the handy owner.

are some, as well as good compromises, shown in the first section, "The Boats"), one has to turn to other sources. Short of building a boat, good places to look are the back corners of the backyards of boat dealers; the front lawns of persons thinning out their inventories of "things" with a yard sale; and in the classified pages of boating magazines, especially small-circulation publications like *Messing About in Boats*, where readers love to dicker over oddball (by today's standards) boats. If you have a good idea of what you want and have the time and patience to follow up leads, you will find a wide choice of hull types and materials.

We saw just such an odd cast-off behind the garage of an acquaintance in a neighboring town. We passed the word to a friend who was boat shopping and he, in turn, negotiated to buy the 15-foot aluminum hull for $100. He went to work on the high-sided shell of the old runabout, and with pluck, plywood, and a few hundred more bucks, turned out a creditable center-console boat (see bottom photo). Steve's biggest investment was a new 30-h.p. Nissan outboard which, in this short boat, is run from the tiller with an extension handle. In the three or four years he has had this boat, Steve has cruised and fished hundreds of miles of Maine coastline and rivers.

Other low-powered cruising and fishing boats have been made from old fiberglass runabouts that have lost their gloss but not their strength, ex-sailboats whose round hulls make exemplary cruisers, abandoned wood fishing dories, handsome wood motorboats, and an endless variety of craft in between. Having modified or converted a number of small boats in our sparsely equipped shop (you don't have to be a professional boatbuilder to do most of this straightforward work), we have noticed that older boats, in general, seem to have heavier scantlings than newer models, which makes them easy to work on. Soundness of skin and strength of framing are critical to a safe boat, and it is always the responsibility of the builder—or you, the modifier—to assure that both are adequate.

Beyond that, how pretty or how intricate the work is entirely up to you—and your pocketbook.

—DRG

Surveying Fiberglass Boats

In 1988, while sailing along the west coast of Florida, I discovered the boat of my dreams, and it just happened to be for sale. It was a 38-foot full-keel ketch, typically Taiwanese and loaded with teak. Although it had been sadly neglected for several years, I spotted a beautiful boat beneath the cosmetic shortcomings, one that could be bought *cheap*. Unfortunately, it was the final day of my vacation, and I only had time to obtain an equipment list and asking price from the broker, who also supplied me with the names of several local surveyors.

After returning to Minnesota, I studied the equipment list, researched the boat, and ultimately made an offer about 30 percent lower than the owner's asking price. He accepted without a counterproposal, which means I probably offered too much. I knew I could fix the cosmetic problems myself, and my research made me reasonably certain of its sailing characteristics, but without an in-depth inspection I had no idea of the boat's true overall condition.

I arbitrarily phoned a surveyor from the broker's list, he sent a substantial list of most impressive credentials, and I hired him. Several days later I received his survey. Beyond the obvious cosmetic problems and a stuffing box that needed repacking, he had found no serious problems. All things considered, it was a good survey with no expensive surprises, not even the reasonable invoice of $300.

I called the broker, made arrangements to sleep on the boat for a few days, then headed back to Florida to look over the boat more closely and get local estimates for obvious repairs and upgrades. By the time I was finished I had a fair idea what it would take to make her shipshape.

Still trusting in the survey and expecting no serious problems, a friend and I went for a test sail with the owner. With him at the helm, we exited the canal and made ready to hoist the sails. I was more excited than on the day I got my first bike.

The first thing I noticed when I removed the sail cover was several small holes in the mainsail and a 2- to 3-inch bow in the spruce boom. Mainsails and spruce booms are expensive, but the surveyor had not listed them as substandard. Both problems were so obvious that it seemed unlikely he had ever taken the sail cover off the boom. So much for the excitement of a new bike. I began to wonder what else he had missed.

To make a long story short, I found many other obvious problems, including a rotten deck core. My dream boat had turned into an expensive nightmare. That was my first and last experience with a "professional" surveyor, and the lessons I learned are not unique to the purchase of a big boat.

Obviously, surveying the typical outboard runabout is far less complex than surveying a 38-footer, but all things being relative, the emotional and financial impact of a poor choice can be just as disastrous.

There are many 16-foot fiberglass flowerpots sitting in the backyards of complacent buyers.

EDUCATE YOURSELF

You probably won't depend on the credentials of an out-of-state surveyor when purchasing your runabout. You'll have to be comfortable with making the final analysis yourself—and there is much you'll need to know. There are many 16-foot fiberglass flowerpots sitting in the backyards of complacent buyers.

At this point, you should have a fairly good idea of what you're looking for in terms of hull and interior design, make, and age. You may also have some idea of the kinds of cosmetic and structural problems you might find. Of course, it is of little use to understand what problems may exist unless you know how to recognize them. And the best way to learn to recognize them is to spend as much time as you can crawling over, under, and through as many different kinds of boats as you can find. Besides, it's just plain fun. And the education gained won't be beneficial just to someone out shopping for a used boat. Those who currently own an older boat will find it helpful in creating preventive maintenance schedules and making tough decisions about repairing or trading.

THE GELCOAT

Unless you have extensive experience in fiberglass repair, avoid boats with obvious and severe hull or deck damage. These will be just too complex and expensive to repair or restore. Besides, there are too many *good* used boats available to warrant the risk.

Obvious damage aside, don't be overly concerned with the initial appearance of the boat. Keep in mind that we're looking for a steal, and the seller is already aware of the cosmetic problems. If you can point out more serious problems, you may be on your way to buying your boat for pocket change.

Unless the boat is in current use, and thus receiving periodic care, you can expect the gelcoat to have little or no shine left. That lack of luster will be especially noticeable on horizontal deck surfaces directly exposed to the sun's ultraviolet rays. It will be even more evident on those decks with colored gelcoat.

Reds, blues, and black seem to fade more dramatically than lighter colors. You can restore dark colors with rubbing compound and multiple coats of a good marine wax, but only to a point. Depending on the sun's intensity in your area, a dark pigment may have to be rubbed out twice a year. In fact, it is possible to *destroy* the gelcoat with excessive use of rubbing compound, leaving a complete

An old fiberglass runabout could be converted to a lobsterboat, but the hard use would make the boat a questionable effort for restoring to pleasure use. By contrast, the 20-foot Romarine shown here, designed and built as a workboat, will make a fine and long-lived pleasure boat.

paint job as the only practical and cost-effective repair. If you want to avoid painting the boat, I suggest you avoid colored decks. A white deck is far easier to restore and maintain than one with a colored gelcoat. If you purchase a boat with colored decks in relatively good condition, keep a tarp on it when not in use or it will eventually fade.

The same applies to many metal-flake finishes. In extreme cases of deterioration you can actually feel the metal flakes poking through the gelcoat. At best these finishes demand

a maintenance-conscious owner who will keep the boat covered when not in use. Inspect all such finishes carefully.

Close inspection of the gelcoat will likely reveal a phenomenon known as crazing. This may show up anywhere on the hull or deck as a series of hairline cracks radiating outward from a center point. They often remind me of a daddy longlegs. There is much speculation about what causes these unsightly little cracks. Some contend that they result from flexing, perhaps caused by di-

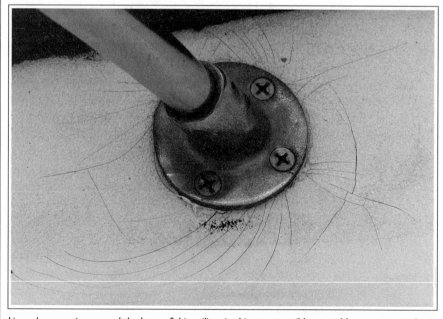

Lines show crazing around the base of this railing, in this case possibly caused by pressure on the flange.

A poorly designed plywood quarter knee on this fiberglass hull has broken away from the fastenings.

rect impact. Others suggest that they occur when the hull or deck section is removed from the mold. Yet others speculate that it is caused by the chemical breakdown of a given batch of resin. Crazing may also result from a gelcoat that has become brittle because it was applied too thickly. All of these things may contribute to crazing, but I prefer to classify them simply as phenomena—minor mysteries to science and pains in the neck to the boat painter.

Crazing poses no threat to the boat's structural integrity, but if you are planning to paint your boat any color other than the original, it will cause you problems: Crazed areas simply will not accept paint. The smallest cracks can be filled with a sandable primer, but most will survive the best preparation and prime job. If your new paint is darker than the original gelcoat, the lighter-colored cracks will be very noticeable.

I've seen boats literally covered with crazing, and my only suggestion is to avoid those boats unless you're prepared to live with the cracks. On the other hand, I've seen few older boats that didn't have at least a few bad spots, so expect them.

THE HULL

A solidly built fiberglass boat will appear bulky, with a rounded bow stem and decklines: fiberglass was never intended to make sharp corners. If you poke around in enough boatyards and look at enough boats, you'll soon learn to recognize the subtle differences in appearance between a well-made boat and one where the builder skimped on materials. There are other indicators of general hull quality.

Stand at the boat's stern and look forward along the sides of the hull. The gelcoat may be dull and scratched, but the finish should be flat and smooth, with no visible pattern. Many builders used woven roving for the first layer of fiberglass. If the gelcoat isn't thick enough, the characteristic basket-weave pattern of the roving will show through the gelcoat. All too often, further inspection will show that a single layer of roving constitutes the only layer of fiberglass used in the sides of the hull. The older Glastrons and many bassboats come to mind. Boats built this way were easily holed above the waterline, and even though they may

have survived for 15 years, they aren't the type of hull that you want to invest time and money in restoring.

On certain designs the hull thickness may be evident from the inside, if you can find an area where the vinyl or carpet is loose. Feel under the gunwales at the hull/deck joint. Boats in the 16-foot range seldom have hull sides thicker than ¼ inch. The thicker the better.

At each corner of the stern you will usually find aluminum corner caps attached with one or two stainless steel screws. Remove the screws and caps. On some designs you'll be able to determine the thickness of the hull side as well as that of the transom. The type of hull/deck joint used also will be evident.

Spend some time pushing on the sides of the boat with your hands. This simple procedure may be the most effective test of hull rigidity. Under pressure, there should be little or no flex in the sides. Press *hard* right under the hull/deck joint, along the entire length of the hull. Any flex or separation indicates insufficient hull thickness and/or leaks at the joint. Again, to find a benchmark, try flexing different boats until you find one that flexes too easily.

The second area to inspect closely is the bottom of the hull. Because of the floor it will be difficult, if not impossible, to determine the thickness of the bottom, but in most cases adequate construction in the sides indicates the same in the bottom. Hidden problems in the bottom generally are revealed through a close inspection from the outside.

Gouges and scratches are to be expected, especially along the keel, which is constantly subjected to contact—with beaches, trailers, and often rocks. Consider them as normal wear, and plan on repairing them when you paint the boat. However, if the keel shows obvious signs of severe damage, the boat is probably not worth your effort.

Pay close attention to any area that looks obviously different, such as dented or bulged areas. These often will have small cracks seeping water or showing recent signs (dirty or rust-colored stains around the cracks) of having been wet. In many cases, discolored cracks indicate a leak. You may even find a single drop of water hanging from a crack several days after the last rain. If this is the case, you can bet that the foam flotation is saturated with water and serving no purpose. Replacing the flotation will mean replacing the floor, regardless of its condition. The leak can be repaired from the inside after the foam has been removed, leaving only a cosmetic repair to be done on the outside. But if you're not up to the entire project, avoid the leaker.

At this point, we'd better briefly discuss cored, or sandwich construction, hulls. A core material, such as foam or end-grain balsa wood (the most common core for boats 15 to 20 years old), is sandwiched between multiple layers of fiberglass to make the boat stiffer and lighter. Balsa-core construction is much more common in larger craft because of its superior strength-to-weight ratio over solid fiberglass. However, I have come across balsa cores a few times in boats in the 18- to 20-foot range, and once in a 16-foot bassboat. On each occasion the boats were suitable only for the scrap pile.

I certainly have no objections to balsa cores, and because of the superior strength-to-weight ratio, I expect you'll see an increase in the use of cored hulls in boats of this size. However, if damage to the fiberglass skin allows water to enter in sufficient quantities to saturate the core, sooner or later the skin and core will separate, and the now unsupported skin will become very fragile.

Separation will be evident from bulges or waves in the hull. A gentle push on the high spots will cause them to buckle freely. Even if you've never seen it before, you'll know. In most cases, repair or replacement will be cost-prohibitive in boats of this size. Avoid cored hulls unless the hull is in exceptionally good condition. You can find out from the builder whether your prospective renovation candidate has a core, and if so, what type.

The final area of concern is the hull/deck joint. Here we are only concerned with the aluminum extrusion that covers the joint and, to a certain extent, becomes part of the joint's integrity. It isn't uncommon to find fairly severe damage at the

Crawl through boats until you've seen first-hand what effect the sun has on tarps, upholstery, and floor coverings.

hull/deck joint. Generally, the damage will be forward on either side, often the result of collisions, either with another boat, a day marker (it happens), or more probably with a pesky dock post.

Typically, damage to the fiberglass of the hull or deck sections in this area can be repaired easily. Damage to the aluminum extrusion is another story. Inspect it carefully. If it is kinked, dented, or bent to the point that it can't be straightened, finding a replacement can be difficult and expensive.

If the boat manufacturer is still in business, they may be able to provide you with a new extrusion, or at least point you in the right direction. Extrusions can be expensive, though, so check the cost of a replacement before buying the boat.

If the boat hasn't been in production for many years, finding a replacement extrusion may require a bit of searching. If your prospect is sitting in a boatyard, begin by checking the boat next door. Most builders in the 1960s and 1970s used only two or three different types of hull/deck joints. Consequently, many extrusions are interchangeable, and you may be able to find a junker boat with an entire piece or a section that may be cut to replace the damaged area.

The problems of finding extrusions may also extend to the transom cap, stern and bow caps, and windshield channels. If these parts are missing, damaged, or of unique design, try to find replacements before closing the deal on your boat.

THE INTERIOR

Armed with nothing more than a flashlight and an awl, you should be able to draw accurate conclusions about the overall condition of the boat's interior. This is where you will find the most time-consuming and expensive repairs, and it is also the one part of the survey that may serve to lower the asking price considerably. The owner is certainly aware of the obvious and visible cosmetic problems and has probably set his asking price accordingly. However, he may not be aware that the boat needs a $500 floor or a $700 transom. Find those problems and point them out. *Then* bargain.

Start by inspecting the upholstery, which will almost certainly need replacing on most older boats. Unless you're handy with a commercial sewing machine, it may also be one of the most costly repairs you'll encounter; depending on the number of pieces involved, you may spend $200 to $400 on a new suit of upholstery. You can save a lot of money by removing the old upholstery pieces and taking them to the shop to use as patterns. When looking for sewing bids, be sure to make it clear that you will remove the old material from the seats and reupholster the new ones yourself.

It is a good idea to get an estimate or two for replacing the upholstery before making an offer on a boat. It will give you a better understanding of the overall cost of restoration—and put you in a better bargaining position with the owner.

Seat bottoms, backs, and bases of boats built in the sixties and seventies usually are construction-grade plywood, and, with all the inadequately sealed screws attaching the hardware, they are often rotten. With your awl, probe the backs and bottoms thoroughly. If you can't yet distinguish between sound and rotten plywood, my only advice is to crawl through more boats, poking away with your awl until you become familiar with the different feel. In short, the awl will penetrate rotten wood with little effort; the more rotten the wood is, the easier the awl penetrates.

When probing the seats or bases, also probe the floor around the seats, which is often one of the first areas to rot. The seats usually are attached to the floor with screws, and inevitably the screws have allowed water to reach the plywood laminates. Rot radiates outward from this area, which means that eventually you will have to replace the entire floor. However, if the soft spots are limited to a small area, such as around the seats, it means that you have discovered the problem in its early stages, and the stringers and frames probably have not been affected. Either way, the entire floor will have to be replaced to ensure a proper repair.

THE TRANSOM

As you probe the floor with your awl, work your way aft and repeat the process on the entire surface of the transom. More than likely you'll inspect the floor carefully, because it probably is covered with a vinyl or carpet covering, which may hide visible signs of rot. Don't cheat on the transom simply because it has no similar covering. Generally, transoms of boats built in the sixties and seventies were sprayed with resin and chopped fiberglass. Beneath this shiny surface may lurk a rotten plywood transom core. Pay special attention to all hardware mounted into or through the transom, such as outboard mounting bolts, towing eyes,

Rob Groves

Cored construction. Think Oreos. The goop in the middle that you eat first is, on the boat, either foam or end-grain balsa wood. The rest is fiberglass.

Jim Anderson

Used boats frequently show their years of wear, especially in the upholstery. It can be repaired or replaced, but in either event it may be a costly project.

and drain tubes. Often, rot will begin around the hardware and spread outward.

There are a few additional areas that may indicate the condition of an outboard boat's transom. Take a look at the legs of the outboard mounting bracket. If the bracket legs have punctured the fiberglass hull, you can be sure the transom core will crumble once exposed. Also, sight along the outside of the transom from corner to corner. Ideally it will be straight, although that is seldom the case. Many builders tended to overestimate their boats' horsepower ratings. Even when the ratings were realistic, many owners just ignored them. Big, powerful outboards are heavy and possess a high degree of torque when pulling up a skier, and all outboards tend to bounce when trailered. Those combined factors often result in an outward bow to the transom and serious stress cracks on the inside corners of the splash well. The stress cracks don't necessarily mean that the transom is rotten, but they may indicate that it is getting soft, and this certainly means that you have a difficult repair to the splash well—one that may require separating the hull and deck sections to gain access to the back of the splash well. If you have gone that far, you may as well replace the transom, too.

There is one final area that may indicate the condition of the transom. When removing the corner cap to inspect the hull thickness, the top edge of the transom may be exposed on some designs. On others, it may be possible to feel the top edge of the transom from inside the boat. Some builders completely sealed the top edge of the transom with resin because they recognized its potential for rot. Many did not. If you can get a look at the top edge of the transom, it should be bright, with all the laminates intact. A dull-gray color and

Signs of real trouble can be seen on this Lady. The corner caps made of steel have rusted beyond repair. The lower corner where side and transom meet has been patched, and the gouged motor cutout on the transom indicates hard use. The boat does not appear worth repairing—unless you already own it.

slight delamination don't always indicate a rotten transom, but they do indicate that it has taken in some water. The top edge should be saturated with resin as a preventive measure.

I have not encountered major transom problems in inboard or sterndrive designs. I expect this is due partly to the design itself, which demands more care in construction, and partly to the deck, which efficiently protects the transom. However, because a damaged transom on an in-

board or sterndrive boat will be very difficult and expensive to repair, give the whole area a thorough survey.

HIDDEN WOOD

I don't think the average boater is aware of just how much wood is used in fiberglass boat construction. With the exception of stringers and frames, it is all construction-grade plywood—and all subject to rot.

We have already talked about the floor and the transom, and I mentioned earlier that plywood is also used in seat backs, bottoms, and bases. There is more. Most consoles have a piece of plywood on the back side that serves as backing for mounting instruments. Some designs used upholstered plywood side panels and bulkheads under the consoles. Many builders added a piece of plywood under the gunwales for extra support and for attaching deck hardware. You may find a small strip on the inside of a shoebox hull/deck joint or under the decks of older V-hulls. Bassboats have a piece glassed to the underside of casting platforms to support pedestal seats and provide purchase for mounting hardware. Occasionally, you'll find plywood storage compartments and rod boxes or lids for live wells.

Some of these applications are more susceptible to rot than others, but a proper survey should include close inspection of all of them. You will probably find yourself standing on your head and wishing your arm were a foot longer, but a thorough job of checking all these hidden wood parts may prevent some nasty surprises.

Now that you have inspected the gelcoat, interior, hull, floor, transom, and the hidden wood, you should have a fair idea of how extensive your renovation will be. Don't be intimidated by the prospect of replacing the floor or transom. It may be hard work, but the expense is minimal. If the hull and deck are of sound design and in fair to good condition, the remainder of the boat can be completely rebuilt. And remember: Pointing out a rotten floor or transom to the seller can lower a boat's asking price dramatically.

ACCESSORIES

If there is an outboard involved in the purchase, it will probably represent a substantial portion of the purchase price and warrant a survey of its own. I suggest you have it tested by a qualified mechanic and, if possible, take it for a test run.

However, you need no technical expertise to check the throttle, shift, and steering cables. Operate the throttle and shift controls and turn the wheel in a full sweep several times. Throttle and shift cables are relatively inexpensive; if they are frozen due to age and rust, I wouldn't be overly concerned. On the other hand, a frozen steering cable may run as

If you poke around in enough boatyards and look at enough boats, you'll soon learn to recognize the subtle differences in appearance between a well-made boat and one where the builder skimped on materials.

much as $250, depending on the size of the boat.

If the steering cable moves at all, chances are good that a complete lube job at the motor will restore it to its original ease of operation. If you can't budge it, the cable itself has rusted beyond repair. I've tried several times to free them up with a variety of lubricants with little success. Replacement is the only sure cure.

While examining the throttle and steering cables, take a look at the 12-volt wiring harness. In most cases the wiring harness runs aft from the dash, within the same wire ties as the other cables. If many of the wires are broken or cracked, it is usually easier to rewire the entire boat than to repair or replace selective wires.

Without taking the boat for a test run, or at least hooking up the battery, it will be difficult to check items such as lights, speedometers, depthfinders, tachometers, bilge pumps, live-well pumps, and radios. Depending on the boat's age and condition, plan on replacing those items where any question exists. At worst you will stay on the high side of your projected cost, and you may even be in for a pleasant surprise when you discover that they work.

As you look over the accessories, jot down any extras that may be included in the deal, such as docklines, anchors, rod holders, spare props, life jackets, etc. You'll need all these items anyway, so you should consider them when making an offer.

SUMMARY

As I said earlier, the secret to surveying a used boat is education. Once you've decided on a design, research the builder and find out if the company is still in operation. Prior to making an offer, try to list what parts will be needed, and get estimates from your local dealers and boatyards.

Crawl through boats until you've seen first-hand what effect the sun has on tarps, upholstery, and floor coverings. Probe floors and transoms with your awl until you can tell the difference between rotten and sound wood. Examine known leakers so you'll be able to spot similar symptoms when you come across them. You'll see no fiberglass flowerpots in the backyards of smart boat-buyers.

—Jim Anderson
(*Runabout Renovation,*
International Marine, 1992)

Buying Used Aluminum Boats

A secondhand aluminum skiff is one of the safest purchases you can make in the used-boat market. This is not to say you can't go wrong, but if you follow the procedure for buying a new boat, as detailed in the section beginning on page 7, and then watch for the points noted below, chances are you will come out OK, perhaps getting a boat almost as good as new at a savings of hundreds of dollars. The reason for this is simple: everything is there for you to see—dings, dents, rivets, welds, broken parts—you name it.

The aluminum itself should be sound if the boat is not too old and has been given reasonable care. Aluminum alloys are tough, but if corrosion or electrolysis have eaten anything away, you can spot it by the heavy white residue corroding aluminum exudes instead of rust. Severe corrosion will look flaky or eaten away and have a flat, weak sound when tapped rather than the ring of solid metal. If in doubt, reject the boat or get an expert to look at it. If the bottom has been painted with antifouling paint, give everything a second close look. Some metal-based bottom paints can eat through an aluminum boat in just a season or two.

Otherwise, study the condition of the boat. Dents, deep scratches, missing fastenings, and the like indicate abuse or hard use and should raise a caution flag. If some fastenings are rusted, or the boat has been modified extensively, look carefully to see if the strength of the hull has been compromised.

Examine the transom area closely. Most aluminum skiffs are designed to be trailered, but not everyone drives the same way. If the loaded trailer has been banged over rough roads and ditches without consideration for the rig, you can be certain the transom has undergone some severe stressing because of the weight of the motor. This is particularly so if the rig is towed with the motor tilted up, because the extended lower unit serves as a lever and torques heavily against the upper half of the transom. If not well engineered, the transom

The water test, by the way, is the ultimate key to getting a good boat. Years of hard use (or only months, in some abusive cases) may finally cause an aluminum hull to leak. . . .

may be damaged, rivets sprung in the transom knee, the splashboard pulled away from the transom, and the quarter knees partially pulled away from the sides.

If the transom block is unprotected wood, it may be badly gouged by the motor clamps and have to be replaced. Check to see if you can do this job properly by yourself or if you will have to have it done by a boatbuilder at considerable cost. Are the seats still in good condition? Remember, they almost always are major structural members in the boat.

Look at the boat from the side, bow, and stern from a short distance away on the chance the hull may have been bent out of shape in an accident or by being jammed between a large vessel and a dock. If it is off slightly, the cause may have been in the manufacturing process, in which case it is no cause for alarm. But if the hull is off true by a lot, or if the bottom shows a twist, you will be better off looking elsewhere for your boat.

Probably the best indication of the boat's worth is its general condition. Some owners are remarkably careless in the way they use their boats. This is most apt to show as dents, deep scratches in the finish or in the metal itself, splintered seats, and broken parts. It has probably been run aground a number of times, so look at the bottom carefully and examine the exterior keels to see if any of them are structurally damaged. Other owners use their boats very little and then only in fair weather (which may be why the boat is for sale). As a result, the paint inside and out is almost like new (except for possible fading), the only noticeable wear is where footgear has worn the paint off the floor frames, and the stem piece and skegs (or keels) are hardly scratched. That was the state of the Starcraft skiff I saw for sale on a rural lawn. The owner even let me borrow it to try with my own motor. The boat was almost like new, and I couldn't wait to write the check. The skiff never disappointed me.

The water test, by the way, is the ultimate key to getting a good boat.

Years of hard use (or only months, in some abusive cases) may finally cause an aluminum hull to leak—usually nothing more than weeping around a rivet or along a seam, but a leak, just the same. An honest owner will probably tell you about it in advance, but check the boat in the water anyway.

After the careful examination and test ride, if you want the boat but still have doubts, ask an experienced aluminum-boat owner to make his own survey. Between the two of you, a decision should be possible.

—DRG

CONVERSIONS

Dressing Up a Whaler

Selecting a boat suitable for cruising the Intracoastal Waterway with two people and a Welsh Corgi puppy on board sounds like a relatively simple task. But when restrictions are placed on your selection—it must be trailerable behind a four-cylinder Jeep Mini Cherokee, easy on fuel, maneuverable and safe, have easily maintained quality construction, and be under 18 feet—the task becomes a bit more difficult.

We first chose a 15-foot Zodiac inflatable, because of its excellent fuel economy and unbelievable capacity.

I trailered it to Hilton Head, South Carolina, for a week of testing in the surrounding waterways and found that a long voyage can be made in this boat, but it sure was not going to be done by me. The bouncing and the awkwardness of tiller-steering an outboard would make extended runs impractical. Adding mechanical steering and controls was possible but would impose restrictions on usable interior space. I drove home ready to go back to the drawing board.

Halfway back I recalled an old 17-foot Boston Whaler stored upside down behind the Zodiac dealer's warehouse. Within 24 hours of my arrival home, I had negotiated a trade for this bare 1974 Whaler hull.

Structurally the hull was excellent, but cosmetically it needed help. Chips and scratches were evident and the sun had taken its toll on the gelcoat.

I dragged the hull to Bruce & Johnson's Marina in Branford, Connecticut, where Tom Kellenbach sanded and primed the hull, filled the nicks and scratches, and gave her an

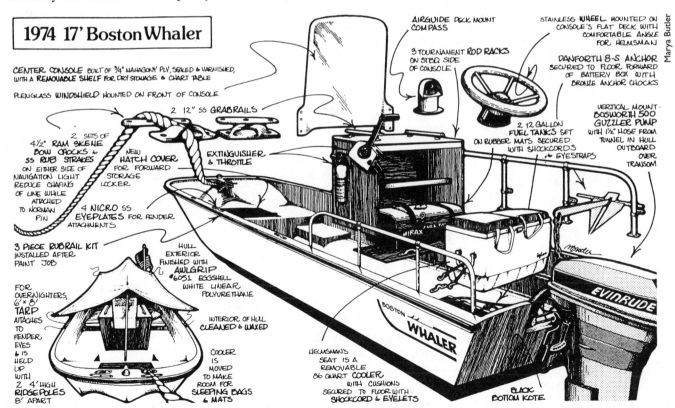

1974 17' Boston Whaler

CENTER CONSOLE BUILT OF 3/4" MAHAGONY PLY, SEALED & VARNISHED, WITH A REMOVABLE SHELF FOR DRY STOWAGE & CHART TABLE

PLEXIGLASS WINDSHIELD MOUNTED ON FRONT OF CONSOLE

2 12" SS GRABRAILS

AIRGUIDE DECK MOUNT COMPASS

STAINLESS WHEEL MOUNTED ON CONSOLE'S FLAT DECK WITH COMFORTABLE ANGLE FOR HELMSMAN

3 TOURNAMENT ROD RACKS ON STBD SIDE OF CONSOLE

DANFORTH 8-S ANCHOR SECURED TO FLOOR FORWARD OF BATTERY BOX WITH BRONZE ANCHOR CHOCKS

Marya Butler

VERTICAL MOUNT BOSWORTH 500 GUZZLER PUMP WITH 1½" HOSE FROM TUNNEL IN HULL OUTBOARD OVER TRANSOM

2 SETS OF 4½" RAM SKENE BOW CHOCKS & SS RUB STRAKES ON EITHER SIDE OF NAVIGATION LIGHT REDUCE CHAFING OF LINE WHILE ATTACHED TO NORMAN PIN

NEW HATCH COVER FOR FORWARD STORAGE LOCKER

EXTINGUISHER & THROTTLE

2 12 GALLON FUEL TANKS SET ON RUBBER MATS SECURED WITH SHOCKCORDS & EYESTRAPS

4 NICRO SS EYEPLATES FOR FENDER ATTACHMENTS

3 PIECE RUBRAIL KIT INSTALLED AFTER PAINT JOB

HULL EXTERIOR FINISHED WITH AWLGRIP #6051 EGGSHELL WHITE LINEAR POLYURETHANE

FOR OVERNIGHTERS, 6' x 8' TARP ATTACHES TO FENDER EYES & IS HELD UP WITH 2 4' HIGH RIDGEPOLES 8' APART

INTERIOR OF HULL CLEANED & WAXED

COOLER IS MOVED TO MAKE ROOM FOR SLEEPING BAGS & MATS

HELMSMAN'S SEAT IS A REMOVABLE 86 QUART COOLER WITH CUSHIONS SECURED TO FLOOR WITH SHOCKCORD & EYELETS

BOSTON WHALER

EVINRUDE

BLACK BOTTOM KOTE

Awlgrip #6051 Eggshell White finish before tackling installation of the three-piece rubrail kit. Below the waterline, he applied Interlux Black Bottom Kote. We decided not to refinish the interior glass: Cleaning and waxing managed to restore it nicely.

I definitely wanted a center console, but not one made of glass, so the project was handed over to Bill Sorensen, chief carpenter at Bruce & Johnson's. He fashioned a sheet of ¾-inch mahogany plywood into a superbly crafted and functional center console with a removable shelf that doubles as a chart table. The steering wheel was mounted with a gentle angle on the flat deck of the console, resulting in a very comfortable helm position. Sorenson even fashioned a new hatch cover for the forward storage locker.

The console was sealed and varnished, the steering assembly and stainless wheel were installed, and she was ready to come home for the finishing touches. A bow rail was omitted, partly because I liked the ease of access to the water (or land) from the bow, and partly because I appreciate the lines of the boat more without the rail.

For fuel, two 12-gallon Mirax D1212 "Boston Whaler" tanks were installed in well-ventilated areas, with a portable 6-gallon OMC tank for reserve. The large tanks sit on rubber mats and are held in place by shock cord and eye straps.

The console was kept simple, with a few modifications for navigation and safety equipment. Included is an Airguide deck-mount compass, two 12-inch stainless steel grabrails, and a small Plexiglas windshield. Mounted on the port side of the console is a Kidde M-10 BC fire extinguisher, and to starboard are three

Kevin Vanacore's restored Boston Whaler was converted for coastal cruising. Sleeping area is created by moving the big cooler seat and setting up a tarp on a ridgepole.

tournament rod racks. Inside the console are dry areas for binoculars, charts, radios, and other valuables.

A removable 86-quart Igloo cooler with cushion serves as the helmsman's seat and cold storage. Additional seating is provided by the Whaler's molded-in seats at the bow section. The use of a few boat cushions makes this a comfortable area in calm water.

I spent as much refurbishing this Whaler as I would have paid for a new one, but then my boat perfectly fits me and my uses.

For sleeping, we remove the cooler and lay two foam pads on deck with our sleeping bags on top. A 6-foot-by-8-foot tarp tied to the side rails and supported in the middle by two 4-foot ridgepoles serves as a shelter tent.

I added two 4½-inch Skene bow chocks and stainless steel rubstrakes on either side of the navigation light to reduce the chafing of dock and anchor lines attached to the Norman pin. Four Nicro stainless eyeplates are mounted on the forward gunwale sections for fender attachments.

On the after bulkhead is a vertical-mount Bosworth 500 Guzzler Pump with a 1½-inch hose running into the tunnel and over the transom to dispose of rain and washdown water. A Danforth 8-S anchor is secured to the floor forward of the battery box with bronze anchor chocks. Careful attention was given to placement of a telescoping boathook, paddle, and other essentials.

All told, I spent as much refurbishing this Whaler as I would have paid for a new one, but then my boat perfectly fits me and my uses. What more could one want?

—Kevin Vanacore
(*Small Boat Journal* #44)

A 15-Foot Plywood Cruiser

For 20 years I had been buying and building bigger boats to suit the needs of a family of six and an ego that thought bigger was better. Now that the children were grown and much of my boating was solo, I asked myself, "What do I really need in a boat?" High on the list was fishing and exploring the shallow areas of Choctawhatchee Bay on the Gulf Coast of Florida, with an occasional trip offshore. That called for a small, trailerable boat, easy to load and launch, one that combined shallow draft with reasonable seaworthiness.

I made the rounds kicking trailer tires, listening to salesmen tell me why I needed this boat or that. Then, one evening while thumbing through Harry V. Sucher's *Simplified Boatbuilding: The Flat-Bottom Boat*, (unfortunately, the book is out of print, but you may be able to obtain a copy from your library or a used-book dealer), I found just the boat—a 15½-foot flat-bottomed plywood skiff.

> *My humble boat could be birthed in the local lumberyard and berthed in my backyard.*

There are no exotic parts in the materials list; my humble boat could be birthed in the local lumberyard and berthed in my backyard. Needed for building are two sheets of ½-inch AC fir plywood, two sheets of ¼-inch plywood, 50 linear feet of 1 x 2 spruce, wood glue, assorted brass screws, and 5 gallons of polyester resin. The finished boat is a solid skiff with glass-taped seams. All exposed wood is saturated with three coats of resin and covered with two coats of marine hull and deck paint. Cost to this point: $600.

I pushed a 21-foot, 2,000-pound fiberglass sailboat with a 6-h.p. motor for a couple of years, and with my new "big is *not* better" philosophy, I decided to buy a 6-h.p. Evinrude outboard. The engine and remote controls cost $1,000; the cable-and-pulley steering system and assorted cleats and chocks added another $50. After six months of work,

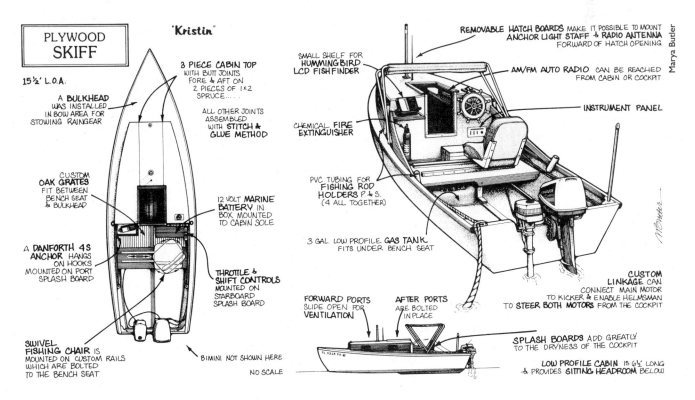

Marya Butler

PLYWOOD SKIFF

'Kristin'

15½' L.O.A.

A BULKHEAD WAS INSTALLED IN BOW AREA FOR STOWING RAINGEAR

3 PIECE CABIN TOP WITH BUTT JOINTS FORE & AFT ON 2 PIECES OF 1×2 SPRUCE.....

ALL OTHER JOINTS ASSEMBLED WITH STITCH & GLUE METHOD

CUSTOM OAK GRATES FIT BETWEEN BENCH SEAT & BULKHEAD

12 VOLT MARINE BATTERY IN BOX MOUNTED TO CABIN SOLE

A DANFORTH 4S ANCHOR HANGS ON HOOKS MOUNTED ON PORT SPLASH BOARD

THROTTLE & SHIFT CONTROLS MOUNTED ON STARBOARD SPLASH BOARD

SWIVEL FISHING CHAIR IS MOUNTED ON CUSTOM RAILS WHICH ARE BOLTED TO THE BENCH SEAT

BIMINI NOT SHOWN HERE

NO SCALE

REMOVABLE HATCH BOARDS MAKE IT POSSIBLE TO MOUNT ANCHOR LIGHT STAFF & RADIO ANTENNA FORWARD OF HATCH OPENING

SMALL SHELF FOR HUMMINGBIRD LCD FISHFINDER

AM/FM AUTO RADIO CAN BE REACHED FROM CABIN OR COCKPIT

INSTRUMENT PANEL

CHEMICAL FIRE EXTINGUISHER

PVC TUBING FOR FISHING ROD HOLDERS P. & S. (4 ALL TOGETHER)

3 GAL. LOW PROFILE GAS TANK FITS UNDER BENCH SEAT

CUSTOM LINKAGE CAN CONNECT MAIN MOTOR TO KICKER & ENABLE HELMSMAN TO STEER BOTH MOTORS FROM THE COCKPIT

FORWARD PORTS SLIDE OPEN FOR VENTILATION

AFTER PORTS ARE BOLTED IN PLACE

SPLASH BOARDS ADD GREATLY TO THE DRYNESS OF THE COCKPIT

LOW PROFILE CABIN IS 6½' LONG & PROVIDES SITTING HEADROOM BELOW the boat was ready to launch.

For the next three years *Kristin,* named after my youngest grandchild, served my needs well. But this past year I began thinking of camp cruising, and with that came the decision to build a plywood shelter for my boat. To keep weight as well as windage to a minimum, I designed a 6½-foot-long, low-profile cabin with sitting headroom, using stitched and glued ⅜-inch lauan plywood to keep down weight. The only framing consists of two 1 x 2 spruce strips running parallel to the hatch from the after bulkhead to the forward end. The three-piece top butts on this frame. All other joints are stitched every 6 inches with stainless safety wire and bonded with 4-inch-wide glass tape inside and out. Three coats of resin were applied to all wood surfaces, and the cabintop was painted with two coats of marine enamel. The sides and after bulkhead were left natural.

For light and ventilation, four rectangular ports were made of ¼-inch Plexiglas. The after ports are fastened permanently with ½-inch brass bolts, but the forward ones are made to slide in tracks made of two layers of ¼-inch Plexiglas.

The companionway hatch is standard sailboat style with removable covers that can be stored below. By not having a sliding hatch cover, I am able to mount a radio antenna and a custom staff with anchor light made of old aluminum spar stock and Plexiglas tubing on the cabintop. Splash boards of lauan plywood were fabricated after the cabin was stitched in place; these help keep the cockpit dry while blending the cabin lines into those of the boat.

The original console was removed and a mahogany spoked steering wheel mounted on the starboard side of the bulkhead. Just beneath the

wheel is a 4 x 12 instrument panel made from a sheet of ⅛-inch-thick aluminum that holds three toggle switches for the anchor light, running lights, compass, and cockpit courtesy light. The engine kill switch is also mounted on this panel.

An AM/FM auto radio is mounted just under the hatchway with a remote speaker at the forward end of the cabin; the controls are reachable from the cockpit or the cabin. Power is supplied by a 24-volt marine battery in a box mounted to the cabin sole behind the instrument panel and vented to the cockpit. On the port side of the bulkhead is a small shelf to hold a Humminbird LCD fish finder, and below this, a chemical fire extinguisher.

Custom-made oak grates fit between the bench seat and the bulk-head. The 3-gallon, low-profile gas tank tucks neatly under the bench seat, and I may add another to extend the cruising range. There are four fishing-rod holders made from PVC tubing, two of which are behind the bench seat for trolling and two outboard on the splashboards.

A swivel fishing chair mounted on a set of rails bolted to the bench seat allows me to move my weight athwartships to keep the boat in trim. I can also rotate the chair 180 degrees for trolling and fishing.

A Danforth 4S anchor hangs on aluminum hooks on the port-side splashboard, while throttle and shift controls are mounted on the starboard splashboard. Under the latter set of controls is the cockpit courtesy light.

With the two, 2-inch-thick Naug-

ahyde-covered foam pads laid on the cabin sole, sleeping is as comfortable and roomy as in any V-berth. When not in use, the pads are held to the cabin sides by bungee cord. Life jackets and PFD cushions are also tucked behind the bungee. A pull-down table is mounted on the starboard quarter with a cutout for a wash basin.

Alongside the 6-horse Evinrude, which is mounted on the centerline, is a little 2-horse kicker used mainly as a trolling motor, but also serving as backup power. I've found that when the seas get lumpy, running both motors at low speed gives more thrust and better control. For this reason, I fashioned a linkage that is permanently mounted to the 6-horse and can be quickly connected to the kicker, permitting me to steer both motors from the cockpit.

—Art Mosca
(*Small Boat Journal* #64)

Shortly after the story of his boat was published in the January 1989 issue of Small Boat Journal, *Art Mosca began receiving letters from resourceful readers who tracked down his address in order to ask questions about the boat and to inquire for plans. One of them drove 400 miles to see the boat, and as Art writes somewhat wistfully, "He made an offer I couldn't refuse, and that boat now resides in Alabama."*

Art stays active in boating, however, by building custom stripper canoes—and testing them on camping trips.—DRG

> *With my new "big is not better" philosophy, I decided to buy a 6-h.p. Evinrude outboard.*

The MFG Just Won't Die

My 76-year-old parents needed a boat—something safe, comfortable, and simple for exploring Virginia's Yeocomico River, local bottom fishing, and evening rides out on Chesapeake Bay to watch the sunset.

Since neither was as strong or as agile as they once were, they had to have a way to keep the boat with a minimum of care. Their area was too rural to take advantage of a forklift-operated "boatel," but a friend who runs a small country boatyard allowed us to launch the boat at minimum cost anytime we wanted.

After this problem was resolved, a concept began to take shape. The boat should be an outboard, 15 to 16 feet in length and capable of cruising efficiently at 12 to 14 knots. That would be enough speed to get them anywhere they might want to go within 45 minutes, without requiring a big motor and without making the boat pound uncomfortably. I figured that with the right hull, 15 h.p. would be enough.

To be efficient in this speed range, the boat would have to be light at the transom. For riding comfort and dryness, my parents should sit amidships, preferably in comfortable swivel seats. This arrangement would have the added advantage of putting them side by side, away from the engine, so they could talk without having to raise their voices.

To keep the rigging as simple as possible, they could steer with an extension tiller. Although they had been mixing oil and gas in our outboards for years, it would be convenient to have the motor fed from an automatic mixing tank, like OMC's Accumix system. An electric starter would keep things easy for my father.

The least expensive way to do the job seemed to be to find an old fiberglass runabout with a sound hull, strip it to its interior, and build a bench seat. An alternative would be to find a secondhand aluminum skiff and rig it out. There were plenty of old runabouts around, but they were wide, stubby hulls. Modifying one of them would cost some money for supplies, plus lots of time. I had shifted my attention to aluminum skiffs, when the right boat turned up.

She was a 1957, 15½-foot MFG runabout built in Erie, Pennsylvania. This early fiberglass boat had a mahogany deck and gunwales, mahogany seats, and mahogany keel and keelson bolted together through the hull, a mahogany transom knee, and a transom made of two pieces of mahogany sandwiching the fiberglass. Her hull appeared to be molded after the round-bilged, lapstrake Lyman skiffs popular in the 1950s, and she even had fiberglass ribs made to simulate the steam-bent oak ribs of the Lyman.

Despite the round bilges, she was quite stable with the solid feel and easy motion of a bigger boat. It was obvious that she would be more comfortable for them than an aluminum skiff. When my 8-h.p. outboard got her up on plane with throttle to spare, I knew she was the boat for my folks.

Peterkin, as she was christened, has been in my family now for several summers, and she is a great success. The illustration shows how she is rigged: two swivel seats amidships, the fuel tank and battery secured just behind the seat, extension tiller, and a 15-h.p. Evinrude with a Doel-Fin hydrofoil to offset the tendency of her round-bottomed hull to squat. A 9¼- x 9-inch propeller, rather than the standard 9½- x 10-inch prop, was found to be a better choice for the boat's size and weight. To our surprise, the engine planes her with four adults aboard. Cruising speed is about 12 knots at 1-gallon-per-hour fuel consumption.

My parents have spent more time on the water since they got the boat than they did in the previous 10

1957 15½' FIBERGLASS RUNABOUT

TWO SWIVEL SEATS

EXTENSION TILLER

FUEL TANK & BATTERY SECURED AFT

15 H.P. EVINRUDE WITH A DOEL-FIN PLANES 'PETERKIN' WITH FOUR ADULTS ABOARD

Marya Butler

years. Speed, stability, motion, and comfort are all just right. My mother's back is not the best, but her cushioned seat takes good care of her. And my father likes having an elegant boat that draws appreciative comments. He has never been one to show off anything, but he enjoys answering questions about where she came from. There were plenty of boats like her around the Yeocomico 30 years ago, but she is the only one now.

Steering with the extension tiller felt awkward to him at first, especially when docking, but he has gotten used to it and likes having direct contact with the engine. He also likes being able to stand up and steer. The boat's speed is good for what he calls "coasting," poking back into the Yeocomico's various creeks and coves. She is fast enough to get around but slow enough for good watching.

Maintenance of all the wood parts was a worry at first. But we had to have her surveyed for the insurance company, and the surveyor suggested that nothing more than a biennial dose of wood preservative on the keelson and floorboards, plus the obvious attention to varnish and bottom paint, would take care of her needs. She came with a custom-fitted cover that protects everything when she is not in the water. Putting her to bed for the winter takes half a day, and it

> When my 8-h.p. outboard got her up on plane with throttle to spare, I knew she was the boat for my folks.

takes a weekend to get her ready again in the spring.

If *Peterkin* had not come along, I would have gotten an aluminum skiff for my parents, and they would have been happy with it. The basic concept of swivel seats, extension tiller, and modest—not minimal—power is certainly transferable to other boats.

This sort of boat has plenty of ap-plications beyond its use by two septuagenarians watching sunsets on Chesapeake Bay. It is an easily trailered exploring boat, a fine picnic boat, a superb trolling boat (the modest engine allows a broad range of speed control down to very slow), and a trustworthy boat to teach young people the ways of the water. (My sister's children spend a lot of time in *Peterkin*.) If it works well on big tidal rivers, it should work equally well on reservoirs and lakes.

We lost something when Lyman stopped making new boats and MFG switched to more "modern" designs. With all due regard to modified-V and other hull forms, there is still a role for round-bilged hulls intended for modest planing speeds.

—John Page Williams
(*Small Boat Journal* #67)

Everyman's Exploration Boat

The sting of sleet in the wind-driven rain was proof enough that we were a long way north of our usual cruising grounds in Maine. Our heavily laden skiff rocked easily on the long swell as we pondered our next move. The silence was immense, broken only by the sound of wavelets against the aluminum hull and the distant thunder of surf.

We were 450 miles up the Labrador coast from our starting point at the Quebec border and some 45 miles north of Nain, the last inhabited community. More than 150 miles of wild, mountainous coast lay between us and Hudson Strait—oh, how we wanted to keep on going!

"It doesn't look too good," I growled to Geof, who was sitting just under the canopy, staring at the chart. He said nothing for a minute or so.

"We're looking at 10 or 15 miles of exposed coast and no promise of shelter at the end of that," he said finally. "We can probably make it around the Cape and get a good look at the Kiglapaits, but if we get weathered in up there, we're in trouble. We're running out of time."

The Kiglapaits were the first big mountain range north of Nain and our second choice as a climbing area. Our original goal was the Kaumajet range, another 50 miles north, but we had given that up two days earlier when we realized that four weeks simply was not enough time to do all we had planned. Now a nasty easterly was shutting down our hopes of even making the Kiglapaits, and once again a stark fact was brought home to us—although Labrador appears small on most maps, its coast is huge.

"Let's can it," I said. "We've got a couple of interesting peaks right here at Port Manvers and can only take two days to climb anyway."

Thus we reached our farthest north on a two-man expedition to one of the least-known coasts in North America south of the Arctic Circle. We had been planning for a year and a half, had been traveling for two weeks by car, ferry, and boat for a total of 1,600 miles from our starting point, and were now stopped. But we were far from disappointed—it had been an exciting trip so far, and we still had two weeks to go. Alexander Forbes had been right when he wrote:

Why go so far afield to map a desolate, uninhabited and, to most people, useless land? There are several answers. The bold and rugged landscape, the intricate coast line and the lack of forests make Labrador an ideal region in which to apply and perfect certain new methods of aerial mapping. Deep fiords and winding lakes, ice-sculptured mountains of complex structure, lingering glaciers and the sparse vegetation of the far north offered an almost virgin field for geological and botanical studies. Ships now and then approach these shores, but do so at their peril. The charts and sailing directions are inaccurate. By locating shoals and harbors and by describing anchorages and their approaches, a practical service could be performed that might mean the saving of lives and property. If these were not reasons enough, another—less logical but perhaps more impelling—was the haunting lure of a wild and almost unknown country.

(From *Northernmost Labrador Mapped from the Air*, by Alexander Forbes, The American Geographical Society, 1938.)

The Forbes book, with its spectacular air photos of mountains, islands, capes, and bays, was the source of our inspiration. But we had no scientific excuse for our travels, only a "less logical but more impelling" reason—for the sheer adventure of it.

Thus began an article I wrote for *Small Boat Journal* back in 1981 describing one of the most exciting boating ventures of my life. The purpose of presenting it here is to show that reason and high-minded purpose need not be the only excuses (if you need any!) for planning and carrying out a major boat voyage; the sheer adventure of it figures prominently in some of the most scientific expeditions, and one need not apologize for it.

If you want something to sharpen your senses, think big and go small. But go!

> No, you don't have to be a Thor Heyerdahl or an H. W. Tilman to sally forth on your biggest adventure, but as the ancient Chinese philosopher once said, you'd better have your act together.

Since that time, I've watched friends visit the Labrador coast with a variety of craft: kayaks of several types, a custom aluminum outboard, even an inflatable. In each case, careful thought had been given to the boat type, with either the boat tailored to the trip or the trip tailored to the boat. Such planning is imperative, for in a land without roads and with water both fresh and salt nearly everywhere, one's boat is as important as food. In the past, most water expeditions have been in liveaboard vessels, and in some cases the larger craft are still the sensible choice, for many reasons. But as you look into the travel possibilities for your venture, you will be surprised to find that more frequently than not, small boats are not only the right answer but in some instances are the *only* answer.

How does one go about selecting a boat and then rigging it out for a specific trip? Well, experience helps, and I don't mean this flippantly. On the contrary, when you make the decision to undertake a major small-boat voyage, you are accepting the advantages and limitations of little boats, to say nothing of the responsibilities for a safe journey for you and your companions. Thus, in encouraging you to "go exploring," I assume a level of experience capable of dealing with the everyday surprises and challenges one might expect on such a trip. This means knowledge about weather, boat and motor repairs, navigation, small-boat seamanship, first aid, and a dozen other skills that an experienced explorer takes almost for granted. No, you don't have to be a Thor Heyerdahl or an H. W. Tilman to sally forth on your biggest adventure, but as the ancient Chinese philosopher once said, you'd better have your act together.

It may help in your own planning to hear how we went about selecting and rigging our Labrador craft. Let's pick the *Small Boat Journal* article again:

The choice of the boat was dictated by our needs and our pocketbooks. We wanted one large enough to carry us and our gear safely over big waters. From our reading and from contacts in Newfoundland, we knew that at least half our travel would be in protected waterways and that small boats were a common means of conveyance along that coast. At the same time, our boat had to be light enough to be hauled out of the water by the two of us, since we would be leaving it for extended periods of time. It had to be tough to endure beaching and hauling. And it

Deep in the wilds of coastal Labrador, the 18-foot aluminum skiff Torngat is right at home nudged up against a granite ledge. The wooden foredeck and spray hood were made to be removable; rig made it possible to sleep aboard.

had to have enough speed to cover 100 miles in an average day. Complicating all this was the need for as small a motor as would do the job, because weight would greatly affect hauling and launching.

Aluminum seemed the only answer. At first we considered having a custom boat built, but the lack of time and money ruled this out. A careful perusal of aluminum boat catalogs showed an almost consistent break between the largest simple, open skiffs, at 16 feet in length, and the fancier runabouts in the 18- to 22-foot range. The former were too small, the latter too heavy and too expensive.

The answer came in a brochure from Lund American Inc. of New York Mills, Minnesota, where we found just the boat we were looking for. It was the Lund S-18, an 18-foot

aluminum skiff with a 1,500-pound capacity that weighed less than 400 pounds. Its simple interior could easily be modified, and Geof, a professional boatbuilder, was confident he could make a lightweight raised deck for the bow, something we considered a necessity if such a boat was to stand up to the seas we anticipated. I knew enough about Lund boats to know they were well built. Cementing the decision was the fact that the price was right, under $1,500 at that time.

Having found our boat solved only one problem, for as our modern times make so abundantly clear, nothing is easy. The next job was getting it, since the nearest regular delivery point for Lund Boats was Columbus, Ohio, a mere 1,000 miles away. So, at the height of the 1979 early-summer gas shortage, I drove to Col-

umbus to pick up a boat I had never seen outside a brochure. What a relief when I got it on the trailer and had a chance to look it over! It appeared to be custom-made for our needs and, despite its light weight, was even more strongly built than I hoped.

Time soon became a factor in everything we did. Attempting to find the low side of our power needs, I tried a 15-h.p. motor, and while it pushed the boat comfortably when running light, it wasn't up to the load intended for it. The Lund official with whom I had arranged the purchase of the boat recommended a 25-h.p. motor as best for our requirements even though the S-18 is rated for a maximum of 55 h.p. My final choice was the Mariner 25, at that time built in Japan by Yamaha and only recently introduced in the United States. I bought it mainly on its reputation as

Foam flotation has been removed from the second seat from the bow and the metal cut to make an opening forward under the raised foredeck. The opening was lined with plywood, some of the foam replaced, and the cutout seat (now two smaller ones) reinstalled. In recent years, a new full-width plywood seat has been built and the after side of the cutout sheathed in plywood. The resulting closed area is used as a rope locker.

a respected and durable work motor and was never disappointed. It ran flawlessly and required nothing more than a fresh set of spark plugs halfway through the trip.

Our gas mileage was about 5 miles per gallon—not bad considering what we were asking of the motor. A 35- or 40-horse might have improved our mileage somewhat, but the added weight would have made hauling-out a far more difficult task.

Our average speed of 10 to 12 m.p.h. sounds slow by the standards we are used to in this country of high-powered boats, but it was a comfortable pace for both boat and crew and one that could be maintained on the open-sea stretches as well as the smooth-surfaced "runs," as the protected reaches are called in Labrador. This speed was also our most economical. One might think that at such a slow speed the boat would run at a squat. This was not the case, thanks to a Doel-Fin stabilizer fin attached to the lower unit of the motor that gave a good amount of "lift" to the stern.

Fuel was carried in two standard 6-gallon metal tanks and in four 6-gallon plastic gasoline containers. We carried our own oil and mixed it when we bought fuel. Sparkplugs and an extra propeller were the only spare parts we carried.

While we bought the Mariner, the spare motor, a 5-h.p. Suzuki Model 5DL, was on loan for testing. Prior to the trip we determined that it was quite capable of driving our loaded boat at hull speed without effort and would do so with excellent economy. This decision to rely on a second motor rather than carry an inventory of spare parts (Murphy's Law says you won't have the right ones with you) proved a good one, and I've followed that practice ever since.

We began modifying the boat, a task that took several months of on-and-off work. Small lockers were cut into the after seats and carved out of the foam flotation, the light weight of the motor more than compensating for the small amount of foam removed. A grabrail of ½-inch I.D. galvanized pipe was installed between the rear and center seats. The second seat aft of the bow was cut out to open access to the cuddy under the deck, and the little bow seat was converted into a shelf for items we wanted to keep permanently dry. Aft of the deck and attached to it was a canopy made out of coated ripstop nylon, the same material used in tents. This setup gave us a tiny cabin

The foredeck is shown mounted on a wood shelf bolted to the sides. The aluminum bows for the spray hood fit into holes drilled in wood blocks screwed to the sides.

forward that not only provided a haven for the man off watch but also served as a sleeping area for both of us when we weren't camping in the tent ashore. Once we figured out how to adapt the area for our sleeping bags, we spent about half our nights aboard, a big convenience when it was stormy or when we arrived at some hard landing spot late in the evening. Heavy ground tackle in the form of 15- and 20-pound fisherman anchors and ⅜-inch nylon anchor rodes assured us of worry-free nights.

At first the breast-high grabrail appeared oversize and unnecessary, but once at sea we found it invaluable. Whoever was at the tiller had to stand throughout most of his watch, and the solid rail to hold on to took much of the strain off one's legs. It was also a great safety factor since the center well was filled with cargo and anyone moving forward or aft had to step from seat to seat. The center rail greatly reduced danger of going over the side into 38-degree water. (Details on building grabrails can be found on page 200.)

The key to increasing the seaworthiness of our boat was the raised deck, which extended 7 feet aft of the bow. Geof first built a self-draining shelf securely bolted to the hull about 4 inches below the gunwale. The deck was cold-molded of ¼-inch lauan plywood doubled on both the sides and the top and then covered with fiberglass. A V-shaped coaming angling forward served as an effective waterbreak. A rugged Jonesport cleat at the forward end of the deck and 12-volt running lights on the sides, powered by a hotshot battery, completed the deck unit.

The deck was held to the shelf by six ¼-inch bolts and could be removed in just a few minutes. This was helpful during storage in winter

Emergency gear includes a rope ladder attached to a grabrail for climbing back aboard, an EPIRB radio beacon, a well-stocked first-aid kit in a soft-sided beer cooler, and a small tool kit in a tackle box.

(just turn the boat over on a rack) or if the skiff was to be used for a period of time when the deck was not needed. The deck turned out to be watertight and durable—at one time, four Eskimo children were jumping up and down on it.

The road rig was a secondhand, 2,000-pound-capacity, galvanized Shoreline trailer towed by an International Scout, the latter welcome on the last 60 miles of rough road to Red Bay in southern Labrador, where we left the truck and took to the water.

Navigational and emergency gear was adequate for coastwise cruising in a small boat. Our principal navigating tool was a spherical compass

> *If you want something to sharpen your senses, think big and go small. But go!*

Geof had used on a small sailboat. We lucked out. We didn't have time to compensate it before leaving but found it was right on the button anyway. Extreme compass deviation is an occasional but common problem on the Labrador coast. One is warned of some of the worst places in notes printed right on the chart, but we found others where the compass would be off 10 or 15 degrees for several miles and then return to normal.

Anyone used to the well-charted, carefully buoyed waters of our U.S. coasts is in for a surprise, and perhaps a shock, upon discovering that aids to navigation are for all practical purposes nonexistent along the Labrador coast. Thus, navigation is from point to point, and even in good weather one must follow compass bearings or chance getting lost among the scores of confusing bays and islands.

Our emergency gear consisted of a borrowed EPIRB, an emergency radio beacon whose frequency is monitored by commercial and military craft (and now by satellite) and that can be activated at the flip of a switch. Smoke signals, parachute flares, international orange flag, and heavy 9½-foot oars were on hand for desperate times, and a well-stocked first-aid kit was kept under the bow deck. A 4-foot-long small rope ladder was fastened to one of the pipes of the grabrail and then tucked under the seat out of the way. Had we capsized, or had one or both of us gone overboard, this ladder could have been quickly unlimbered either from aboard the boat or from the water and would serve as a big help for getting back aboard. One has to bear in mind constantly that a person in this cold water will lose strength quickly, making it very difficult for a single person on the boat to haul another aboard with brute strength.

We carried a good selection of tools for both motor and boat repairs. We also took the winch off the boat trailer and mounted it on a piece of ¼-inch-thick aluminum plate made especially for this purpose. With this rig we were able to haul both boat and motor up the beach above the tide line.

Our camping equipment was basic stuff, in line with our preference for keeping things simple. Home ashore and in the mountains was a Moss two-person tent. The kitchen consisted of a one-burner Optimus 111B gasoline stove (a poor choice; see page 220), two aluminum pots, a frying pan, and a 1-quart container of stove fuel. (The amazing Optimus, we found, would operate quite well on the same gasoline/oil mix we used in the outboard motor.)

Personal utensils consisted of a small wooden bowl, an insulated cup, and a spoon. Food was mainly dry grains, pasta, rice, cheese, dried milk, flour, and pancake mix. Two handlines with 10-ounce diamond jigs supplied us with fresh cod in minutes whenever we wanted fish, and we were able to buy instant coffee and eggs at coastal villages. Mostly we lived off food we brought from the States or had purchased in Newfoundland.

Each of us had two sleeping bags, one of lightweight down and the other filled with Dacron, the former being for our mountain ventures while the synthetic bag was preferred

> *Navigation is from point to point, and even in good weather one must follow compass bearings or chance getting lost among the scores of confusing bays and islands.*

in the damp environment of the boat. I am thin-skinned, so I was most comfortable during the subarctic nights with the down bag placed inside the Dacron every night of the trip. The synthetics proved their value when water eventually got to our sleeping bags. We were warm even when the bags were damp, and our body heat did a good job in eventually drying them out. Clothing was basically wool and acrylic pile, the latter far superior to down in wet conditions. Commercial fishermen's foul-weather gear kept us dry in the worst downpours.

In looking back over the 12 years since our Labrador adventure and weighing the value of our equipment then versus the vast array of high-tech stuff that has come on the mar-

ket since, there is little I would change were I planning for the same trip today. Mainly we were backpacking by boat and thus traveled light, although we had the luxurious capability of carrying some favorite extras. In any event, we were well fed, warmly clothed, and nearly everything aboard could serve double duty or more and yet be quickly and easily repaired in case of damage or breakdown.

Most "epics" happen because something goes wrong. Our trip had but one of these, and even then it hardly met the definition. On our return down the coast, we chose to save some time by cutting across the 10-mile-wide mouth of a bay. The weather was fair and the conditions gentle as we started out, but halfway across we were headed by a strong offshore breeze that generated a wicked cross-chop exactly the wrong size for our 18-foot boat. What followed was two hours of creeping, bone-jarring progress toward a distant headland that never seemed to change in size. The ride was so rough we both developed headaches, but that was about the extent of the damage. The moral of this story? There is none. If you spend a lot of time on the water, expect at least a few rough times.

And how do I feel about our choice of boat, motor, and trailer? They did the work expected of them without failure, and all three are still hale and hearty after many more thousands of rugged miles since that exceptional first northern voyage. They still meet most of my boating needs. And they are a resounding testament to the fact that good quality lasts.

—DRG

Working with Canvas

Whenever the urge to go cruising grips us, there is an immediate desire "to build a house" on our small boats. There are arguments in favor of this, particularly if your boat is large enough and will always be used as a cruiser, but where space is at a premium or housing is secondary to other uses, a very effective shelter can be one made of fabric. When elaborate construction and sewing are required, you may be smart to turn to a sailmaker, but where the work is fairly straightforward, chances are you can do it yourself. In the following piece, Paul Butler will get you off on the right stitch. —DRG

Fabric spray shields and cockpit tents are comfortable, space-saving, and lightweight. They can significantly increase your living space, make a rough passage a bit safer and drier, or turn sleeping aboard on a cold, wet night into a pleasant experience.

Fabric structures should be as low as possible to keep windage to a minimum. Well-designed fabric shelters may sometimes be left in place when underway. If you want to, you can sew canvas flaps and mosquito netting into the fabric.

A wide variety of fabric types, weights, and colors is available. Quality is related to price—you get what you pay for. Some fabrics stretch, fade, or wear more than others, and even shock cords may not be able to take up the slack of cheap fabric or wet, untreated canvas. We've found heavyweight fabric advantageous in building these structures. And, when in doubt as to the best fabric weight for a specific applica-tion, we call our supplier and ask his opinion.

No matter how it is designed or which fabric is used, a structure that flaps, sags, or leaks is as bad as none at all. A good support system is the key to success. Every boat offers different options for securing and supporting fabric structures. Battens, ridgepoles, upright poles, and shock cords can provide tension and support. Fabric also needs slope to effectively shed moisture. Even a heavy dew will fill pockets in a flat and loose-fitting piece of fabric. And a bit of flex is necessary, because a stiff and unyielding fabric structure will strain lines, bend supports, and stretch fabric.

Narrow boats with small spray shields don't usually pose difficult design problems, but wide hulls often require a more complex structure to provide proper support.

SIMPLE SUPPORTS

Options for framing and support of a fabric structure are limited only by the imagination. A ridgepole is the simplest support and does a creditable job. Ridgepoles usually run fore and aft down the centerline, although they can also be positioned on one side of a hull for a "lean-to" shelter. We've even used a 10-foot sculling oar supported by a forward tripod and a notch in the transom.

Telescoping supports may also be situated inside the structure, braced up from the thwarts or the sole. I made three good aluminum supports from an old tripod. I adjust them by

This small, professionally made dodger on an aluminum skiff reveals some of the difficulties faced by a non-pro attempting to replicate this neat rig. A coaming that fits the gunwale has been made to secure the snaps of the fabric. The canvas has then been cut to fit the same curves, and a zipped clear plastic opening has been added forward. The material must be cut and sewed to fit the aluminum frame in such a way that it is tight but not binding—all in all, a challenging project for a novice.

tightening two knurled knobs on each leg. These supports can be placed in a grommet or reinforced patch in the fabric.

BATTENS AND BEAMS

Support battens may be rigged under or above the fabric or sewn in between layers. One method for supporting fabric is an external batten much like a mountain tent. All you need is a pocket at either end for the batten, and small loops or ties along the rest of the batten length. If these ties are small-diameter shock cord, they can be adjusted to keep the fabric at exactly the correct tension to shed water and wind. This structure only requires tie-downs at corners and along the edges to be self-supporting.

You may find fiberglass, plastic, or aluminum battens that work well and do not require any finishing, but wood battens are the best looking. They finish nicely and bend to a uniform curve. Hardwoods such ash or mahogany or straight-grained softwoods such as spruce or fir make fine battens. All wood battens should be well sealed to keep their strength, since soaked wood will lose much of its stiffness and may snap in response to a gust of wind or a sudden load. Three coats of epoxy, followed by varnish if the batten is to be exposed to sunlight, are best for sealing.

Wood battens made for supporting a fabric structure usually need to be wider than thick to prevent twisting and make rigging easier. A successful size for us has been ¼ x 1½ inches, but each application seems to require some experimentation as to best size and shape. Start big and keep shaving the batten with a block plane until it bends easily to the shape you want. Keep in mind that laminated and epoxy-sealed battens will be stiffer than plain, unfinished

One of the simplest spray dodgers is a tarp stretched over a three-piece frame, the canvas being fitted to the curve of the gunwale. The two pieces of frame forming the triangle at the after end of the dodger are braced by a ridgepole running to the bow. One problem with this rig is the difficulty in keeping the fabric taut.

Marya Butler

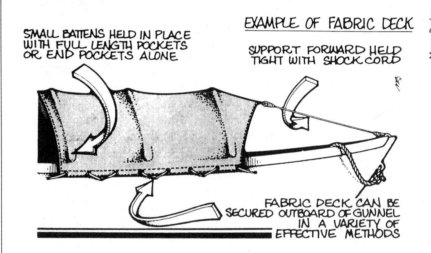

SMALL BATTENS HELD IN PLACE WITH FULL LENGTH POCKETS OR END POCKETS ALONE

EXAMPLE OF FABRIC DECK

SUPPORT FORWARD HELD TIGHT WITH SHOCK CORD

FABRIC DECK CAN BE SECURED OUTBOARD OF GUNNEL IN A VARIETY OF EFFECTIVE METHODS

EXTERNAL ROD OR BATTEN SUPPORT

CAN BE DESIGNED TO SHED WIND & RAIN & PROVIDE FLEXIBLE ADJUSTABLE COVER

TENT MADE FROM 2 PIECES OF FABRIC WITH SUPPORT LOOPS SEWN INTO CENTERLINE SEAM

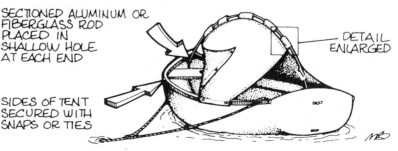

SECTIONED ALUMINUM OR FIBERGLASS ROD PLACED IN SHALLOW HOLE AT EACH END

DETAIL ENLARGED

SIDES OF TENT SECURED WITH SNAPS OR TIES

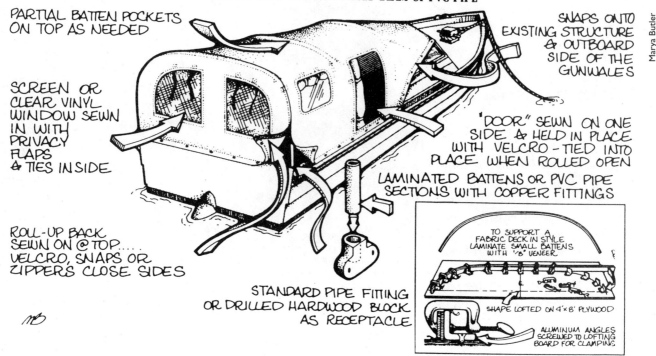

FANCY COCKPIT TENT with LAMINATED BEAM or PVC PIPE

PARTIAL BATTEN POCKETS ON TOP AS NEEDED

SCREEN OR CLEAR VINYL WINDOW SEWN IN WITH PRIVACY FLAPS & TIES INSIDE

ROLL-UP BACK SEWN ON @ TOP..... VELCRO, SNAPS OR ZIPPERS CLOSE SIDES

SNAPS ONTO EXISTING STRUCTURE & OUTBOARD SIDE OF THE GUNWALES

"DOOR" SEWN ON ONE SIDE & HELD IN PLACE WITH VELCRO - TIED INTO PLACE WHEN ROLLED OPEN

LAMINATED BATTENS OR PVC PIPE SECTIONS WITH COPPER FITTINGS

STANDARD PIPE FITTING OR DRILLED HARDWOOD BLOCK AS RECEPTACLE

TO SUPPORT A FABRIC DECK IN STYLE LAMINATE SMALL BATTENS WITH 1/8" VENEER

SHAPE LOFTED ON 4'x 8' PLYWOOD

ALUMINUM ANGLES SCREWED TO LOFTING BOARD FOR CLAMPING

Marya Butler

battens, but they will also retain uniform strength under all weather conditions.

You may wish to drill small holes in the ends of the battens to provide a tie-off point. Straight battens may be slipped out of the batten pockets and rolled in the fabric, allowing a large assembly to be stored easily in a small place. In many fabric structures, the battens are different lengths, and having each batten labeled makes the shelter easier to rig. If the batten pockets start to wear,

consider wrapping the batten ends in duct tape.

Fabric deck shelters can be supported with beams that fit into sockets or notches in the gunwale or deck structure. Sometimes these beams can be permanent and the fabric covering removed or left in place according to the weather. By laminating, you can make the beams almost any shape.

These beams are best lofted and laminated right on the lofting board. Make the lofting board of ¾-inch

plywood and do all the layout right on the board, then screw down short sections of aluminum angle and use the lofting board for laminating the beams. We build ours out of ⅛-inch veneer.

TIE-DOWNS

The outboard ends of fabric deck shelters, tents, and spray shields can be held in place with snaps or loops and hooks. They can be attached to

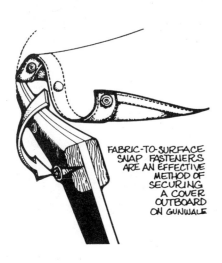

FABRIC-TO-SURFACE SNAP FASTENERS ARE AN EFFECTIVE METHOD OF SECURING A COVER OUTBOARD ON GUNWALE

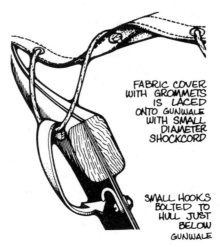

FABRIC COVER WITH GROMMETS IS LACED ONTO GUNWALE WITH SMALL DIAMETER SHOCKCORD

SMALL HOOKS BOLTED TO HULL JUST BELOW GUNWALE

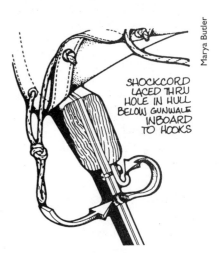

SHOCKCORD LACED THRU HOLE IN HULL BELOW GUNWALE INBOARD TO HOOKS

Marya Butler

the outwale, under the outwale, or, in the case of hooks, even inside the boat if you drill a small hole under the gunwale to provide access for a small hook.

We favor shock-cord loops and hooks over snaps as a means of attachment. Shock cord stretches in response to pressure or slack and will keep a fabric panel at about the same tautness whether wet, dry, hot, or cold. Using cords of various sizes and lengths also allows a degree of fine-tuning. Be sure to get the quality cord that comes in rolls in various diameters, from ⅛ inch (good for small adjustments and lace lines) up to a whopping ½ inch (which defies efforts to stretch it more than a few inches).

If hooks are permanently attached to the boat, the fabric structure, once adjusted, can be set up easily, even late at night or in wind or rain. With any fabric structure, you may need to rig additional lines fore and aft to provide proper support tension. We always throw a few small C-clamps in the boat for overnight trips, since you can easily clamp a structure to-gether in an emergency. Small plywood pads protect the hull from marring.

A couple of words of caution: Anchor your boat so it can weathercock into the wind. If the wind blows into the tent from the backside, your ears will pop every time the thing flaps.

Also, test everything before your first night aboard. For some reason, nothing ever seems to happen to fabric deck shelters or tents until late at night or in miserable weather, when you least want to get up and deal with it.

—Paul Butler
(*Small Boat Journal* #53)

Nothing ever seems to happen to fabric decks or tents until late at night or in miserable weather.

ENGINES

Introduction

Like the automobile engine, the outboard motor has undergone a lot of refinement and change in recent years, a souped-up evolution sparked by occasional shortages and rising prices of fuel, international competition, higher expectations on the part of customers, and revolutionary changes in manufacturing and marketing.

As a result, we feel safe in saying that the modern outboard motor is a fine piece of machinery—durable, reliable, and economical—a statement some old-time outboarders will view with skepticism and considerable mirth. "Modern outboards—if you want to call 'em that—at least the U.S.–made ones, are junk," they will reply.

If this harsh criticism was ever true—and there are many who consider it baloney—it is no longer the case. Whether the motor is Mercury, Yamaha, Johnson, Nissan, Evinrude, Honda, Mariner, Suzuki, or Force, the big-name brands are, as a class, fine machinery. They are so for the simple reason that competition has forced them to be that way.

The American outboard motor story is not unlike that of the rise and fall and rebirth of the auto industry. In the decades following World War II, American outboards grew in horsepower, reliability, and prestige. Then, in the seventies and eighties, quality of the U.S. products dipped and Japanese-built outboards took over a larger and larger share of the market. As innovative and reliable as the Japanese autos, the Asian out-

The rise of the four-cycle outboard under the leadership of Honda is a good example of the type of competition that has changed the outboard industry.

boards won over many Americans because they were better products.

The U.S. outboard industry took a pasting before it smartened up and began reclaiming some of the lost market through improved engineering, new ideas, and better quality control. While the motor makers have profited from this turnaround, the real beneficiaries are the outboard users, who once again can shop with

a reasonable expectation that the motor they buy will serve them well.

While competition has helped bring about a better assurance of quality, it has also both helped and complicated the process of selecting an outboard motor. The complications are in the huge choice of motor sizes, options, and even engine types and propulsion systems. Gaining in variety and popularity are four-cycle engines, the highly efficient and clean-burning power plants that are beginning to make inroads in a field long dominated by the relatively simple two-cycle motor. As for propulsion, the outboard jet is now a standard item with a variety of horsepowers, and is offered by several outboard manufacturers.

The rise of the four-cycle outboard under the leadership of Honda, with its growing choice of state-of-the-art engines, is a good example of the type of competition that has changed the outboard industry. The U.S. saw the introduction of the modern four-stroke outboard in the 1950s, when Homelite produced a 55-h.p. motor derived from the Crosley engine

block. This was manufactured for Fisher-Pierce, now Boston Whaler, and was named the Bearcat. An 85-h.p. version was developed from the English Coventry Climax racecar engine. Long out of production and with parts becoming scarce, Bearcats (like many old Boston Whalers) are still running today in nearly every boating region of the country, with most of them concentrated in the upper Midwest. But development does not stand still, and a New York–state dealer in Bearcat parts pretty much summed up the situation when he told us, "The Bearcat is a dinosaur beside the new Hondas."

One could argue that the Bearcat was a good idea before its time, but the fact remains that American outboard companies will now be playing catch-up again. With today's rising emission standards and the need for still greater fuel efficiency, one can be pretty certain that the four-cycle outboard motor will play an increasingly important role. Yamaha is now marketing a small four-stroke, and you can bet that its line will soon expand. To their credit, U.S. outboard-motor makers are not holding back this time, and there are indications that continuing improvements in the two-cycle field, reportedly in the area of direct injection, will keep those motors in the battle for attention.

Diesel outboards have been around for many years, but they have never won a place in the hearts of U.S. boaters. The Italian-made, air-cooled Carniti was claimed to be the only diesel outboard in the world until recently, when fresh competition came from—where else?—Japan. The Italian diesel comes in just one size—the 6-h.p. Carniti, offered by Pennsylvania Development Co. (3810 Crooked Run Road, North Versailles, PA 15137). Weighing 147 pounds and selling for $1,500, the

The American-made four-stroke outboard reached its zenith more than 20 years ago in the 85-h.p. Bearcat, shown here mounted on one of the slab-sided Boston Whalers of that period.

The diesel outboard motor has never caught on in a big way among small-boat users. Development of the motor has been centered in Italy with the Carniti, but Yanmar's trim entry may signal broader competition.

Carniti is described in a brochure as being "for displacement and auxiliary power, not planing. They are ideal for fishing boats, workboats, pontoon boats, houseboats, sailboats, inflatable boats, and heavy loads."

Now from Japan comes the 36-h.p. Yanmar diesel, a powerful, fuel-stingy mill that has a lot going for it—except its price of $12,795.

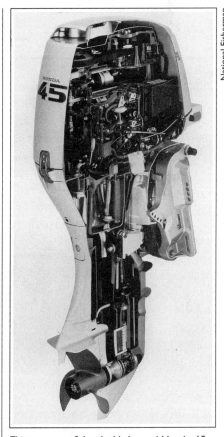

This cutaway of the sleekly housed Honda 45-h.p. four-stroke reveals a more complicated design than the simpler but less efficient two-stroke motor. The trade-off, however, is a quiet, clean, fuel-stingy, powerful engine that is pacing a growing field of contenders.

Already winning converts among commercial fishermen and marine operators, the Yanmar may change reluctant attitudes toward diesel outboards as soon as the price comes down. Further information is available from Mack Boring & Parts Co., 2365 Route 22, Union, NJ 07083.

If the diesel outboard has failed to make an impact, the same cannot be said for the electric outboard, once scorned as a weak freak and now an important means of secondary propulsion for fishing boats and a primary source of power for canoes and dinghies.

With so many motors and options available, the small-boat skipper is inclined to act like the kid in front of the candy counter, saying, "I want one of each." Like the same youngster squeezing two nickels in his pocket, the adult knows that reality will force him or her to make choices instead. And that may not be easy. In this section, we take only a brief look at the machinery, almost all of which will do an adequate job within its limits, and concentrate instead on suggesting ways to help buyers select and maintain motors that will suit their particular requirements. This is important because boatowners are dealing with a medium—water—that at times is mysterious even to those who boat on it regularly. We emphasize this seemingly obvious fact because many of the problems affecting outboard motors are not so much mechanical malfunctions as water-induced surprises, such as smashed propellers, bent drive shafts, clogged cooling systems, water-contaminated fuel, corrosion, and other events uncommon to land-based power plants. If you know about and can deal with these potentialities, living with outboard motors will be far more bearable, and if you take one further step by carrying out a schedule of routine maintenance on your motor to head off mechanical breakdowns, you may even discover there is some fun in your relationship.

—DRG

Selecting an Outboard Motor

Selecting the proper outboard power for a boat can be just as important a decision as buying a car and, in some cases, just as expensive. A motor in the 150- to 275-h.p. range, for example, can cost more than $15,000, and the *average* price of an outboard is about $4,000, a sizable percentage of any boat's cost. Also, because there is such a wide selection of boats and motors, it is easy for a buyer to become confused. For these reasons, it helps to be a savvy shopper.

The key factor to consider when selecting an outboard is horsepower. How much do you need? That depends on the hull design, the weight of the boat, the load you want to carry, and the use you plan to make of the boat. Though there are no hard-and-fast rules for determining horsepower, here are several guidelines that will help you make the right decision.

THINK 25

Ever since 1909, when Ole Evinrude first pushed a rowboat up the Kinnikinnic River in Milwaukee, Wisconsin, with a 1½-h.p. "kicker," the small-boat industry has been devising powerboat hulls of every conceivable shape, from flat bottom to deep-V to cathedral, tunnel, step-plane, and more (for more detail on hull shapes, see "It's All in the Hull," page 2).

Overpowering a boat is a lot worse than underpowering it. . . .

As a rule, flatter hulls get up on plane quicker and run faster than V-hulls with the same horsepower, since the flatter the hull, the less drag or resistance. However, a flatter hull will tend to pound in a chop, making a less comfortable ride in rough water. Deep-V designs are well suited for riding rough seas but require about 25 percent more horsepower to get up on plane and maintain the same speed as a modified-V design of similar size. As a result, modified V's are the most popular designs available.

While these boats have a sharp entry forward, they tend to flatten out along the bottom, leaving no more than 12 to 16 degrees deadrise at the transom. In comparison, the deadrise for deep-V hulls typically measures 18 to 20 degrees or more.

The other important factor that requires consideration is the weight your outboard will have to push. This is a function of the boat's size, the methods and materials used in its construction, and the use to which it is put. A boat that is going to carry

The choice of motor and horsepower is very dependent on the size and weight of the boat and its intended uses. This rugged fiberglass Pro-Line with its offshore capability is well suited to the 135-h.p. Merc on its bracket. An open aluminum skiff of the same length might do very nicely with 100 less horsepower, but its uses would be confined to more protected waters.

SELECTING AN OUTBOARD MOTOR   **79**

Variety is the game on this row of little boats. From left, starting with the large skiff, are a Sears Gamefisher, a Mighty Mite, a Cruise 'n Carry, a Tohatsu, and a Mercury.

or pull heavy loads clearly needs more horsepower than one that will only have a passenger or two aboard. If you are shopping for a complete rig, you can probably save a considerable amount of money by getting a boat-motor-trailer package with a hull design to suit your boating conditions.

According to outboard engineers, the amount of horsepower required to efficiently operate a fully loaded semi-V boat can be determined by using a 25:1 ratio: For every 25 pounds of gross weight, you will need 1 h.p. So, a loaded boat weighing 1,400 pounds would do well with one of the 55-h.p. outboards.

In considering power options, the engineers also advise us that a reasonably reliable rule of thumb is that a 10 percent increase in power results in about 4 m.p.h. more speed. But since more horsepower also costs more (and often weighs more), there is a point at which the extra speed may not be worth the extra bucks.

When considering the purchase of a new or used boating rig, or just the replacement of your old motor with a newer model, tally up the total gross weight of what you want to move across the water. You can find the weights of motors and boats in the manufacturers' brochures. Passenger and gear weight can be handled by the bathroom scale. Armed with such information and using the 25:1 formula, you can determine the size motor required for best overall performance. This formula is predicated on the fact that most popular boat hulls start to get up on plane at from 12 to 17 m.p.h., and cruise at 25 m.p.h. A cruising speed of 25 m.p.h. is reasonably fast, yet is about an optimum speed for planing hull fuel economy.

If you think you are buying a larger motor than necessary, consider that you will be able to operate it under reduced r.p.m., saving considerable fuel expense. A boat-and-motor combination capable of maintaining 25 m.p.h. at 4,000 r.p.m., or about ¾ throttle, when fully loaded with fuel, gear, and the normal passenger load, will go considerably far-

ther on a gallon of fuel than the same boat with a smaller-horsepower engine run wide open at 5,000 to 5,500 r.p.m.

However, no single formula will work for every boat-and-motor combination, so there are other guidelines besides the 25:1 ratio to consider.

Boats under 20 feet long built since 1972 are required by the U.S. Coast Guard to have a capacity plate. On outboard boats, the plate must show *maximum recommended horsepower* for the outboard motor. You don't want to exceed this; not because it is illegal, but because it is dangerous. Overpowering a boat is a lot worse than underpowering it, and unlike in cars, where a powerful engine may not be much larger than a regular one, outboard motors rapidly increase in weight as the horsepower goes up. Weight, as we have said, is *always* a critical factor aboard a boat, particularly so if it is hanging off the bow or stern.

Another way to choose horsepower is to use the maximum recommended horsepower as a guide. If you will be using the boat in a variety of ways and with fairly heavy loads, a good choice will be a motor from 75 percent to the maximum. Seventy-five percent should be adequate for a lightweight boat; use a higher figure for a heavy boat. Boat weight does make a difference, probably because the maximum power rating is based on a formula and is an approximation rather than an absolute. Some manufacturers have gone to the trouble of figuring out the most efficient horsepower for their line of boats. You probably won't go wrong following these recommendations, though you can determine whether they are in line by using the maximum rated horsepower as your ceiling and the 25:1 ratio as your base.

However, the range of choices is much wider. Many aluminum skiffs, for instance, will give good performance with as little as one-third the maximum horsepower, and unless you are a speed freak, one-half the max will do the job satisfactorily in most cases. Thus, if the maximum recommended horsepower is 35, a 15- or 20-h.p. motor is fine for general needs. It should go without saying, of course, that if you are pushing the lower limits in horsepower, be prepared for sluggish going whenever you are carrying heavy loads.

On larger, heavier boats, a great deal depends on how and for what you will be using your boat. If it is a rugged center-console fisherman that will be ranging far and wide, you will probably want a motor within 10 or 15 percent of the maximum. If the boat is for easy cruising and puttering around the lake, then 50 to 65 percent of the max will probably be all you need.

For inflatable boats, pontoon boats, and canoes, the National Marine Manufacturers Association (NMMA) has established separate guidelines for maximum allowable power:

Inflatable Boats (with transoms)

$$\text{Factor} = \frac{\text{Boat}}{\text{Length (feet)}} \times \frac{\text{Max.}}{\text{Beam (feet)}}$$
(to nearest whole number)

Factor Range	Horsepower Formula
0–42	h.p. = 7.5
42–80	*h.p. = $1\frac{9}{9}$ × (Factor – 40)
Over 80	*h.p. = ½ × (Factor + 10)

*Horsepower may be rounded up to the next multiple of 5 unless the calculation results in an exact multiple of 5.

Inflatable Boats (with motor brackets)

Length	Horsepower
Under 9 feet	3 h.p.
9–12 feet	5 h.p.
12 feet and over	7.5 h.p.

Pontoon Boats

The maximum horsepower capacity of outboard pontoon boats shall be calculated by the formula below:

$$\text{h.p.} = \frac{\dfrac{\text{external volume}}{\text{of pontoons}} \times \dfrac{\text{pontoon}}{\text{length in feet}}}{\text{pontoon diameter* in inches}}$$

*If pontoons are not circular in cross section, use the diameter of the largest circle that can be inscribed on the pontoon.

Canoes

Length	Horsepower
Under 15 feet	3 h.p.
15–18 feet	4 h.p.
Over 18 feet	7.5 h.p.

Unfortunately, similar guidelines do not exist for helping one decide what horsepower motor is required to efficiently propel sailboats

and launches with displacement-type hulls. In the case of sailboats, where an outboard motor is used only to assist the sailor in the absence of wind, in emergencies, or in docking, the maximum horsepower required is the minimum needed to propel the boat at hull speed against wind and tide. Actually, "static thrust," the measure of how well an engine pulls against an unmoving object, is a more useful figure here than horsepower. Static forward thrust for most popular outboard models runs from 30 to more than 200 pounds, reverse thrust from 30 to 200 pounds. Though space here is too limited for a full discussion about powering displacement boats, the following figures should put you in the ballpark.

Displacement Boats

Length	Horsepower
Under 15 feet	2–4 h.p.
15–22 feet	4–8 h.p.
22–25 feet	9.9 h.p.

DEALER RELIABILITY

Though each of us has only so much money to spend for fun on the water, price alone should not be a deciding factor in selecting an outboard. Like automobiles, outboard motors consist of hundreds of individual parts, and in spite of sophisticated engineering, computer-controlled production, and quality-control standards, every once in a while a lemon comes off the assembly line. This is when dealer reliability, fairness, and service become very important.

Good dealers will give you straight answers to your questions, because they know they will have to answer to them later if something goes wrong. They will have skilled outboard mechanics who get regular training on changes in new models, and who can usually solve routine problems quickly. If you are lucky (and asking around will help here, too), the dealer or one of the mechanics will be an outboard wizard whose magic may one day save you hundreds of dollars. A good dealer will also offer you a reasonable price for a new or used motor, in most cases, but it is only fair to remember that those trained mechanics and detailed knowledge of the entire motor line do not come cheaply. This important local business is worth our support.

The manufacturer's suggested retail price will give you a starting point for determining the price of a motor. You probably won't pay any more than that price, but you might be able to shop around and find a motor for less. We suggest you give careful thought to the above com-

ments about a dealer before deciding whether or not the price is fair. If the motor is to be used only occasionally on a pond boat and you have the mechanical ability to service it, a mail-order outboard may be all you need. If the motor is going to be used regularly under ordinarily rugged conditions and you want reliability backed by prompt dealer service, then your motor will probably cost more. A well-made outboard, given good care, should last for many years, even if used frequently; in fact, in salt water, regular use is usually better than having the motor sit idle on the transom for weeks, because running helps keep interior parts and exterior mechanical linkages lubricated.

All brands now offer a one-year warranty on parts and labor, and some offer longer guarantees at no

extra cost. If your motor will be subject to heavy use, a long-term protection plan, which does cost extra, might be worthwhile. As for resale, most of the big brands carry a good trade-in value or can be sold privately without much effort.

Outboard motors, particularly the smaller portables, like any machinery, respond to tender loving care. If they are slammed around in handling, parts will be jarred loose or broken, and if the lower unit is tipped above the powerhead, there is a good chance water will leak into the cylinders and thus speed wear and damage. A potential second buyer is unlikely to be enamored with a motor that is covered with dents, dings, and other signs of hard and careless use.

No matter what boat you own or plan to buy, there is an outboard motor to fit your needs. To

A second motor is good backup on any boat that cannot be rowed or paddled into the wind. A common problem, however, is the 20-inch or higher transom on larger boats that calls for a long-shaft motor. Outboard motors under 10 h.p. are generally short shafts (15-inches) for use on smaller boats, and if the motor is purchased with a long shaft, it not only costs more, but its utility is somewhat limited. A compromise is a small outboard bracket attached at the right height on the outside of the transom so that a short-shaft motor can be used as a spare and still retain its full utility.

give you a better idea of what is available and to help you narrow your choices, we've organized the size ranges generally used for different boats and on-the-water activities. These range from mini-outboards for canoes, dinghies, and small sailboats to the powerhouses found on offshore fishing boats. In between is a wide selection of versatile midrange motors, popular for fishing, skiing, and cruising.

MINI-MOTORS

The smallest members of the portable motor families range in size from 3.5 h.p. on down to 1.2 h.p. and cost from about $675 to $875. They are just the ticket for use on dinghies, prams, canoes, and even small inflatables. These lightweight motors feature integral fuel tanks, manual tilt adjustment, and manual steering. Most are available in short-shaft motors only, and they do not have a reverse gear. Instead, most can be pivoted at least 180 degrees.

Don't expect too much in the way of speed from these little fellows, but they do save rowing or paddling. For long canoe trips with lots of gear aboard, select at least a 2-h.p. motor, or even 3½ or 4. (See "Canoe Power," page 38.)

PORTABLE POWER

Bess Evinrude coined the advertising slogan "Don't Row! Throw the Oars Away! Use the Evinrude Detachable Row Boat Motor." From that beginning, when one could lash the "kicker" on the running board of the family touring car and use it on a variety of clinker-built rental craft, boaters have appreciated a motor light enough to carry.

Now, portable outboards weighing from 33 to 83 pounds are available

Now available on many midsize motors is tiller steering, which in the past has been pretty much limited to motors under 50 h.p. Mercury, for instance, offers tillers on 40-, 50-, 60-, 75-, and 90-h.p. motors. The gearshift is mounted on the front of the motor, but most of the bells and whistles (power trim, oil injection, electric start, etc.) offered on remote engines can be had on these.

in a number of horsepowers. Prices range from $1,000 for a 4-h.p. motor to as high as $2,500 for a 15. These are manual-start, one- or two-cylinder engines with either loop-charged or cross-flow fuel induction (both integral systems that help with fuel efficiency). Some of the larger engines in this size-range are available with electric starting, remote controls and steering, through-prop exhaust, and oil injection.

A 15-h.p. works well on a 14-foot fishing boat carrying two anglers and their gear. A 9.9-, 8-, or even 7½-h.p. would be a second choice. For a 12-foot hull, a 6-h.p. is fine. Motors in this size-range are frequently chosen as auxiliary motors for sailboats and larger powerboats.

Sail auxiliaries come in both two- and four-cycle models with shaft lengths from 15 to 25 inches. For larger sailboats in the 24- to 26-foot range, a 9.9-h.p. would be my choice. Electric starting is nice but not neces-

sarily required. Daysailers would make a good choice from the standpoint of low cost with good thrust by selecting a 4-h.p. Since these motors are set up as auxiliaries, they make excellent emergency or trolling motors for large motorboats.

MIDRANGE MOTORS

This most popular category of outboards is comprised of 18- to 55-h.p. motors, which are used on boats in the 14-foot to the lightweight 18-foot class. Their prices range from $2,500 to around $5,500. These are generally manual-starting, loop-charged, two-cylinder engines available in short- and long-shaft models, with manual tilt adjustment. Most feature through-prop and pulse-tuned exhaust. Options include electric starting, remote controls and steering, and shallow-water drive. Most of the engines in this size-range come with oil injection and power trim and tilt as options. For the most part the motors are permanently mounted on the boat transom, since they are too heavy to be lifted off easily.

At the lower end of the range (18 to 25 h.p.), one can expect good performance on the larger aluminum and smaller fiberglass fishing boats used on inland lakes, large rivers, and saltwater bays. For greater load carrying, consider 30 to 35 h.p. on the large, beamy 16-footers.

Look to the 35- to 55-h.p. electric-start motors for powering the popular aluminum 15- and 16-foot bass and striper fishing boats. They often have carpeting, pedestal seats, live wells, and other gear such as fish locaters, electric positioning motor, and batteries, which all add weight, and consequently require more horsepower to operate.

All the engines in this horsepower-range are capable of introducing the youngsters to the fun of water-skiing.

FISH AND FUN POWER

A family on a tight budget will find a 60-h.p. motor on a quick-to-plane 15- to 16-foot aluminum or fiberglass hull quite adequate for fun on the boards as well as fishing. Safety is a prime consideration for water-skiers, so you need to think in terms of the minimum power required to tow a skier from deep water on either one or two skis with both a driver and an observer in the boat. Larger fiberglass boats require a bit more power. Pulling two or more skiers or doing fancy maneuvers on slalom skis is easily handled by motors in the 80- to 140-h.p. range. Having the right propeller is very important for water-skiing; therefore, seek out a marine dealer who specializes in boating equipment for water-skiing to help you with your choice.

Motors in this category cost from $5,000 to $9,500 and have such standard features as electric starting, remote controls and steering, power trim and tilt, oil injection, and through-prop and pulse-tuned exhaust. Most are loop charged with two to six cylinders, including the new V-4s.

OFFSHORE MOTORS

With the development of larger motors and bigger boats, outboarders are going farther and farther offshore in search of gamefish. Five years ago, it was rare to find anything over 20 feet that you could hang an outboard motor on; today, 30-footers with outboards are common. Some of the 19- and 20-footers in our size-range can handle single motors of 150 to 225 h.p., but this is pushing into the "big"-boat field as far as we are concerned, and their prices reflect the line between small and big, running from $10,000 to more than $12,000.

Selection of the proper outboard power-and-boat combination ensures satisfactory performance, longer engine life, and protection from the cost of trading off an unwise selection. All it takes is a little homework to get a maximum return for your investment.

—Graeme Paxton
(*Small Boat Journal* #45)

Jet Drives

A jet-drive outboard can take you where you could only dream of going with a prop-drive motor—up and down shallow rocky rivers, across reefs and shoals, and over other waters that would demolish a propeller and lower unit. Jet drives have the further advantage of not presenting a dangerously spinning propeller.

Their operation is simple. An impeller driven by the driveshaft draws water through an intake grill on the jet-drive unit. To propel the boat forward, the spinning impeller discharges the water at high volume and pressure through a nozzle directed astern. For reverse, a cup or bucket swings over the jet stream, directing its flow in the opposite direction.

Though a jet can theoretically attain the speed of a propeller drive, the nozzle size and impeller pitch would be impractical for most appli-

The lower unit of a jet outboard motor bears little resemblance to the prop version. There is a propeller of sorts, but it serves as the impeller of a pump that sucks in water at the lower front end of the unit and then blasts it out the rear nozzle. The pivoting device below the nozzle opening is the reverse mechanism; when it swings up into the ejecting stream of water, it changes the force of thrust by 180 degrees.

cations. Conventional jet drives are designed for average speed under reasonable loads. Furthermore, outboard jet drives undergo about a 30-percent horsepower loss as a result of the effort required to pump water through the impeller housing. Maneuverability, especially at low speed, also suffers. Because a jet drive lacks the rudder effect provided by the outboard's lower unit, steering tends to be uncertain until the engine gets a solid thrust of water behind it.

Another problem often cited is that the jet drive may scoop up gravel, sand, and vegetation, wearing down the impeller or clogging the intake. The ⅝-inch grate over the intake screens out all but the smallest debris. More-expensive stainless steel impellers (available from Wooldridge Boats), rather than the stock aluminum impellers, can reduce wear and tear in difficult operating conditions.

Not every boat can accommodate a jet drive. Wide, flat bottoms work best; appropriately, the original jet boats were called *sleds*. Missourians discovered that the engines worked equally well on their flat-bottomed jonboats. According to jet-drive manufacturer Richard Stallman, jets also work satisfactorily on shallow-V boats with no more than 3 degrees deadrise. "Deep-Vs, round bottoms, and soft-bottom inflatables are the worst," he says.

Jet drives install on the transom like conventional outboards, with their mounting height the most critical adjustment. They must be installed so that the leading edge of the intake is flush with the bottom of the boat. Mount the outboard too high and the unit sucks in air and the impeller cavitates; too low and the lower unit creates frontal drag and is vulnerable to damage. Unless the boat is built especially for a jet-drive outboard, you may have to add shims

Well named, OMC's Roughneck tunnel jet center-console 19-footer is a high-tech adaptation of the traditional jonboat. This unusual view shows the blast of water issuing from the Johnson V-4 outboard jet motor. The shallow tunnel directing the water to the motor lets the all-welded boat operate in as little as 6 inches of water with a jet and only slightly greater depth with a conventional outboard.

Nothing is perfect. Here, a skipper attempts to remove rocks jammed into the intake unit of his jet. This is an early add-on unit; in contrast, most of today's jets come installed on the motor.

Outboard Marine Corp.

ENGINES

to the transom to attain correct mounting height.

With the jet drive properly installed, the boat can operate in inches of water. However, a water depth that is equivalent to the draft of the boat and then some is desirable to get going. Starting in about 1½ feet of water ensures that the impeller picks up clean water rather than rocks and sand from the bottom.

All outboard-drive lower units in the United States are manufactured by Outboard Jets (Division of Specialty Manufacturing Co., 2035 Edison Ave., San Leandro, CA 94577; 415-562-6049), a company established by Richard Stallman in 1962. Retrofit units, priced from $980 to $1,470, are available for most popular brands of outboards and most horsepower ranges.

A few years ago, Yamaha introduced a line of outboards with the jet drive already mounted. Suzuki, Tohatsu, OMC, and Mercury followed suit with their own ready-to-go jet-drive outboards. The jet outboards currently available come in a range of horsepower sizes and with all the features found on their prop-driven counterparts.

—Richard Lebovitz
(*Boating World* #82)

Silent Power: The Little Electrics

Twenty years ago, electric motors represented a somewhat obscure form of propulsion. Fishermen, mostly largemouth-bass fishermen, used electrics to slip silently into casting range of their quarry. That was about it. For such sport, these little motors proved ideal. They were noiseless; they started with the flick of a switch; and they could be fitted with foot controls, leaving both hands free for casting.

The early electric "trolling" motors, as they were known, had one significant drawback, however: they lacked muscle. Even light craft outfitted with them couldn't fight the push and tug of strong winds and currents. As the popularity of electrics grew among anglers, so did the need for more power. Bassboats became highly refined fishing machines that fairly groaned under the weight of 150-h.p. outboards and electronic gear. Walleye fishermen developed their own specialized boats and a technique called *back-trolling* (trolling bait from a boat going backward) that was perfectly suited to electrics. Mexican cast-netters began to use silent power to sneak up on schools of shrimp, and as straight auxiliary motors to power small tenders to and from shore. Saltwater fishermen, particularly the bonefish and tarpon guides on Florida's flats who pushed their 20-foot skiffs with long, heavy poles, found quiet electrics a welcome substitute. But the motors had to have more guts.

More powerful electric motors were not long in coming. Unlike gas outboards, which are measured in horsepower, electrics generally are rated by the pounds of thrust developed by the propeller. Originally, 12 to 14 pounds of thrust was more or less standard. Thrust ratings surpassed the 20-pound mark in the early eighties. Today, you can buy electrics that develop more than 50 pounds of thrust!

As a result, electrics now are able competitors to light gas outboards. They have enough push to maneuver a small sailboat into port or to take a family camping in a big freighter canoe. So long as their power is sufficient to do the job at hand, they offer considerable advantages over gas motors.

This fiberglass bassboat, with its heavyweight motor, variety of gear, and crew of two, would seem to be more than the tiny electric motor in the bow could handle, but modern electrics are standard on such boats and offer a quiet and effective means of working the shallows.

ENGINES

ELECTRIC PLUSES

Electrics can be started, speeded up, and stopped with the flick of a switch. Steering can be done by hand or foot. Except for a barely perceptible hum, they are noiseless and odorless. They leave no oil slick on the water or exhaust in the air, and you don't have to tote along extra gas and oil, which somehow always manages to spill. Unlike small gas engines that suffer from fouled plugs and carburetors in constant need of adjustment, electric motors are virtually foolproof, because they have few moving parts and require no fine-tuning.

By the time you purchase an electric motor and its special battery pack and charger, the cost is about the same as an equivalent gas model. But electric motors have a longer life span, and the cost of power—electricity at the plug versus gas at the pump—is considerably cheaper. Granted, batteries don't last forever, but you can expect about 500 hours of continuous use from a battery powering a 20-pound-thrust engine. Compared to the half-gallon-an-hour gas consumption in a conventional two-horse outboard (a generous estimate), there are substantial savings when you go electric. With the application of photovoltaic modules (solar cells) to charge the batteries, you don't even need a conventional source of electricity, just sunny days.

Versatility is another of the electric's admirable features. They are an unparalleled fishing aid in fresh or salt water. With a foot-controlled model, your hands are free to cast at all times. You can use them to troll at speeds from a snail's pace to 5 m.p.h. and to hold the boat next to a school of fish without dropping anchor. They also function as fine auxiliary motors. I've relied on mine to take me back home when my outboard got cranky, and they have replaced my oars as a means of propul-

An electric is a good primary source of power on a canoe or other lightweight boat. The battery's location on the floor inside the boat, the quietness of the motor, and the low cost of fuel (once you have paid for the charger) are big pluses.

sion in shallow water or when I've had to maneuver into tight spots.

I float-fish rivers a great deal, and in all but swift, shallow waters electrics allow me to cast instead of row. They afford me access to lakes and reservoirs where gasoline motors are prohibited. They power my canoe, loaded with a week's worth of camping and fishing gear, on wilderness trips, and they enhance the tranquility I seek when I want to get away from it all.

THRUST FACTORS

Modern electric motors develop between 8 and 54 pounds of thrust. The more powerful motors, generally those with more than 30 pounds of thrust, require two 12-volt batteries to drive them. Also, high-thrust motors require more amperes, which drain a battery faster. Other qualities like cost and construction being equal, the thrust/ampere relationship is also a pretty good test of value. The brand that delivers the most thrust for the least amperage will run the longest between charges.

Some manufacturers are reluctant to talk about these motors in terms of horsepower, so comparisons with gas motors can be difficult. An exception is Minn Kota, which offers a series of "HP Electrics" that are rated in horsepower rather than pounds of thrust. Three- and 4-h.p. models give a good idea of the power electrics can now produce. My unscientific tests suggest that 15 pounds of thrust comes close to 1 horsepower.

One rule of thumb is that an electric motor should have a bare minimum of 1 pound of thrust for every 100 pounds of gross weight it is pushing. Personal experience suggests that this minimum is only enough to move a boat around on quiet water, but not much more. If you want auxiliary power performance, double that figure. My fully rigged fishing boat, with friends added, weighs around 1,100 pounds. My motor develops 23 pounds of thrust. I don't need any more power, but there are times when I wouldn't want less.

By the same token, it makes no

sense to overpower a hull. You gain virtually no speed, and you lose battery hours. When you have too much power, your boat reaches a maximum efficient speed and then seems to resist going any faster, even when you shift into higher thrust ranges. I look for bubbles. Once displacement hulls develop bow waves that crest and bubble, and planing hulls burp bubbles in their wake, you are not making the most efficient use of electric power.

MOTOR OPTIONS

After you determine the thrust you need, consider the mounting options. Transom mounts with hand controls are the all-around workhorses and the most popular design. They are the best for auxiliary (or primary) power, and for all-around fishing. Some transom mounts also convert to bow mounts with reversible powerheads for back-trolling. The idea is to achieve a very slow but controlled drift. Minn Kota even has an autopilot that can be set to steer the boat while you fish.

Bow mounts are favored by fishermen who cast to their quarry. Such mounts remove anglers from the clutter around the transom and afford them a clear view of what lies ahead. Bow mounts also provide more responsive steering, because the motor pulls the boat rather than pushes it. Hand-controlled and foot-controlled models are available. Foot controls add about $150 to the package price, but if you are a caster, they are well worth it.

Because the powerhead spoils the prop wash from an electric motor in reverse, all motors have 360-degree steering rather than a reverse gear. Three-speed to five-speed settings are available on the lower-thrust motors where gears are used to transfer the power to the propeller. In some

Foot controls for electrics are common, especially on larger boats where the motor may be mounted on the forward deck. Some motors, such as this Evinrude Scout, can also be purchased with hand controls.

larger motors with a turbine-type power unit, there is an infinite power control switch. Some motors have a quick-release bracket that allows you to leave the mounting bracket on the transom and take the motor home— a nice feature if you dock rather than trailer your boat.

Most motors can be used in salt water, but a few cannot. I would prefer to have this added protection,

whether I planned to boat in salt water or not. Some powerful electrics have a breakaway feature engineered into the tilt mechanism should the motor strike an underwater object. This feature has great merit, because a heavy boat underway has more than sufficient inertia to bend a shaft. Finally, look for solid construction in any motor you buy: stout shafts, strong mounting jackets, and heavy-

National Fisherman

duty cowlings and controls.

Propellers on electric motors usually have shear pins. Most of them are fashioned from tough, plasticlike material that is incredibly durable. My motors have taken some hard knocks, but I've never broken a prop. If you are a fisherman, weed-free props are a pleasure. The best design I've seen is a powerhead that acts as a weed guard.

Batteries for electric motors are a different breed from those used in cars. While a car battery will not damage an electric outboard, crank batteries, as they are known, are designed to deliver a powerful surface charge to spin up to 300 horses around inside an engine block. This type of construction does not lend itself to continuous use, and they tend to be short-lived when regularly drained of power and recharged.

Deep-cycle batteries are larger than car batteries, have more plates, deliver greater amperage, and cost more. The typical crank battery delivers 85 amperes; the typical deep-cycle battery, 105 amperes. In terms of performance and durability, deep-cycle batteries are unmatched. They are not harmed by being drained dry of their charge, and they deliver more power over a longer period of time than crank batteries. Furthermore, they can be drained and recharged about 100 times. I am an unusually active angler, and my boat battery also powers the lights in my pickup camper at night. I normally get two to two-and-a-half years of service from a battery.

CHARGE AND DISCHARGE

The life of a battery between charges is determined by dividing the number of motor amperes into the battery's ampere rating. For example, a motor that draws 20 amperes at full thrust, hooked up to a 105-amp battery, should deliver about five hours of continuous use. This is not an exact equation, because extraneous sources invariably sap some energy, but it is close enough. Also, this equation assumes these motors are being used at top speed. Lower speeds draw fewer amps. When I am fishing, the motor is off about half the time, or running on low speeds, so I only need to charge my battery every three days. I have never fully drained it of its charge.

The efficiency of batteries and motors is affected also by the diameter and length of the cables connecting the two. The longer the cables, the more power is lost. Most manufac-

One rule of thumb is that an electric motor should have a bare minimum of 1 pound of thrust for every 100 pounds of gross weight it is pushing.

turers recommend 6- or 4-gauge wire for battery connections farther than 5 feet from the motor, and cite performance improvements as high as 40 percent over conventional 12-gauge wiring harnesses. Positive, clean terminal connectors that screw or clamp to the battery can increase power by another 5 to 10 percent over clip-on connectors.

Cleaning terminals, an occasional bathing in fresh water if your electric has been in salt water, and keeping your battery or batteries charged is about the only maintenance required. Higher-thrust motors often have battery-level indicators that warn you when recharging is needed. You can also buy battery gauges that will tell you how much charge is left

in your battery. Of course, you can also use a hydrometer, available at any auto-supply store. Hydrometers also indicate how much of a charge a battery needs when partially discharged, so they are handy to have whether or not your motor has a discharge warning.

Battery chargers convert 110-volt AC to DC current. The higher the ampere rating of the charger, the more quickly it will charge a battery. So the same equation works with chargers as with motors—a 20-amp charger will take about five hours to fully charge a completely drained 105-amp battery. A 20-amp charger, with a timing device and an automatic hold that maintains a battery at full charge, costs around $200. It will also charge your car battery.

One other option is to use a large marine engine or a car engine to charge your trolling battery. My experience has been that outboard-motor alternators are the less-desirable option. I find that I'm not underway long enough to keep my trolling battery up, and the danger of unintentional discharge is too great. Never operate an electric motor and an electric-start outboard motor from one battery. You could easily run that battery down to a point where it will not spin your gas engine. Even with a two-battery system, you should have some sort of a cutoff mechanism that removes your starting battery from the line while your trolling battery is in use. Otherwise, you could conceivably drain both batteries dead.

A car engine has proven to be a most satisfactory system for keeping a trolling battery charged. I mount mine under the hood and use an automatic cutoff switch to tie it into the alternator. When I turn off the ignition, contact points inside the switch separate so the extra battery cannot drain my car battery when I use it in conjunction with camper appliances. As a rule, my travel habits are sufficient to keep the extra battery charged by the act of driving from place to place, and this system simplifies my life in that I don't have to look for electrical outlets when I'm on the road.

I love these little motors because they deliver simple, dependable service that has simplified a lot of problems that once were associated with being on the water. And if your tastes are anything like mine, electric motors will probably do the same for you.

—Norman Strung
(*Small Boat Journal* #39)

Straight Talk from a Dealer

There is no lack of advice available on outboard motors and boats. If you doubt this statement, just ask a boat or motor question of *anyone* who owns one. From there you can go on to a vast number of books, videos, experts writing in magazines, and even the man in the street. The latter will probably say he knows nothing about boats or motors and doesn't want to, "so don't bother asking me." At least there is nothing conflicting in his comment, which is more than you can say for much of the advice you will get from friends and other sources.

In an effort to find solid answers to some of the more common questions, we found that two situations seem to prevail. In the first case, there may be more than one correct (perhaps "acceptable" is a better word) answer to some questions. In the second case, although the answers may sound right, they can still be wrong or the advice just doesn't apply to your particular situation.

The best advice usually comes from someone who is basing his or her reply on experience, and if that person makes a living selling and repairing motors and boats, chances are he has put "conventional wisdom" to the reality test and can agree with it or challenge its premises with hard-earned authority. So we turned to a friend of ours who is one of the most respected boat and motor dealers on the Maine coast. He is Lincoln Davis of Stetson & Pinkham of Waldoboro, Maine, whose firm not only does a sizable business in small pleasure-motorboats but also serves a large commercial market, supplying boats and motors to commercial fishermen and other mariners. We selected questions ranging from the simplistic to the complicated, all of which we have heard more than once and for

> Outboards of 30 h.p. or less can be winterized by their owners quite adequately as long as the motors . . . have lubricated splines in the drive.

which we have heard more than one "correct" answer. Here they are:

Question: *Should I flush my motor after each time I use it in salt water?*
Linc: You can, but it isn't necessary. After all, some outboard motors are mounted on boats that stay in salt water all season. However, the motor should be flushed with fresh water and get a thorough washing before it is put away for the winter.

Question: *What does flushing do?*
Linc: Obviously it will help break down any salt deposits in the cooling system, but more important, aluminum chlorate crystals form in the cooling passages and eventually act like hardening of the arteries, in this case blocking the flow of cooling water. Flushing with fresh water helps clear out these crystals. To be effective, the motor should be run in fresh water for at least 10 to 15 minutes.

Question: *Is it OK to leave the motor mounted on my boat in the backyard during the winter?*
Linc: It is done all the time, and in fact this is a perfectly acceptable place to store the motor as long as it is *in an upright position*. The motor should never be stored on its side or back in a warm place, such as next to the furnace, since water may run into the cylinders and corrode them as well as accelerate corrosion in the cooling system. If water freezes inside the motor, it can break things, which is why it should be stored upright so that all water drains from the cooling system.

Question: *Should I have my motor winterized by my dealer or can I do it myself?*
Linc: Being a motor dealer, I like to service motors. But outboards of 30 h.p. or less can be cared for by their

owners quite adequately as long as the motors are of the newer breed that has lubricated splines in the drive. This self-service should include lubricating moving parts, checking the lube in the lower unit, cleaning the motor, and giving a short squirt of lightweight lubricant like WD-40 into the cylinders through the spark plug holes. Be sure to pull the propeller and grease the spline. All too often we get motors for service where the prop is so badly corroded to the spline that it cannot be removed. New props are expensive. Motors over 30 h.p. should be serviced at least once a year by the dealer—without exception. There are too many expensive things that can go wrong.

Question: *You said "check the lower unit lube." Are you saying it shouldn't be changed?*
Linc: There is no need to change it until it smells rotten. What you do want to look for is water in the lower unit. If the lube has a cloudy look to it, it is probably contaminated by water and should be changed. Water can enter the unit through a leaking seal, but just as likely it may be forced in by sharp temperature changes such as a hot lower unit going into ice-cold water.

Question: *I find talk about propeller pitch and size confusing. How important is this stuff?*
Linc: With motors of 30 h.p. or less, you will do just fine with the prop that comes on the motor, with rare exceptions. One would be if you are moving heavy loads and your motor is not able to produce its full revolutions. In this case, you may want a prop with a flatter (lower) pitch. With medium and large motors, propeller size is much more important—and not infrequently misunderstood even

by those who should know. For instance, our motor manufacturer supplies us with a book on recommended propeller sizes for larger motors. I've found it useful as long as I always drop down one size from the recommended prop.

Question: *Why is prop size so important?*
Linc: The wrong propeller can lead to over-revving or under-revving of the engine. It would seem that over-revving (running too fast) would damage the motor. It will, in time, but I believe under-revving is more damaging because of the heavy strains being placed on the engine—like trying to take a loaded truck up a hill in high gear.

Question: *So what do I do about*

> *Composite (plastic) propellers are in many cases now equal—or close to it—to those made of aluminum. They are considerably cheaper.*

propeller problems?
Linc: Try to find someone in the dealership who knows something about propellers or, lacking that, take your problem to a propeller shop, if there is one within traveling distance. Propeller design and selection require a large amount of science, but there is art involved, too.

Question: *Most outboard props are made of aluminum. Are composite and stainless steel wheels any good?*
Linc: Stainless steel is the best propeller material, and the most expensive—about three times the cost of aluminum. Its strength and durability are its big advantages. It is worth going to a stainless steel prop when you find it would save you frustration

and money because you are beating up so many aluminum wheels. It happens. Composite (plastic) propellers are in many cases now equal—or close to it—to those made of aluminum. They are considerably cheaper.

Question: *Should I try to file down or hammer out nicks and dings in my aluminum propeller?*
Linc: Only if they are bad enough to cause vibration in the motor. The sophisticated design of today's wheels will allow for a surprising amount of banging around before they start causing trouble.

Question: *Is it OK to use an automobile battery for starting my motor?*
Linc: There was a time 15 or 20 years ago when I would have said there was little or no difference between an auto and a "marine" battery except, of course, the price. That is no longer true, and you will be much better off today using a battery designed for marine use.

Question: *Do you mean one of those expensive deep-cycle jobs?*
Linc: No, I am talking about a starting battery that is ruggedly built for marine use.

Question: *What if I have a little cabin and use battery power for my cabin lights when cruising; is it OK to run the lights off the starter battery?*
Linc: You can, but I wouldn't recommend it. Better to get a second battery of the same type as your starter and have a battery switch so that you can use one or the other, but not both at the same time. This will ensure that you don't run down your starting battery, but will let you recharge both when running your

motor. On small boats such as we are talking about, deep-cycle batteries are needed only for heavy-draw devices like electric trolling motors.

Question: *What is the biggest problem with batteries aboard boats?*
Linc: Far and away the answer is corrosion and dirt on the terminals. Whenever you think your battery has gone dead, check the terminals first. Remove the lead wires, clean and buff both the clamps and the terminals, and then make sure the leads are tightly fastened to the terminals. That in itself will solve a lot of so-called battery problems.

Question: *Why do some outboard motors show exactly the same specifications and still differ in horsepower?*
Linc: Manufacturers build motors in groups in order to save money. Common differences are 9.9 h.p. and 15 h.p., or 25 h.p. and 30 h.p. Sometimes there will be more than two horsepower ratings in a group. The motors differ only in carburetion,

with the higher-rated motors being pushed harder.

Question: *Am I better off with a lower-rated engine in a group?*
Linc: Yes, if it will do the same job for you.

Question: *Is this the secret to so-called "commercial" motors?*
Linc: To a large extent, yes. Several engines in the mid-horsepower ranges are being detuned by makers so that they can be run from the tiller. These will run better on today's generally lousy gasoline and last longer, since the components are not being stressed to the extent that they are in the higher-horsepower recreational motors. Detuning is mainly a matter of changing the carburetion, tuning the exhaust, and adjusting the timing.

Question: *Will aluminum boats corrode in salt water?*
Linc: Yes, and this protects them from further corrosion. Modern aluminum boats are built with marine alloys. The exposed aluminum will

undergo fine surface corrosion, which will then protect the metal underneath. Unless exposed to electrolysis, aluminum boats do fine in salt water.

Question: *What causes electrolysis?*
Linc: Certain metals will create an electric charge when near or in contact with aluminum in salt water, and this will corrode the aluminum. Certain bottom paints are particularly bad in this respect and may ruin an aluminum boat in a season. If you must use bottom paint, make certain it is compatible with the metal. Trailer boats don't need bottom paint, by the way.

Question: *The manufacturer of my aluminum boat says I should wash it off after using it in salt water. Is this necessary?*
Linc: No. You may want to wash off the dried salt for aesthetic reasons, but it won't hurt the boat if you don't.

—DRG

Rigging an Outboard

Slap an engine on the transom, and any boat will run—but will it run safely and efficiently? Properly rigging an outboard is the only way to get optimum performance out of the many possible boat-and-engine combinations. Usually, it's a job for experts; but a reasonably technical person who has the time and interest can do the job right, too. Just keep in mind a few simple rules and procedures.

According to Dave Martin, manager of Mercury Marine's Boathouse

Bulletin Program, the key to proper rigging is transom height. Many people mistakenly measure along the face of the transom. But transom

> *The key to proper rigging is transom height.*

height is actually measured along a perpendicular from the top of the transom to the bottom of the boat. For short-shaft engines, the standard height is 15 inches; for a long shaft,

20 inches. That should position the engine straight up and down with the antiventilation plate (sometimes referred to as the *cavitation plate*) even with the bottom of the boat.

Don't presume that the transom automatically provides the correct height. The "standard" 20-inch transom on the boats at one of the *Small Boat Journal* Powerboat Sea Trials ranged from 19¾ to 20½ inches. Measure, then adjust the engine height using the screw clamps (on smaller engines) or bolt holes (on larger engines) provided on the mounting bracket. Martin says that you can get better performance from today's powerful engines and excellent props by positioning the engine slightly higher rather than lower on the transom when the measurement is not exact.

If you have to bore holes through the plywood core in the transom of an aluminum or fiberglass boat, be sure to apply a good-quality sealant before installing the bolts. This will protect the wood from delamination. And be sure the engine is centered. An off-center engine will lift out of the water when the boat is turned in the opposite direction, increasing the likelihood of ventilation and spray.

Of course, as soon as you lay down a rule, you find an exception. Many small fishing motors and larger engines that push heavily loaded boats at slow speed will work best when they are run with the anti-ventilation plate an inch or two below the boat bottom. But on sport boats, ski boats, and high-performance craft, the antiventilation plate may be mounted 1 to 4 inches above the boat bottom. Raising the engine reduces the lower unit's drag and increases speed; however, such engine installations generally require shimming or a jack plate and some type of high-performance propeller. It is best to check with the manufacturer or a knowledgeable dealer before using any of these special engine installations. (See "Why Jack an Outboard?" page 94.)

OTHER NECESSITIES

Before putting the boat in the water and fitting the proper prop, you should check the installation of the control box, cables, battery, and fuel tank. The boat manufacturers don't always provide a suitable mounting

Exterior brackets are becoming popular on larger outboard boats, both as a means of saving room in the boat and as a means of increasing the efficiency of the motor. Brackets usually increase rigging complications unless the setup is part of the construction process.

Crestliner Boats

Crestliner builds a bracket into the transom of some of its models. In addition to eliminating the "add-on" look, the company lists other advantages: increased cockpit space, less engine noise and exhaust fumes, and improved boat handling and performance. Crestliner's V196 Phantom SST with the Space Saver Transom (SST) is shown here. Note that the after end of the bottom is located just under the "Phantom" mark, or several inches ahead of the after end of the bracket where the motor is attached.

place for the control box, and you may have to improvise so that it is in a convenient location. One of our Sea Trial boats required a ½-inch plywood spacer between the control box and the mounting plate to provide

enough clearance to operate the controls easily.

Your hand should rest comfortably on the controls, and you should be able to move the controls backward and forward without bumping into

Why Jack an Outboard?

The optimum height relationship of the propeller to the bottom of the boat is dependent on many outside variables. When operating at low speeds or trying to carry a heavy load, a lot of blade surface area in the water is required. This means that most of the prop must be below the bottom of the boat. At high speed on a good performance hull, however, the blade area requirement is much lower. By raising the engine mounting height, part of the prop (and the gear case) is lifted out of the water, *greatly* reducing drag. Speed improvements of more than 10 m.p.h. are common when going from one extreme to another.

Currently, the better-designed hulls and props achieve their maximum speeds with typical transom heights of 26 to 29 inches. Since it is difficult (sometimes impossible) to get a loaded boat on plane with the engine permanently mounted that high, the use of a hydraulically adjustable transom jack lets you enjoy the best of two worlds. It gives you the ability to set your outboard in the full down position for getting on plane, pulling out skiers, low-speed cruising, or drag-racing takeoff. Once the boat's speed increases, the unit can be raised to the most efficient transom height for the prop's load. Without a hydraulic transom, there is no way you can even think of running your prop's optimum transom height and still have an enjoyable family ski and pleasure boat.

Land and Sea Inc.'s Action Bracket fitted with one of the company's new jack plates, which permits the motor to be raised and lowered without changing its angle in the water.

With a hydraulic transom and infinite dash control of its travel, you can find the best combination of installation height, trim angle, and prop in minutes instead of weeks (without making Swiss cheese out of your transom!). This also makes the normally difficult job of safely jacking a big V-6 engine on a 20- to 23-inch transom a cinch.

—Land & Sea Inc. catalog
(P.O. Box 96, North Salem, N.H. 03073)

---

the steering wheel or any other obstruction. The lanyard on the ignition safety stop switch should also be able to reach your clothing, so that it can be readily fastened to you.

Cables are generally routed out of the way under the gunwale. Some of the plastic clamps now on the market are convenient for bundling them together and easily removing them for repairs. And don't be stingy with cable length. Martin runs the throttle and shift cables under the front of the engine, making a full loop around before connecting them. "This arrangement is clean and neat," he says, "and no matter which direction the engine turns, the cables will never bind."

Your battery should have a restraining device to keep it from moving around. Though clamps alone may do, a box is preferable. In addition to being resistant to the electrolyte, the plastic box protects the battery terminals. The box must be securely fastened, and spacing material resistant to the electrolyte should be placed inside to restrict battery movement within the box. The box should be installed so that the battery does not rest on any bolt heads. Also, a battery should not be installed directly above or below a fuel tank, fuel filter, or fitting in a fuel line.

If you don't box your battery, choose one with top terminals rather than side terminals. The Coast Guard's Product Safety Assurance Branch says a number of fires have occurred from metal fuel tanks bumping into terminals and causing the battery to short out.

In any case, anchoring a portable fuel tank makes as much sense as anchoring a battery. Plastic hold-down trays are available for this purpose, and they have the extra benefit of keeping the deck free of fuel-can rust or spilled fuel and oil.

Though the owner of a new boat need not worry about the condition of the hull and prop, the owner of an older boat should be sure that the hull is clean and the prop in good shape.

A fouled bottom and a bent or badly dented prop will affect performance and fuel consumption, and propeller vibrations could cause engine damage.

IS IT PROPERLY PROPPED?

With the boat properly set up and the manufacturer's recommended prop installed, you can now run the boat to see if you need to adjust the diameter and pitch of your propeller. This requires the use of a tachometer, and the boat loaded with the normal amount of weight you expect to carry. With the correct propeller, the engine will run at wide-open throttle

Fires have occurred from metal fuel tanks bumping into terminals and causing the battery to short out.

within the manufacturer's recommended maximum r.p.m. range. If not, you will need to change to either a higher- or a lower-pitched prop (higher pitch if you have to bring the r.p.m. down, lower pitch if the r.p.m. are under the optimum range and must be increased).

The beauty of this procedure is that you only have to rig the boat right once, then just make regular checks of the hull and prop. The effort you put into proper rigging of your motor will pay off for years to come in better performance, reduced fuel consumption, and less trouble on the water.

—Richard Lebovitz
(*Small Boat Journal* #54)

ENGINES

How to Maintain Your Outboard or Sterndrive

For a variety of reasons, including saving money and the simple joy of doing it yourself, a lot of boaters would prefer to do their own chores on their outboards and sterndrives. Unfortunately, many shy away from the task, not because of laziness but because of concern that the job may be too difficult. In truth, the procedures involved in maintaining both outboards and sterndrives are easy—as simple as or simpler than those used in maintaining your automobile. Outboard care is the easier procedure, so we will look at this first.

OUTBOARD MAINTENANCE

Oil

Buying the proper two-cycle oil is crucial to the life of your engine. Fortunately, choosing the right kind is simple. Look for an oil with an approved rating, either TC-W2 or TC-W3. (The TC stands for two-cycle, the W for watercooled. The 2 and 3 are slightly advanced versions. Use the rating recommended by the engine manufacturer for your particular model.) Since your outboard burns oil in its cylinders (unless you have a four-stroke engine), you don't have to worry about periodic oil and

Be obsessively vigilant regarding fuel leaks.

filter changes—as you do in your car—but that doesn't mean you have no oil-related maintenance.

Of course, I'm referring to the oil (or more properly, lube) in your outboard's lower unit. Regular maintenance on this unit is crucial but simple. You should change the lower-unit drive oil at least once a year; more often if you put more than 200 hours on your engine. The procedure is simple: Make sure the drive is warm so the oil will flow, trim it until it is roughly vertical, place a pan beneath it to catch the oil, remove the top plug (the one by which you checked the oil level) to provide a place for air to enter the oil chamber, then remove the bottom plug. Give the lube plenty of time to drain, then replace the lower screw.

Examine the oil carefully for signs of contamination, such as discoloration, iridescence, or cloudiness. Then replace the lower plug and prepare to refill the unit.

Drive Unit

Most drive lube comes in a tube, with a nozzle that fits into the fill hole. Cut off the end of this nozzle, insert it into the fill hole, and squeeze until you see oil begin to drip back out, indicating the drive is full. Insert and tighten the plug, wipe off the drive, and properly dispose of the old lube.

Touch up the paint and replace any zincs that are more than half gone. Also note that if your outboard operates in salt water and its zincs show virtually no wear, this might be a sign that they aren't doing their job. Look for corrosion in any component that does not have a good connection to the rest of the drive. Make sure you look carefully for subsurface paint bubbling, a sign that corrosion has entered one place and is traveling between alloy and paint. These areas should be scraped clean, primed, and painted. Never paint or wax zincs.

If you are running in polluted water or salt water, this is also a good time to flush the interior cooling passages with fresh water. Use a special adapter that clamps around the raw-water intakes, which are just forward of and above the propeller on either side.

At this time you may also want to remove the propeller and shine a light inside to check on the condition of the internal zinc in the lower unit. Make sure to reinstall the propeller with a new lock washer or cotter key and grease the propeller shaft so that it will be easy to remove the prop next time. Also check the condition of the propeller. Repair any nicks, dents, or other imperfections. A damaged propeller may be out of balance, which can cause vibration and eventually ruin your propeller seals.

Make sure the bright steel hydraulic rams on the trim cylinders have a coat of oil. They depend on frequent use to maintain the oily coating. If the coating degrades, the rams will rust, damaging the seals inside and allowing the hydraulic fluid to leak out.

One good way to keep your sterndrive or outboard well maintained is to use flushers like the one shown here to keep internal cooling passages clear and clean. You can connect this model for a sterndrive or one of the many similar devices for outboard motors to a garden hose to run water through the system after the boat is hauled out of the water. Flushing after use in salt water is often recommended.

Now pull the engine cowling, then hose off the engine with a light spray to remove salt, dirt, and grease. After it dries, spray all metal components with a light coat of lightweight oil such as WD-40. You don't need much. Also wipe down the spark plug wires with a protective spray, and check for loose connections, particularly at the spark plug boots. Look for any signs that water is accumulating in the engine pan; that could mean a deteriorated engine cowling gasket.

Fuel Filters

Many new outboards have a small fuel filter with a cleanable element under the engine cover. In most cases it will have a translucent body, so you can check for contamination without opening it. If you have any doubt, open the unit, pull out the filter screen, and examine it for debris.

Separate exterior fuel filters usually require changing once a year. There are a number of types—spin-on, cartridge, and in-line—and all are easy to remove and install. However, when you install a new fuel filter you should, if possible, fill it with clean fuel to prevent the carburetor from sucking air at start-up.

Be obsessively careful about fuel leaks. Gasoline is extremely dangerous. Always make a thorough check for fuel leaks after installing a new fuel filter. At the same time, check all connections, fuel and oil (if equipped with oil injection) lines, and squeeze bulb for leaks and deterioration. If they're soft, gooey, or stay depressed when you pinch them, they're probably degraded from alcohol in the fuel and must be replaced.

Ignition System

Anyone with a modicum of mechanical ability should be able to remove, clean, gap, and reinstall a set of spark plugs, or gap and install a new set. Just remember to gap them carefully according to the engine manufacturer's recommendations, and don't overtighten them.

Once a year, as part of your ignition service, you also should check the engine's ignition timing. This can be a difficult job for a novice, as it requires accurate use of a timing light. If you've never used a timing light, have someone show you how to connect one and use it, preferably on your engine. You can get general guidance from a number of automotive books.

Other Service

Some older outboards might have grease fittings or other lubrication points, such as at the throttle linkage and bracket pivot points. Check your owner's manual for specifications. As a basic guideline, keep all movable links and cables well lubricated so they move easily.

If you live where temperatures fall below freezing, you may have to prepare your outboard for winter layup. This is another procedure you either can do yourself or leave to a mechanic. Basically, winterization involves removing any water from the engine cooling system, shutting off the fuel supply and running the engine until it quits to get all the fuel out of the fuel system, topping off the fuel tanks to prevent condensation, and adding a fuel stabilizer. You also should pull each spark plug and spray the plug hole with a rust preventative or special protective fog, which you can buy from your local dealer or marine supply store. Outboard Marine Corporation, Mercury Marine, and MDR all market spray protectives. For more specific recommendations, check your engine owner's manual.

STERNDRIVE CARE

Oil

Your boat's engine and drive unit must have a clean supply of lubricating oil to run long and well. Always use an oil rated S or S and C in your sterndrive engine. Other types of oils or oils that carry no rating may cause severe damage and accelerate wear on your engine. The second letter of the API (American Petroleum Institute) designation represents the complexity of the additive package, typically starting with A, the lowest level with the least-advanced additives, and progressing upward alphabetically. Always choose the highest letter available. In other words, if you have a choice between SE or SG, choose SG, regardless of what type of engine you have.

Now let's talk about how to change it. First, never change oil when it's cold: It won't flow freely and it will be difficult to get all the dirty oil out of the engine and sterndrive. The oil needn't be hot—warm is fine.

When you want to change the oil in your automobile, you simply slide a container under the oil pan, remove the drain plug, and let the oil run out. That procedure is unlikely to work in most sterndrive boats, because you probably can't get to the drain plug to begin with, and there probably isn't a flat spot under the engine on which you could set a container.

One solution is to pump the warm oil out of the oil pan through the dipstick hole. Most manufacturers of newer sterndrives have made a provision for this by threading a fitting onto the end of the tube into which the dipstick fits. You simply remove the dipstick, thread a hose to this fitting, and pump the warm oil out of the engine.

On older sterndrives not equipped with this fitting, you'll have to snake a hose down the dipstick hole, making sure you don't push the hose too far, causing it to curl up in the pan and out of the oil. In either case, the mechanism commonly used for pumping is a simple centrifugal pump that fits on the end of an elec-

The second letter of the API designation represents the complexity of the additive package. Always choose the highest letter available.

tric drill. Its advantages are low cost and portability. Due to its small size, however, its power is limited. Another disadvantage is that you need a supply of 120-volt current to power it.

Another solution is a 12-volt pump, which has a supply cable that simply clamps to your battery's terminal via alligator clips. It's more powerful, but also larger and more expensive. A third alternative, usually found only in larger boats, is a permanently mounted oil-change system.

Once you have a container full of dirty oil, you have to find a way to dispose of it responsibly. This can be a real problem in some places, although many states now require anyone who sells oil to accept used oil in return. This shouldn't even require mentioning, but unfortunately it does: Don't pour the oil on the ground, down the sewer, or into the water. It will only end up polluting the environment.

Many boatowners pour the used oil back into the oil containers and store them in a safe place until their municipality has an annual "Amnesty Day" on which toxic chemicals are accepted for disposal. Some service stations and recycling centers accept used oil, and there are oil-recovery firms in many urban areas; check your Yellow Pages under "Oils—Waste." With a little perseverance, you can find a proper place to get rid of your oil.

Oil Filter

Chances are you're familiar with your car's spin-on oil filter, a metal canister designed to be discarded completely when removed. The filter on your sterndrive engine is precisely the same unit. Indeed, here's one instance where, if you can buy one cheaper at an auto-supply store, you can substitute the automotive for the marine with no problem. Just make sure you've got the right filter. If you have any doubt, bring the old one to the auto-supply store and the clerk will look up the model number for you on a cross-reference chart.

Removal and installation are the same as with your car: Use a special oil filter wrench to remove the old one. Coat the rubber gasket on the new one with fresh oil, then screw it on until the gasket contacts the metal mating surface. Then turn it another three-quarters of a turn to seal it. An added step you may want to consider is filling the filter or canister with clean oil before you install it. Many mechanics do this, because it keeps the engine from running dry for the first few seconds after an oil change. If you choose to do the same, remember to keep track of how much oil you add. Overfilling an engine with oil can be both messy and dangerous.

After you change the filter, be sure the exterior of the filter is absolutely clean so you'll be able to detect any leakage quickly. If you do your own maintenance on your car, you may be used to a somewhat dirty engine, a fact of life because it's exposed to road grime. Dirt should never be tolerated on a marine engine. The engine, all its components, and the surrounding environment (including the bilge) should be scrupulously clean, not only to help you determine when something is wrong, but for safety reasons as well. Remember, your car's engine is exposed to the open air; your boat's engine operates in a relatively closed environment where sloppiness can lead to pollution, slips, and even fire.

Once you've installed the oil fil-ter, start the engine and let it run long enough for the oil to warm. Check for leaks. If there are none, this part of your job is finished—except, of course, for finding a proper way to dispose of the dirty oil filter.

Fuel Filters

As we noted before, most carburetors have a small internal fuel filter where the fuel line enters. Except under extraordinary circumstances, this should never need cleaning. Many older sterndrives have no other fuel filter, a risky proposition. If your engine didn't come with one, you should install one, preferably one of the water-separating types.

Fuel filters usually require changing once a year. There are a number of types—spin-on, cartridge, and in-line—and all are easy to remove and

With a little perseverance, you can find a proper place to get rid of your oil.

install. However, when you install a new fuel filter you should fill it with clean fuel so the carburetor won't suck air when you start the engine.

Be obsessively vigilant regarding fuel leaks. Gasoline is extremely dangerous. Always make a thorough check for fuel leaks after installing a new fuel filter.

Ignition System

Let's go over each part of the sterndrive ignition system from a self-service angle. Once a year you'll need to replace the ignition points and condenser, unless your engine has electronic ignition. If you're steady and precise you can do this, but accuracy in setting points is crucial. You can use a mechanical feeler gauge, but you'll probably get better accuracy using a dwell meter. While you are at this, replace the distributor cap and rotor.

Remove, clean, gap, and reinstall the spark plugs, or gap and install a new set. Just remember to gap them carefully according to the engine manufacturer's recommendations. Don't overtighten them.

Once a year, as part of your ignition service, you also should check the engine's ignition timing. As with an outboard motor, it requires accurate use of a timing light, so you may need to get some technical help or look for general guidance in a number of automotive books.

Other Service

The only other periodic service required by your sterndrive engine might be cleaning the flame arrestor around the oil filler cap. Also, top off all fluids, including the fluid in the power-steering pump, if so equipped. The primary cautions here are to use only the approved fluids and solvents, which should be listed in your owner's manual.

Some older sterndrives may also have grease fittings or other lubrication points, such as at the throttle linkage. Again, check your owner's manual for specifications. (No manual? You should have one. Try getting in touch with the manufacturer of your sterndrive, or check with the nearest dealer.)

Winter Layup

If you live where temperatures fall below freezing, you may have to prepare your sterndrive for winter layup. This is another procedure you either can do yourself or leave to a mechanic. Winterization involves removing water (not coolant) from the engine cooling system; ensuring that the coolant is of sufficient concentration to protect against freezing; changing the oil and filter; topping off the fuel tanks to prevent condensation; and adding a fuel stabilizer. You also should pull each spark plug and spray rust preventative into the hole. For more specific recommendations, check your engine owner's manual.

Regular maintenance on the drive unit is simple and is done exactly the same as for an outboard (described earlier).

—Richard Thiel
(*Keep Your Outboard Motor Running* and *Keep Your Stern Drive Running,* International Marine, 1992)

The Ticking Fuel-Tank Bomb

Built-in fuel tanks bear watching, providing you can get at them in the first place. Aluminum tanks foamed in or strapped beneath the cockpit sole can be reached through a hatch in some installations, but it is not uncommon for them to be covered by the sole (deck), which must be cut away if the tank requires repairs.

"I consider the fuel-system installation to be the most important element in a powerboat," wrote Contributing Editor Keith Lawrence in *Powerboat Reports* of July 15, 1990, "and I am continually appalled at the cavalier treatment that it receives in many, if not most, powerboats." Corrosion beneath hold-down straps or between foam and tank frequently leads to leaks, and expensive repairs. "Oil-canning" (flexing) of thin tank sides might cause a fracture in the metal, particularly next to an area of stiffness such as the weld of a baffle. If aluminum tanks are used, says Lawrence, they should be bolted to solid framing through heavy welded feet, with no contact where corrosion might start. The tanks should also be coated with an epoxy-based anti-corrosive coating.

Properly designed and built fiberglass tanks are considered among the safest of all types, with polyethylene tanks close behind—and both well ahead of aluminum. Because of their small size, some of the center-console boats mount the fuel tank in the console rather than beneath the sole, where it can be regularly checked for leaks. Another alternative is deck-mounted polyethylene fuel tanks, either fixed or portable.

Whatever system is used, great care is needed because of the shaking a tank takes aboard a small boat. Good installation is a must.

—DRG

Tips for Saving Fuel

Conserving fuel is a simple way to reduce your boating expenses, prolong your time on the water, and extend your boating range. Unfortunately, many boaters don't see saving fuel as a priority. The first question people ask when they go to buy a boat is "How fast does she go?" Yet, when those same people go to buy a car, they ask instead, "How many miles to the gallon?"

On the road or on the water, saving fuel still makes good sense. Here are some practical ways to go about it.

PREPARATION

If you are a trailer boater, fuel saving begins before you pull out of the driveway. We'll assume your trailer and tow vehicle are matched for load capacities (see "Selecting a Trailer," page 111). We will also assume your car is in tune and its tires are properly inflated. But what about your *trailer?* Have you checked its tires for proper inflation? Are the wheel bearings properly lubricated? Is it carrying the proper load, and is the load evenly distributed? And is everything tied down inside the boat to keep the load from shifting and to minimize wind resistance?

Spring is a good time to check the condition of your boat and engine, which should be checked again at the middle and end of the season. The hull bottom, lower unit, and propeller should be smooth and clean—free of marine growth as well as nicks and gouges. A coat of fresh paint on the hull may be all that is necessary, or you may need to repair the gelcoat. If the propeller blades are bent or damaged, have the prop

BOAT LOADING

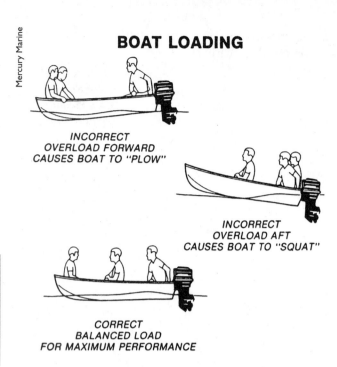

INCORRECT
OVERLOAD FORWARD
CAUSES BOAT TO "PLOW"

INCORRECT
OVERLOAD AFT
CAUSES BOAT TO "SQUAT"

CORRECT
BALANCED LOAD
FOR MAXIMUM PERFORMANCE

MOTOR ANGLE ADJUSTMENT

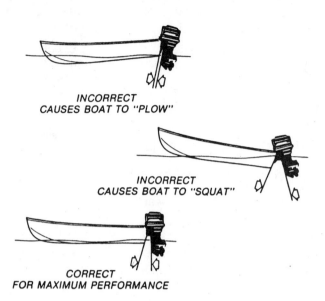

INCORRECT
CAUSES BOAT TO "PLOW"

INCORRECT
CAUSES BOAT TO "SQUAT"

CORRECT
FOR MAXIMUM PERFORMANCE

Mercury Marine

repaired or replaced. Lay a straight-edge against the hull bottom to check for hook or rocker caused by improper loading on the trailer. Though these problems can and should be corrected, you can avoid them in the first place by seeing that your boat has adequate support, especially at the transom, where most of the weight is located.

Give your outboard motor a thorough inspection. Clean or replace the spark plugs; check the wiring and the rest of the ignition system, including the timing. Inspect the carburetor for proper float level, correct jetting, and smooth choke operation. While you are at it, change the gear oil, check the oil level, and lubricate moving parts, as indicated in your owner's manual.

You are just about ready to go, but before you leave the driveway or dock, have you thought about where you are going? You can save gallons of fuel by planning your destination and taking the shortest route or the road that is easiest on your vehicle and rig. You can also save fuel by exploring places closer to home rather than driving or boating long distances. Granted, part of the pleasure of trailer boating is being able to explore faraway destinations, but some of the best boating spots lie right at the back door of most boaters.

Transom brackets that can improve performance by 5 to 20 percent are now offered as optional or standard equipment by many boat manufacturers.

OPERATION

Boats and motors are not a very efficient combination. They have to overcome the resistance of both wind and water, and they lose a fairly high percentage of their available horsepower through the propulsion system. Still, there are ways boaters can improve their rig's efficiency and bring down fuel consumption.

Every engine attains its maximum horsepower rating within a specific r.p.m. range. If the prop and engine are not matched to the boat, the engine will operate either below or above this range. If below, you need a lower-pitched or smaller-diameter prop; if above, you need a higher-pitched or larger-diameter prop. The engine or propeller manufacturer, or boat and motor dealer, can help you with your choice.

Correctly mounting an outboard is also important. Your engine should be centered on the transom and at the height recommended by the manufacturer. Transom mounting height is measured along a *perpendicular* from the top to the bottom of the transom—not along the back of the transom itself. Raising or lowering the engine height affects performance, so be sure you understand the implications before diverging from the manufacturer's recommendations (see "Rigging an Outboard," page 92).

If you are carrying any item

ENGINES

aboard that is not absolutely necessary, leave it behind. Weight increases fuel consumption more than any other factor. Furthermore, when you load the boat, be careful to distribute the weight of the gear and passengers evenly. Too much weight forward will cause the boat to nose-dive and plow through the water; too much weight aft will cause the boat to porpoise. Properly trimmed, a planing boat will run at a bow-up attitude of about 2 to 3 degrees. If you are singlehanding a tiller-steered outboard, you can exert better control over weight distribution by using an extension handle. Good, inexpensive handles are available from marine dealers, or you can devise your own (see "How to Make an Extension Handle," page 105).

Boat trim is also affected by engine angle. For smaller engines, you adjust the tilt pin so the antiventilation plate lies parallel to the surface. Larger engines with power trim and tilt can be automatically trimmed in or out while underway to adjust for hull peculiarities, boat speed, water conditions, or weight placements. However, keep in mind that whenever the plate is at any angle to the surface, it induces fuel-robbing drag. Another way to adjust trim is to add trim tabs to your boat. These can be simple fixed tabs or hydraulically operated, adjustable tabs, depending on the size of the boat (for more on trim tabs, see the next two essays).

Other mechanical means of increasing fuel economy are transom brackets and jack plates.

Sportfishermen and owners of high-performance powerboats have been using transom brackets for some time, but they are just beginning to reach a broader market. Transom brackets are now offered as optional or standard equipment by many major boat manufacturers. By positioning the prop in cleaner water back of the transom, they can im-

Some improvement in performance and gas consumption may be gained by the addition of a hydrofoil, or stabilizer (arrow), to the motor cavitation plate. This is particularly true with a heavy workboat like this one, which may have a tendency to squat when loaded.

prove performance by 5 to 20 percent. Jack plates, regularly used in racing craft to raise the engine and reduce lower-unit drag, are beginning to appear in conjunction with brackets (see "Why Jack an Outboard?" page 94).

While you are weighing the ex-

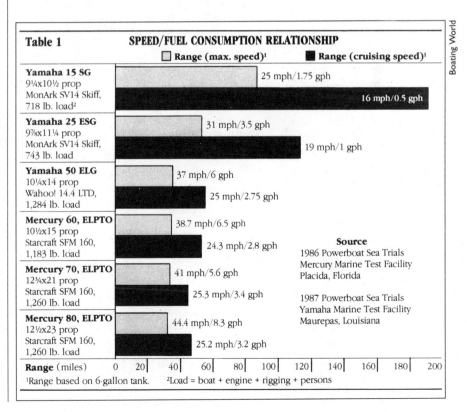

Table 1 — SPEED/FUEL CONSUMPTION RELATIONSHIP

☐ Range (max. speed)[1] ■ Range (cruising speed)[1]

Engine	Range (max. speed)	Range (cruising speed)
Yamaha 15 SG 9¼x10½ prop MonArk SV14 Skiff, 718 lb. load[2]	25 mph/1.75 gph	16 mph/0.5 gph
Yamaha 25 ESG 9⅞x11¼ prop MonArk SV14 Skiff, 743 lb. load	31 mph/3.5 gph	19 mph/1 gph
Yamaha 50 ELG 10¼x14 prop Wahoo! 14.4 LTD, 1,284 lb. load	37 mph/6 gph	25 mph/2.75 gph
Mercury 60, ELPTO 10½x15 prop Starcraft SFM 160, 1,183 lb. load	38.7 mph/6.5 gph	24.3 mph/2.8 gph
Mercury 70, ELPTO 12¾x21 prop Starcraft SFM 160, 1,260 lb. load	41 mph/5.6 gph	25.3 mph/3.4 gph
Mercury 80, ELPTO 12½x23 prop Starcraft SFM 160, 1,260 lb. load	44.4 mph/8.3 gph	25.2 mph/3.2 gph

Source
1986 Powerboat Sea Trials
Mercury Marine Test Facility
Placida, Florida

1987 Powerboat Sea Trials
Yamaha Marine Test Facility
Maurepas, Louisiana

Range (miles)   0   20   40   60   80   100   120   140   160   180   200
[1]Range based on 6-gallon tank.   [2]Load = boat + engine + rigging + persons

Boating World

pense of a bracket or other mechanical means against the projected savings, don't forget that the simplest way to conserve fuel is to slow down. Fuel consumption increases dramatically with increases in speed, so throttle down to cruising speed (about ⅔ to ¾ throttle) and enjoy the scenery. With some boat-and-motor combinations, you will be able to double your range and cut your fuel consumption in half, arriving at your

destination only a few minutes later than if you headed out wide open.

Finally, if you are boating on the coast, keep an eye on the tides. Try to plan your trip to run out and in with them, rather than against them. And no matter where you are boating, watch the weather. Battling winds and waves siphons just as much fuel from the tanks as overloading or running wide open.

Of course, you can always carry

more gasoline aboard to increase your range, but that means more weight, which in turn means more fuel consumption—just what we are trying to avoid in the first place.

—Richard Lebovitz
(*Small Boat Journal* #60)

A Fuel-Saver's Report

Author John Page Williams (Exploring the Chesapeake in Small Boats), who is education director for the Chesapeake Bay Foundation as well as a small-boat expert, considers center-console skiffs in the 17- to 20-foot range among the very best all-round small boats. If proof is in the pudding, his is well done, for he has owned his 17-foot center-console Mako for more than 20 years. In a recent letter, he commented in detail on propellers, weight, and trim tabs, three subjects of special interest to anyone who wants to run a boat at its top efficiency. With his permission, we quote from that letter:

It is important to fit the boat with a tachometer and use it to pick a propeller of the correct diameter and pitch. For general use, the wheel should have as much diameter and as little pitch as possible, to let the engine turn up to the top of its operating range (which is listed in the owner's manual). The wheel should also be cupped, to provide lift and thus to help the boat plane at relatively low speeds. Sizing the wheel this way will provide good power, a slow idle speed for trolling and maneuvering in close quarters, and minimum strain on the engine. Propeller work is precision stuff, so the skiff owner should find a good wheel shop to advise (retail boat dealers often don't understand) and to make modifications. The guidelines above should help the skiff owner to ask good questions at the shop.

A good rule of thumb for power on shallow-V (modified-V) skiffs (my Mako, for example, has 12 degrees of deadrise at the transom) is to have a weight-to-horsepower (prop-rated) ratio of 25:1 to 30:1, counting into the weight figure the maximum gross load of hull, engine, fuel, batteries, gear, and people. I have run my Mako successfully with a ratio

of 42:1 (an old crank-rated Merc 65), but it took some brilliant work by my wheel shop for that engine to move the boat effectively with a full load. The present prop-rated Merc 90 breathes much easier with a load in seas, and the increase in fuel consumption is negligible. This relatively light three-cylinder engine is perfect for my purposes.

The skiff's 9-by-12-inch Teleflex hydraulic trim tabs add an important element of seaworthiness and comfort. The tabs keep her on plane at speeds as low as 12 knots (as opposed to 17 before I installed the tabs), allowing her to slow down in big seas and ride them like a rocking chair, where she would otherwise be skipping from wavetop to wavetop or slogging along in a squat. In smaller seas, I can adjust the engine's power trim to the most efficient angle and then use the tabs to trim the boat so that her sharp forefoot is cutting the seas, instead of using the engine's trim to do the job less effectively and compromising its efficiency. In effect, the tabs allow me to choose which part of the skiff's bottom strikes a wave first. Finally, the tabs allow me to adjust trim from side to side. This capability is most important when quartering into a chop, a running angle that is uncomfortable and wet in almost any boat. In this situation, I lower the windward tab, elevating that side of the boat and lowering the leeward side. She dries right out, and the ride softens up.

I've had tabs on *School* for the past three seasons. They have more than proven their worth. Teleflex's customer service people have been terrific in helping me install the system and troubleshoot the one problem I have had with it. These tabs have definitely made a very good boat even better.

—*John Page Williams*

Trim Tabs and Hydrofoils

The more educated boaters become in their avocation, the more they expect of their boat's performance. Modern boaters are no longer content with a craft that simply gets them from point A to point B. Rather, they ponder things like fuel flow, time-to-plane, engine stress, and optimum handling. Indicative of this trend is the fact that features once accepted as luxuries, such as power steering and power trim, are now viewed as necessities.

It is not surprising, therefore, that there is a growing interest in the subject of trim tabs and hydrofoils. "What do they accomplish, and how do they work?" "Will either enhance my boat's performance?" "Is the gain worth the expense?" "Are there any drawbacks to their use?" All are questions that savvy-seeking boaters want answered.

TRIM TABS

The exact origin of trim tabs is uncertain, but nautical history does tell us that the early ones were made of wood wedges or shingles attached to the hull bottom to extend aft of the transom. Although the manufacturing process has become much more sophisticated, the basic principle stays the same. Modern trim tabs are an extension of the hull bottom. They consist of two tabs (also called *plates* or *planes*) made of steel, aluminum, or plastic that are mounted at the bottom of the transom. Some models are permanently fixed, and others have a threaded strut so they can be mechanically adjusted, but the better models are adjustable from the helm via a switch that activates hydraulic cylinders.

Trim tabs can serve several purposes. The most common use is to assist a boat in getting up on plane. When the tabs are lowered, the force of the water tries to lift them, but

> *The biggest benefit a hydrofoil is likely to offer a boat is quicker planing time.*

since they won't "give," the upward force raises the stern of the boat instead. This, in turn, drops the bow, which allows the boat to plane more quickly. How much more quickly depends on the boat design, weight distribution, the size of the engine(s), and other factors. I've been on some boats where the use of trim tabs made a tremendous difference in coming

on plane, and others where the effect was barely noticeable—although the latter is rare. If a boat planes well in general but requires all the passengers to move to the bow to pull up a water-skier, trim tabs should be considered. Trim tabs can also be worthwhile if a boat exhibits excessive bow rise or rides down by the stern. Obviously, a quick-planing hull is safer to operate, allowing earlier visibility of another vessel crossing in front of you or of floating debris.

Trim tabs can also be used to adjust the angle of a boat while it is underway, both fore and aft, and laterally, and at slow or high speeds. Lowering the tabs will keep a boat on plane at slower speeds and lower engine r.p.m. This feature is especially appreciated in slow-speed zones and by anglers who troll. It can also eliminate aggravating bow steering common on

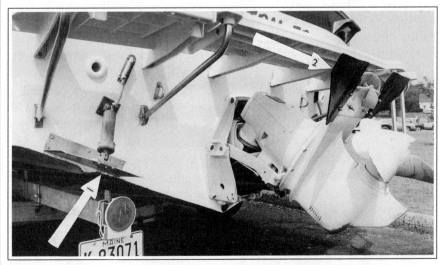

Belt and suspenders appear to be needed on this deep-V hull. Hydraulic trim tabs (1) are mounted on both sides of the power unit while stabilizers (2) have been attached to the cavitation plate. Both devices help counter this hull type's desire to dig into the water when power is applied.

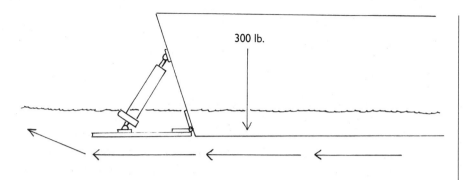

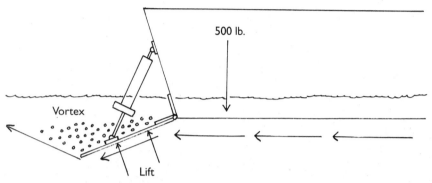

The trim tab serves as a small extension of the bottom (top sketch) under normal load. With the addition of weight (bottom sketch), the skipper lowers the tab, and the flow of water along the bottom presses against the tab, providing a lifting action. Because it breaks the smooth flow of water along the hull, the tab does create drag, but without it the hull would run at a steeper angle, thus creating an even greater drag. The size of the tab is exaggerated here in order to show its effects.

most boats at slow speeds.

On large bodies of water a head sea can create an uncomfortable, jarring ride. Lowering the tabs to a mid-position will smooth the ride by keeping the bow lower to slice the waves rather than slamming down on top of them. This attitude may allow a little more spray to come over the bow, but the added comfort is worth it. However, caution has to be exercised not to lower the tabs so much that you "stuff" the bow into oncoming waves. (It is best to practice on gentle seas first.) In a following sea, put the drives and tabs up. This will lift the bow to offset the waves lifting the stern.

Trim tabs can be used to balance the boat laterally by activating only one tab. If your boat is listing due to wind or an uneven load, lowering the tab on the listing side will level the boat. A quartering following sea can also cause list, because waves lift the stern unevenly. If one side of the transom is higher than the other, drop the tab on the lower side for a level and drier ride.

Will trim tabs increase your fuel efficiency? If used properly, in most cases, yes. To achieve the best results, the tabs should be as large as practical for the size of the boat. Most boats are designed to be properly trimmed when running at full throttle with a light load. Naturally, then, a planing hull will deliver its worst fuel economy while initially coming on plane. As you throttle forward the bow rises and the heavy stern drops, creating a wall of water that must be climbed in order to plane. Cutting down the amount of time it takes to do this will increase fuel economy. Considerable fuel savings also can be realized by using tabs when you have a heavy load, like fish boxes filled to capacity after a successful day's angling. Ac-

cording to the manufacturers, most boaters increase fuel efficiency by 10 to 20 percent after installing trim tabs, although some have documented improvements of 35 percent. Depending on the brand and size, trim tabs will cost between $300 and $900.

HYDROFOILS

It is, in fact, the cost of trim tabs that often prompts one to look at alternative methods of enhancing a boat's performance. Hydrofoils, for instance, are touted as another means of improving fuel efficiency, planing time, and handling. Depending on which manufacturer's product you use, the price ranges in the neighborhood of $20 to $90.

Basically, *hydrofoils* (also known as *stabilizers*) are a marine application of aerodynamic technology. A true hydrofoil is patterned after an airplane wing. The top side of the wing is curved to create a greater surface area than the bottom. This causes water to travel farther above than below, which creates a low pressure or vacuum on the top, resulting in lift.

Doelcher Products pioneered the attachable hydrofoil with the introduction of the Doel-Fin in 1975 (see illustration on page 65). Since then numerous other manufacturers have come and gone with variations of their own. Some designs now employ drag as a means to produce lift—such as by turning down the trailing edge. (Trim tabs also use drag to produce lift.) While trim tabs are applicable to any engine installation, hydrofoils are designed for only outboard and inboard/outdrive-powered (I/O) boats, since the hydrofoils bolt onto the drive's antiventilation plate above the propeller (see the photos on pages 101 and 103).

In theory, hydrofoil suppliers believe wings and propellers are meant to work with each other. One states it this way: "You need a propeller to develop thrust to compensate drag, and you need a wing, or foil, to develop lift to compensate weight. And by nature of design, all outboards and outdrives have stern weight."

The biggest benefit a hydrofoil is likely to offer a boat is quicker planing time. As with trim tabs, the degree of improvement depends on several factors, such as boat design, weight distribution, and amount of horsepower. A hydrofoil can also help a boat stay on plane at lower r.p.m. All of this takes some of the stress off the engine and, in many cases, increases fuel efficiency.

Unlike trim tabs, however, hydrofoils cannot be adjusted in and out of the water. Consequently, on some boats the benefit of lift might not offset the extra drag the submerged unit creates once the boat is on plane. (Attwood addresses this dilemma by designing its Hydro-Stabilizer in gull-wing fashion so that the fins are out of the water after the boat gets on plane.) So while most hydrofoil manufacturers claim that you'll see improved top-end speed with their product, few guarantee it, which is a

point you should inquire about before purchasing. In fact, you may see a decrease in speed, because the drag factor multiplies exponentially the faster you go.

Generally, boats not equipped with the power trim are going to see more improvement from a hydrofoil than boats with power trim. The height of the antiventilation plate in relation to the boat's keel is another important factor in the effectiveness of a hydrofoil. Ideally, they should be about the

> *Will trim tabs increase your fuel efficiency? If used properly, in most cases, yes.*

same height. If the plate is lower, it will improve time-to-plane but may decrease top-end speed, and if it is too high, it may have little effect whatsoever.

Other benefits of hydrofoils include the ability to pull up waterskiers quicker and with less engine strain, to reduce prop ventilation, and to eliminate porpoising or bouncing of the bow. According to some hydrofoil manufacturers, fuel savings can range from 10 to 40 percent. You may also witness improved handling

in following seas, because as the boat's stern lifts, it has to displace water on top of the wing, which creates a vacuum, or suction, on its bottom. Hydrofoils are also excellent for inflatables that have a tendency to ride high in front.

Concern has been raised because engine manufacturers have taken the stand that hydrofoils and other bolt-on accessories like trolling plates nullify the warranty of the drive's antiventilation plate. Hydrofoil manufacturers contest that this is not a concern, and to reassure their customers, some are including coverage of the drive unit's antiventilation plate under their own warranty.

In summary, trim tabs and hydrofoils might greatly enhance the performance and enjoyment you get from your boat. Hydrofoils are more limited in their application than trim tabs, but they're also considerably less expensive. Tabs, if you can afford them, offer a wide variety of applications and can be adjusted to provide a drier, more comfortable ride no matter what conditions you run into.

—Randy Scott
(*Boating World*, #83)

How to Make an Extension Handle

The complications and space-robbing features of a wheel steering system for your outboard boat can be avoided with the installation of an extension handle to the tiller of your motor. With such a device, you can stand while steering or move forward to better trim a lightweight boat when you are running it alone. Manufac-

tured extension handles are for sale at some of the better-equipped boat and motor dealers, but you can make your own for only a few dollars and an hour or so of construction time.

The easiest way to make an extension handle is to take a wood rod the same diameter as the grip on the motor tiller and cut it off at the de-

sired length. Next, cut an 8-inch piece of black PVC pipe the inside diameter of which is the same as the outside diameter of the extension handle. Then cut a ⅛-inch-wide slit lengthwise in the PVC so that this piece can be tightened around the tiller grip and extension handle. The best way to make the slit is with a 10-

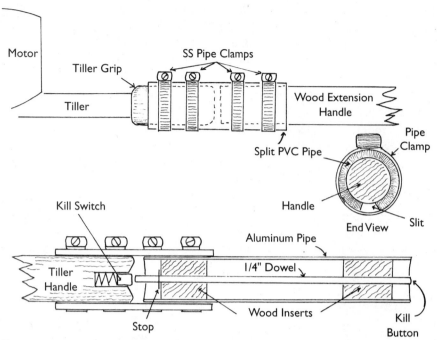

Two types of tiller extension handles are shown here. On the top is a simple wooden extension held to the tiller by a split PVC pipe and pipe clamps. On the bottom is a similar device using an aluminum tube. The sliding dowel inside the tube serves as an extension of the kill switch in the handle of the tiller.

inch table saw; the kerf of the blade is just the right width if all measurements are close, but by making a second pass through the saw you can widen the slit if necessary to ensure a tight fit.

The PVC pipe can now be pushed half its length onto the tiller grip and the extension handle pushed in from the other end until it butts against the tiller grip. There should be enough spring in the slit PVC pipe to adjust to the contours of grip and extension handle. Now slip on four stainless steel adjustable pipe clamps over the PVC pipe, two on the tiller end and two on the extension. Tighten them securely, and your extension handle is complete. (If there is the slightest slipping by the PVC connector, widen the lengthwise slit in it and re-install. This connection must be tight and solid for the extension handle to operate safely.) Simple and durable, this rig should last the life of the motor. We have used the same handle for a dozen years, and it is still as good as new.

A length of aluminum tubing can be substituted for the wood, if you prefer, with the part where you will be gripping it covered with electrician's tape, cork tape like that used on fishing rods, or a bicycle handlebar grip. The wood needs nothing in the way of a grip, being warm and smooth in its natural state.

In one case we wanted a handle for a motor that could only be turned off by pressing a kill-switch button in the end of the tiller grip. We got around this problem by using aluminum tubing with tight-fitting 2-inch-long wood inserts at each end of the tubing. The inserts were drilled to accommodate a thin hardwood dowel of the same length as the extension handle, which served nicely as a mechanical extension of the kill switch. Pressing in on the dowel where it protruded at the end of the extension handle forced the other end against the spring-loaded kill switch in the tiller grip, turning off the motor. When the pressure was released, the spring under the switch pushed the dowel back to its original position. A small metal stop in the dowel kept it from coming out of the extension handle. All the wood components were saturated with linseed oil to stabilize the wood against swelling or drying. This handle worked just fine for the two seasons we used this motor.

—DRG

Protecting Your Prop

Outboard motors and shallow water don't mix. When you fish or explore in shallow water and you don't use an electric motor, rocks, stumps, sandbars, and other obstructions can damage your outboard prop and lower unit, unless you protect them.

Before you incur an eye-opening, forehead-slapping repair bill, use these ideas to safeguard your prop and lower unit.

Older low-horsepower outboards use shear pins that offer some prop protection. A shear pin is a long cylindrical piece of soft metal about 1 inch long and 1/8 inch thick. It fits into a slot between the prop and the propeller drive shaft. In normal use, the shear pin is strong enough to turn the propeller. When an obstacle hits the propeller, preventing it from turning,

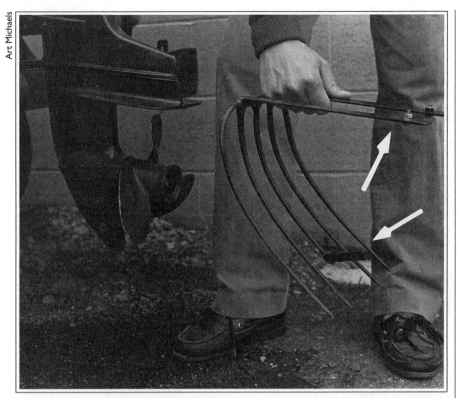

A dung fork makes a simple and effective prop guard. The parallel bars welded to the fork are bolted to the cavitation plate on the motor. A short clamp welded to the center tine fastens to the motor skeg.

A four-tine dung fork has been adapted as a guard for this motor, but its attachment to the lower unit with pipe clamps reduces its reliability, since the clamps may loosen in use, causing the guard to become a potential damaging object.

the shear pin's soft metal breaks, disengaging the prop. Fixing the setup requires replacing the shear pin.

On newer small-horsepower outboards, a toothed plastic hub fits between the propeller and the drive shaft. When an obstacle hits the prop, preventing it from turning, the prop disengages from the teeth in the plastic drive.

Both arrangements are designed to save the propeller and the propeller drive shaft from damage when an obstruction stops the propeller from turning. In many instances, they work.

In some instances, they don't work. Hitting an underwater obstruction can break a propeller piece off, bend the propeller shaft, and damage the outboard lower unit's other internal parts. For this reason, boaters with small-horsepower outboards might need the more thorough protection that prop guards provide. Guards include forks, cages, and other designs that protect the propeller, lower unit, and skeg.

FORKS

A fork is a simple, inexpensive small-outboard prop guard. If a fork is mounted solidly, it can prevent or reduce the damage you incur from clobbering an underwater obstruction.

The best tool is a four- or five-pronged dung fork, which has thin, round, pencil-like blades that cause negligible drag in the water. It's the best compromise for strength against obstruction, drag in the water, and weight.

Spading forks are more common than dung forks in hardware stores, but the blades are wide enough to interfere noticeably with maneuvering and handling. They're also not as long as dung fork blades, so they might not provide enough protection

Art Michaels

Art Michaels

Propeller guards come in as many shapes and sizes as there are motor designs. This device uses fins to shunt aside obstructions, but as can be seen, while the guard protects the lower unit of the motor from rocks or other large objects, the prop remains fairly vulnerable. The rugged design of the guard is a big plus.

Quite good all-around protection is provided by this guard, and its solid attachment to the motor helps ensure that the guard itself does not damage the propeller in a collision.

for your outboard's skeg.

To mount a fork securely, it needs flat steel rods welded to the top, which are bolted to the top of the cavitation plates. Rod lengths vary according to the engine lower unit configuration and amount of horsepower. A fork also needs a small, welded U-shaped brace on a middle fork, which is bolted to the skeg.

CAGES

A cage is another inexpensive prop guard. Cages most often feature formed, welded steel rods that follow the outline of the lower unit from the cavitation plates to a point below the skeg. The larger the cage, the more it detracts from performance and boat handling.

OMC PROP GUARD

OMC offers a different kind of prop guard for its 9.9- and 15-h.p. outboards. The company's cagelike cast-aluminum prop guard is about 3 inches wide and encircles the prop. It protects the prop from some obstructions that might strike from beneath or from the sides, but it doesn't

protect the prop from some obstructions that might hit it head-on, and some of the lower unit remains vulnerable.

The OMC prop guard comes in a kit with hardware and instructions. You can order this prop kit from a dealer, but fit it only to Evinrude or Johnson 9.9- or 15-h.p. outboards in model years 1974 to current models.

OTHER DESIGNS

Look hard enough and you'll find a great variety of prop guards, nearly all of which are homegrown inventions. Other designs are welded steel contraptions in astonishing shapes. A few of these guards work amazingly well; others don't.

One design is made of light, strong aircraft aluminum and looks like wings attached to an engine's lower unit. It is designed to bend on impact, thus sparing the prop and lower unit. This device is cumbersome and interferes somewhat with performance, but it does protect the prop and lower unit well.

DISADVANTAGES

Consider the disadvantages of placing a prop guard on your outboard. For one thing, installing a prop guard might void the warranty on your motor, so check with the dealer before you mount a guard.

After you install a prop guard, regardless of which design you choose, never run your outboard in shallow water in reverse. Operating your engine in reverse in a shallow or pebbly area can be like throwing a hand grenade at your lower unit. Running in reverse, a prop guard can pick up rocks and debris and fling them into your prop. The prop can then fire the stones into your lower unit, or ricochet them off the guard into the lower unit. A small-horsepower motor's prop can propel a pebble hard enough to penetrate a lower unit.

Some do-it-yourselfers use hose clamps to position prop guards on lower units, but guards installed this way can loosen. When a loosely placed prop guard hits an obstruction, the guard can contribute to

prop and lower-unit damage.

For this reason, when you install a prop guard, leave it securely in place. Removing the guard occasionally can diminish its ability to protect your prop by weakening the installation.

On most small outboards, the cavitation plate and the skeg contain no working parts. Nevertheless, if you install a prop guard, don't drill holes in the gear housing or where you add lubricant.

Another disadvantage of installing a prop guard is that it might lower the engine's resale value. Installing a prop guard properly requires drilling bolt holes into the engine's cavitation

Installing a prop guard might void the warranty on your engine, so check with the dealer first.

plate and skeg. Removing the guard and trying to sell the engine might render it unattractive to someone who doesn't want a prop guard on an engine.

COST AND INSTALLATION

Prop guards cost anywhere from a few bucks to nearly $100, depending on the engine design, materials used, and difficulty to install. The average cost of a fork with installation on a small-horsepower outboard is about $50—a reasonable investment, because prop damage and lower-unit repairs often cost much more.

If you boat in an area where you need a prop guard, a local dealer who

sells and services your brand of outboard probably can recommend which design works best on your engine. When you shop for a prop guard, remember four qualities of the best prop guard designs and installations:

- They protect the prop, the lower unit, and the skeg on all sides.
- They minimize loss of power and maneuverability.
- They don't make the motor cavitate.
- They are securely mounted.

In areas where boaters need prop guards, most outboard dealers use their own installation procedures and guard designs, because the configurations of outboard lower units differs among brands and among each brand's horsepower models. In addition, these dealers most often have considerable experience with prop guard design and installation, and they prefer certain designs and installation procedures for engines they sell and service.

When you shop for a prop guard, get recommendations from boaters who use designs that interest you, and consult your outboard dealer. If skinny water lures you and you don't use an electric motor or jet drive outboard, you need a prop guard. Invest in one now before you pay dearly later.

—Art Michaels

BOAT TRAILERS

Introduction

A boat trailer is about the simplest piece of rolling stock imaginable: a few pieces of channel steel, some rubber rollers, a winch, wheels and axle(s), and lights. But when you see the price, the cost of simplicity takes on new meaning. Boat trailers are expensive; even the cheapest little pond-boat carrier costs several hundred dollars, and some of those at the top end of the range in which we are interested can cost several thousand.

What this tells any buyer is that either someone is making a lot of money on trailers or there is something there that doesn't immediately catch the eye. Having lived with a variety of good and bad trailers, ranging from one built from a $25 set of Model A wheels and axle (which stills carries firewood behind my tractor) to a four-wheel horse trailer costing as much as a good used car, we are confident in saying there is a lot that meets the eye, if you know where to look, but even then there are surprises.

Just as weight is a critical factor in boats, so it is in boat trailers. There is a vast difference between towing 500 or 2,000 pounds behind a car. As the load approaches the weight of the tow vehicle, it often demands equal rights, and it may let you know this by shoving your car around while you are doing 65 on the Interstate. Warnings about correct load weight and careful speed on the highway are everywhere in the trailer's owner's manual, but many people ignore such cautionary advice, if they bother to read it in the first place. Fortunately, the trailer manufacturers—unques-

> *As the load approaches the weight of the tow vehicle, it often demands equal rights. The tail is quite capable of wagging the dog.*

tionably on the advice of their lawyers—tend to be conservative in their recommendations, and additionally, most boat-trailer owners quickly come to realize that the tail is quite capable of wagging the dog. But there are enough exceptions to make anyone who has owned trailers give wide berth to speeders.

A lot can happen when a heavy boat is racing down the highway— little things like cushions flying out of the cockpit and landing on the windshields of following cars, or big things like a wheel disintegrating from the effects of a burned-out bearing. The driver may be unaware of what is going on back there until the trailer begins to fishtail wildly with a force that all but rips the steering wheel from his hands. Many such unwelcome events stem from the nature of the beast, where the wheels are dunked in salt water, hammered on bumps and potholes, left to sit without moving for weeks on end, then spun at a speed that may be a third faster than the wheels on the tow car, all the while being swayed back and forth against the bearings and lock nuts. That's asking a lot of a couple of little stamped steel wheels.

One of the best investments a trailer boater can make is a pair of big rearview mirrors, particularly one of the wide-view kind for the left side, where one can see the inside trailer wheel occasionally dropping off the pavement or climbing over a curb on a misjudged turn. It is nice, too, if you can see both taillights or at least their reflections so you can act swiftly to repair them if they go out.

At a busy launching ramp, you will see many theories on trailer handling in action. There are the dunkers and the dry launchers, those who are deliberate in easing their boats off the trailer and those who do water wheelies by backing into the drink, quickly shifting gears, and jerking the trailer out from under the boat. The latter maneuver always impresses the bystanders, especially if something goes wrong, but it doesn't leave any room for correction, such as having forgotten to put in the drain plug or neglecting to thoroughly untie the hold-down lines.

Here, too, is where you can see various accessories in action and decide if they are things you might want. Some boatowners swear by guide-ons, those tall posts that help line up the boat for loading. If you have struggled alone to load a boat in a sharp cross-breeze or running tidal current, you can appreciate the idea. Others prefer power winches, although the need for them on boats in our size-range is arguable, as there are very powerful hand winches available at a fraction of the price of an electric hauler.

In the material that follows, you will begin to see why boat-trailer use is not quite as simple as it seems. Learning to use a trailer quickly and easily is an acquired skill rather than an instinctive talent. In fact, one finds that dealing with a trailer is adjusting to an Alice-in-Wonderland world where everything seems to be backward; but, for many of us, trailer towing time and boat time are about equal, and the idiosyncrasies of these "simple" beasts cannot be ignored.

—DRG

Selecting a Trailer

Though much consideration goes into the selection of a boat, the purchase of a trailer is often an afterthought. This is unfortunate, for so much of one's boating pleasure depends on a trailer that functions reliably and safely.

There are many sizes and models of trailers to choose from, not to mention accessories, so it is easy to become confused or to make a hasty choice. Take your time. A trailer that isn't suited to your boat, as well as the terrain and distance you want to cover, will probably spoil your boating fun, and maybe even your boat.

Manufacturers have to offer trailers suitable for a wide assortment of boat types and sizes, from light but very wide catamarans to narrow monohull sailboats to powerboats with shallow- and deep-V hulls. In fact, it is now common to purchase complete rigs of boat, motor, and trailer, and in this case, the trailer is most likely well matched to the boat, perhaps even being built to specs supplied by the boat manufacturer.

However, thousands of boats are purchased separately, leaving a new owner to figure out what will be best to carry his pride and joy all those miles over dry land. The first step in finding the right trailer is to skim the catalogs, picking out the models that are designed for your boat's length and weight. This will narrow the field down so much that any feeling of bewilderment will probably evaporate.

You will soon find that most manufacturers offer "economy" and "premium" models. Economy trailers are not poorly made, just less elaborate than premium models. They often use the same hitches, springs, hubs, wheels, tires, and rollers as the more expensive ones. However, an economy trailer may have fewer crossmembers in its frame, which means

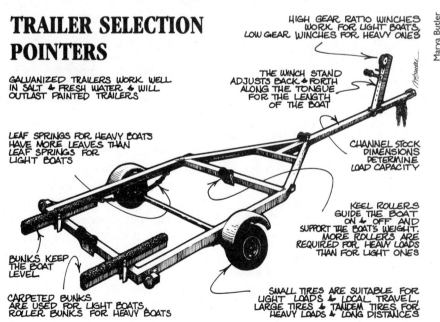

TRAILER SELECTION POINTERS

GALVANIZED TRAILERS WORK WELL IN SALT & FRESH WATER & WILL OUTLAST PAINTED TRAILERS

LEAF SPRINGS FOR HEAVY BOATS HAVE MORE LEAVES THAN LEAF SPRINGS FOR LIGHT BOATS

BUNKS KEEP THE BOAT LEVEL

CARPETED BUNKS ARE USED FOR LIGHT BOATS. ROLLER BUNKS FOR HEAVY BOATS

HIGH GEAR RATIO WINCHES WORK FOR LIGHT BOATS, LOW GEAR WINCHES FOR HEAVY ONES

THE WINCH STAND ADJUSTS BACK & FORTH ALONG THE TONGUE FOR THE LENGTH OF THE BOAT

CHANNEL STOCK DIMENSIONS DETERMINE LOAD CAPACITY

KEEL ROLLERS GUIDE THE BOAT ON & OFF AND SUPPORT THE BOAT'S WEIGHT. MORE ROLLERS ARE REQUIRED FOR HEAVY LOADS THAN FOR LIGHT ONES

SMALL TIRES ARE SUITABLE FOR LIGHT LOADS & LOCAL TRAVEL, LARGE TIRES & TANDEM TIRES FOR HEAVY LOADS & LONG DISTANCES

Marya Butler

Subtle points make a difference. A boat trailer with a long wheel base usually tows and backs much better than one with a short wheel base. Note how the wheels on this trailer are far aft on the frame but still only a short distance back from the center of weight. The 12-inch wheels also lift the boat high enough so that it can be towed with the motor in the down position, which is easier on both the transom and the motor mount. A lightweight rig like this tows without any fuss behind a small pickup or compact car.

fewer and more widely spaced support rollers for the keel. This wider spacing can give adequate support to a light boat, especially one that has a strong keel, but fewer, more widely spaced keel rollers provide less directional guidance when a boat is being winched on the trailer and will not provide enough keel support for a heavy boat.

The difference between economy and premium models, as well as trailers rated for different loads, may also lie in the size of the steel channel stock used for the frame side-rails and cross-members. Channel stock 3 or 4 inches deep would be adequate for a lightweight aluminum utility boat, while stock 5 or more inches deep is recommended for heavier craft of the same length.

In addition to frame depth, a frame's width and thickness—even the type of steel—all figure into the load capacity of a trailer. For example, one manufacturer uses 3-inch-deep channel stock of 12-gauge steel for a 450-pound-capacity trailer and 3-inch stock of 11-gauge steel for a 600-to-1,000-pound-capacity trailer. For a 1,200-to-1,400-pound-capacity rig, 11-gauge, 4-inch stock is used.

Besides boat size and weight, consider too how you are likely to use your trailer. Boaters who tow only short distances do not require trailers built as durably as those taking long, fast trips to distant boating areas, nor do they require trailers with as many features to make launching and hauling easier. For instance, if you are going to launch and haul your boat frequently, or are likely to encounter wind and current at the launching ramp, having plenty of rollers to guide your boat onto its trailer will save lots of irritation.

For efficient production, trailer makers try to develop a moderate

> *Since bunks and rollers are bolted on and come in many styles and sizes, they can be arranged in almost endless ways.*

number of well-thought-out basic components, which can then be put together in various combinations to create trailers suited for varying needs. For example, there might be a short, a medium-long, and a long frame, and three or four tongues of different lengths. These parts can be selected and put together to create beds able to hold boats of different lengths. A basic frame can have a two-wheel or a four-wheel running gear bolted on to accommodate boats of various weights.

Similarly, basic or elaborate hull support rollers and bunks can be attached, as well as winch stands of different heights and winches of different capacities. Therefore, if you do not see exactly the trailer you need in a local dealer's display yard, don't give up on him and go elsewhere. Remember, the ones carried in stock are models a dealer feels are most likely to suit the average customer.

Talk to the dealer and go over the manufacturer's literature with him. It is usually possible to figure out how to assemble basic components to fit your special requirements. You may then be able to arrange for his next shipment to include a trailer especially assembled to meet your needs.

Even if the dealer can't help you, local welding shops can. Suppose you have built a Chesapeake sharpie that is 22 feet long but weighs only 800 pounds. Catalogs show 1,000-pound-capacity trailers that could carry this weight, but they will only accommodate 15- to 16-foot boats. A welding shop could weld together channel stock that will neatly lengthen the tongue of one of these trailers.

RUNNING GEAR

Most trailers use wheels and tires smaller than those used on cars, a practice begun in the years following World War II, when the boating boom was just getting underway. It is not that they are cheaper or in better proportion to the load being carried. Rather, small wheels position a straight axle closer to the ground, so one ends up with a trailer and boat that ride as low as is feasible, for the sake of stability on fast turns and in blustery crosswinds.

When reasonably new and supple, and when used under average conditions, these small tires are reliable. But very long, fast runs on sizzling summertime pavement can get them hot enough to weaken their construction and cause premature failure. A small wheel has to rotate more than a large one while traveling the same distance. The 5.70 x 8 tires widely used on boat trailers have to turn 1,111 times to cover 1 mile, whereas the 205 x 14 tires used on many small cars make only 782 revolutions per mile. This, along with underinflation

and bearing burnout, is why you so often see disabled trailers parked alongside expressways leading to resorts.

In recent years, many trailer makers have been offering models fitted with 13-inch wheels and tires in the same size-range as those commonly found on automobiles. This setup appeals to boaters who frequently travel long distances and might need to locate replacement tires in out-of-the-way places. These larger wheels and tires work out nicely with larger deep-V outboards and slack-bilged sailboats, because they can tuck under the hull. They also give a better ride. Small tires drop farther into potholes and climb more over bumps. To keep the center of gravity low in some boats, trailers equipped

> *It is not unusual to find trailers of different load capacity identical in every respect except the tires.*

with large-diameter tires may be fitted with drop-center axles.

Two 8-inch wheels and tires cannot safely carry many larger boats. The solution to this problem has been to use tandem wheels, which puts four of them under the load. In addition to carrying a heavy boat safely and dependably, this arrangement gives a good ride on bumpy roads. Because only one wheel on a tandem drops into a pothole or encounters a bump at one time, tandem wheels tend to even out the irregularities. The articulated linkages used to attach tandem axles to trailer frames have a rocking action that further reduces the amount of up-and-down motion transmitted to the frame and load.

The purchase and maintenance costs of tandem wheels are higher, and they resist sharp turns, which

makes maneuvering in close quarters more difficult. Nonetheless, the tendency of tandem wheels to track straighter can be useful when backing a large rig to a launching ramp.

It is not unusual to find trailers of different load capacity identical in every respect except the tires. Trailers rated for light loads often use two-ply tires, but when the same size is used on trailers rated to carry heavy loads, the tires will have four or even more layers of fabric in their construction. However, tires can be constructed in various ways, using different kinds of fabric, so do not be surprised if you find a two-ply tire carrying a four-ply load rating.

You will find the ply count, maximum load capacity, and minimum inflation pressure all molded into the side of the tire. For example, the numbers 4.80 x 8A, found on a typical small-boat trailer tire, indicate that the tire is 4.8 inches wide, fits an 8-inch rim, and has an A-range load rating of 390 pounds at 30 psi (pounds per square inch). In contrast, a B-range or C-range tire of the same size will have ratings of 590 pounds at 60 psi and 745 pounds at 90 psi, respectively. Once you have bought a trailer, faithfully observe the tire pressure recommendations given by its manufacturer. And be on guard in case some well-meaning person lowers the tire pressure of your trailer to automobile pressures.

SPRINGS

Over the years, various spring types have been used on boat trailers. Coil springs are lightweight and don't soak up and hold water like leaf springs, but they are floppy and cannot hold axles in correct position by themselves. When they are used, it is necessary to accept the weight and cost of fore-and-aft and transverse radius rods. Also, the absence of interleaf friction means that a vehicle using them can bob up and down excessively, so hydraulic shock absorbers must be installed to snub this action. Dust shrouds built into these make it hard to thoroughly hose off salt water.

Most boat manufacturers today favor leaf springs, mounted fore and aft on each side of the trailer. The friction between their leaves effectively snubs the tendency for the trailer to keep bobbing up and down after striking a bump, so shock absorbers are not needed, and neither are axle-positioning radius rods. The number and thickness of the leaves depend on the load. While two-leaf springs may be adequate for a 400-pound load, five-leaf springs may be necessary for a 1,300-pound load.

Trailer leaf springs are deliberately made shorter and stiffer than those found on automobiles. This stiffness is desirable to resist swaying in fast turns and on windy days. If a boat is securely fastened to a trailer, it will not bounce up and down on the hull supports and will not be bothered by the harder ride. Homemade trailers using automobile axles and springs often tend to sway and weave alarmingly when underway because the long, supple car springs are too flexible to keep things under control.

As you inspect various makes and models of boat trailers, you will notice that they have holes drilled in their frame siderails. They are put there to allow the running gear assembly to be shifted forward or aft as necessary to achieve good balance. An outboard boat with a large motor, battery, and long-range fuel tank all located in its stern will have a center of gravity somewhat farther back than a trailerable sailboat with most of its weight amidships.

By moving the axle and wheel assembly back and forth while at the same time adjusting the winch stand (and bow chock) at the forward end, you can position the boat to balance nicely on the trailer and therefore tow well.

CAPACITY

Trailers that carry the certification label of the National Marine Manufacturers Association meet rigid design standards, including a load capacity rating. Choose a trailer whose load capacity matches your boat.

You may not be able to find a trailer that is rated at the exact weight of your boat, but since the capacity ratings are on the conservative side, putting a 1,150-pound boat on a 1,000-pound trailer will not cause it to promptly break down. However, as it gets older, its tires or hub bearings could show the effect of this modest overload. The general rule is to get a trailer rated a few to several hundred pounds more than your rig. This gives enough surplus capacity to take care of the luggage, camping equipment, and other things that sooner or later will be loaded aboard.

Don't overdo it, though. It is unwise to get a trailer rated to carry a weight substantially in excess of the weight of your boat. If you were to put an 1,800-pound boat on a trailer rated for 4,000 pounds, you would pay more than is necessary, the heavier weight would penalize the towing

> *The general rule is to get a trailer rated a few to several hundred pounds more than your rig.*

car, and the stiffer springs would give the boat an unnecessarily hard ride.

COATINGS

Most trailer makers offer a choice between painted and galvanized models. Paint finishes can vary widely in durability. Cheap trailers or those made by small firms with limited facilities might have only one spray coat of fast-drying lacquer. Other firms offer good-quality, durable, multicoat jobs using the most advanced paint application methods. Ask how a paint finish was applied, and you will be able to form an opinion as to whether it is a poor or an excellent job.

Unfortunately, even the best paint finish is subject to scratching or chipping, and where bare metal appears, rust will set in. Hot-dip galvanizing forms a scratch-resistant surface and has the advantage of coating the interior surfaces of box-steel frames and tongues, which cannot be reached by spray painting. Galvanized trailers appeared first in saltwater areas, but their high resistance to rust has also made them popular among inland boaters. According to one manufacturer, galvanized trailers will last five times as long as painted ones. And they generally cost only $50 to $100 more.

BUNKS AND ROLLERS

All trailers have keel rollers for the sake of easy launching and hauling. But something has to be provided to prevent the boat from tilting from side to side. Strips of wood covered with carpeting, called *bunks,* are often used for this purpose. They are low in cost, distribute pressure uniformly, and when properly adjusted do not create enough friction to keep a light-weight boat from sliding off and on.

Larger trailers for heavier boats tend to use gangs of rubber rollers. An experienced dealer will know how the hulls of his boats are made and can help you select hull supports that will bear against reinforced rather than unsupported areas of the bottom.

Since bunks and rollers are bolted on and come in many styles and sizes, they can be arranged in almost endless ways. The pictures in trailer catalogs will help you get ideas on how to set up your new trailer.

Black rubber rollers have been used for many years because they have good resistance to attack by rubber's big enemies, air and sunlight. However, they tend to leave black marks on hulls, which is why some trailer makers prefer gray rubber rollers. When made of properly compounded material, they also have good resistance to the elements.

After a boat sits on its trailer for a long time, such as during winter storage, its weight can produce flat spots on rubber rollers. The amber-colored rollers on the market don't leave black marks on hulls, and they resist flattening. If you already have rubber rollers, you can minimize flattening by tapping suitable wooden wedges between trailer and keel to take weight off the rollers.

Some trailers, especially those made for smaller boats, are hinged about midway in their length and tilt as the boat is launched, thus easing the hull into the water. A tilt trailer can be backed until the water is just below the wheel hubs while the winch area where you are standing is on dry land.

This provides water deep enough to float most of the lighter boats and lets you launch without wetting your hubs and the trailer frame. Hauling is equally dry and easy.

WINCHES AND LINES

Winches come in a bewildering range of sizes and styles. A winch meant for use on a light trailer (a 700-pound-capacity trailer, for example) may have a gear ratio of no more than 2:1. This means the drum makes one revolution for each two turns of the crank. One meant for a heavier rig (anywhere from 1,000 to 2,000 pounds) will likely have a gear ratio of 4:1 or even 6:1. With a ratio such as the latter, the crank will be easy to turn, but many turns will be needed to haul a boat onto the trailer. So some winches are of the two-speed type. When the winch is in low gear, a heavy boat can be hauled up onto the rear of the trailer quite easily. Once it is "over the top," the winch can be shifted into its higher gear so the boat can be moved forward on the trailer more rapidly and with fewer turns of the crank.

Some winches also have brakes, a useful option when trailering a heavy boat. Trying to keep a hefty

Carpeted bunks (top) provide good support for lightweight boats, but the friction may make launching difficult. Roller bunks (bottom) correct the friction problem (possibly over-correct it on a steep ramp!) and are a virtual necessity for heavier boats, especially if launching and hauling are frequent.

Hinged or tilt trailers "break" where the boom connects with the frame, a useful feature for light-weight boats, since there is no need for submerging the trailer wheels.

Many trailer boaters find guide-ons a handy feature, particularly if they usually launch and haul alone or if they submerge their trailers. This owner has mounted the trailer lights on the top of the guide-ons—far from the salt water! Notice that the tow vehicles here are pickup trucks and that all the other vehicles in the accompanying photos are midsize cars or larger. Long, sometimes steep ramps, such as those on salt water, require considerable power for hauling.

hull under control on a steep ramp by "unwinding" the crank slowly results in much too slow a launching, and if you lose your grip on the handle, a brakeless winch can go out of control—and the spinning crank handle can give you a wicked rap on the knuckles or even cause serious injury. Deft use of a winch brake enables a heavy boat to be launched both quickly and safely.

Because an electric motor can rotate a winch drum faster than a human can do it, and because motors don't get "winded," electric winches have become popular. They make it possible to haul out a large boat quickly at a busy ramp, and they make boating possible for a person who for some physical reason must not indulge in strenuous activity. Also, since the switch of an electric winch can be operated by pulling on a long cord attached to it, it is a boon to the solo boater, who can stand beside his boat and guide it straight onto the trailer, operating the winch by means of the cord.

Winch lines made of steel cable are strong, and a long line can be wound onto the drum due to the small diameter of the cable. But the small diameter makes the cable hard to grasp when guiding a boat onto the trailer. As a steel cable ages, it can develop broken strands that stick out and are very hard on the hands (good leather gloves are a hide saver). Sunlight and rot don't attack steel cable, but rust does. Fortunately, you can see such deterioration long before it has weakened the cable seriously. Periodic application of a light preservative oil will greatly lengthen the life of a steel cable.

Synthetic rope winch lines are strong enough when of suitable material and diameter, and they won't rot or rust. They are easy on the hands. But long exposure to sunlight breaks down the petrochemical-based material from which they are made. Use a simple fabric or plastic cover to shield the winch and its rope from direct sunlight, and swap the rope end-for-end on the winch once or twice a year.

Because of its greater diameter, synthetic rope fills up the winch drum faster than does steel cable. Provided the drum can hold enough line, this is a useful characteristic. When the line is pulled out to begin the task of hauling a boat, effective drum diameter is small and mechanical advantage is good. The boat comes out of the water and goes "over the top" with little straining. As winching continues and line winds around and around the drum, effective drum diameter increases and so does the rate at which the boat moves forward to the bow chock.

What we have said here with regard to some of the many aspects of boat trailers should give you enough feel for the subject to enable you to make a wise choice.

—Bob Whittier
(*Small Boat Journal* #48)

BOAT TRAILERS

Two Accessories You Can Make Yourself

Three easily added boat-trailer accessories—two of which you can easily make yourself—are a jack, safety chain, and a walking board.

Since a trailer tongue should carry about 10 percent of the total weight of the rig, this figure averages 30 to 50 pounds for lightweight boats and 100 to 200 pounds for heavier rigs. Trying to pick up the tongue from the ground is backbreaking work, so the installation of a jack just behind the coupling makes life an awful lot easier and not only lets you hook and unhook the rig from your car at the mere turning of a crank, but also will lift the bow high enough to drain the boat while it is stored in the backyard.

The safety chain's sole purpose is to keep your boat out of the back seat of your car. Made of ¼- to ⅜-inch galvanized chain, it is fastened securely to the tongue just beneath the bow. It is rigged with a scissor hook that attaches to the bow ring of the boat, and comes taut just as the bow is snugged into the chock on the winch.

A trailer-tongue jack saves a lot of back pain, and the swivel wheel (caster) permits moving the trailer around when it is off the vehicle. Most jacks will lift the bow of the boat high enough to drain water through the drain hole when the rig is stored outside.

In the event of a panic stop, the weight of boat and motor might be enough to crush the winch stand and slide forward into the back of the towing vehicle. With the safety chain, the winch stand and chain working together can hold the weight of the boat under all but the very worst circumstances.

The walking board is just that, a board bolted to the trailer bed that will let you walk safely and comfortably aft to attach the winch hook to the bow of the boat for hauling, to untangle lines, or to guide the boat onto the trailer. Anyone who has tried to keep his footing on the narrow, slippery trailer frame members to do the same jobs will appreciate the walking board. A 10- or 12-inch-wide, straight-grained, ¾-inch-thick pine board will serve on most trailers. If you are on the heavy side and the gap between frames is wide, you might want to go with a 2 x 8 or 2 x 10 plank instead.

—DRG

Choosing a Tow Vehicle

A good tow vehicle is one that can pull a loaded trailer without strain on either the vehicle or its driver.

Most car and truck manufacturers specify the maximum towing capacity for each of their vehicles. But how are these ratings figured? Is it just a matter of engine displacement and maybe vehicle weight,

or is it more complicated?

It's more complicated—a lot more complicated—than that. Neither the curb weight of the vehicle nor its engine size is the main determinant of towing capacity. Nor is the primary factor in rating towing capacity the car's horsepower, or whether it has front-wheel rather

than rear-wheel drive.

In fact, a vehicle's capacity to tow a trailer depends on a combination of more than a dozen different elements. The following is a list of these rating factors—variables the car makers think about before assigning ratings for a vehicle's maximum towing capacity.

CAR WEIGHT

The weight of the tow vehicle affects steering as well as load-carrying capacity. The rule of thumb used to be: Don't tow a loaded trailer heavier than your car. Weight is still a factor in determining towing capacity, but not as pronounced as it was a few years ago. Some cars have trailer weight limits as small as 25 percent of curb weight (weight of the car with full fuel tank but no occupants or luggage) or even less, while others are rated to tow significantly more than their own weight.

REAR SUSPENSION STRENGTH

Overload springs, load levelers, heavy-duty shock absorbers, and other such additions (usually offered as optional extras rather than as standard features) can help a tow car accept bigger loads.

TRAILER TOWING PACKAGE OPTIONS

Adding a factory-installed trailer towing package specifically designed by the manufacturer to improve a vehicle's towing capability can improve maximum towing capacity no end. In fact, these package options often can be the biggest single influence on rated tow-vehicle capacity. Take, for example, the little Volvo 240, weighing 2,985 pounds. With no trailer towing package, it is rated to tow 2,000 pounds. Add the optional tow package, consisting mainly of an automatic transmission fluid (ATF) cooler, and the tow-capacity rating rises to 3,300 pounds—more than the vehicle weight itself.

What's in a towing package? The specific items vary from make to make, but an unusually complete trailer towing package might include the following components:

- Heavy-duty radiator
- Heavy-duty transmission or trans-axle oil cooler
- Heavy-duty turn signals
- Special trailer towing suspension, front and rear
- Dual exhaust system to boost horsepower
- Factory-installed frame hitch
- Heavy-duty signal flasher
- Auxiliary power steering fluid cooler
- Heavy-duty engine oil cooler
- Higher-ratio axle gearing
- Heavy-duty front brakes
- Heavy-duty wide tires
- Larger U-joint
- High-amp alternator
- Heavy-duty battery
- Factory-installed trailer wiring harness, including take-outs and relays for trailer lights, battery recharging (for house trailers), electric trailer brakes, and both halves of a weatherproof connector plug with pigtails to hook up to a trailer.

Factory-packaged systems can be extensive—but at a typical cost of $300 to $500, not expensive, considering what you get. On the other hand, retrofitting an existing vehicle with the same equipment can set you back several thousand dollars, especially if you pay a mechanic to do the job rather than do it yourself. And most retrofit jobs aren't easy. Oil coolers, transmission fluid coolers, supplemental engine coolant radiators, heavy-duty suspension, higher-ratio axle gearing—all are available as "kits" in the auto aftermarket. If you install only one or two components to correct a specific problem—such as overheating in hilly terrain—the cost may be justifiable. But usually the best economic choice is to trade up to a vehicle already equipped to do the job.

SUITABILITY OF HITCH ATTACHMENT POINTS

Certain cars have easy-to-bolt-on hitches that can be obtained through trailer retailers from aftermarket suppliers like Hitch World (a U-Haul subsidiary), Reese, Draw-Tite, or Da'Lan (a foreign car and truck hitch specialist). Other cars won't fit any off-the-shelf hitches known to man.

Trailer Classification	Class I	Class II	Class III	Class IV
Maximum GVWR (lbs.)	2,000	3,500	5,000	10,000
Coupler Designation	No. 1	No. 2	No. 3	No. 4
Minimum ball diameter (inches)	1⅞	2	2	2⁵⁄₁₆
Minimum breaking-point requirements:				
Longitudinal tension and compression (lbs.)	6,000	10,500	15,000	3 times the gross trailer weight
Transverse thrust (lbs.)	2,000	3,000	4,000	Equal to gross trailer weight
Vertical tension and compression (lbs.)	2,500	4,500	7,000	1.3 times gross trailer weight

Strength Ratings for Trailer Couplers and Balls

If you happen to own one of these "nothing fits" automobiles, you may have a problem with no easy solution. In some cases (if you own a 1989 Jeep Cherokee, for example) the only right way is to order the hitch to be factory-installed when the car is built. To be safe, check hitch requirements and availability before you buy your new tow vehicle.

Incidentally, unless you want to risk voiding your auto warranty, forget using a bumper hitch on any new car. Before the days of shock-absorbing bumpers, bumper hitches were extensively used for light and medium loads, since they were easy to install and inexpensive. But today such hitches are not recommended except for the very lightest loads, and in several states *all* bumper hitches are banned.

Truck hitches are something else again; step "hitches" mounted on a step at the center of the bumper of many light trucks are not considered bumper hitches in the usual sense.

SUITABLE TRAILER HITCH AND BALL CONFIGURATION

Hitch and ball size and type vary according to the size and type of load to be towed. See the table on page 118 for the classifications you can choose from.

WHEELBASE

Length between front and rear wheels affects steering and traction. The longer the wheelbase, the better for towing, all other things being equal. Example: A heavy tongue weight on a short-wheelbase vehicle such as a Honda Civic (not recommended for towing) can wreck the car's handling characteristics.

HIGH ENGINE POWER AND TORQUE AT RELATIVELY LOW R.P.M.

Any tow vehicle's engine should have sufficient horsepower and torque to accelerate promptly when entering a highway and to climb the steepest hills expected to be encountered without having to reduce speed excessively. Power should be obtainable at moderate engine speeds to avoid constant downshifting. That usually means having an engine that derives extra power from a large

Adding a factory-installed trailer towing package specifically designed by the manufacturer to improve a vehicle's towing capability can improve maximum towing capacity no end.

cylinder displacement, rather than a turbocharger to boost power. In fact, some manufacturers (Saab and Chrysler, for example) recommend against using turbocharged engines on tow vehicles.

REAR-WHEEL DRIVE (RWD) VERSUS FRONT-WHEEL DRIVE (FWD)

FWD cars have more weight on the front wheels and less on the back wheels compared with RWD cars. And weight distribution—how the car weight and the tongue weight are distributed between front and rear wheels—affects traction, steering, and ability of the car to absorb the extra load of the trailer. With typical vehicle weight on the back wheels of only 36 or 37 percent for FWD vehicles (versus 44 or 45 percent for RWD models), the FWD cars have less traction to pull big loads, especially on steep grades (such as launching ramps) where weight distribution is shifted off the front wheels and onto the back ones. It is largely for this reason that Chrysler Corporation rates even most of its big cars to tow a maximum of only 2,000 pounds.

DRIVE GEAR RATIO

The so-called axle ratio (i.e., the number of engine revolutions made for each revolution of the drive wheels) affects rear-wheel torque: The higher the ratio, the faster the engine is turning for a given road speed, and the higher the torque. Higher ratios give greater pep and pulling power, but poorer gas economy.

COOLING CAPACITY

Automatic transmission fluid (ATF), transaxle lube, power steering fluid, engine oil, engine coolant—all can heat up more than usual when subjected to the adverse conditions of towing a heavy trailer. Manufacturers of vehicles designed for such heavy-duty conditions offer special cooling equipment as options.

BRAKE CAPACITY

Some cars have higher-capacity brakes than others, and vehicles towing big loads may need trailer brakes to help control the combined moving mass of both vehicles. Most states require trailer brakes for loads over 3,000 pounds. But five states—and many automakers—require trailer brakes on some models for loads over a piddling 1,000 pounds.

HEAVY-DUTY TIRES

Fat and thick tires with a wide tread area provide not only better traction, but a margin of safety where heavy loads are involved. They're recommended for towing by some manufacturers, and required by others.

POSSIBLE MANUFACTURER'S LIABILITY

Some automakers seem more sensitive than others to the possibility of lawsuits if something should go wrong while one of their cars is towing a trailer. I asked one corporate auto marketer, whose cars seemed to be at least the equal of other brands rated for 1,000 to 2,000 pounds, why his weren't recommended for towing at all. "In this day and age," he responded, "the whole hang-up is liability. We may change our minds later, but for now, we just don't want to take a chance."

The moral of this story is that, if you try towing a trailer without first checking your owner's manual and warranty, you could be in for big trouble. With the new closer-to-the-limit car designs, car makers say that towing a load that is too heavy might overheat and consequently damage the engine, transmission, and brakes, and could overstress tires, damage suspension, cause steering problems, or scrape the muffler and rear end as the car bottoms out on the road. And low-powered engines might mean having to slow down on grades to the point that the car

You will almost always find detailed trailer towing information in the owner's manual of a vehicle.

is a menace to traffic.

How can you avoid the problems of towing with an underrated vehicle? First figure out how much load you have to tow. Check your registration papers or sales literature for exact numbers, and don't forget to add a couple of hundred pounds for miscellaneous gear stowed aboard the boat while trailering. Then consult your vehicle dealer to find which cars are rated to tow how big a load, and which are not recommended for *any* towing.

Finally, be sure to use a car that is fully suited to the towing task at hand, as determined by the people who should know—the manufacturers. Judging from my experience, you can't always rely on what the salesman says. In my own research, I was given incorrect tow rating information by five different sales and customer service representatives for five different vehicle brands.

Consequently, your best bet is to check the manufacturer's literature rather than just asking the salesman. You will almost always find detailed trailer towing information in the owner's manual (usually available for study in the showroom simply for the asking), if it is not spelled out in the usual sales brochures on the racks in the showroom.

In summary: These days you can't assume that any heavy car with a big engine is suitable to tow a trailer. There are many factors beyond weight and power that affect towing capacity. But if you use care and diligence in picking your new tow car, you'll get years of boat-trailering pleasure in return.

—Steve Henkel
(*Boat Trailers and Tow Vehicles,*
International Marine, 1991)

The Tricks of Handling a Trailer

There's nothing complicated about a boat trailer; it is merely a device to haul your boat from point A to point B. Yet, often people who purchase trailers have no idea how to tow a boat safely. This becomes obvious when you are following a novice on the highway and see him struggling to keep both the trailer and the tow vehicle on the road.

Towing requires a completely different perspective by the driver. The total length of the rig is often two or three times longer than the family car, making normal driving tasks such as turning or entering the highway more complex. Additionally, the only thing you can see in your inside rearview mirror is not the traffic behind or the car you just passed but the bow of the boat, looking as if it is about to launch into the back seat.

Launching and loading create their own special problems, which can lead to some embarrassing, if not disastrous, moments on the launching ramp, from such minor events as jackknifing your trailer while backing up to the water to more spectacular feats such as backing your whole rig into the drink. There is hardly a veteran of trailer boating who hasn't forgotten to insert the drain plug before launching. In fact, this move is so common, you almost are *not* a veteran until you do it!

Though it is impossible to anticipate every trailering problem you might encounter, here are some procedures I've found useful for getting my rig safely to and from the water.

TOWING

While driving home on one of America's superhighways on any warm Sunday afternoon, you are apt to see one or more boats on trailers disabled on the shoulder of the road. Standing nearby will be an irate owner, steaming about a burned-out wheel bearing, a blown tire, or any number of other minor mishaps. Although the vast majority of these incidents are due to poor maintenance, at least 10 percent can be traced back to too light a trailer with too heavy a load.

Overloaded trailers tend to whip or swing wildly (also known as fishtailing) when traveling at turnpike speeds, a highly dangerous and potentially lethal situation. Therefore, the first questions you should be asking are what kind of equipment you will be hauling in the boat and how much does it all weigh. Then and only then can you make the correct decision on load capacity of the trailer needed to do the job.

A good rule of thumb is to calculate carefully the total weight of the boat, motor, accessories, fuel, batteries, water, and any other items placed on the boat while trailering. Add 33 percent to the total weight of the rig and you will have a good ballpark figure on what the trailer capacity should be. Adding this extra percentage compensates for factors such as rough road conditions or increased load from additional equipment.

Just because the trailer has the correct rating for the load you're carrying, don't assume that you can tow the rig at highway speeds without further considerations. A trailer must also have the correct tongue weight.

A critical safety link between the tow vehicle and trailer is the trailer's safety chain. Since the entire weight of the trailer and cargo will come down on this chain if the ball and hitch fail, be certain the chain is adequate in size, is well secured at both ends (hooks on the tow vehicle should face aft, as shown), and has sufficient slack for turning, and that the two chains cross one another to divide any shock equally. Chains with bent-wire links are rarely strong enough for this vital purpose.

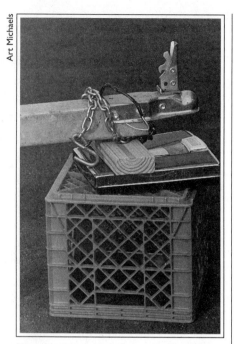

Tongue weight can have a major effect on handling. Here, a set of bathroom scales is used to check the weight of the tongue at the hitch.

If the tongue weight is too light or too heavy, the trailer will whip or sway when towed at high speeds and adversely affect the handling of your car. As a general rule, most manufacturers recommend that the tongue weight should be equal to at least 5 percent of the total weight, though percentages can range as high as 15 percent. It is always a good idea to follow the manufacturer's recommendations.

Setting the correct tongue weight is easy. Just place the tongue on a bathroom scale, loosen the winch post, and move the boat forward or backward while watching the scale. Once the correct weight is achieved, torque the winch-post bolts to the manufacturer's specifications. Also, check to see that there is still solid support at the transom.

Now that you've matched the trailer to the load and set the correct tongue weight, carefully look at the most important items between your rig and the road—the tires and wheel bearings. A blowout on a congested superhighway is likely the most haz-ardous towing situation you will ever face. Therefore, select the largest tires with the highest load rating that will fit your trailer. The benefit of purchasing larger tires becomes obvious on that first trip down the highway: Both the tires and the wheel bearings will be cool to the touch after several hours of trailering.

Low tire pressure can also cause a tire to overheat and blow out, so it is a good idea to check the inflation pressure regularly. A quality tire gauge is worth every cent you pay for it. Use it to check the tires while they are cold. When the tires are hot, the gauge will give a misleadingly high reading.

When a wheel bearing fails at highway speeds, just getting the rig off the road safely can be a hair-raising experience. Bearing protection devices (such as Bearing Buddies) are a worthwhile investment, but they are far from foolproof. Lubricate them frequently to prevent water and dirt from entering the bearings and causing undue wear. Also, inspect the seals at least once a season and remove and repack the bearings at the end of each year. The $15 to $20 fee for this service is a real bargain.

ROAD HANDLING

When passing another vehicle while towing a boat, use both sideview mirrors *only*. Before pulling out into the left lane of traffic, glance into the left side mirror to check for other vehicles. A blind-spot or convex-type mirror is extremely helpful in performing the maneuver. Then turn on your left signal to indicate your intention to move into the left lane, and pull out gradually. Once you are in the passing lane, gradually increase your speed. Don't put your pedal to the metal; the excessive acceleration may make controlling the rig difficult.

Once you pass a vehicle, turn on your right signal to indicate you want to get back into that lane. Be sure you are well beyond the car you have just overtaken by checking the right side mirror. If you have a blind-spot mirror on the right side, remember that objects in it will appear farther away than they really are. Then, after making sure you have ample room, *ease* the rig back to the right lane and turn off the signal.

The force of the wind can create extremely hazardous driving conditions for trailering boats. A boat substantially increases the surface area you must deal with, and a gust of wind coming from the side will produce a sail-like effect.

You can eliminate some of the problems caused by high winds by folding down Bimini tops and removing side curtains. But the best thing you can do to compensate for wind, as well as bad road conditions, is to *drive a bit slower*. Once your rig goes into a skid or starts to jackknife, there is little you can do to regain control. If you must drive slower than normal—when going up a steep hill, for instance—be sure to turn on your emergency flashers. Otherwise, drivers may assume your speed is close to the limit, and the result could be an expensive and dangerous rear-end collision.

Turning presents yet another problem. With the trailer in tow, you have more than doubled the total length of your rig. So, in order to make a turn, you must be sure the trailer wheels clear the curb by swinging the turn far wider than normal. If you are unsure about this procedure, practice making turns in a large parking lot while watching the position of the trailer tires in the sideview mirror. Because the average vehicle is about 6 feet wide and the average trailer 8 feet wide, the tires are usually visible and make good reference points when turning and backing.

Gary Diamond

A dry launch is possible with most roller-equipped trailers, even with a heavy rig like this Pro-Line. The trailer is backed into the water only to the edge of the wheel rims. The boat is then given a gentle shove, and it will float free, leaving all the vital trailer parts dry.

LAUNCHING

You can't launch or load or, for that matter, park a trailered boat without knowing how to back up. Yet, for many people, this is the most difficult task in trailering. With trailer in tow, you have not only doubled the length of your rig, but it now pivots in the middle. At first, the trailer may seem to have a mind of its own as it heads in the opposite direction from your steering. To overcome this problem, place your hand on the bottom of the steering wheel, and if you want the boat to go to the left, move your hand to the left; to go to the right, move your hand to the right. Again, the best place to practice trailer maneuvers is in a large (and preferably empty!) parking lot.

Backing up without having someone to guide you is always a risky business. Things like light poles, curbs, ditches, and even other vehicles have a way of appearing out of nowhere. Our advice is simple and forthright: If you must back up without help, *always* get out of the car and check the area before you go in reverse. Backing down a steep launching ramp without first checking is an open invitation to trouble. If you do have someone guiding you, station them on your side of the vehicle where you can see and hear them.

Though some trailers, such as self-loaders and carpeted bunk models, are designed to be submerged, some are intended only for freshwater use. If you have an all-roller trailer, there is no reason to submerge it. Yet, a large percentage of boaters put everything in the water including a portion of their tow vehicle. Submerging the trailer or car in salt water results in just one thing—its quick and untimely demise.

All-roller trailers are specifically designed to make launching and loading easy. Before backing down the ramp, tilt the motor, if you have one, to the full up position and lock it in place. Check to make sure the drain plug is properly secured in the boat and attach a suitable length of rope to the bow cleat. To launch, simply back the rig to the water's edge, submerging the tires only to the bottom of the rim. Then place a chock behind at least one of the rear wheels of the tow vehicle for safety, apply the parking brake, and shut off the engine (if your car has a manual shift, leave it in low forward gear; if it is an automatic shift, leave it in park). Then unhook the safety chain, take the bow line in hand, and give the bow a gentle shove. The craft will slowly roll from the trailer to the water without hitting bottom in the process. I've launched 25-foot powerboats all along the Eastern Seaboard and have yet to encounter

Art Michaels

In the wet launch method, the trailer is submerged for launching and hauling. Drawbacks include having to wade to handle the winch, sometimes having to submerge the after end of the tow vehicle, and accelerated corrosion of trailer frame and running gear.

Gary Diamond

Gary Diamond

In hauling, the bow is guided between the first two rollers and, in this case where the trailer is equipped with self-centering rollers, the boat is correctly positioned on the trailer. It is then simply a matter of reeling in with the winch. Again, there is no need to submerge the trailer's wheels.

any difficulties using this method.

By using the dry method of launching, you never get anything wet other than the bottom of your trailer tires. Wheel bearings, lights, rollers, and vital parts (including your feet) remain completely dry, allowing your trailer to live to a ripe old age.

LOADING

Loading your boat back on the trailer is no more difficult than launching. Again, only back the trailer to the water's edge—*don't submerge it.* Then position the bow of the boat between the first two rollers and begin

cranking the boat onto the trailer. Roller trailers are usually self-centering and will correctly position the boat as tension is applied to the winch cable. Naturally, a power winch makes the job of loading faster and easier, but even if you are limited to a manual winch, the job isn't too difficult. As a safety precaution, always stand to one side of the winch as you crank the boat onto the trailer. If the cable were to break under maximum tension, you could be seriously injured. Be sure to crank the boat all the way onto the trailer and firmly position it against the winch-post stops.

Then attach the safety chain and haul the boat away from the launching ramp so others may launch or load their boats. Finally, attach the tie-down straps, reposition the engine, and secure all the gear in the boat. Before you get in to drive away, make one last check all around the trailer and in the boat again; you'll be surprised how often you miss something that could cause you grief once underway. Now you can head home without any gnawing anxieties about wet wheel bearings, blown-out lights, or rusted roller bearings.

There are lots of advantages to trailering your own boat. Not only do you have peace of mind knowing your craft is safely stored at home, but you also have a tremendous advantage over larger boats that are moored at a marina and therefore have limited cruising range. Given a little bit of preventive maintenance and used with a fair dollop of common sense, your trailer will likely outlive its owner. Abuse that same trailer, and you could be the next irate person standing on the shoulder of the highway on a hot Sunday afternoon.

—Gary Diamond
(*Small Boat Journal* #61)

Hitch & Ball, Inc.

If your tow vehicle doesn't already have one, you will need to buy a hitch and ball and either install them yourself or have it done for you.

Hitches, couplers, and balls all use the same capacity system as shown in the accompanying table: Class I for towing loads up to 2,000 pounds, Class II for 2,000 to 3,500 pounds, Class III for 3,500 to 5,000 pounds, and Class IV for 5,000 to 10,000 pounds. There is also a "fifth-wheel" hitch that can be set into the bed of a truck over or forward of the rear wheels to carry even more weight than a Class IV frame hitch. But fifth-wheel hitches are for extremely large boats—and beyond the scope of this book.

I recommend installing a hitch that is strong enough to match or exceed the manufacturer's rated maximum towing capacity for your vehicle. That way, if you move up in boat size before you replace the vehicle, you won't be forced to replace your frame hitch.

The strength of a frame hitch depends not only on its material and construction but also on the strength of the tow vehicle body and frame. Smaller hitches sometimes attach to the back bumper as well as to the frame, immobilizing the so-called crash-resistant or "5-m.p.h." bumper and thus preventing the slight yield-

Trailer and Hitch Class	General Category	Maximum Capacity Towing Weight t.w. (lbs.)	Tongue Weight (percent of t.w.)	Type of Hitch	Typical Tow-Vehicle Attachment Points
Class I	Light duty	2,000	10%	Fixed ball platform	Bumper plus two points on frame
Class II	Regular duty	3,500	10%	Fixed ball platform	Bumper plus two points on frame
Class III	Heavy duty	3,500 to 5,000	10%	Receiver type	Four or more points on frame
Class IV	Extra-heavy duty	5,000 to 10,000	10%	Receiver type	Four or more points on frame

Trailer and Hitch Classes and Capacities

A neat solution to the problem of needing more than one size ball for your trailer hitch is the Convert-A-Ball hitch system. A single shank is bolted to the bumper or receiver. A 1⅞-inch or 2-inch ball can be mounted on the shank with a steel pin that is attached to the ball, thus eliminating the need to bolt on a solid ball each time a different size is needed.

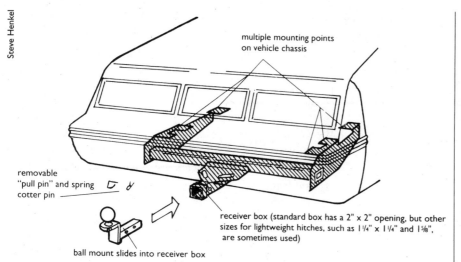

multiple mounting points
on vehicle chassis

removable
"pull pin" and spring
cotter pin

receiver box (standard box has a 2" x 2" opening, but other
sizes for lightweight hitches, such as 1¼" x 1¼" and 1⅝",
are sometimes used)

ball mount slides into receiver box

A receiver-type hitch lets you remove the ball mount when it is not in use or when you want to change ball sizes.

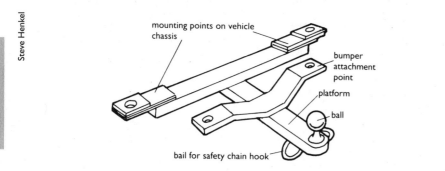

mounting points on vehicle
chassis

bumper
attachment
point

platform

ball

bail for safety chain hook

A fixed-platform hitch is designed for lightweight duty only, but since it is bolted to the rear bumper, mounting it immobilizes the "5-mph" bumper shock-absorbing feature of modern passenger cars.

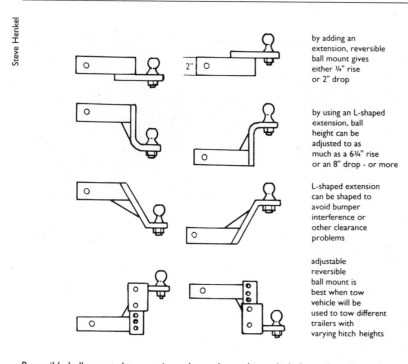

by adding an
extension, reversible
ball mount gives
either ¾" rise
or 2" drop

by using an L-shaped
extension, ball
height can be
adjusted to as
much as a 6¾" rise
or an 8" drop - or more

L-shaped extension
can be shaped to
avoid bumper
interference or
other clearance
problems

adjustable
reversible
ball mount is
best when tow
vehicle will be
used to tow different
trailers with
varying hitch heights

Reversible ball mounts let you raise or lower the angle at which the trailer will travel.

ing on impact that is designed to help protect the vehicle body. If that is the only type of hitch that will fit your vehicle, you have no choice, but it's better to use a frame-only hitch, so the bumper can function in collisions as it was designed to do.

If you opt for a small, lightweight Class I hitch (perhaps out of necessity if you have a small, lightweight car), you may be able to bolt it on yourself. Heavy-duty hitches are more complicated and difficult to attach, so if you are thinking of a big hitch, I recommend hiring a commercial hitch installer to do the job. U-Haul, the nation's biggest hitch installer, can do it for you; so can any dealer for Eaz-Lift, Draw-Tite, Reese, Da'Lan, or one of a number of hitch manufacturers. You can get addresses and telephone numbers for dealers in your area from the Yellow Pages, or you can try your own auto mechanic. It's likely to be quicker and maybe safer to use someone who specializes in hitches.

I recommend buying a receiver-type hitch rather than a fixed-platform type, even for light-duty service. With the receiver type, you can remove the ball platform or "hitch bar" (also sometimes called the *drawbar*) and store it inside the vehicle when not in use. That keeps it out of the weather, forestalls rust, and prevents theft of your ball (another favorite target of waterfront thieves). Moreover, if you are a certified boat nut like me and have two or more trailers with different-size couplers (such as a 1⅞-inch size on one trailer and a 2-inch size on another), and perhaps different hitch height requirements as well, you can carry a variety of ball/platform combinations to suit your changing needs.

There are several ways to adjust hitch ball height after your frame hitch is installed, so that your boat and trailer will ride on the level

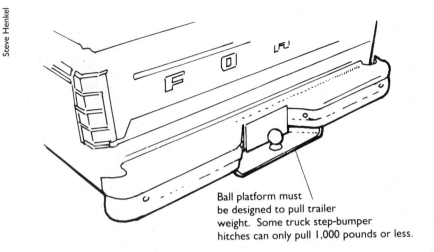

Ball platform must be designed to pull trailer weight. Some truck step-bumper hitches can only pull 1,000 pounds or less.

The step-bumper hitch, often called a step 'n tow, is common on pickup trucks.

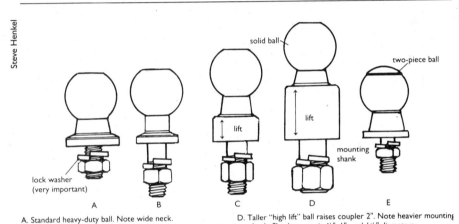

lock washer (very important)

A   B   C   D   E

solid ball

two-piece ball

lift

lift

mounting shank

A. Standard heavy-duty ball. Note wide neck.
B. Standard light- or medium-duty ball. Note narrower neck.
C. "High lift" ball raises coupler 1".
D. Taller "high lift" ball raises coupler 2". Note heavier mounting shank. Shanks come in ¾", 1", and 1¼" diameters.
E. Two-piece ball - not recommended except for lightest loads.

Hitch balls come in a variety of types and sizes.

rather than bow-up or bow-down. To raise or lower the ball on the tow vehicle, you can (1) try replacing the frame hitch with a lower or higher one (not usually a practical option—most hitches for a given vehicle will be about the same height); (2) use a "high-lift" ball to change the ball height of an existing hitch; or (3) in conjunction with a receiver-type hitch, use a "step-up," "step-down," or "two-way" ball mount to adjust the ball height. That way you can change the height of your ball by 1 to 6 inches or more. A fourth option is to use a step-up coupler on the trailer, which works well when towing with, say, a high-chassis truck or sport utility vehicle (SUV).

Step-bumper hitches are sometimes mounted on the rear bumpers of pickup trucks. Sometimes the standard step bumper is comparatively light-duty (under 1,000 pounds of towing capacity or even less), and an optional, beefed-up bumper may be ordered to increase trailer towing capacity.

—Steve Henkel
(*Boat Trailers and Tow Vehicles*,
International Marine, 1991)

Troubleshooting Your Light System

Water and electricity don't mix. Hence, mostly as a result of their occasional immersion in water, boat-trailer lights, wires, and plugs sooner or later tend to malfunction. The end result is always the same: the lights flicker or go out. But the causes vary. Here are some common electrical problems and their solutions.

Individual Light Bulbs Burn Out Frequently That's often because the glass bulbs are hot from use during the trip to the launching ramp, and when they hit the cold water at the ramp, they crack or break. Even "submersible" lights generally are not waterproof, and they may let in enough water to kill bulbs.

There are three good solutions to this problem. First, you can buy a truly waterproof light set. As of this writing, Wesbar's encapsulated unit is the only one I am aware of that is fully waterproof. Second, you might build a trailer "light bar," which can

be mounted on top of your boat during travel and removed before launching (see "Building a Long-lasting Light Bar," page 128). Third, you could put your lights on high guide bars or "stalks" to keep them high and dry. A fourth approach won't solve the problem but may help to lengthen the time between burnouts; that is to disconnect your light plug upon arrival, then wait a half hour or so until the trailer bulbs have cooled off. If none of these so-

Building a Long-lasting Light Bar

Keeping trailer lights in working order is a constant hassle, particularly so if you submerge the light system when launching or retrieving your boat. In his piece on troubleshooting trailer lights, Steve Henkel mentions one alternative: a "light bar." Such a device is easily built by anyone handy with tools and will solve nearly all of your trailer light problems. (Note we say "nearly all"; anything electrical can fail, and at the end of this piece we offer a solution for when all is darkness and there is no light.)

A light bar is nothing more than a basic trailer lighting system mounted on a 2 x 4. The rig is tied to the gunwales near the after end of your boat and plugged into the plug on the tow vehicle. The bar is removed before you launch the boat, stored in your vehicle, tied on again after you have hauled out, and left in place on the boat until your next trip or removed and stored when you get home. We have three trailers (two boat and one utility) and two tow vehicles, and we use the same light bar with all our rolling stock. Talk about reducing frustration!

The bar wants to be as long as the beam of your boat plus about 4 to 6 inches extra on each side. We used a 2 x 4 for the bar; you could also use a 1 x 6 or the like. Anything lighter or narrower can be broken easily, or may have a tendency to roll on its axis because of the weight of the lights.

We used 1- x ⅛-inch aluminum bar to make the simple light brackets. We then attached two taillights purchased in an autoparts store and hooked them up with standard four-wire flat cable used for wiring trailers (see diagram). A standard four-prong flat plug was wired in at the tow vehicle end of the cable. If

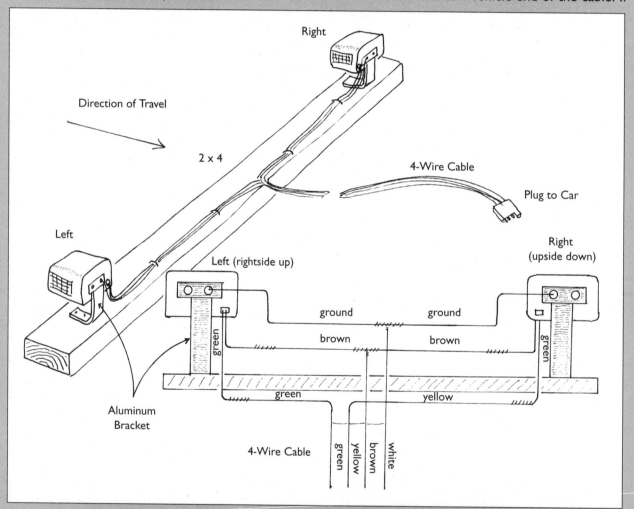

Standard auto taillights are identical, so one has to be upside down. Short green and brown wires extend from body of each light; left green is spliced to cable green; right green is spliced to cable yellow. All browns are spliced together. Attach a single white ground wire to retaining nuts on light brackets and splice into cable white ground.

you find buying the various pieces needed confusing, complete taillight kits can be bought from trailer dealers, many marine stores, and mail-order houses. The BOAT/U.S. catalog, for example, offers a light kit that includes lights, wire harness, and trunk connector for $19.95.

When you complete your bar, just check to see that all the lights (directional, brake, and tail) work, and repeat the checking process every time you hook it up. Things very rarely go wrong, but if they do, it is a piece of cake to troubleshoot this rig. (The biggest problem when one or more light circuits does not work is usually nothing more than dirt and/or corrosion on the plugs, both male and female. Clean these and be sure they are solidly seated before trying to do anything else.)

Durable? The light bar we have now, used regularly on all three trailers, has lasted for 10 years. I put on new lights last year, not because the old ones weren't working, but because they were starting to show their age.

Our boat is aluminum, so we lay the bar directly on the gunwales and tie it to the seat braces with rubber bands made from bicycle inner tubes.

There are a couple of things to watch out for when using a light bar. First, the cable is long, and since it is exposed, you must be careful that it doesn't bounce over the side of the boat and drag on the road. This can shred it and short it out in no time—I know from experience. Second, where the cable goes over the bow and down past the winch to the tow-vehicle plug, it must be secured to the winch post, again so that it will not drag on the ground. Leave enough slack between trailer and vehicle to compensate for turns.

Finally, there will probably come a time when your trailer light system breaks down on the road at night and you won't have the means to fix it. Handy at this time is a plain old flashlight with a piece of red plastic secured over the lens with a rubber band or a piece of string. Tie this to the left rear corner of your boat with the light facing aft. If the light has fresh batteries in it, it will last for a couple of hours or more and will help keep following cars and the highway patrol from running into you.

—DRG

lutions appeals to you, you can always carry a bunch of spares and continue to replace the bulbs at frequent intervals.

Light Sockets Corrode, Causing Lights to Operate Intermittently, or Flicker, or Go Out
Any of the solutions for bulb burnouts is likely to help here, too. Another fix is a regular program of cleaning the corrosion off the contacts in the socket and then smearing the contacts on both socket and bulb with a little grease or petroleum jelly. To determine whether the socket is the problem, use a voltmeter/ohmmeter, available at Radio Shack for less than $10 the last time I looked. Simply remove the lens and bulb from the suspected socket, connect the trailer wiring to the tow vehicle, turn the trailer lights on, switch the meter to "50 VDC" (volts), and press the prods against the two contact points inside the socket. If you get a steady voltage reading even when you wiggle the prods around a bit, the socket

> *Poor ground connections are the most common source of boat-trailer electrical difficulties.*

is probably not the problem; try changing bulbs to known good ones. If you get an intermittent voltage reading, the socket probably *is* the problem. Try cleaning up the contacts, or replace the socket. If you get no reading at all, try wiggling the wires behind the socket; maybe there's a loose connection back there.

An Open Circuit Develops, Causing Lights to Go Out This could be from a broken terminal point, such as at a light fixture, trailer-to-tow-vehicle plug, or ground connection point, or it could be from a broken wire. The first place to look is at all ground terminals; *poor ground connections are the most common source of boat-trailer electrical difficulties.* Do not rely on the coupler connection with the tow vehicle ball to make a good circuit to ground; it won't. Instead, carry a ground wire through the plug from the tow vehicle, and extend it all the way back to the taillights, clipping it right into the lighting circuit as well as the trailer's steel frame. Then you won't have to worry about whether the steel frame is doing its job as a conductor, since the wire is also doing the same job, and better.

If terminal points are not the source of your problem, you'll have to search along the connecting wires for faults. Because wire insulation can sometimes remain intact even when the conductor inside is broken, it can be difficult to pinpoint the site of an open-circuit problem. But if you inspect every inch of wire carefully, you'll eventually rout out the fault.

Wiring Develops a Short Circuit The chief source of boat-trailer short circuits is chafed wires pinching against the trailer frame or against each other, and eventually wearing through their insulation. To establish that there is a short circuit in the first place, use the volt/ohm-meter switched to "ohms," a measure of electrical resistance. Note that when the two prods touch each other, the needle swings all the way over the scale to zero ohms (no resistance), indicating there's a short circuit between the prods. If the needle doesn't move at all (shows an infinite resistance) when you place the prods on two contact points on a wire, it means there's an open circuit between the two points.

With the trailer power plug disconnected, place one prod on "ground" and the other on each of the three plug prongs in turn. The meter should show a high (but not infinitely high) resistance, since the high-resistance light bulb filaments are part of the circuit. If the resistance between prongs is close to zero, there is a short in the circuit.

Turn Signals Blink Too Fast, and/or Flasher Unit in Tow Vehicle Burns Out Frequently You need a heavy-duty flasher for

your vehicle. They are available in most autoparts stores.

Plug Already Installed on Trailer Won't Mate with Plug Already Installed on Tow Vehicle You can replace one or the other plug with one that does mate, or buy an adapter plug that mates with both halves.

Wesbar, for instance, sells two versions of a "round-to-flat" four-pin adapter.

If you are replacing a plug, be careful to match the colors of the wires, which have been standardized for boat-trailer use. See the accompanying wiring diagram for information on which color is supposed to go

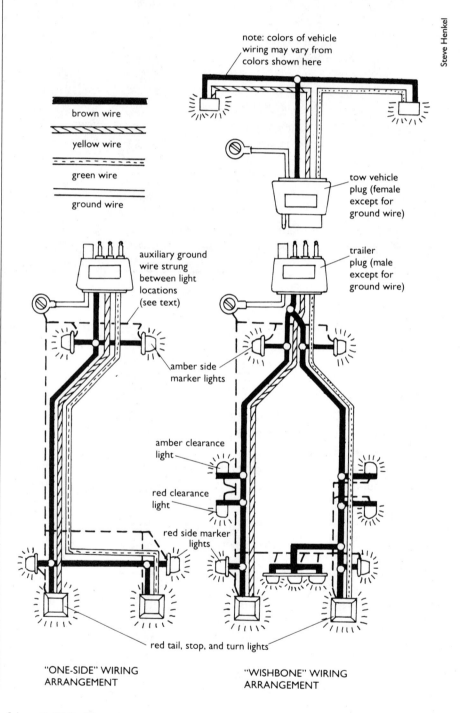

note: colors of vehicle wiring may vary from colors shown here

brown wire

yellow wire

green wire

ground wire

tow vehicle plug (female except for ground wire)

auxiliary ground wire strung between light locations (see text)

trailer plug (male except for ground wire)

amber side marker lights

amber clearance light

red clearance light

red side marker lights

red tail, stop, and turn lights

"ONE-SIDE" WIRING ARRANGEMENT

"WISHBONE" WIRING ARRANGEMENT

Schematic Wiring Diagram

Steve Henkel

where. If you are hooking up lights on a new trailer or tow vehicle, the diagram and accompanying notes should give you all you need to know to do the job.

Tow Vehicle Has Turn-Signal Light Circuit Separate from Brake Light Circuit If, for example, you have amber blinkers but red brake lights, you'll need to buy a taillight "black box" converter, available from Cole-Hersee, Shelby Industries, Wesbar, and a number of other suppliers.

Turn-Signal Lights on Tow Vehicle Don't Flash Simultaneously with Trailer Lights Try reversing the yellow and green leads at the connector plug. Make sure that the brown leads from each side of the plug are mated, and that the white ground wire is solidly grounded on both sides of the plug.

After a Short Circuit Is Found and Fixed, Neither Trailer nor Tow Vehicle Lights Work Check the lighting fuse in the tow vehicle. (See your vehicle's owner's manual for location.) It is probably burned out.

—Steve Henkel
(*Boat Trailers and Tow Vehicles,*
International Marine, 1991)

The Critical Wheel Bearings

Conventional wisdom calls for repacking boat trailer wheels with grease at least once a year, and more often if hubs are frequently immersed in salt water. As part of this repacking process, you can inspect bearings, grease seals, and axles, and replace anything that needs replacing. For a view of what you're getting into, see the accompanying illustration. There are a dozen steps in the repacking procedure, as described below.

1. *Jack up wheel.* Working on a level surface, and preferably with no boat on the trailer, raise one trailer wheel off the ground by putting a jack under the axle. Before jacking, chock the wheel or wheels on the other side to prevent rolling. On empty tandem trailers, you may be able to elevate one set of wheels without the use of a jack simply by depressing the tongue as low as it will go to raise the back axle, or raising it as high as possible to elevate the front axle.

Many axles are hollow tubes, which after a time begin rusting, sometimes from the inside out, thus weakening the skin. Therefore, if you use a jack with a small cross-sectional area at the end of its ram, place a pad such as a short length of 2 x 4 between axle and jack to help prevent crushing the axle surface.

2. *Clean up work site and prepare hub.* Wipe the tire, wheel, and hub clean of road dust, dried mud, and grease at both front side and back. That way there's less chance of dirt getting into the hub innards during the regreasing process.

You can either remove the tire and rim from the hub or leave them in place. Removing them gives you a little more space to work in, but if the hub resists being pulled off, being able to grab the edges of the tire will give you extra leverage.

After cleaning up the area and removing the tire and rim, if you choose to do so, spread clean newspapers on the ground below the hub so that if the hub or bearings inadvertently fall to the ground during disassembly they won't pick up new dust or dirt. The newspaper also gives you a clean place to lay out your tool kit.

3. *Remove bearing protector or dust cover.* If you haven't already discarded your old dust covers and installed a set of bearing protectors, I strongly recommend that you switch to them now. The protector (or dust cover) is a press fit into the hub. The easiest way to get it off is to hold a piece of softwood (such as a

Wheel hub and bearings require regular maintenance (once or twice a season, at least) if they are to survive frequent immersion in water. If you "dry launch" without putting the hubs in the water, the bearings will last for years.

2 x 4) against the top outer edge of the protector and tap gently with a hammer, spinning the wheel and working gradually around the perimeter of the hub. This will inch the protector outboard, and eventually it will be loose enough to pull off by hand. Alternatively, you can wedge a broad-bladed screwdriver between the hub and the inboard edge of the protector and pry it off by twisting the screwdriver blade and working gradually around the perimeter. If it is not pushed on too tightly, you might also be able to wiggle it off using a pair of channel-lock pliers clamped along its axis.

4. Remove cotter pin and spindle nut. Wipe the grease off and inspect the pieces. See if the cotter pin is beginning to get mangled; if so, replace it. The spindle nut may be loose enough to start by hand; otherwise, Vise-Grips should be enough.

5. Remove thrust washer, outer bearing cone, and hub. To do this, grasp the tire (or edge of the hub if you've removed the tire and wheel) on both sides, tilt the top slightly toward you, and pull toward you just a bit. Your purpose is to dislodge the thrust washer and outer bearing cone, which you can then lift out, clean up, and set aside. If a gentle pull doesn't do the job, apply more pressure, but avoid pulling so hard that the bearing pops off onto the ground. Usually the inner cone and seal will then slide off. If they don't, try jerking a second time. If you still have no luck, try tapping the hub assembly off from the back side—but be sure not to dent or score the seal, which is made from thin, pressed steel. If the hub still doesn't come off, you might need a wheel puller. Before using one, remove the tire and rim from the hub if you haven't already done so, so the wheel puller can get a grip on

the outer edge of the hub. If you don't have a wheel puller and the hub just won't slide off, it may be time to reinstall the wheel and let your local mechanic handle the rest of the job.

Assuming you successfully remove the hub, array the parts on newspaper, being careful not to mix up either the outboard bearing cone or the race with its inboard counterpart.

6. Remove grease seal and inboard cone from hub. The best way to do this is to place the hub or rim flat on two parallel blocks of wood, with the seal and cone at the bottom and clean newspapers spread out underneath. After wiping away the grease in the hole in the hub, shove a piece of wood (such as a hammer handle) into the hole, set its end on the face of the inner cone, and tap gently around the perimeter until the grease seal and cone pop out onto the newspapers.

7. Clean off grease and examine all parts. After wiping away the main body of grease with paper towels, you can use kerosene, diesel fuel, or most commercial solvents to dissolve whatever grease remains on any of the pieces you have removed. Avoid gasoline or other highly flammable materials. Wipe all parts clean with paper towels. After cleaning the bearings, spin the rollers in the cones to see if they are free-turning. Examine all parts for rust, pitting, scoring, heat discoloration, or other signs that they need replacing. Check the grease seal for rust and to be sure it's not pitted, scored, bent, or dented,

and that rubber parts aren't torn, frayed, or old and embrittled. A good rule is to replace the seals automatically whenever repacking the hubs, to lessen the chance of grease leaking out onto the axle (and water leaking in) through an imperfect seal.

If the axle spindle itself is pitted, badly worn, or scored, it may be a sign that a bearing has frozen and the inner race has been rotating on the spindle rather than on its rollers. You can carefully file off any slight bumps on the spindle, using emery cloth to finish the job.

If the seal surface on the rear of the spindle is roughened by rust, scoring, or pitting (resulting in a poor mating surface with the seal), you can usually repair it with a Bearing Buddy Spindo Seal Kit, available from Unique Functional Products (135 Sunshine Lane, San Marcos, CA 92069; 619-744-1610). The kit includes a stainless steel collar that fits over the damaged spindle, plus a special O-ring and replacement seal sized to the changed diameter of the spindle.

8. If a bearing needs replacement, remove the race from the inside of the hub. Even if only one of the two bearings appears to need changing, consider replacing both; otherwise, the second one is bound to wear out soon. Be sure to buy exact duplicates. A size designation is usually engraved on the side of the bearing rim to help you match new with old. Also, know that bearings are always replaced as a unit; i.e., the race and the mating bearing cone. Never attempt to "mix and match" parts from different bearings.

To remove a race (which is a press fit in the hub), tap it out using the same technique as for the grease seal.

9. Repack bearings with grease and begin reassembly. Reinstall

> *Even if only one of the two bearings appears to need changing, consider replacing both; otherwise, the second one is bound to wear out soon.*

both inner and outer races, if removed, by tapping them back into place. Then clean your hands to make sure you don't contaminate the new grease with dust and grime. Hold a gob of premium-quality wheel-bearing grease in the palm of your hand, drop the inner bearing cone into it, and knead the grease until it permeates the insides of the cage (the space between rollers). If you don't want to handle messy grease directly, fill a plastic Baggie with grease, drop the cone in, and knead from the outside. When the inner cone is saturated, set it in its race. Then tap the grease seal gently into the inner side of the hub using a softwood block or rubber hammer to obtain even pressure around the seal's perimeter. Fill the hub with enough new grease to prevent massive air pockets when the hub is installed. Then slip the hub over the spindle.

10. *Finish reassembly. Install a grease-packed outer bearing cone, the thrust washer, and the castle nut (or drilled nut, or hex nut with a keeper) that fits over the end of the threaded spindle.* Then begin the bearing adjustment process.

When the nut is hand-tight, spin the wheel and tighten the nut some more until the hub just begins to bind as it turns. Now grab the two sides of the tire or hub and wiggle and push to be sure the hub is firmly seated. Again spin the wheel, and tighten the nut once more until the hub just starts to bind. When you're sure the nut (and nothing else, such as the tire dragging slightly on the ground) is causing the hub to bind slightly, back off one notch (or one hole or one flat)

A good rule is to replace the seals automatically whenever repacking the hubs.

on the nut. The wheel and hub should now spin easily and smoothly; if the hub still binds a little, back off another notch (or hole, or flat). Shake and wiggle the wheel again to be sure there is practically no play. When you're fully satisfied that the bearing is adjusted for smooth operation but doesn't have excess play, put the cotter pin or keeper in place.

Daub the bearing protector almost full with new grease, and smear the mating surfaces with more grease so the protector will slide in easier.

Even smeared with grease, it should be a tight fit if it is the right size for the hub. Tap it carefully into place using a wood block to protect it from damage. Check to be sure it's fully seated.

If you are installing a cap rather than a bearing protector as recommended, leave some air space for expansion rather than filling the cap with grease.

Pump the protector with a grease gun until the piston moves off its seat almost but not quite to the top. At that point, stop adding grease, so that the piston can push out a little more when the hub heats up during travel and the grease inside expands.

11. *Lower wheel to ground and remove jack and chocks.* This process is the reverse of Step 1.

12. *Clean up.* Wipe off any excess grease from the hub or bearing protector; install a grease cover such as the plastic covers sold for the purpose, or a sandwich bag secured with a couple of rubber bands. Wipe off your tools, and go boating!

—Steve Henkel
(*Boat Trailers and Tow Vehicles,*
International Marine, 1991)

ELECTRONICS

Introduction

We live in an electronic age. The average household plays host to a dozen or more solid-state gadgets and machines that rely solely on the ethereal workings of printed circuitry, spinning disks, and glowing CRTs. Not surprisingly, the transistor has now taken to the water, in force. Whether it is a simple weather radio or an awesome GPS (Global Positioning System) receiver, the electronic machine has been adapted and strengthened to operate reliably in the marine environment.

Probably the greatest test of the durability of an electronic device is to use it aboard a small boat, where wetness and rough handling are a way of life. Given this fact, a skipper must temper the desire for transistorized goodies with the reality that one can buy a lot of expensive equipment that may never be used before it recycles itself. The reasoning behind this is simple: a shallow-draft boat that spends all its time close to shore just doesn't need Loran, radar, GPS, and the rest of the marine electronics alphabet.

Two electronic devices that can prove useful, however, are a radio and a depthsounder. Still popular among coastal and lake fishermen for close-in gabbing, CB (Citizens Band) radio has been pretty much superseded for general use by VHF (Very High Frequency) radio. With the advent of rugged little hand-held models, reliable radio communication is now available for just about any small boat.

> Probably the greatest test of the durability of an electronic device is to use it aboard a small boat, where wetness and rough handling are a way of life.

Depthfinders, too, have been toughened up for small-boat use, and the number of LCD (liquid crystal display) fish finders, digital sounders, chart recorders, and similar machines is amazing. Best of all, most of them can be had in the $100 to $500 range, an amazing reduction in price from just a few years ago.

The sportfishing market has been the big incentive for depthsounder manufacturers to weatherize their products, but any small-boat skipper can enjoy the benefits of knowing what is below the keel. Several companies even offer a portable sounder with LCD screen that is contained in its own carrying case so that it can be taken home or used on rental boats.

Portability means that electronic gadgetry is a prime target for thieves. Some boat manufacturers have addressed this problem by designing lockable cabinets that protect your electronics from the wiles of both the weather and the rip-off artists. Some of these storage compartments have glass or Lexan covers that permit use without having to move any equipment around. Anyone handy with tools can build such a compartment for his or her own boat. But we still recommend that you take your valuable machines home with you if you must leave your boat at a dock or mooring.

—DRG

A VHF at Your Beck and Call

While VHF radios have long been an essential part of the electronics array of large pleasure boats and commercial vessels, they are now finding their way aboard more and more small boats. Lower prices and smaller sizes have even made VHFs vital safety equipment on boats as small as kayaks.

If there's a medical emergency on board and you need to summon help or have help ready when you arrive in port, what can be more effective than explaining the problem via radio?

Small-boat users are also recognizing VHF's versatility as a communications tool. VHF enables you to talk with approaching vessels to ensure safe passing, signal drawbridge and lock operators, contact marinas to arrange for repairs or supplies, or even call home through a shore-based marine telephone operator. Although the marine VHF-FM (Very High Frequency, 156.0 to 162.55 MHz) radiotelephone has been in use for more than 15 years, a lot of boaters don't really understand what VHF is all about. Every so often I hear "10-4" and other 10-signals, indicating that there is still confusion with the CB (Citizen's Band 26.9 to 27.3 MHz) channels, a hopelessly clogged and unregulated mess unsuitable for boaters.

VHF actually replaced the much older and bulkier HF-AM (High Frequency, 2.5 to 3.0 MHz) band. HF had a range that often extended hundreds of miles under the right conditions, particularly at night, clogging up both nearby and distant receivers. And only a couple of HF channels were available.

By comparison, VHF has at least 55 transmit/receive channels, and more may come in the future. But its range is limited to about 20 miles with other boats and 50 miles with shore stations. The range for hand-held units is even smaller.

For the skipper who needs long-distance communications, a single-sideband (SSB) system is available. And in order to avoid the same problems that occurred with HF, the FCC has imposed a requirement that no vessel can install SSB without first installing short-range VHF. As a result, short- and long-range communication is now better than ever. This VHF/SSB system does have shortcomings, though. Reliable medium-range communication between boats—say 30 to 50 miles—is lacking. Also, VHF doesn't make it over land very well. Nevertheless, VHF is the marine radiotelephone system we'll have to live with for the foreseeable future. And there are ways we can make it cover the necessary distance.

The maximum power for VHF is 25 watts—the power of most permanent-mount units. Exceeding that wattage is illegal and won't help significantly anyway except in very limited situations. That is because VHF signals travel in straight lines rather than bouncing off the ionosphere as SSB radio waves do, so VHF's range is limited by the horizon. That's also why VHF is called a *line-of-sight* system.

More important than transmitter output wattage is using the right antenna system. Buying the most expensive VHF transceiver and then saving a few bucks on a bargain-

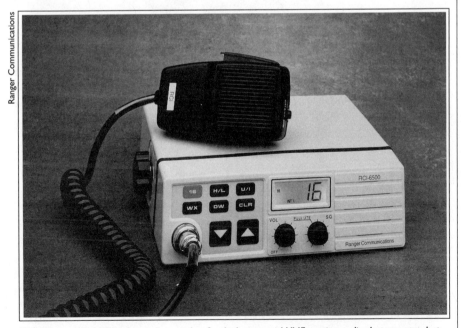

Ranger Communications

The Ranger RCI 6500 is a good example of a dash-mounted VHF marine radio that can stand up to the rugged demands of small-boat use. Priced at about $350, the unit is encased in a weather-resistant housing.

basement antenna is like buying the best stereo system and hooking it up to tinny speakers. There are four factors that significantly affect your antenna's performance: location, elevation, gain, and cable.

An antenna should be installed at least 3 feet away from any other antenna or metallic object that can interfere with its radiation pattern and on the highest elevation practical for your boat. Height is especially important, because VHF signals travel in straight lines. You can get a good approximation of your antenna's theoretical straight-line "horizon" by multiplying the square root of your antenna's height in feet by 1.75. This gives the theoretical distance in miles (i.e., a 16-foot antenna would have a 7-mile horizon). Now add the horizon for the antenna of the boat you wish to contact, and that will be the theoretical maximum distance apart the boats can be and still talk to each other.

There are exceptions to this rule. Increased range is possible during periods of temperature inversion, when the temperature is slightly higher a short distance above the ground or water surface. Extra range is also possible when the lower layer of the air near the water is exceptionally moist, such as during periods of little or no wind, or during warm months when the sun heats the water. Any of these situations cause much of the VHF's radio frequency (RF) energy to be "ducted" or channeled for surprising distances, even over land.

The best time to take advantage of these phenomena is during the early morning hours, shortly after sunrise. Under the right circumstance, stations more than 100 miles away can be heard clearly even by boats with low antennas. Because some mild "ducting" conditions almost always exist, the theoretical transmission range is often more than doubled—providing the system is operating efficiently.

On small, open fishing boats, especially those with center or side consoles, the antenna often gets in the way of casting. To overcome this difficulty, the skipper has two choices: He can opt for a long antenna mounted on the gunwale where it can lie flat when not in use, or he can go for a short (36-inch or less) antenna on the console that is always upright but doesn't have the height or gain, and therefore the range, of the longer antenna when raised.

Though VHF antennas are omnidirectional (their waves radiate in all directions), they concentrate their signals or sensitivity horizontally. The amount of horizontal concentration, or radiation compression, is called *gain*, and is measured in decibels (dB). The most basic antenna with no gain is called a *unity*, or *zero decibel* (0-dB), antenna. The next step up in performance is a 3-dB antenna, which makes 25 watts perform like 50. Then there is a 6-dB antenna, and finally even a 9-dB antenna. Each 3-dB increase has the same effect as doubling the wattage. Thus, a 25-watt transceiver hooked up to a 9-dB antenna would perform like a 200-watt unit with a 0-dB antenna.

Though that may sound great, there is an unwanted side effect to radiation compression. The 0-dB antenna radiates around its entire axis in a pattern that's almost like a donut with the antenna in the center of the hole. But the higher the gain, the

The hand-held VHF transceiver has made reliable radio communications available to the smallest of boats. The Standard Communications Horizon Hand-Phone 6, shown here in its leather carrying case, is a powerful 6-watt radio containing all U.S., Canadian, and international channels. It is heavily gasketed and sealed to protect it from water and weather. Listing at $660, it can frequently be purchased in the $350 range.

more this radiation pattern is squashed until it radiates around the antenna in a tight beam. It's like comparing a floodlight and a spotlight of the same candle power.

The disadvantage of excessively high gain through radiation compression comes from the boat's tendency to rock in choppy seas. The swaying of the antenna causes the signal to be squirted far above the horizon, out into space where no one is listening, or aimed into the water, where it is quickly lost. That's why sailboats typically use only 3-foot, 3-dB-gain antennas, whereas small powerboats can use 9-foot, 6-db-gain antennas.

Finally, the coaxial cable that connects your transceiver is important. A coaxial cable is a transmission line with an insulated central conductor surrounded by an insulated outside conductor. Because it has more cross-sectional area of conductor to carry current, larger coaxial cable will offer radio energy less resistance with less loss than will smaller cable. For example, RG-58AU or RG-58A/U coax (both ¼-inch diameter) should not be more than 20 feet long or it will cause quite a bit of signal loss. If more than 20 feet separates your transmitter and antenna, use RG-8/X or RG-8X coax (slightly more than ⅜-inch diameter), because it has a much lower signal loss per foot.

A saltwater environment sooner or later causes all sorts of corrosion damage that can severely hinder your transceiver's performance. This is especially true of the antenna cable and its connectors. Even though the exterior insulation may look perfect, if

> *More important than transmitter output wattage is using the right antenna system.*

any moisture finds its way inside, the cable's electric properties will be altered to such an extent that performance will suffer considerably. That is why the purchase of the high-quality cable is money well spent. Cable with a PVC jacket and dielectric core, properly terminated and sealed with silicone, is more moisture resistant than plastic-jacketed cable. It is not advisable to substitute TV or CB coax for VHF cable.

If your boat is already carrying a 12-volt battery, it makes sense to consider installing permanent-mount VHF.

For other boats, including small outboards, kayaks, and rowboats, a hand-held VHF is the obvious choice. Operation is basically the same, though these units have considerably less transmitter power, and their short antennas limit their range. Still, most VHF hand-helds are 3 watts and a few are 5 watts. Even those with 1 watt are designed to operate within a 20-mile boat-to-shore-range, sufficient for most boaters. For additional range, most will hook up to an external antenna. By the way, all VHFs, whether 3 watts or 25, must have a low-power switch (1 watt).

Hand-helds require periodic recharging to keep them operating. Also, it is a good idea to keep them in a specially made watertight plastic bag to protect them from the weather or an accidental plunge into the water.

Although size and cost once kept marine radios out of the small boat, this is no longer the case. There are now permanent-mount models no larger than a book, and hand-held models are even smaller. And both types are available at discount prices of less than $200—not a lot of money for an extra measure of safety.

—Bob Stearns
(*Small Boat Journal* #53)

The Many Kinds of Depthfinders

Ever since he first stuck a pole into the water to test the depth of some creek, river, or pond, man has been looking for better ways to accurately measure the distance from the water's surface to the bottom. In spite of this, for literally thousands of years, the leadline, consisting of a lead weight and marked line, was the standard method for measuring depth.

Not until the sinking of the *Titanic* in April 1912 was a concerted effort made to measure depth electronically. Shortly thereafter, the U.S. Navy, the Electro-Acoustic Company of Kiel, Germany, and Reginald A. Fessenden, a scientist with the Submarine Signal Company in the United States, all developed depthfinders operating on the same principles as today's sophisticated devices. In fact, the flashing-type depthfinder Fessenden developed in 1920 is similar to those still in use.

A depthfinder is primarily a machine that sends high-frequency soundwaves downward through water and receives echoes reflected off the bottom. Because sound travels through the water at a speed that varies little with temperature or frequency, all the unit does is measure the elapsed time between the transmission of a signal and its reception. The only limitations to how far down the gear can measure are the strength of the transmitted signal and the sensitivity of the receiver to the much weaker returning echo.

Depthfinders have four components: a transmitter, a transducer (which is nothing more than an underwater antenna), a receiver, and a device to translate the duration of the echo's round trip from boat to bottom in seconds into a distance measurement (feet, meters, or fathoms).

The transmission sends precisely timed pulses of electrical energy to the transducer, which converts the pulses into mechanical energy in the form of acoustic waves. The transducer alternately serves as a speaker, sending out sound waves, and as a microphone, intercepting sound waves and feeding that information to the receiver, which amplifies the signal to a useful level. The manner in which this information is displayed determines the type of unit: digital, flasher, chart recorder, video, analog, or liquid crystal display (LCD).

Until the transistor replaced the bulky vacuum tube in the 1960s, recording depthfinders were just too big and power hungry for all but the largest yachts. Today, however, the small-boat skipper has a wide and perhaps confusing variety of depthfinders to choose from, each suited for a particular application but often capable of more than one.

One of the toughest decisions facing the potential buyer of a depthfinder is which operating frequency is best. Most use 50 KHz or 190 to 200 KHz, and many manufacturers offer their models in either frequency. Each has both strong and weak points. (The flasher, digital, and analog types are not offered in a choice of frequency. That has already been decided by the manufacturer.)

Both 50-KHz and 190-to-200-KHz depthfinders will show depths up to 1,000 feet (or perhaps a little more), but for depths up to 2,000 feet or more, the 50 KHz model is unquestionably superior. On the other hand, 50 KHz doesn't fish well in under 100 feet of water and should not be used in depths of 25 feet or less; but it does show fish at depths as great as 400 to 600 feet (or more, if the schools are large). The 190-to-200-KHz models only show fish reliably to about 300 feet, but they do

so in detail that is unmatched by any of the lower frequencies. The ultimate depthsounder will be one that can operate on either frequency at the flick of a switch, and very likely that is not too far off.

If you do most of your angling in water that is under 500 feet, you would probably be better off with a 190-to-200-KHz unit. If very deep water fishing is your preference, then the 50-KHz models bear close inspection.

The transducer cone angle can be important in some situations, especially with the 190-to-200-KHz chart, video, or LCD depthfinders. Some manufacturers offer a choice between wide (20 degrees or more) and narrow (12 degrees or less). Wide beam angles see more area as the boat passes over the bottom, but they don't allow the unit to reach the same maximum depth and see both fish and bottom as the narrow beams do.

For very shallow water (50 feet or less), the wide cone is the best choice. For deeper water (over 100 feet), the narrow beam allows the user to position his craft over a wreck or bottom

> *If you do most of your angling in water that is under 500 feet, you would probably be better off with a 190-to-200-KHz unit.*

The cone angle of a sounder is important with regard to detail. A wide cone shows more bottom but is limited in depth penetration. The narrow cone shows less bottom but has sharper detail and a greater depth reach, and it shows fish better.

Aquameter Instrument Corp.

ELECTRONICS

structure with greater accuracy. A few manufacturers offer a switchbox that allows both transducers to be used with the same depthfinder.

The transducer can be installed on the transom, through the hull, or inside the hull. Which option you choose depends on your particular boat and how you use it.

As a rule, most small-boat owners seem to prefer the transom-mount systems, while most larger craft seem to wind up with through-hull installations. Sailboat owners usually use through-hull or glue-down transducers, while owners of small and medium I/O and outboard powerboats have their pick of all three types.

For a through-hull or transom-mounted transducer, the hull material does not matter; however, a glue-down transducer inside the hull can be used *only* if the hull is solid (not cored) fiberglass.

DIGITAL DEPTHFINDERS

By far the most accurate and most compact depth indicators available today, digital depthfinders are also the easiest to use. Just turn them on, and the exact depth in feet, fathoms, or meters is instantly displayed in LCD numbers from ½ to 1 inch high. Some models read as deep as 2,000 feet under good conditions, and yet are still no larger than a few inches wide.

All use less current per watt of signal output than any other depthfinder, making them attractive to sailboat owners.

Because of their precision, these depthfinders are ideal for various change-of-depth alarm systems. Most of the better models have both shallow and deep alarm settings, and even the less expensive models usually have at least one of these. Used together, these two alarm systems serve as an excellent "anchor watch" that never sleeps, quickly waking the skipper if the anchor drags into water that is too deep or too shallow. Digital sounders are not designed for detecting fish.

Because of their compact size, digital depthfinders are offered in both panel flush-mount (e.g., in the dash) or stand-alone designs. Prices are in the $150 to $400 range.

FLASHERS

Flashers represent the least expensive and least sophisticated depthfinders that are still capable of reliably showing fish as well as indicating depth. Rugged and relatively uncomplicated, their only moving part is a rotating disk with a neon bulb that flashes at the appropriate spots on a calibrated circular dial to represent the bottom and fish. A number of manufacturers use LED displays, and at least one manufacturer offers a flasher that utilizes a circular LCD "dial" in place of the rotating disk with the neon bulb. Whichever you buy, check to be sure the display is bright enough to be read in direct light. Some models also have depth alarms.

Flashers have no memory capability, not even an interface for a tape recorder, and the information they provide is very basic. If you don't happen to be looking at the dial when the depth suddenly changes, you'll miss seeing that ledge or other bit of underwater structure—or the momentary mid-depth flashes that represent fish.

But when basic depth and limited fish information are acceptable, they're hard to beat in the $80 to $300 price range.

CHART RECORDERS

Serious anglers who want a depthfinder capable of displaying and preserving detailed information, including not only the exact shape of the bottom but everything between the boat and the bottom—especially fish—still show strong preference for the paper chart recorder. The top models on the market can separate echoes as close together as an inch or two, but the best separation is 3 to 6 inches. This makes it possible for the user in most cases to determine if he is seeing one large fish or a tightly packed school of small fish.

The computer microchip has found its way into chart recorders, allowing the user to select almost any combination of upper and lower limits and thereby expanding the scale for fine bottom detail, even in very deep water. As an example, let's assume you are looking at the bottom in 1,000 feet of water, and you would like to look at only the lower 10 feet. You simply select 1,000 as the lower limit and 990 as the upper limit. This enlarges the lowest 10 feet to the full width of the paper, which on the usual 4- to 6-inch-wide paper would be like magnifying it almost 100 times!

Since all scales are selected via a digital keypad like the one on a touch-tone telephone, the number of possible range combinations varies from many thousands to almost a

> *Serious anglers who want a depthfinder capable of displaying and preserving detailed information still show strong preference for the paper chart recorder.*

million, depending on the make and model. The same keypad can be used to reduce the surface clutter, change the pulse length of the transmitted signal for better definition at the particular depth range selected, and change the recorded information from feet to fathoms or meters.

Another feature the better chart recorders include is "white" or "gray" lining (both are the same), a means of separating objects close to the bottom from the bottom itself. An angler looking for fish that normally stay close to the bottom, such as grouper or sea bass, usually wants this capability.

Two relatively new features for some chart recorders are a built-in interface for Loran C (usually of the same make), which allows the user to record Loran coordinates at the push of a button, right on the chart paper beside the wreck or other promising fishing hole; and a small digital window (usually LCD) in one corner of the display panel that indicates the exact depth. Some also interface with GPS, thus ensuring extremely precise positioning.

The better chart recorders typically cost between $500 and $1,200.

VIDEO DEPTHSOUNDERS

A cathode ray tube (CRT), just like the one in your TV set, can also be used to display depth information. The display looks very much like that appearing on paper chart recorders, except that the information can be displayed in black and white or color. Each color represents the strength of the returning echo, from the weakest to the strongest. For instance, blue might indicate a very weak echo, and bright orange a very strong one. In-between echo intensities might be represented by red, yellow, and green.

Some users feel the various colors offer more information, particularly when it comes to identifying fish species. This, of course, requires extensive knowledge of the area to be fished, as well as a good understanding of certain other habits pertaining to the species, such as school size, depth, and how far they are above the bottom.

On the plus side, video depthsounders don't require expensive chart paper. However, they're larger than a chart recorder, consume more power, and can't match the very fine

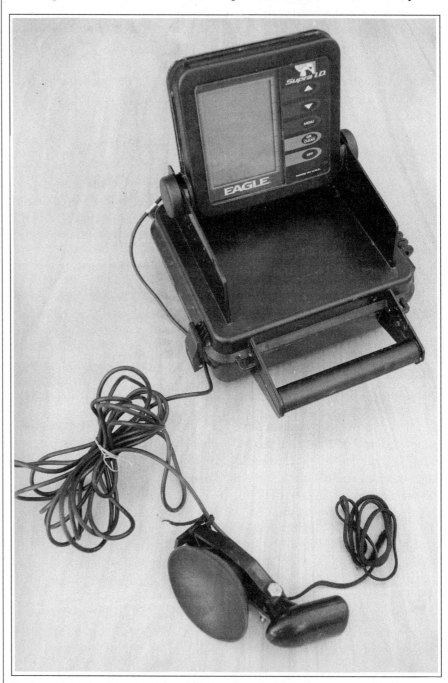

The most popular small-boat depthsounder is the liquid crystal display (LCD) type. This Eagle Supra ID can be bought for as little as $125 in the permanent-mount model or, for another $25 or $30, in a fully portable configuration such as the one shown here. Included is a battery case for the two 6-volt lantern batteries to which the viewing unit is attached, and a suction-cup mount for attaching the transducer to the transom. Its scroll-through menu offers a variety of fish-finding features. The portables have the advantage of being ready for instant use aboard virtually every small boat.

detail available from the better chart recorders. They also don't have a permanent memory, though optional tape recorder interfaces are available for this purpose.

The better CRT depthfinders do have the ability to freeze the display for any length of time. Many also have the ability to "recall" (scroll backward) the part of the display that has just moved off screen. Most have the same basic depth selection and "zoom" features as a chart recorder, plus the ability to display the exact depth in digital form in one corner of the screen.

LCD DEPTHFINDERS

These are the latest innovations to hit the market. They use a liquid crystal display panel, just like those on watches and small calculators, only here the panel is 4 to 5 inches high and 2 to 5 inches wide, depending upon make or model. As yet, no one has developed a color display suitable for this application, but very likely that's not too far off.

Depth information appears on an LCD depthfinder very much like that on a black-and-white video unit. LCD units have essentially the same depth and zoom capabilities (depending on make and model) as the chart and video depthfinders, but they lack the detail (resolution) of the better video recorders, because the density of the pixels (those dotlike bits that form the picture) are presently only 800 dots or less per square inch.

As you would expect, the units with the higher pixel densities are the most expensive, but even those don't have anywhere near the resolution of the best chart recorders. However, engineers working on this type of display now produce panels with pixel densities of 2,500 pixels per square inch.

In addition to graphics, some manufacturers have models that offer digital displays of boat speed and water temperature data, plus depth.

The LCD depthfinder is light, compact, and has no moving parts. It requires considerably less current to operate than a video depthfinder, and a bit less current than a chart recorder. And it needs no paper.

LCD depthfinders are priced from a bit less than $200 to just over $1,000. Many anglers are finding that the less-expensive models cost about the same as the medium- to high-priced flashers, and while their low pixel densities form crude pictures, they still have far more information to offer than a flasher.

They all measure depth, but choosing the right depthfinder requires a closer look at your needs as well as the unique technical abilities of each type. The dealer who sold you your boat or is selling you a depthfinder should be able to help you with that choice, too.

—Bob Stearns
(*Small Boat Journal* #55)

Installing a Depthfinder

Installing a depthsounder is a relatively easy project that requires only a few basic tools and consists of three simple steps: (1) installing the mounting bracket for the unit, (2) hooking up the unit to a 12-volt power source, and (3) installing the transducer. In most cases, the project can be completed in a couple of hours.

It is important to pick a location where the information displayed by the unit can be seen easily. At the same time, consideration must be given to the built-in weather resistance of the unit. Those built by the better manufacturers are usually weatherproof and require no additional protection from the elements—

A poorly placed transducer won't see the bottom even half as deep as it is supposed to, or detect fish at all.

even around salt water. Others might require a simple plastic splash cover. Read the owner's manual for installation instructions and maintenance requirements before starting any phase of the project.

The top of a console, behind the windscreen, or even under the overhang of a top cover are all good places for installation. Just make sure it doesn't obstruct your view of the water ahead when you are at the helm. If your console or helm area is small, the position you select for the depthfinder should not restrict the full-range movement of throttle and/or gearshift control.

The power hookup should be

fused, just to be safe. If you are not picking up the 12 volts from an already fused buss panel, then use the in-line fuse supplied by the manufacturer. Never use a fuse that has a greater amp rating than specified by the manufacturer. It's also most important that the power hookup be completely protected from saltwater intrusion, so be careful how you route wires and make splices or connections. A little silicone sealer in the right places never hurts, either.

Proper placement of the transducer is the single most important consideration if you want to get everything you can out of your depthfinder. A poorly placed transducer won't see the bottom even half as deep as it is supposed to, or detect fish at all.

Best performance is obtained when the transducer is mounted directly in the water, either on the transom or through the hull. You can place the transducer inside the hull *only* if the latter is built of solid fiberglass that is completely free of air bubbles. Wood, foam- or balsa-cored glass, and aluminum hulls will not allow the signal to pass through the hull and return without such great attenuation that almost everything is lost.

In order to "shoot through" the hull, you must be able to reach the inside (bilge) surface of the outer hull and position the transducer so that it is pointing straight down. Before epoxying the transducer in place, it is a good idea to first build a small dam around the spot where you intend to install the transducer and flood it with ¼ inch or more of water. Once you have taken the boat out to a suitable depth for testing, place the transducer inside the dam and see what type of bottom readings you get.

Aquameter Instrument Corp.

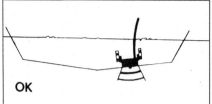

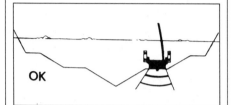

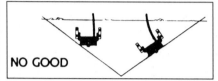

Transducer placement is the single most important factor affecting a sounder's performance. The transducer must be fitted through, or closely to, the hull and be able to send a signal. In the "No Good" sketch, the transducer at left is not close enough to the deep-V hull; the one at right will not read depth under the hull; instead, its cone will be directed off to the side.

Then try hanging the transducer over the side to see if the readings are any better. If they are, you will either need to find another spot inside the hull or select another method of mounting the transducer.

If you find a good inside spot, clean the area thoroughly with acetone (remember to wear protective gloves) or some other good solvent, dry thoroughly, and use a generous amount of epoxy glue to anchor the transducer in place, making sure there are no air bubbles in the glue.

If an inside transducer location is not going to work, then your choices are either on the transom or via a through-hull fitting. Most small-boat skippers, understandably, would rather go the transom route than drill holes through the bottom and void their manufacturer's warranty. Also, trailer rollers could damage a through-hull transducer on a trailered boat.

Pick a spot on the transom as far away from the centerline as possible to eliminate noise or turbulence from outboard or sterndrive lower units, or the prop wash from an inboard. The bottom of the transducer should be flush with the bottom to eliminate drag, and it must point as close to straight down as possible, or the depth readings will be weak and in error. It also must be placed where some special hull configuration (i.e., strakes) won't cause a flow of air bubbles across the face of the transducer.

If a suitable transom spot isn't available, then perhaps a through-hull installation is your only choice. This requires the careful installation of a fairing block to direct the water flow ahead and behind the transducer and to point the transducer straight down. Attention should also be given to metal compatibility. For example, bronze transducers should not be used on aluminum hulls. If you are in doubt about proper installation procedure, it is best to seek professional help.

The ultimate test of a good transducer installation is when the readings are just as good underway at slow speeds as when the engine is off. Also, with the sensitivity turned down a little, you should be able to get bottom readings in at least 50 to 100 feet of water while on plane at speeds up to 50 m.p.h. and more.

—Bob Stearns
(*Small Boat Journal* #55)

ELECTRONICS

SEAMANSHIP

Introduction

Seamanship is a sense of the sea, a knowledge of what can and cannot be done, what should and should not be done, and how and how not to do things in a boat. And it does not stop at the edge of tidewater. The "sea" in seamanship is there because the word is old. A seaman in the days of sail was expected to know his trade, and once that was learned, he had acquired the basics of seamanship—but only the basics. Nothing has changed in that concept.

A good seaman, man or woman, never stops learning. What one doesn't acquire intentionally is dumped on one by the sea anyway, and this problem of trading blows and knows goes on as long as one is aboard a boat. It is more than straight learning, however. A person on the water is in a hostile environment, since it is impossible for a human to survive there indefinitely without special aids and equipment. Therefore, to a greater or lesser degree, some of the aspects of seamanship become instinctive, a true sense of the sea. This is evidenced in the right response to an emergency on the water, in an ability to put the cover back on a can of worms that were ready to take over the ship. We have watched in fascination as a good seaman has calmly and efficiently dealt with a shipboard problem that could quickly have developed into a catastrophe.

It is a lack or lapse of seamanship that gets us in trouble on the water. A good seaman sees a problem developing and meets it head on; a poor seaman may not even recognize it as a problem, and thus will be completely astonished when it occurs. We watched just such a scene unfold

> To a certain extent, seamanship is a state of mind.

one lovely moonlit summer night on a lake. We were on a point of land, and a hundred yards away was a small island. We heard the roar of a powerful outboard motor coming up the lake. Seconds later the dim outline of a speeding boat appeared, heading toward the break between the island and the point. "I don't believe this!" my wife said to me as the motorboat hurtled toward trouble. There was a loud crash as the lower unit of the motor struck a line of rocks just under the surface. The motor raced, then stopped, and a babble of voices and curses erupted in the suddenly still night. We called to see if they were all right and received another string of obscenities in reply. "There are almost as many rocks there as you have in your head!" we responded, drawn to reply in kind by their actions. There were a few more choice comments sent our way, and then the boat disappeared into the night, this time under two-paddle power.

There were at least four flagrant lacks of seamanship here. The first was just plain illegal—running at night without lights. The second was running in poor visibility at a speed far beyond what was safe. The third (and here is where experience comes in) was going between a point and an island, always a gamble if you don't know the water, because points and nearby islands more often than not have shallow water between them.

The fourth lack of seamanship was the total disregard by the skipper of his responsibility for the lives and safety of those aboard his boat. This last point, which is far and away the most important here, is one unknown or taken too lightly by many pleasure-boat skippers more concerned with getting at the joys of life on the water than learning the responsibilities it involves.

Seamanship is boat handling in the minds of most people, and there are solid grounds for that belief. If a person cannot control his craft in a reasonably competent manner, it is difficult to think of him as a good seaman. Equally, though, the person at the helm should be able to judge how other vessels, particularly larger ones, are controlled. With a little craft, the small-boat skipper can maneuver quickly and easily; in fact, there are few boats larger than yours that can respond as fast as you can—it is that old factor of weight again. Lightness is a huge advantage for the small guy, helping him to stay out of trouble and also not to be the cause of it. But random darting about can lead to confusion on the part of the skipper in the larger craft, so the small-boat driver should know the U.S. Inland Rules of the Road and follow them until such action is deemed unsafe.

The Rules of the Road were devised long before the days of VHF radio let approaching captains talk to one another to communicate their intentions. The Rules established procedures of action that all captains were expected to know. That the Rules did not guarantee safe passage in all cases, usually because of a lapse of good seamanship on the part of one or both captains, is seen in the long record of collisions—between and among vessels of all sizes. The responsibility to avoid collision is just as much the duty of the driver of a 16-foot motorboat as it is of the captain of a 7,000-ton freighter.

If you're going to operate your boat in busy maritime waters or on major rivers, you are expected to know the U.S. Inland Rules of the Road as well as any navigation rules your state may have established. The Inland Rules are covered precisely and well in John Mellor's *Small Boat Guide to the Rules of the Road*. For the little-boat skipper, concerned as he is with survival in world of larger craft, the following Rules are of special importance:

- Vessels in your right (starboard) front quarter (actually a fat quarter of 120 degrees) have the Right of Way over you. In other words, they do not have to change course; you do. Vessels to your left (port) front quarter must give way to you.
- A vessel being overtaken has the right of way even after the overtaking vessel has moved ahead.
- In a narrow channel, approaching vessels should pass port to port.
- A sailboat under sail has the Right of Way unless it is overtaking you. (If a sailboat is under both sail and power, for safety's sake, consider it under sail.)

As we said earlier, these Rules are to be followed in order to avoid confusion, but when you are in a small boat, don't assume that someone in a larger vessel is going to respect your Right of Way; in fact, our experience indicates compliance with regard to small boats is a 50-50 proposition—damn poor odds in anyone's book. We have been cut off more times than we can remember by larger boats whose skippers either ignored the Rules, did not know this basic bit of marine law, or figured might meant right. In any event, it was unimportant; sensing a game of chicken in the offing, we chose to cluck—and duck out of the way.

The Inland Rules recognize the importance of this defensive attitude in Rule 2, the so-called *Rule of Good Seamanship*. It reads:

(a) Nothing in these Rules shall exonerate any vessel, or the owner, master, or crew thereof, for the consequences of any neglect to comply with these Rules or the neglect of any precaution which may be required by the ordinary practice of seamen, or by the special circumstances of the case.
(b) In construing and complying with these Rules due regard shall be had to all dangers of navigation and collision and to any special circumstances, including the limitations of the vessels involved, which may make a departure from these Rules necessary to avoid immediate danger.

This Rule—apparently written by three lawyers who weren't speaking to each other—condensed down to two words, should be the creed of all small-motorboat skippers: Drive defensively.

This section covers other aspects of seamanship, in addition to many techniques of boat handling unique to small boats. In fact, just about everything you need to know in the way of basic small-boat seamanship is here. The one thing lacking—and only you can add it—is practice in doing things in a good and seamanlike fashion. And this means time on the water—which is the best part of learning. The following takes us from words to reality:

For more than an hour we had been making good time down the Strait of Belle Isle, and we had just left the mouth of Chateau Bay behind us. Ahead

> Condensed down to two words, the creed of all small-motorboat skippers should be: Drive defensively.

were 30 miles of unrelenting coast with no protection whatsoever under the massive cliffs. The light southwest breeze that had headed us all morning was freshening and, as the chop built, we were forced to reduce speed. By noon we were down to a crawl and our 18-foot aluminum boat was pounding badly.

Geof was at the tiller, easing the boat along the best he could, while I pondered our alternatives. We could go back to Chateau Bay and hole up for the night, thus breaking our fast run down the coast of Labrador, or we could go on and knock ourselves silly. With luck, we would arrive at the entrance of Red Bay by dark, but it would be hard to find in the gloom.

Staring morosely back along the coast, I watched two specks resolve themselves into a pair of fishing boats that we had passed just south of Battle Harbor. They were plowing along at a good pace, paying no heed to the 2-foot chop that had brought us almost to a halt. Suddenly the answer to our problem was obvious.

"Geof, try swinging in behind that boat and snuggle up just as close as you can to his transom," I said as a fishing vessel passed some 50 yards inshore of us. "Keep out of the white water from the prop, but otherwise close up tight."

Geof turned sharply to the starboard, and we rattled toward the nearer fishing boat, smashing through its wake in a shower of sunlit spray. Then the seas suddenly quieted. They rolled under us in long smooth swells rather than the hard-etched wavelets that had been giving us such grief only moments before. My companion skillfully guided us to within 30 feet of the fishing boat, and we settled in just to the starboard of his propeller wash. Geof matched his speed to that of the other boat. A big smile creased his whiskered face.

Two men came out of the pilothouse to stare at us with puzzled looks on their faces. Geof waved and pointed to the white-capped seas rushing past us on both sides. They raised their arms in a gesture of camaraderie and went back

into the cabin. An hour later, the fishing boats were taking spray over the tops of their houses, but except for the larger swells rolling under us, our ride continued as comfortable as before. We indicated to the fishermen that we were headed for Red Bay, and later in the afternoon, they swung close to shore and pointed to a break in the wall of cliffs—the back way into our destination.

This bit of good fortune is an example of how a small-boat skipper must be alert to opportunities, especially those that can contribute to the comfort and safety of boat and crew. Seamanship is an accumulation of experience combined with common sense and a smidgen of luck. Certain aspects of seamanship, such as weather judgment, basic boat handling, and the Rules of the Road, are

> It is a lack or lapse of seamanship that gets us in trouble on the water.

required of all skippers, be their boats large or small. But other types of seamanship pertain to the craft one is handling, the needs being different depending on the size of the vessel and whether it is under power or sail.

To a certain extent, seamanship is a state of mind, one geared to the water rather than the land. As with a flier soaring along far above the landscape, a skipper in the middle of a bay cannot step out of the craft onto the ground and walk away. The craft, whether airplane or boat, must go safely in its medium, and its captain must adjust his mind to think in non-land terms, and know enough about what he is doing to arrive back at the land in one piece.

"Are you saying that banging around in small boats is an *intellectual* exercise?" you may ask. "Give us a break! This is supposed to be *fun*."

Sorry, Skip, but intellectual it is, in that small boating is analytical, calculating, logical, rational, serious, and even introspective. You can also meld this batch of 25-cent words into just two: common sense.

There is another important use of the mind the sensible skipper keeps handy on his mental workbench, and that is anticipation, a subtle weighing of consequences one's actions may produce. We were running in company with a second boat down a bleak section of the Maine coast toward a notorious point and bar. It was midmorning of a lovely summer day, and our goal was to go a few miles beyond the point and return in early afternoon. As we neared the point, the smooth water was riffled by a light zephyr from the southwest, and that hint of sea breeze brought me up short. I stopped the boat to look around. Fair-weather clouds were beginning to puff above the land; the sky remained clear over the sea—classic conditions for a brisk sea breeze, and it was coming early in the day, an indication that it may blow seriously. Returning with a strong wind at our backs against a dropping tide could mean rough trouble off the point. I signaled to the other boat that we were cutting the trip short. They argued for going on but relented when we headed back the way we had come. By lunch time, the sea was a mass of whitecaps, and as we basked in the sun on a protected island beach and enjoyed watching the graybeards roll by a short distance away, no comment as to the right choice was needed. Trouble is not trouble when it is anticipated and avoided.

But never get smug! Just recently, we were pulling away from an island and were watching a fishing boat working close off our port quarter. We swung behind it to give it a clear field of operation. Once clear, we accelerated toward the next island and glanced to starboard. A motorboat had "come out of nowhere" and was bearing down on us only a short distance away, clearly with the right of way. We did the only thing we could: we stopped, and he pulled behind us and continued on with a wave. Embarrassed and disgusted with ourselves, we waved back sheepishly and continued on, reminded once again that inattention is one of the biggest causes of accidents.

As can be seen, small-boat seamanship is not some mystical attribute for the selected few, but rather a combination of common sense, practical knowledge, and practice—and attention to business! Most anyone can become a reasonably competent seaman by reading the vast literature available, listening to those who have been there, simply observing the watery world that is the chosen medium, and then applying that experience through practice. Thousands have done it before you.

—DRG

Rough-Water Handling

One of the clouds that small powerboats sail under is that they are dangerous when the weather goes bad. As with so many generalizations, this is a bum rap. It stands to reason that they are dangerous at and above some stage in the weather, just as any vessel is, but in fact most small boats are considerably more seaworthy than most of us want to find out about. And, as is so often the case with small boats, seaworthiness is as much the product of the skipper as it is of the boat designer.

Since safe boat handling in rough water is an acquired skill with many facets in its makeup, let's take a look at some of the parts before we take to the water. As a matter of fact, let's first define what we are talking about, since one person's idea of what constitutes hard going is nothing more than another person's "salmon chop"; i.e., good fishing weather.

Wind *is* weather when it comes to boating. Rain or even snow can be endured with no more ill effects than water down the neck, or cold feet. Fog can be spooky or frightening, but it isn't very dangerous in itself. Wind, though, is something else. It may be a bright and breezy day ashore, while out on the water you are on the edge of catastrophe because of frothy seas. For that reason, when a skipper listens to a weather forecast, his first interest should be predicted wind speeds, for they will either make or ruin the day, depending on what he plans to do.

Water is rough because the wind is blowing in your face or has been blowing somewhere over the distant horizon. By contrast, there is the special case when water is running

> *Most small boats are considerably more seaworthy than most of us want to find out about.*

downhill and humps into rapids and standing waves; we will look at this a little later.

Waves generated by distant winds end up as rounded swells by the time they reach us, and while they may sometimes seem awesome, especially from a small boat looking up from a deep trough at moving walls of water, they are not particularly dangerous as long as they have a good depth of water under them. But as big swells approach the coast and enter the realm of the small boat, they hump higher as they "drag" in the shoaling water and their tops may outrun their bases, breaking in the classic curling comber or spilling their crests in a bubbly toupee of foam. More than one small-boat skipper has been caught close inshore with his eyes on fishing or other attractions, only to be surprised and sometimes rudely dumped by one of these breaking swells.

If you do choose to take your boat into this breaker zone, always remember that potential danger is both ahead of and behind you. The smart skipper is in constant visual touch with what is around him and has only a brief glance for his fishing or birdwatching companions. Everyone aboard should have on a PFD when venturing into this zone, because the unexpected is to be expected; calamity can be on you in seconds.

An alert boater will never turn off the motor in this area, because it is all too easy to flood a hot engine in your excitement to move out of danger. At the same time, you will be considering the potential of several approaching swells and not just the one that is about to roll under the boat. This at-

A rugged coast such as this makes a fine training ground because it offers many types of water.

tention will let you scoot out of danger when an obvious breaker is humping on the outer ledges. If it appears you misjudged and that the next wave will break, you have a couple of choices. If you and your boat are cat quick and there is room, you may be able to dash right or left, avoiding the worst of the dumping wave and banking into the wash just before it comes aboard.

The alternative—and you may not have much choice—is to turn into the breaking wave, order your passengers to hit the deck—literally—and apply a squirt of gas to get your boat moving ahead. But *don't* keep accelerating; once your boat is moving, back off the throttle to steering speed and let the momentum of your boat break through the wave crest. As it does, you will probably come down with a bang on the back side, for the wave is moving faster than you may think. If you hit the crest with any speed, your boat may leave the water altogether, and along with it much of your control.

There is another phenomenon that takes place near shore, particularly so if the swell is smashing against cliffs or ledges. When a wave breaks on a smooth beach, its force is expended in dispersing the water over the sand, and the return runoff is relatively weak and often concentrated in streams, known as *rip currents,* that pour *away* from the shore. When that same wave strikes a cliff, however, some of the power may be released in a burst of spray, but much of the force merely bounces off the rock and heads back to sea to strike the next incoming wave head-on. The collision may send up an explosion of spray higher than the first while the very steep-sided wave created is quite capable of flipping a boat. These *reflective waves,* as they are called, keep the waters riled and rough for 50 to 100 yards offshore. This area of confused seas and swift currents also confuses baitfish, which become easy targets for larger fish that move in and out of this zone looking for a free lunch.

For obvious reasons, entering the breaker zone is serious business, and it can be downright dangerous if you don't know your own capabilities or those of your boat. But for some small-motorboat skippers, being able to skirt the breaker line is important, since it may be where the fish are. As we have said before, and will again, you can acquire the skill needed, but don't expect it to happen overnight. One way to add to your store of wave knowledge is to find an offshore reef with a good depth of water behind it and then work your boat in the waves generated by the reef. In the right conditions, you will find a variety of wave sizes from low humpers to mildly spilling breakers. The important thing, of course, is to start small and work up as you gain experience and confidence. A few sessions of this practice will let you work closer to shore, but in doing this, you should also work slowly from the easy to the hard. If you know your limitations and work well within them, you will eventually discover that your boat handling—and fishing—are greatly improved.

Moving into rough water created mainly by swells close to shore is, in a sense, going looking for trouble. You are there by choice. This may not be the case when you are dealing with wind-generated waves, and any boater who spends much time on the water must learn to handle them. There are several factors that must be considered.

A particularly important point the inshore boater should understand is *fetch*—the distance a wave travels from its source. Waves are not just suddenly there in all their size and fury; rather, they grow, from ripples to chop to graybeards to giant swells. We were once told that a wave cannot grow more than 1 foot in height per mile, and we found that "fact" to be reasonably true under normal circumstances. Then we watched a powerful northwest squall come tearing down a 3-mile-long Maine lake.

The waves grew 1, 2, and then 3 feet high. We were impressed. The wind kept howling at about 50 m.p.h.: the waves grew to 4 feet, and then 5. (The heights are reasonably accurate; I was measuring them against the height of a shoreside cabin that was being deluged by the spray as the waves hit a rock retaining wall.) Some of the height was due to shoaling of the water and reflective waves off the retaining wall, but it still appeared that they were stretching the 1-foot-per-mile rule. (You can draw your own conclusions by looking at the photo taken at the time, bearing in mind that photos have a tendency to flatten wave heights.) So much for immutable theory.

However, exceptions simply prove the rule, and it is safe to say that a 20-m.p.h. wind blowing off the land 2 miles away will build much smaller seas than a similar windspeed blowing up a bay with a 10-mile fetch in which to grow. Ocean swells are the product of great fetch, among other factors. Meanwhile, those 2-to-4-footers that are spawned by an afternoon sea breeze may come from the same direction as the swells, but with only a few miles of fetch behind them, because they are the product of a localized wind.

The height of waves is also of interest to the small-boat skipper. One of the most misjudged of all the features of moving water, wave height is measured from the bottom of the trough to the crest of a wave, and because it is impossible to measure this rapidly varying height with a ruler, we tend to judge wave height by such subjective factors as imagination and plain terror. However, it is possible to get a reasonably accurate reading of wave height using comparisons. For instance, if the gunwale of your boat is 18 inches above the surface, you can sight along that, and if the wave crests are at that height when your boat is level at the bottom of a trough, then wave height is approximately 1½ feet. If you are sitting at the tiller in a skiff, your eyes are approximately 3 to 3½ feet above the surface. If you can sight along several wavetops in a row when you are in the trough, then 3 to 3½ feet is a good guess. If all you see is water when you are in a trough, the waves are higher. Other heights can be measured with variations on that wavetop theme. Best to lean on the conservative side, however, for waves are usually lower than they seem, especially when they are tossing a small boat about.

The distance between wave crests has considerable influence on both your comfort and your perception. A long distance between crests makes the waves seem lower; a short distance, higher. If you are at a river mouth that is pouring an outgoing tide into a shorebound chop, the steep 3-footers generated can seem twice as high. If you are slamming

A freshwater lake can quickly be whipped into a fury by a hard-charging squall. Here, wave heights test the theory of 1 foot of height for each mile as they roll in after a fetch of only 3 miles.

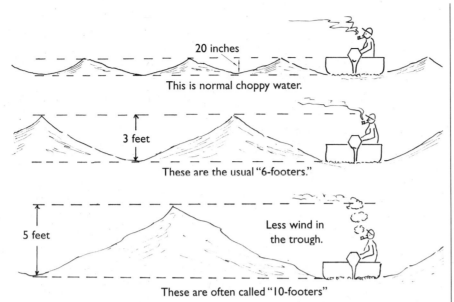

20 inches

This is normal choppy water.

3 feet

These are the usual "6-footers."

5 feet

Less wind in the trough.

These are often called "10-footers"

Wave height is difficult to judge, but rough approximations can be made from the trough using this guide. As waves get larger, their height is apt to increase dramatically in the eyes and mind of someone in a small boat. For a boat of the size shown here, the "6-footers" would probably be the most dangerous.

into these waves and the wind is sending sheets of spray into your face, your wife has her eyes closed and is biting her lip, and the kids are crying, the 3-foot waves may seem enormous.

BOAT HANDLING

The automobile-like motorboat, with steering wheel, throttle, windshield, upholstered seats, and high speed capability, brings a lot of people onto the water who are more familiar with smooth highways than rough seas. With a mindset based on getting from one point to another as straight-lined and quickly as possible, they miss much and frequently subject themselves and their boats to unnecessary hard knocks. They feel that if speed and a rugged hull cannot handle the conditions, then it's too rough to be out.

We would like to encourage a dif-

ferent approach, one that accepts the fact that though a boat may drive like a car, it is operating in an entirely different medium, one that can change dramatically in a short time, that hides a variety of hazards both on and under the surface, and that may require skills one would never dream of needing until faced with a line of breakers

Entering the breaker zone is serious business, . . . but it may be where the fish are.

suddenly looming out of the fog.

Persons in self-propelled craft and sailboats are forced to approach the water on much more intimate terms than those experienced by powerboaters, and they soon develop an awareness of the "live" medium beneath them, a sense that detects even subtle changes in current and wave height. Lacking power, they

must improve their boat-handling skills, give with the thrust of wind and wave, seek easier routes, and judge the ever-changing weather. The motorboat skipper will profit mightily by acquiring this same "sea sense," or "road sense," as it would be described in highway terminology.

The waves of greatest importance to our discussion are those generated by local winds, as mentioned above, and not the larger swells rolling in from the ocean. Still, it is possible—in fact quite common—to have the surface wrinkled by both a large swell and smaller wind waves, and it is the latter that cause trouble. This is because every boat has a range of waves that give it a hard time; smaller ones don't bother it, larger ones don't bother it, but, oh, those in between! Because they are roughly the same distance between crests as the length of the boat, these waves cause the craft to pitch and plunge dramatically. This fact is true for all vessels, from the smallest dinghy to the largest oceanliner. One of the basic arts of boat handling is learning to deal with these wrong-size waves in a way that is safe, even if not particularly comfortable.

Let's imagine you are in your motorboat and heading into a rising wind. As your boat begins to pound, you slow down, but as the seas get higher, you find you are still climbing steeply and then suddenly dropping off the crest with a resounding bang before plunging into the back of the next wave.

If something is wrong, you first try to change it. You can change wave size—at least the length between crests, which is most important in our case—simply by changing direction. If you bear off 45 degrees in either direction, you will almost double *your* distance between crests, and this should reduce or eliminate the pounding (see the illustration). If you continue to pound on the steeper waves, turn your boat another 30 degrees as you approach these higher crests and go over the top almost *sideways*. By doing this, you shorten the length of your boat dramatically (it is now only as "long" as the beam), and chances are you will roll smoothly over the crest. Care must be taken not to be caught broadside by a breaking wave crest, since the water of the wave is moving in a circular motion and could roll your boat over.

This assumes, of course, that you have reduced your speed to accommodate the conditions. For instance, when we are in bad going in our motorboat and an especially nasty wave is in the immediate offing, we cut the throttle to idle and let the buoyancy of the boat do its job. This slowing or stopping the forward progress of the boat works in the same way as that of a kayak steadied by a quick paddle brace. In either case, the wave passes under the drifting boat harmlessly. A properly trimmed small boat will ride very rough water if left on its own.

What we have said about heading into waves applies equally to following seas, but in this case speed *must* be reduced to the conditions or you will find your boat burrowing into the back of the next wave instead of lifting to it. We like to have the boat trimmed with weight centered just aft of amidships when dealing with following seas in order to lighten the bow. If your passengers are crowded in the cuddy forward, or if yours is a small runabout with two heavy persons sitting just behind the windshield, you may find you are taking water over the bow as you plunge into the wave troughs. Getting that "movable ballast" out of the bow and farther aft

By angling off when faced with head seas you can ease both the ride and your mind. Notice how the boat on the left is facing waves on a wave–boat length ratio of about 1.25:1, while the same size boat at right is dealing with the same waves but at about a 4:1 ratio, a much more comfortable sea. By zigzagging into the waves, you may make better time even if you double your distance over the water. Either method eats into your fuel supply.

can make a huge difference in the way your boat responds. Larger vessels with enclosed hulls and greater weight can take an occasional slug of "green water" over the bow without harm; the same does not hold true for little boats, many of which are undecked forward.

By the way, if you are on an island and the wind comes up to cover the bay with whitecaps before you head home, you may want to think twice before heading out in that mess. For instance, if it is a sea breeze, that local product of a warm summer's day, your best bet may be to hang around on the island for another hour or so on the chance that the waves will get bigger. Odd as it may seem,

the larger waves may provide a far more comfortable ride for your boat. The alternative is to wait out the wind, which frequently goes down with the sun.

Two other types of waves that warrant at least a brief mention are breaking surf and standing waves. The former type is discussed in more detail in "Shore Landings and Takeoffs," page 165. Standing waves are more common to rivers (see page 167), but are present under certain conditions in coastal areas. A standing wave is just that—it doesn't move as do wind-generated waves. A standing wave is created by water flowing over underwater obstructions, and when a heavy current flows into deeper, slower water such as a rapid dumping into a pool. The most important feature of standing waves is that they operate just the opposite from "conventional" waves: With a regular wave, the wave passes

> Our preference is a splash well *and* scupper holes, because any free water in a small boat can be hazardous.

SEAMANSHIP

through the water while the water stays in place (it doesn't, really, but it *almost* does). With a standing wave, the water moves and the wave stays in place.

This switcheroo can have a remarkable effect on a boat. River kayakers, for instance, can almost park on the upstream side of a standing wave and just sit there with the power of gravity offsetting the speed of the water. By contrast, if you are coming down the rapid under power, the standing wave can serve as a takeoff ramp; but if you are controlling your boat by running it slowly in reverse, you can slide over the standing wave as gently as if it were a pillow. A delicate hand on the tiller and throttle so often is necessary in wild places where one would think brute strength would be more useful.

A FEW TIPS

- Even when the wind is blowing briskly not all waves have whitecaps, but those that do are higher and steeper than others, and avoiding them when possible will make your trip a lot more comfortable.
- A series of relatively low waves normally follows shortly behind whitecaps. If you are under power and angling off your intended course in order to ease your passage, this is a good chance to speed up and gain ground directly toward your goal before having to slow and bear off again for the next series of higher waves.
- A cross sea (waves from two or more directions at once) can generate unexpected pyramidal waves that are considerably higher than others. These should be watched for and avoided when possible. This sometimes happens in the lee of islands as the waves bend around the land and collide some distance downwind of the island. The reflective waves near shore mentioned above are an extreme example of this effect.
- Waves are invariably steeper and higher where current is flowing against wind or where waves are coming against the current from the opposite direction (such as an outflowing river mouth where a sea swell is incoming). These waves are at their worst where the flow is strongest. By contrast, the surface may be almost flat at the edges or near shore, a phenomenon frequently created by a back eddy where the flow is *upstream*. But watch out for underwater obstructions in these shallow areas.

> The best way to find out what kind of a rough-water boat you own is to take it out and discover for yourself.

- When running a motorboat in a following sea, try not to stop suddenly, because that steep wake just behind you may wash over the transom and into the cockpit.
- When the sea starts to rough up, be sure everyone aboard has a life jacket on. (Your passengers may feel they are in danger if suddenly told to put on PFDs, which is another good reason to have them wearing life jackets to start with.)
- If it gets uncomfortably rough and you are worried about capsizing, have your passengers and crew sit on the cockpit floor. The resulting low center of gravity and steadiness of cargo (people won't get thrown about much when braced in the bottom of the boat) will stiffen your craft remarkably and make it very difficult for it to be upset.

EASING THE PAIN

Not all hulls react the same to rough water. The flat-bottomed skiff that is so nice to walk around in on a pond may be too stable in rough going and be swamped by waves breaking over the side. A short, wide, high-sided deep-V will slice through waves up to a certain size with aplomb and then become a wandering dog when it is forced to slow down to displacement speed. A round-sided hull will absorb the bumps and grinds of rough water with little effort, but to try and force it to plane is only to dig a deep hole in the ocean (see "It's All in the Hull," page 2, for a discussion of hull types). There are all sorts of compromises between these extremes, but no small boat is perfect, by any means.

The best way to find out what kind of a rough-water boat you own is to take it out and discover for yourself. Crossing your own wake or that of other boats will give you some indication of how she acts, but such practice is no substitute for the real thing. Get out there where it is bumpy and try moving your boat in different directions at different speeds. You may be surprised at the results. We found that our big skiff, with a V-bow flattening into a broad, flat planing surface aft, takes most rough water best when she is partly on plane, around 10 to 12 m.p.h. This speed drops her stern a little with a corresponding lifting of the bow, and the modest pace provides enough momentum to carry the hull through the smaller stuff without slowing her down. This hull configuration will pound unmercifully in seas of 2 to 3 feet, but we have found ways to mitigate the slamming to a bearable thumping. You can do the same with your boat.

If you look about your boat, you

will see a number of obvious and subtle things the designer did to reduce some of the more bothersome effects of rough water. The most noticeable, of course, is the bow. This may have a deep, sharp stem to cut into the waves at slow to moderate speeds. However, if the stem is too deep, it has a tendency to slow the turning response, so the lower part is probably cut away, some with a small curve at the bottom, others with the entire stem raked sharply aft in a sweeping curve. Another obvious feature is the flare of the bow. On some boats—especially those of fiberglass, which can be molded into intricate shapes—the bow will flare out sharply just beneath the deck line, this striking turn of hull being called *flam* (see page 4). Flare and flam are supposed to keep spray from coming aboard—they may or may not do that job well.

Some boats are "wet" and some are "dry," and the bow shape may have a lot to do with it. We've seen sleek hulls that let the water from the bow wave slide right up the side and disperse in the air in a sheet of spray, making for a very "wet" boat; a sim-ple spray rail properly located may virtually eliminate the problem. Not all boats have pointed bows, of course—the traditional broad-bowed garvey being a good example. Originally flat bottomed, the garvey hull has been modified beyond recognition in modern small boats into such forms as the gullwing or cathedral shape—some very successfully, such as the Boston Whaler, and others in varying degrees of mediocrity. In general, the garvey descendants rely on bottom configurations designed to gather a cushion of air beneath the hull to soften their inherent tendency to pound.

Other features designed to reduce the amount of water coming aboard include decks, windshields, cabins, dodgers, breakwaters, side decks, raised gunwales, and full-length spray rails. Aft in many small outboards is a splash well, the purpose of which is to catch water coming over the transom and drain it back into the sea. Boats with self-bailing cockpits usually do without the splash well, relying instead on large scupper holes in the transom at deck level to let the water out. Our preference is a splash well *and* scupper holes, because any free water in a small boat can be hazardous.

Today small motorboats are required to have upright flotation, a lifesaving feature that was built into some motorboats almost from the time the internal-combustion engine was invented. Watertight compartments and tanks accomplished this in early designs, a good example being the sponsons that did double duty as gunwales on some of the canoe modifications built to accommodate small outboard motors. Now closed-celled foam is used almost exclusively for flotation.

The fact that small motorboats must float upright when swamped is reason enough to stay with your boat. This knowledge should also add to your peace of mind whenever the breeze pipes up and the rippled sea turns into a battleground of hillocks and trenches, none of which stand still for a second. Now is the time your little boat will show her strengths and weaknesses, revealing hidden secrets that will make the receptive observer a better skipper.

—DRG

How to Run an Inlet

Inlet running, like most boathandling skills, is best learned by experience built up gradually over time—a luxury seldom granted those of us who don't encounter barred inlets in our boating backyards.

All is not lost, however; there is a quick way to gain "gradual" experience in running inlets at any stage of your boating career. First, let's examine the difficulties. As with other skills, the ability to run inlets begins with an understanding of what we have to overcome and why.

THE PROBLEMS

The difficulties encountered at the mouth of a river or creek (or sometimes at a break in a barrier island) actually begin far at sea in wind-generated waves. The stronger the wind, the bigger the waves. If the wind blows from the same direction for an extended period of time or has the opportunity to blow unimpeded over a great distance, or *fetch*, the waves get even bigger. For more on wave size, see page 148.

Ocean waves generally resemble sine waves, though in real life they are more confused, because several individual waves will traverse a given spot at the same time. The result is a complex wave, similar to a complex sound wave, in which individual wave forms combine to reinforce or cancel each other. This pattern of reinforcement leads to the observation that "every fifth (or third or seventh) wave is bigger." As long as the water depth exceeds one-half the wave length, the seas maintain a

Speed is one effective way to attack an inlet, but as writer Bob Armstrong points out, there are some major hazards connected with the practice, so a skipper must have his act together to do it safely.

SEAMANSHIP

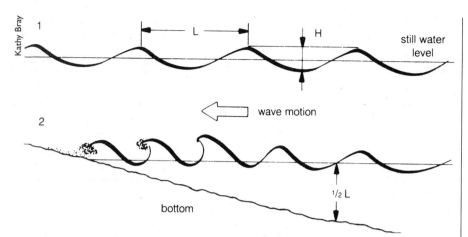

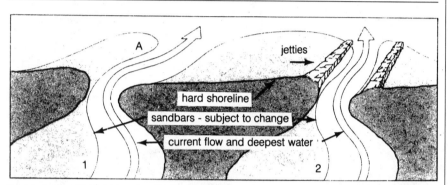

When waves "feel" the ocean or lake bottom (usually when depth increases to about one-half the wave length), the result is steeper, sharper seas, and eventually cresting breakers.

A typical natural inlet is shown in (1). Eventually silt will deposit to the right of point A and the current will either continue farther down the beach or perhaps break through the bar to the left of A (2). The same inlet "improved." The jetties will help stabilize the inlet, but frequent dredging will be required to maintain the channel depth and remove the bars that tend to form along the jetties.

labels in figure:
A
jetties
hard shoreline
sandbars - subject to change
current flow and deepest water
1
2

smooth form and are, except in severe storm conditions, no real threat.

The problem develops when ocean waves move into shallower water. When a wave begins to "feel" the sea bed, its sinusoidal movement is restricted, and the wave slows, permitting the next wave behind it to catch up. The top portion of the wave is less affected and thus tends to overrun the bottom portion, and the result is steeper, sharper, more closely spaced peaks, and eventually, as the sea bed continues to shoal, the familiar curl of a wave approaching the beach. Forward motion and gravity combine to bring the curl downward, forming a breaker. A series of breakers is called *surf*.

The second element of the problem starts with the sand and silt brought downstream by outflowing current. The amount of suspended solids a given current can carry is directly related to its velocity. When an outflowing stream encounters the incoming surf, it slows and deposits some of the silt across the mouth of the inlet to form a sandbar. When the bar develops sufficiently, it changes the course of the stream, which in turn changes the development of the bar. Thus, inlets are in a constant state of change. A major ocean storm or runoff after a heavy inland rain can produce a big change in a hurry. Even in calm weather, change is constant and inevitable.

This presents several problems to boaters. For instance, the meandering course of the outflow can eventually produce a channel that runs parallel to the breakers in the incoming surf. Fortunately, these stretches are often short, but even a few minutes of beam seas in heavy weather can be both uncomfortable and dangerous. Another problem is that buoys must be constantly moved to mark the best water. Thus, it is impossible to chart their location, and a cruising skipper has no way to preview the course through an inlet by studying the chart.

Man's Improvements?

Though constant change is the nature of the beast where inlets are concerned, we humans often can't resist trying to stop it. As a result, we have "improved" many inlets by adding breakwaters or jetties and by dredging and redredging the channel to make it go where we want it to. The truth is that while these artificial changes can slow down nature's changes, they can't eliminate them. Even improved inlets change, though the change is often slowed enough to render them more predictable and easier to run.

STRATEGY AND TACTICS

The most practical way to learn inlet running is to go ahead and do it. But begin gently. For your first attempt, pick a time when you have an offshore wind (wind blowing off the land) and slack water, or the early stages of a rising tide. Starting with an improved inlet helps. If you can't get ideal conditions, two out of three isn't bad, but be sure to avoid onshore winds in your initial attempts. Even under the best conditions, a problem inlet should have enough surge to give you a good indication of what you must work with (and against) and of what to expect under the worst conditions.

If you are starting on an unimproved or natural inlet, be sure to go out through it before trying to come in. This will give you a better picture of the sandbar and surf patterns. In fact, this brings up one of the biggest dangers in inlet running: From the outside it is very hard to determine the state of the seas, since the backs of waves all look very much alike; the clues to roughness are mostly on the inside. With practice, you will note subtle indicators visible from outside, but this degree of observational skill takes time to develop.

Beginning with the easy surge of ideal conditions, practice the proper techniques until they feel natural. If the surge is very gentle, technique won't really matter, but take advantage of the opportunity to get used to feeling the rhythm of the sea. Next, try the inlet on an outgoing tide with all other conditions ideal. You'll notice a difference. When you have mastered that, move on to gentle onshore winds. Ultimately, you'll be ready to face the worst conditions: an outgoing tide against a strong onshore wind.

Throughout your practice sessions, your objective is to maintain control. Just how you do that depends greatly on your boat and how she handles. If you have a lot of power, often you can just pour on the coal and outrun, or at least ride *with*, the seas. If you try to use speed alone, be sure you can go fast enough to skip across the crests or stay with one. Remember, shallowness is one of the problems presented by inlets. This is accentuated in the troughs. More than one speedster has torn off underwater running gear and holed a boat by coming off the crest of a wave and down into so little water that the boat momentarily grounded—hard! So if you opt for the fast lane, do so with care.

A more cautious approach is to enter the inlet on the back of a wave, neither too close to the curl nor too close to the wave behind. This is easier said than done, but you can learn with practice; developing the proper pacing is one of the reasons for practicing under gradually worsening conditions. Entering on the back of a wave is step one; adjusting your speed to stay there is step two (and

Inlets are in a constant state of change. Even in calm weather, change is inevitable.

in my opinion, a wiser choice than barreling onward, even if you have the muscle). If you don't have the power to keep up with the wave system, you'll have to learn to use the power you do have with finesse and let the waves outrun you without upsetting you.

If the seas are overtaking you, try to keep your stern square to the

waves so that there will be less tendency for the boat to swing sideways—a move known as *broaching*. You should avoid this because heavy beam seas can lead to capsizing if their frequency should happen to coincide with the rolling moment of your boat. Repeated beam seas, like the repeated gentle pushes of a child on a swing, can accomplish more in total effect than a large, strong single wave. Staying squared away has to be a prime objective.

Square It Up

At times the sea will win out and swing you around. When it does, take corrective action immediately. Back off on the throttle(s) and turn the steering wheel to swing the bow in the direction you want it to go. Then give a burst of forward power. The purpose of this operation is to swing the boat back stern to the seas, so you'll have to ease off on the throttle(s) and straighten out the rudders as soon as you near the desired heading, or

One effective way to enter an inlet is to ride the back of a wave (top), neither falling behind it and being pooped by the following wave nor getting ahead of it. If the latter happens, the bow will drop over the front of the wave and try to bury itself in the trough (bottom). This slows the boat, letting the following wave catch up and lift the stern even higher, forcing the bow even deeper. This action may cause the boat to broach or, worse still, pitchpole end over end. The looping arrows indicate the circular motion of the water within the waves, a minor force by itself but one that exacerbates some of the other effects. The solid arrows indicate the direction of force—radically different between the top and bottom sketches.

you'll overcompensate and swing the other way. You have to act fast, because you want to be squared away before the next wave can catch you abeam. This sort of throttle-and-steering-wheel game can go on repeatedly until you reach calmer water. It is work, but it will get you through some really tough inlets unscathed.

Pitchpoling, or turning end over end, is another possibility one faces when running a treacherous inlet. Pitchpoling occurs when the bow buries itself in the wave ahead while the wave behind lifts the after section up and over. It *can* happen, though the shape, relative lightness, and shallow draft of most powerboats make it more of a theoretical problem than a practical one. It would be most apt to happen after a wild, out-of-control ride on the curl of a wave followed by a slide down the steep front face (surfing, if you will). While pitchpoling is less likely than broaching, its mere possibility is another good reason for trying to stay on the back of a wave. Here's another: Remember, you only have control when your prop(s) and rudder(s) are in the water. Get too far up onto the top of a wave, and it will lift your after section out of the water.

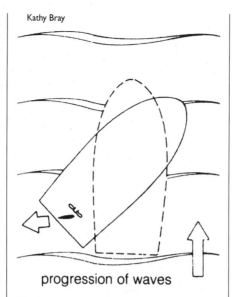

Kathy Bray

progression of waves

The first secret to safe inlet running is to stay square to the seas. While staying square is often impossible, the trick is to get squared away again quickly before the next sea can kick you.

And that can lead to trouble. On the other hand, staying too far back leaves you open to being "pooped"— a calamity in which the wave behind breaks and comes crashing down on you. This presents two not-so-pleasant possibilities. Having a wave's worth of water coming down on you can do considerable damage in its own right, and worse, since the trough is the thinnest water you'll encounter, being pooped can cause the same kind of grounding damage to a slow boat that flying off a crest can do to a fast one.

As I said, keeping a boat constantly squared to the seas and on the back of a wave (if possible) requires nearly constant work with the throttle(s) and steering wheel. And work is the operative word. In fact, a trip through a rough inlet can be downright exhausting. But the results are worth it.

FINAL CAVEATS

No matter how adept you become at running inlets, never lose your respect for the power of the sea. A treacherous inlet can be difficult (and sometimes dangerous) even for the experienced. Size up every situation before entering to make sure that both you and your boat are up to it. When in doubt, stay out.

—Captain Bob Armstrong
(*Getting Started in Powerboating,*
International Marine, 1990)

Anchoring and Mooring Little Boats

There is a vast difference between anchoring a large boat and a small one in our size-class. Virtually all books and instruction have to do with lowering an anchor over the bow, assuring that it is properly dug in and given adequate scope, and then leaving the boat to go ashore in a smaller boat such as a dinghy or inflatable. By contrast, boats we are using are too small to carry a second boat, a practice which is unnecessary in any event. There are all sorts of ways to go ashore from a small boat, moor it securely, and still have it available for use whatever the state of the tide. There are still other ways to moor for shorter periods of time. Below we describe some of them.

Before beginning, though, let's recap what we recommend as necessary anchoring paraphernalia. This includes one or two 100-foot coils and a 50-foot length of ⅜-inch-or-thereabouts nylon line; a 10- to 15-pound anchor; and some odds and ends of smaller line, such as ¼- and ⁵⁄₁₆-inch. This should take care of all the systems described below.

As to what type of anchor is best for a small boat, several choices work well. Early in our boating days, we used a 15-pound fisherman (kedge) anchor, the classic symbol of what an anchor should look like, with flukes and folding stock. This

Two very effective small-boat anchors are this homemade four-tine grapnel and a 20-pound traditional fisherman's anchor with sliding stock. The grapnel is particularly good in weed and on rock; the fisherman's is close to bombproof when its flukes are buried in mud. Both are oversize for the 18-foot aluminum skiff they anchor; when used with a short chain leader, they hold well on a short scope.

worked well as long as the pull was in one direction. The drawback of this anchor type is that one arm sticks up after the other digs in. A boat swinging 180 degrees in wind or tide may cause the line to foul in the arm and pull out the anchor. It happened to us.

The most popular anchor for small boats seems to be the Danforth or its "compatibles," as they say in the computer business. Copies may or may not work as well as the original. The problem we have found with this type is simply one of weight. Those designed for small boats are so light that they tend to drift to the bottom and then bounce along on any sort of hard ground. If you buy one of this type, therefore, we recommend that it weigh at least 12 or 15 pounds. In brief, weight is almost always an advantage with an anchor. Our present anchor, one we have

used for nearly a decade, is a 15-pound grapnel with about a 2-foot-long shank made from 1-inch I.D. galvanized pipe and four curved arms made from solid ½-inch steel rod. A trip ring welded to the arms gives added strength and assures recovery of the anchor if (a) it hangs up, and (b) we remember to tie in a buoyed trip line. It rarely does "(a)," and we remember "(b)" about two-thirds of the time. So far the odds have worked in our favor, but one of these days we will hang up the hook without a trip line, and we'll end up either diving for it or losing it. (We should explain that frequently we keep the anchor bent onto the long bow line of the boat and carry it ashore to hold the boat for short periods of time while we are working on an island. In the course of a day we may anchor or tie up to shore a dozen times, and if we are in a hurry, it is easy to forget the trip line.)

The anchor was the final product of a basic welding course I took one winter, and it has turned out to be a winner. It was designed by my in-

structor and me, and apparently we lucked out on the specs, because the anchor seems to grab on almost any bottom. It is very effective on rocky ground, a condition that usually defeats the lightweight Danforth types.

A friend who spends as much time as I do on the islands in his 15-foot aluminum boat swears by a little folding grapnel. His hook certainly takes up a lot less room than mine. In any event, the grapnel has long been the favored anchor for many small-boat users. (Its hooking ability was much appreciated by crews of the sailing men-of-war, who used grapnels to hold their ship alongside an enemy vessel by throwing the little anchors into the rigging, where they snagged securely. Grapnels are also used for retrieving lost items from the bottom and for finding drowning victims.)

On a brighter note, here are some anchoring and mooring methods we have found useful in our travels. Undoubtedly, you can devise others—and we would love to hear about them.

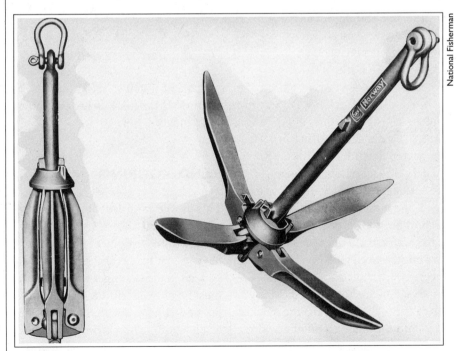

National Fisherman

Available in several sizes, the folding grapnel holds well and folds into a neat package for storage, a welcome feature aboard a small boat.

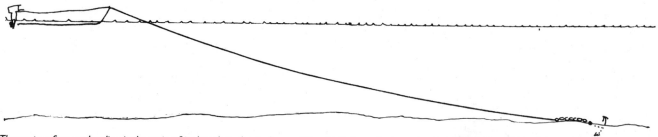

The scope of an anchor line is the ratio of its length to the anchor and the depth from the bow chock to the bottom. Thus, if the depth is 15 feet from the tip of the bow to the bottom and the anchor line is 75 feet in length, the scope is 5:1, a reasonably safe ratio if the anchor is well set and has a leader of 8 or 10 feet of chain that helps hold the anchor flat to the bottom. If there is room and conditions are at all unfavorable, you will rest more comfortably with 100 feet of line holding you to the anchor chain for a 7:1 scope.

SETTING AN ANCHOR

Since several of the methods described below involve the use of an anchor, let's first consider a few basics. All anchors need to lie on their sides in order to dig in. A short length of galvanized chain (6 to 10 feet in our case) will help tip over the anchor and hold it there, a method much preferred over attaching the line directly to the ring on the anchor. The chain also serves as a spring, absorbing some of the yanking as the boat rises and falls on the waves. Because the anchor works best on its side, the anchor line should be long enough to create a shallow angle between boat and anchor. This length of line from bow to anchor is called the *scope* and is described as the ratio between length of line and depth of water. Thus a scope of 5:1 in 10 feet of water would call for approximately 50 feet of anchor line.

A steep scope, say of 3:1 or even less, and a reasonably heavy anchor is probably OK for a lunch stop in calm water, but a scope of at least 5:1 and preferably 7:1 is needed for safe overnight anchoring.

To set an anchor: clear the anchor, check the shackles, tie the anchor line into the chain (a bowline with a simple overhand knot anchoring the bitter end to the standing part will suffice as a knot), fake the line in loose coils on the deck so it will go over the side without catching anything (like a foot!), and *be certain the end is tied to the boat.* Drop or ease the anchor over the side, making sure it is not fouled in the line. Do not throw the anchor. Once the hook is on the bottom, let the boat fall off with the wind if there is a good breeze; otherwise, power the boat slowly in reverse until you have let out the right length of line. When you feel the anchor catch on bottom, give it a solid pull, and then line up two

> **Weight is almost always an advantage with an anchor.**

points and watch to see if the boat is drifting. If the hook is not dragging, your anchor is set.

WIND MOORING

This is the simplest way of all to moor your boat for a short time, although under ideal conditions we have used it for several hours. As can be seen in the sketch, a steady breeze must be blowing off the land and the boat must have ample depth underneath her if the tide is dropping. Fifty feet of line will let the boat drift out far enough to hold in the wind. Be certain that the line is well tied to the boat and the land. We often use an anchor jammed into a rock crevice or dug into the beach to hold the inshore end. The main danger to watch for is a sudden change of wind direction. The method is particularly handy on small islands where there is always an "offshore" wind in the lee.

STERN ANCHOR

Another effective short-duration mooring is to drop a stern anchor as you come in and let out line until you reach shore. When the tide is falling, the stern line can then be tied near the transom without slack. If the tide is rising, an adequate amount of slack must be left in the stern line to let the boat reach shore when it is retrieved. A second long line is securely tied forward, and then the coil is taken ashore. After you get what gear you may want from the boat, it is cast off, and you walk along the shore with the bow coil, towing the boat and letting out line as necessary. As the bow line gets longer, the boat will move away from the shore on the hypotenuse of a triangle. The bow line is made fast to the shore when you are satisfied that the boat is far enough out to be safely afloat until you need it.

Try not to moor sideways to a strong crosswind or swift current; if

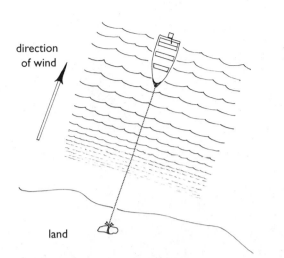

Wind mooring is simplicity itself. Be sure to allow enough line so that the boat will be held well off by the wind and not dodge around in the fluky airs near shore.

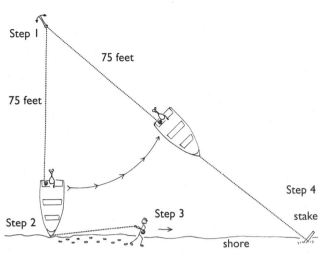

Simple and effective, this rig can be set up in a few minutes. If the shore curves out to the right, the boat may end up solidly moored fore and aft in deep water, an ideal situation for an overnight stop.

you have a choice, take the bow line upwind or up current.

TWELVE-HOUR HOLD

With a tide cycle of slightly more than 12 hours (it may vary in your cruising area), you can take advantage of one of the most secure methods of mooring possible; namely, grounding out. If you plan to stay at a campsite overnight and the tide is high sometime during the evening, you can draw your boat up to the beach at the top of the tide, tie it to shore, and let the tide drop out from under it. If it is 8 P.M. when you tie up, the tide will be back the next morning a little after 8 A.M. to refloat your boat. If the tide is not going to be quite as high in the morning (check your tide calendar carefully so as not to confuse Standard Time and Daylight Savings Time) as it was in the evening, you may have to allow for that by letting the evening tide drop for a half hour or so before grounding out. Either way, if your boat is heavy, you won't be able to get it back into the water until the tide returns, but neither will you have to be concerned about it during the night.

If the tide is at some stage other than high water in the evening, you can modify the grounding-out system as follows: Select the time you want the boat to float in the morning and pull it up to the shore at the corresponding time in the evening, whatever the stage of the tide, and run a

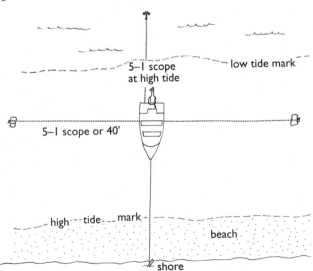

When there isn't much room to move around, you may need to moor your boat at three or four points. The photo shows such a setup with side lines angling off the quarters rather than at 90 degrees to the keel line. In this way, no stern anchor is needed. Each situation dictates the anchoring system you will use, so you should think through several possibilities before making a choice.

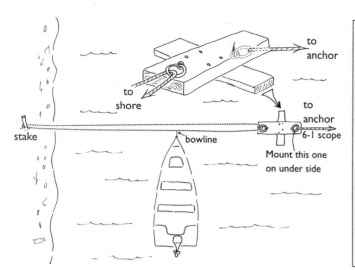

A haul-off is a handy rig in tidal areas since it makes the boat available at any stage of the tide. The photo shows three 14-footers overnighting on the same haul-off.

line from the bow to a tree or other secure tie-off above the high-tide line. Assuming you have selected a spot where the boat can take the ground comfortably, run lines off the quarters about 30 to 40 feet and anchor or tie them off. The boat can now rise or drop with the tide while staying in place and will be ready to go the next morning. (If the boat has to rise several feet because the tide is quite low when you are mooring, you may want to allow a little slack in the side lines or run them out farther in order to relieve the strain as the tide rises. However, if you use a light line like ¼-inch nylon, the stretch in the line will take care of the rise and fall. Remember, the longer the line, the greater the stretch.)

HAUL-OFF

This is a good overnight mooring. An anchor is dropped and set in deep water (it should have at least a 5:1 scope at high tide and the anchor must be firmly set). The anchor line is tied to a rugged float with a ring bolt firmly attached to it. A long line is run through the ring bolt and paid out in equal lengths, the two ends then being tied together to form an endless line running from the ring bolt to shore. (It may be necessary to tie in a second long line of approximately the same length as the first in order to reach from shore to float. This is one reason we suggest carrying lots of spare line aboard your boat. The two lines need to be about the same length so that no knot will have to go through the ringbolt, where it will surely jam.)

A short line can now be tied from the bow of the boat into the haul-off line with a bowline knot, and the boat can be hauled out to the float, where it will ride nicely until needed, when it can be pulled in again. We recommend the crossed-plank design for the haul-off float in order to prevent the line from twisting, which it is in-

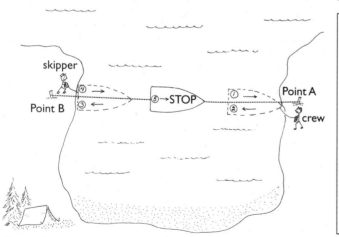

The small-cove mooring is fun to set up and pleasing to look at when completed. The system is described in the text. This boat is moored in a remote little cove in Labrador.

When anchoring in current, it is important that the anchor line go over the bow and not over the side or the transom, where it may cause the boat to capsize in swift water. If the anchor line is tied to the boat, it should have a knot that can be released under strain; fastening it to a cleat is even better. This method will enable you to release the boat quickly in an emergency.

clined to do if a simple buoy is used instead of the float.

SMALL-COVE MOORING

This is a very reliable and esthetically pleasing method to use where you can moor in a small, deep cove (see illustration and photo at bottom of page 160). To start with, you will need a line that reaches all the way across the cove, so you may have to tie in a second length. The procedure is as follows:

1. Run your boat in to point A and let off your crewman with the long rope that has been tied to the bow.
2. Back across the cove while your crewman lets out the rope.
3. Go ashore with a second long line tied to the stern.
4. Signal to your crew on point A to haul the boat to the middle of the cove while you let out the stern line.
5. When the boat is where you want it, both of you tie off to a secure hold such as a tree or boulder.

The boat is now safe and sound whenever you want it. The system can be set up by one person, but the procedure has to be worked out to fit the circumstances, so we will not attempt to describe it here. Think it through along the lines described for two persons, and you will figure out a way. A tip: Steps 4 and 5 will have to be done by you, which means guessing at the length of stern line needed to reach the center of the cove, then faking it down in the boat so that it will pay out without snarling and tying the bitter end to a hold on point B. You then walk around to point A and haul in on the bow line until the stern line comes taut. You can make adjustments at this time, but each one requires a walk to the other point, which will help you work up an appetite, if nothing else!

ANCHORING TIPS

- If your boat will be tided out, be sure the ground beneath it is relatively smooth, without sharp rocks anywhere beneath or near the hull. (Love those aluminum boats!)
- Check your boat before you go to

ANCHORING AND MOORING **161**

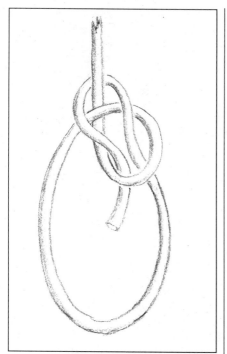

The bowline is easy to tie—and untie—in slippery synthetic ropes. Although a very secure knot, it's a good idea to leave enough of the bitter end to tie an overhand knot around the standing part (the main part) of the rope if the knot will be under heavy tension.

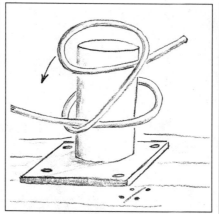

The clove hitch is an excellent "quick fix" knot for lashing on to a hook, securing a line to a pole, or tying up to a dock, as depicted here. It should be snugged up when completed, but it still may "unroll" under pressure if there isn't approximately equal tension on the bitter end. You can counter this with an overhand knot in the bitter end around the standing part.

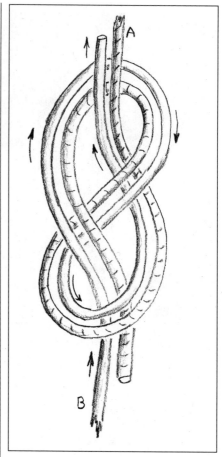

The figure-eight is a simple knot and is normally touted as an excellent stopper knot at the end of a rope because of its bulk and ease of untying, even after being under pressure. However, as shown here, it is a very secure knot for tying together two ropes of about equal size. A figure-eight knot is tied in the end of rope A; the end of rope B is then threaded back through the knot in rope A, following exactly the path of rope A. That's all there is to it. If you want extra security, you can tie an overhand knot around the standing part in the bitter end of each rope.

bed, once during the night, and again first thing in the morning. It is your ticket home and hence worth a little lost sleep. It is not unusual for the wind to come up during the night strong enough to drag a poorly set haul-off anchor or break loose a quartering line. Thus your vessel may drift in on the rocks or close to them while you are asleep and need your attention ASAP.

- If it looks as if any of your mooring lines may chafe on ledge or rocks, you may want to reset or wrap them.
- It would seem unnecessary to remind you to be sure of your knots, but this is so important and easy to goof up, we are saying it anyway. We use just three knots (the clove hitch, the bowline, and the figure-eight) for virtually every requirement, because they are easy to tie, hard to tie incorrectly, hold well with slippery synthetic ropes, and can always be untied.

—DRG

The Delicate Art of Docking

Smart dockside maneuvering is the hallmark of a seasoned boat skipper—and the more adverse the conditions, the brighter the mark. Skill is achieved only through experience, which in turn is derived by two means: mistakes (and the lessons learned) or by slowly building upon a core of fundamental instruction. The former technique is fine for those who can afford repairs to their own and others' boats. The latter is generally quicker, considerably safer, and less costly.

Although much of what follows applies to all boats, we'll limit our discussion to single-screw inboards, I/Os (sterndrives), and outboards. Considering that I/Os and outboards both sport steerable propellers, we'll lump them together as outboards.

Regardless of drive, any ably executed docking maneuver depends upon a well-grounded understanding of how a boat reacts relative to applied forces—wind, current, and most importantly, propeller torque and rudder.

Forget the way an automobile steers, its front end leading, the rest of the chassis obediently following. A boat's steering inputs, rudder and prop, are located aft.

When a turn is made while going ahead, the stern swings in the opposite direction about the boat's pivot point (roughly ⅓ abaft the bow) until the bow points in the desired heading. This basic axiom applies to all boats, although outboards will react more adroitly than conventional inboards with props on fixed shafts and directional inputs by rudder only.

Regardless of many treatises on the subject, replete with more diagrams than a football coach's play book, there are only three basic scenarios: pulling into a slip bow first, backing into a slip, and docking alongside. Conversely (if we're ever to sail again), we have backing out of a slip, pulling out bow first, and departing from alongside. But before taking the wheel, we must understand the governing concept of single-screw operation.

Due to the propeller action, single-screw boats always exhibit a turning tendency, which we can use to advantage, particularly when going astern. Chances are you have a right-hand prop, easily checked by backing at idle speed with the rudder (or outboard) amidships. On boats with right-hand props, the stern tends to go to port when going astern. If the stern goes to starboard, you have a left-hand prop.

Another tenet: Whenever possible, run against the current or wind, whichever appears to exert the greater force. In most instances, we'll want maximum maneuverability with minimum way on the boat, and opposing forces work in our favor. When docking alongside, you'll frequently have a choice, although when coming into a marina, running across the bows of docked boats to reach your slip, the layout generally dictates the approach.

PULLING IN AND BACKING OUT

So much for dogma. Let's get underway. We'll start by pulling into a slip bow first. Imagine your slip is on the starboard side halfway down a water-

Whenever possible, run against the current or wind, whichever appears to exert the greater force.

way lined with slips on both sides. Assuming there isn't any traffic (if there is, wait), idle down the waterway, keeping to your left to gain as much turning radius as possible, but not so close that your stern will greet other boats when you make your turn to starboard.

With your turn made and the boat aligned with the slip, ease in (usually out of gear), then apply a shot of reverse gear to brake motion. No one can tell you when to start your turn, but experimenting in less congested waters will provide the handle required. Temper all this with regard to the wind, which can exert considerable control over a boat with minimum way on.

Hold the rudder a fair shake to starboard (outboards require only minor compensation) when backing out to counteract the prop's effort to swing the stern into the boat on your port side. Experience determines the necessary compensation. Once the bow is clear, hold hard port rudder and idle on back if you're going to proceed to starboard. Then, having gained sufficient clearance off your bow, turn hard to starboard, go ahead, and you're on your way.

If your required turn seaward is to port, hold full starboard rudder as soon as the bow clears the pilings, and give a short burst with the throttle—then immediately back to neutral. Cut hard to port as the boat coasts astern (watching clearance to other boats), then give a short burst of power ahead as soon as there's clearance off the bow to make your turn. Back off to a crawl as soon as the bow comes around.

Backing out in an outboard, with its steerable prop, is considerably easier and more direct, although short bursts with the throttle aid maneuvering in tight situations.

BACKING IN AND PULLING OUT

Backing into a slip with an outboard is essentially a matter of steering the prop where required.

When pulling out from a slip bow first, don't swing hard over rudder until the stern is about to clear the pilings. As soon as you do clear, swing hard over and give a short burst with the throttle to accelerate your turn.

DOCKING ALONGSIDE AND DEPARTING

So much for slips. Now let's find a crowded fuel dock and lay alongside, as in the accompanying illustration. If there's appreciable wind parallel to the dock, we'll come up against it. If

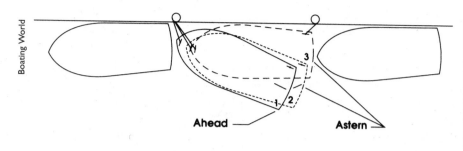

Docking alongside.

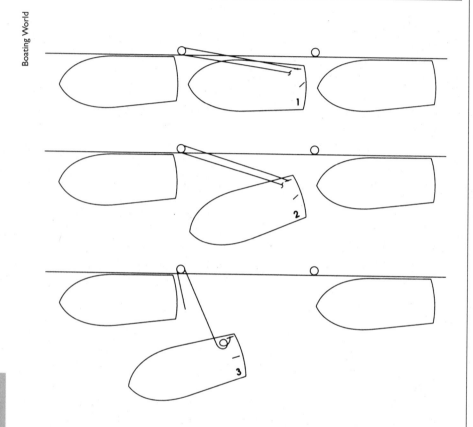

Departing from a dock.

stern in. Similarly, if you come in against a current, it will carry your stern in.

Shoving off can be precisely that when wind and current are inconsequential. With rudder amidships, take off the stern line, then the bow line, then give a smooth shove against the dock from any point forward of your boat's pivot point. When the bow clears, go ahead. Don't put the rudder over while still against the dock. The stern will bear against the dock, preventing a turn, and you will plow into the boat ahead.

To depart when there is a strong head current or a stiff breeze blowing onto the dock, make up a forward spring line from the stern before casting off the bow and stern lines. Make it a running line (cleated at the stern, looped around the dock piling or cleat that's off the bow, and back to the cockpit) as in the illustration, and departure can be made without help from the dock. Swing your rudder hard over toward the dock, and shift into reverse (1). The bow will come off the dock (2), and when it's clear, your mate pulls in the spring line while you go ahead (3).

If your rudder torque going astern will swing the stern off the dock, or if you're in an outboard, cast off the stern line, hold the bow line, and go astern with the rudder hard over away from the dock. When the stern clears, straighten your rudder, continue astern until completely clear, then you're on your way.

Unfortunately, the effectiveness of the written word is limited when the wind blows, the tide runs, and other boats complicate the situation. But the practice and acclimation will brighten your mark, and a knowledgeable friend aboard hastens the process.

—Ray Hendrickson
(*Small Boat Journal* #76)

there's a current running, we'll work against it. Let's assume that there is only one other person aboard or that we're alone, but someone is on the dock.

Idle in at any angle, tucking your bow into the dock (1), then promptly pop in a quick momentary shot of reverse, killing way on the boat as your helper takes a bow line. He then tends his line, keeping your boat clear of the boat astern while you swing hard rudder toward the dock

(2), going in reverse, until the boat swings in and a stern line can be secured (3). Other methods, such as walking the boat in against the current, also serve, but with a small boat, there's nothing simpler than gently poking in there and getting an initial line on the dock to exercise control.

Should the wind be blowing hard against the dock, you'll be giving that initial shot of reverse a bit sooner, and the wind will carry the

Shore Landings and Takeoffs

Anyone can bring a boat up to land or push off from shore, but doing it skillfully takes some practice. Here are a few tips that will remove a lot of the awkwardness from what would seem to be a simple set of maneuvers.

First, though, let's make the job easier by having the right tools. Many small motorboats carry a paddle to propel the boat out into deep water or back to shore. A paddle is a poor choice because of its short length and its weak power, drawbacks that become frustratingly obvious the first time you try to paddle a high-sided motorboat into the face of a breeze. A better choice is an oar from 7½ to 9 feet in length, preferably of hardwood, since it will be used as much as a push pole and pry bar as an oar.

Better still is a setting pole 11 to 15 feet in length. This is nothing more than a push pole averaging about 1½ inches in diameter, with a point carved into the thick end if it is a sapling or the business end if it is a store-bought pole. A soft steel canoe shoe or other pointed metal tip will improve the durability of the working end (we've used a copper pipe reducer very successfully; most hardware stores carry them in their plumbing departments). A heavy boat can be moved and controlled easily with a pole, and as you get into deeper water, it makes a reasonably good paddle, because its wetted area is about that of a paddle blade. The pole can also be used as a pry to move the boat off the shore in a dropping tide and as a ridgepole for a kitchen fly when you are camping ashore.

When pushing off from shore, it is rarely necessary to get your feet wet unless the bottom is extremely gradual and your boat heavily loaded. Rather, push it out until the bow is at the edge of the shore and just holding the boat by a bit of friction under the stem. Climb aboard and move aft with your oar or push pole. Your weight alone is usually all that is needed to lift the bow from the beach; if not, a shove with your pole will do it. Pole out until you have sufficient depth of water to run your motor, and then start her up and back out slowly until you have turning room. But be almighty careful.

Backing under power in shallow water is always potentially hazardous to your motor's health, since the propeller blades are exposed to any obstruction you may hit and the motor cannot tilt up if it strikes something in reverse. On the contrary, the momentum of the boat jams the lower unit against whatever it hits, thus almost assuring damage of some kind.

Going in reverse with a motor operated from the tiller position is much safer, since you can back slowly while actually leaning over and watching the lower unit move through the water. In this way, you can pick your way around rocks and clumps of seaweed with a delicacy that will surprise you. The boat will follow the motor like a docile bovine. While doing this, you can shift into neutral if the motor must go through a clump of floating weed and thus keep it from getting snarled with greenery, or you can raise the motor almost instantly if an obstruction appears unavoidable. By the way, you can tilt the motor out of the water for a few seconds while it is still running and in gear without damaging its inner workings. We must quickly add, however, that this should only be done at or just above idling speed.

Landings on anything other than a smooth sand beach with no waves can be tricky. As you move into the shallows, the urge is to get someone forward to watch for rocks, stumps, or what-have-you. We suggest you learn to read water without having to rely on another person; the art will come in handy when you are operating alone and may save you embarrassment or worse when you attempt to rely on someone who is inexperienced in judging underwater obstacles. When you start to get uneasy as the water shoals, stop the motor, tilt it up, and move ahead under pushpole power. In any event, discourage politely the eager individual who wants to help by going forward to "watch the bottom." Remember, the narrow bow of the boat has little bearing and therefore responds readily to human weight by sinking deeper in the water. As a result, the bow grounds out in several inches of water, and someone is going to have to get their

> *Backing under power in shallow water is always potentially hazardous to your motor's health.*

feet wet to get the boat ashore. Better to keep everyone aft and let the bow ride as far toward the land as it can.

There are some tricks that good boat handlers have developed for special situations. One is landing a person on a ledge, a particularly dicey maneuver if there is a bit of sea running. What is required is deep water right up to the ledge and a decent landing spot for the person going ashore. That person, who must be reasonably athletic, should don a life jacket and then stand in the bow seat or sit on the bow deck in such a way that he or she can slide off easily. His legs should not dangle over the bow, since they may be jammed against the ledge if someone miscalculates.

The skipper must keep the boat pointed straight at the ledge and ease up to within a foot or two of the rock, all the time noting the action of the water and any currents generated. At this point, the boat should be moving ahead ever so slightly, but with the skipper already shifting into reverse. In the 2 or 3 seconds needed for the boat to begin backing away from the ledge, the person in the bow should be able to step ashore safely without having to bridge more than a few inches of water.

This sounds more hazardous in the description than it is in reality; we've done it dozens of times without accidents of any kind. The important thing is to make certain the person going ashore knows what to do and will do it quickly when told to go. As for the skipper, he must be certain conditions are mild enough to carry out the maneuver without danger. And both approach and retreat must be done with a gentle hand on the throttle so that no one is thrown off balance or the boat damaged against the ledge.

An easier method if there is little or no swell to deal with, and if there are suitably placed weeds and rocks,

When conditions are right, try snaking your boat into tiny slits in the wall like this one, or explore the piers of an urban waterfront. This is an exciting way to hone your handling skills and "become one" with your boat.

is to put the bow into a weedy crevice in the ledge and leave the engine idling in forward gear, thus holding the boat tightly against the ledge. If several persons are to leave the boat, it is best to send the strongest person ashore first to help the others.

Maneuvers such as those described here require practice and a responsive boat. Whenever we are working along a rocky shore and have a few extra minutes, we like to go right into the slurp zone and work the boat in and out of tight places. After a while, the motions of boat and water meld together and the boat becomes almost an extension of self.

Eventually, you can look at water some distance away and judge its "boatability."

A final trick, which was developed by sportfishermen working the surf on Cape Cod and points south in their small boats, is the wave-washed beach landing. Carrying their aluminum skiffs on the roofs of their beach buggies or towing them behind on fat-tired trailers, they launch bow first through the surf on a fairly steep beach, using oars for the first few waves and then firing up their outboards. In landing, they wait just outside the surf line and then gun their motors to plane in on the back of a breaking wave, and if all goes well they are able to step out of the boat onto the wet sand.

As may be imagined, all sorts of things can go wrong—and have—in carrying out this maneuver. Trouble starts with misjudging the wave and either riding in on its front to swamp, broach, or roll over, or not getting far enough up on its back and dropping into the trough to catch the next breaking wave right over the transom. In the excitement, you can also forget to unlock the tilt mechanism and be brought up short with the lower unit plowing sand and the motor torquing the transom to the point of popping rivets or ripping fiberglass. It's all in a day's fun.

—DRG

River Expertise

A few years ago I used America's rivers and inland waterways to singlehand my 24-foot boat from Lake Erie to Florida and back. I negotiated a few dozen rivers, about 40 locks, and more than 120 bridges each way. I bucked currents up to 5 knots on the Hudson River at spring flood stage, woke up aground once in a tidal river, and got up-close-and-personal with more tugs, barges, and ocean-going freighters than I care to think about.

I loved the Bahamas, the Florida Keys, and the Tortuga, but for spectacular beauty New York's Hudson River Valley and South Carolina's Waccamaw River are in a class by themselves. While river cruising in any sort of small boat under power is a never-ending learning experience, dealing with locks, currents, bridges, and barges is as fascinating as it is challenging.

Many boaters seem intimidated by river current. They needn't be. Simply follow the charts, use navigational aids, and be willing to accept local knowledge, which can make or break a cruise. On the positive side, current can increase your speed and help save fuel when you are heading downstream. Going upstream, it does not have to be a chore if you play it right and learn to read the water.

Generally, the swiftest water is found in midstream, and slack water is found closer to shore, where it is slowed by friction from bottom and bank. The general rule is that when running downstream, stay in the center of the channel; when heading upstream, stay close to the bank. Shoals tend to build up on the inside of river bends and where small tributaries enter the main river, so in these cases stay closer to the center.

A point to keep in mind is that

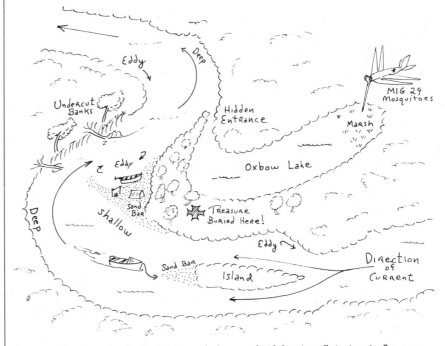

A river winding through valley lowlands may look more placid than it really is since its flow may have been determined days earlier in rainy uplands hundreds of miles away. However, flowing water regularly creates certain features, several of which are shown here.

your boat must be going faster or slower than the current if you want to steer it. A boat going the same speed as the current is controlled by the current, not by you. Thus, if you are going downstream in very fast current and want to slow down, put your engine in reverse so that you can control both speed and direction. If you are headed upstream in fast current and are not sure of the bottom, don't be rushed but instead throttle up just enough to creep upstream. In short, always stay in control, but don't feel that the only way you can go through swift water is at planing speed.

The line between fast and quiet water may be only inches wide, especially just below the tip of a pier, breakwater, or weir. If you try to head out straight into the swift water, the current may well grab your bow and swing it downstream. The better way is to drop downstream a little in the slack water, point your boat upstream, and then ease into the fast water with your bow pretty much heading into the flow, all the while ready to make corrections with tiller and throttle as the current takes hold of your boat. We can't emphasize enough the importance of always having control of your craft in heavy current. An educated seat-of-the-pants touch helps a lot.

Also, in really tricky shoal areas, range markers are quite common. Many boaters are lulled into a false sense of security by believing that navigational aids are strictly for use by large, deep-draft vessels and don't apply to small craft. This isn't so. A lightweight boat may be able to skitter by on the wrong side of a buoy, but some shoal areas are mighty close to the navigational aid, and mud or sand may be waiting just under the surface to grab you, especially in low-water periods. If you are going to play the ignore-the-buoy game, local knowledge is an absolute must.

Debris, docking, and anchoring also require special consideration. Floating debris can be a problem at any time of the year, though it's more prevalent after heavy rains or during spring flooding. When traveling up the Hudson from Albany one spring, I broke three outboard shear pins in one day despite efforts to spot floating and submerged snags. I became proficient at replacing the pins

River expertise in a small boat begins with the realization that moving water must be taken seriously. If alone or with others in tender craft such as this little jonboat, good judgment dictates wearing a life jacket. Such a craft caught upstream of a snag or boulder can be flipped in seconds.

Low dams and weirs are poison for small boats. When the flow is heavy, as it is here, a strong undertow is created on the downstream side, one frequently strong enough to capsize boats and drag people beneath the surface. The circular motion of the current below the dam can hold objects in its deadly grip for many minutes.

quickly, because the water was deep and the current too swift to anchor. So remember to carry plenty of spare shear pins if your outboard motor requires them.

DOCKING AND ANCHORING

Docking in current calls for common sense, planning, a deft hand at the helm, judicious use of spring lines, and practice. Practice is the easiest way to learn, even without a dock. Pick a tree or bush on the riverbank and imagine it is a dock. Then line up your bow and play the current, letting it take you toward your "dock." If possible, always try to dock by heading into the current rather than downstream. If the latter is necessary, practice easing down on the dock while in reverse, again remembering that you will lose control if you are moving at the same speed as the current.

If trying to dock on the downstream side of a dock with the current on your beam, rig an after spring line from the beam or pivot point and simply power forward, which will bring your boat in to the dock and hold it there while you or a crewman put out docklines fore and aft. Timidity is one of the biggest mistakes boaters make when docking. Decide your course of action and then follow your plan deliberately. The common-sense approach? If conditions are adverse, put your ego on hold and call ahead on your VHF or hail someone on the dock for a helping hand.

Anchoring in a quiet cove or below an island in a river can be rewarding, but a few cardinal rules apply. First, get as far out of the channel as possible. Second, avoid anchoring in swift currents or areas where holding ground is poor. Always anchor below an island rather than above it, and don't anchor at a bend of a river where the bottom is often hard and swept clean. Third, know and use the anchor lights. Fourth, if anchoring in a tidal river, check the tide range and river depth before dropping the hook. On some rivers, such

> If there are no aids to navigation, try to follow the general trend of the river and run about a third of the river's width from the outside bank.

as the Hudson, tides can affect water depth even if you are more than 100 miles upstream from the ocean. And fifth, see if your anchorage will be exposed to the wind, because a strong wind blowing against a current can create a nasty chop and cause a boat to "dance" an anchor along the bottom.

DRAWBRIDGES

Drawbridges can be frustrating, depending on the season and the time of day. Most bridges are restricted to certain hours of operation, due to car traffic and other variables. While this is understandable, I remember waiting with 10 other boats for a bridge to open on the Alligator River–Pungo River in North Carolina, only to see one horse and one tractor use the span in an hour.

When approaching a bridge, check either a cruising guide or the signboard on the bridge fender for hours of operation. If the bridge is not restricted, give the bridge tender a long and a short blast on a horn or call on Channel 16 or Channel 13, unless posted otherwise. While waiting for the bridge to open, you can drift, hold your position with reverse, circle, or even anchor out of the channel, depending on current and other boat traffic.

Don't get mad at the bridge tender.

The biggest concern for small boats dealing with drawbridges or swing bridges is other boat traffic that can appear from behind pilings and abutments. This is narrow going for larger vessels, and they should be given the right of way over your maneuverable little boat.

Whitewater Moments

It is quite possible to run a motorboat up or down some rapids, particularly on rivers with a well-delineated channel and sufficient depth for some maneuvering. This is not a practice to be undertaken lightly, however, for a motorboat is far less maneuverable than either a canoe or a whitewater kayak, and if you lose power by trashing your prop on a rock, you lose the ballgame. If you want to learn to run rapids without fail, start by picking an easy one with plenty of depth, a short distance, and a safe runout to recover in if you goof.

A boat designed for the job, a reliable motor, an understanding of how flowing water acts, and a close feel for the boat are basic necessities if you're going to be a good whitewater skipper. Note that oars are in place in case of power loss and that those on board are wearing Class 1 life jackets; you may only have seconds to respond to emergencies in exciting close quarters like those shown here on a mountain river.

A lightweight boat is preferable—we like an open aluminum skiff because it rides easily on top of the water and thus can be quickly turned, and it reacts instantly to a squirt of power. The motor should be powerful enough to jump the boat up on plane, be-cause current speeds run in the 5- to 10-m.p.h. range, which are greater than the displacement speed of the boat hull. The lock should be off so the motor can kick up if it strikes something, and preferably you should have a rubber slip clutch in the prop rather than rely on shear pins. The former usually means you can hit something and keep going; the latter means you head for the showers. A husky 15-foot setting pole can save the day if you lose power for any reason.

Going upstream is relatively easy, because you can creep through the tight places and blast up the easy ones. There is an art to using the set of the current, but learning to do so is one of the secrets of safe passage. Do not have someone in the bow fending off rocks. His weight will make maneuvering difficult, and the powerful current passing under the boat may wrench a pole or paddle from his hands or even throw him overboard. In addition, his pushing against a rock could throw off your navigation to the point of wrecking the boat. This is one-person, very serious work.

Going downstream is more difficult, because you can be going 10 m.p.h. without taking the motor out of neutral. If it is a straight shot to the next pool below and there are no big standing waves waiting at the bottom of a chute, you are probably safe to run just fast enough to maintain steerageway. This will seem like approximately 50 m.p.h. You may find you have better control with the motor in reverse. In any event, this is delicate work. It requires a fair amount of practice to gain the skill and confidence required to run fast water safely.

We've done most of our whitewatering in a powerboat on tidal falls, which are short and generally with ample depth for maneuvering. Even then there is quite an adrenaline shot when you tip over the lip of a rapid and start racing downhill in a 16- or 18-foot boat with land whipping by just a few feet away on either side.

On some fast Western rivers, dory fishing under power is a long-established art, but with the advent of jet-powered outboards, the practice is now more common, and special boats have been developed to take advantage of them (see "Skinny-Water Boating in the Western Jet Boat," page 32).

—DRG

He didn't make the regulations, but he can make you wait longer. If you decide to drift, leave your engine running. I saw a large powerboat drift into a concrete bridge support when its engine wouldn't restart.

When the bridge opens, stick to your side of the channel and remember that downstream traffic has the right of way. Remember, too, that current is often strong in the channel under the bridge. Just before the bridge closes, the bridge tender will usually sound five short blasts.

If you are confident that your boat will go under the bridge without need of the draw, don't go ramming through, but rather ease along under good control and hold this pace until well clear of the bridge and any congestion it causes. However, don't gamble if it is close, unless someone like the bridge tender is watching your clearance. Better to wait than to suffer damage because you are in a hurry.

BIG GUYS ALWAYS WIN

Encounters with barges, ships, and other large vessels should be handled with what I refer to as the "big-boat rule": Even if you think you have the right of way, stay out of their way, because their vessel is bigger than yours. They can't maneuver easily and are often constrained by draft.

Shoals tend to build up on the inside of river bends and where small tributaries enter the main river.

This applies to anchoring as well. For safety and peace of mind, anchor away from channels used by barges, which often run at night and sometimes swing wide on turns.

Also, study the different types of towing methods and be familiar with all markers, lights, and sound signals. While most tugs now push their "tows," some still pull astern with a

towline hundreds of yards long. The line's catenary, or sag, will actually cause it to drop under water. While crossing the St. Johns River ship channel in Florida, I saw a pleasure boat almost hit a submerged towline before the skipper realized his danger. If uncertain of a commercial vessel's intention, or to inform him of yours, call on Channel 13. A horn may not be heard. These highly qualified skippers are generally friendly and have plenty of local knowledge to help you out.

For me, the satisfaction of river cruising comes as much from mastering the navigational challenges as from the scenic beauty. Together, they provide cruisers with memorable experiences.

—Nick Rukavina
(*Small Boat Journal #77*)

Locking Through

At first sight, a lock is intimidating. Suddenly the benign shoreline of trees and grassy banks you have been cruising through gives way to an imposing edifice of steel and concrete, a high-walled prison with dark, dripping walls and a swirling moat. The lock gates through which you must bring your boat may not be immediately visible against the distracting background of walls and piers, buildings, machinery, and warning signs and buoys. It may be even harder to spot the signal light that will tell you if it is OK to proceed.

When in doubt, call time out. Drop

your boat speed to a crawl and take a few minutes to look over what is ahead. First, locate the gates. Usually, they are massive, diagonally or vertically striped steel doors that swing open and tuck into the sides of the lock; occasionally, they will lift instead of swing. If the gates are open, look for the signal light—similar to a highway traffic light—and proceed slowly forward only if it shows green.

Most of the time, the gates ahead will be closed and the light will be red, either fixed or flashing. This means you will have to wait before

you can enter the lock. The length of your wait will depend on the amount and type of other boating traffic and the schedule of operation of the lock. Generally, a commercial vessel has priority over pleasure craft, and its size may not leave any room for your boat in the lock chamber. If it is carrying petroleum or flying a red flag (signaling hazardous cargo), you will definitely have to wait through another locking cycle.

Sometimes lock operation is timed to coincide with bridge openings upstream or downstream. Additionally, many locks will not open after

Entering a lock can be intimidating. If it's a busy time, one or more other boats may be in the lock at once. You'll want to have the general procedure worked out with your crew beforehand.

10 P.M. or before 6 A.M. Try to secure local information on the schedules along your route.

When you have to wait, as you usually will, look for a place to tie up. Many locks have long approach walls, piers, or dolphins (clusters of pilings). If you arrive late, you may be able to spend the night at one of these tie-ups. A few locks have no place to tie up, and you must wait in the river or canal.

SIGNALING

Like most bridges, locks open "on demand," and you should signal the lockmaster of your desire to lock through. Tying up to a dolphin and waiting is not adequate notice. The lockmaster may not even know you are there, and if he does see you, he may think you are just fishing or hanging out.

There are three ways to hail the lockmaster: through a VHF radio, through horn signals, or with the pull cords often found at locks. A radio allows you to call the lockmaster before you reach the lock. The custom-ary VHF channel is 13, but some locks monitor 12, 14, or 16; check locally for the appropriate channel. If you do make contact by radio, you may also ask how long your wait will be and whether you will need to use a particular side of the lock chamber.

Not infrequently, there is nobody at the other end of your transmission.

The lockmaster may be out helping another boat through the lock, or even mowing the lawn. If you don't get any answer, or if you are without a radio yourself, a horn comes in handy. Three long blasts is the common signal on approaching a lock, although some locks ask for two long and two short blasts. Many also have a pull cord near the end of the approach wall or pier that can be used to signal the lockmaster.

Once the lockmaster has been notified, check your lines and fenders. Regular docklines are fine. If you will be descending and using the bollards at the top of the lock wall, lines will have to be twice as long as the drop.

If you know that you will be coming in with the lock wall to your port or starboard, that is where your fenders should be. If you don't know, make sure you have fenders on *both* sides. Cylindrical fenders may be adequate, but they tend to roll on the rough, dirty concrete walls and mess up your topsides. A fender board, usually a 2 x 6 plank several feet long, suspended horizontally be-

One of the most exciting moments is when the lock begins to fill as the upstream lock is opened slightly or water boils up from underwater ducts. Because round fenders have a tendency to roll, a 2 x 6 fender board 4 to 6 feet long may be more effective. The lock usually takes from 15 to 20 minutes to fill.

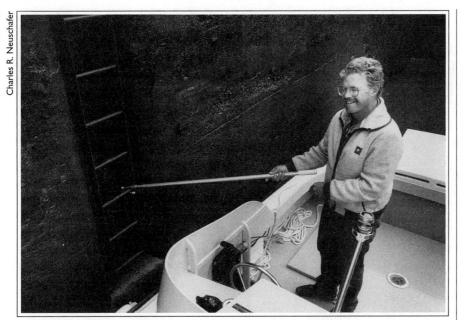

A good technique if you are singlehanding is to hold on to the ladder rungs with your boathook. If lines are being used, never tie them to your boat but rather let them run through your hands. Great strength is not needed to hold your boat in place.

tween fenders and wall, eases this problem.

After the gates have opened and the lockmaster has turned on the green light, proceed slowly forward, close to the wall and parallel to it, being ready to use reverse to stop your forward motion. Bringing your boat alongside the wall of a lock chamber is the same as bringing it alongside a dock, but the feel will be very different, especially if you are proceeding upstream. A concrete lock 50 or more feet wide, a couple of hundred feet long, and 20 to 30 feet deep can make you feel as if you were at the bottom of a huge well waiting for someone to open a gigantic faucet. Keep cool; no one wants you to stay there.

HOLDING OFF

At some locks, the lockmaster will direct you to a particular spot along the wall; he may also throw you first a bow and then a stern line. These lines, which have been made fast to large cleats or bollards at the top of the wall, should not be tied to your boat. If they are, and the water is being raised, the increase in slack will let you drift far away from the wall; if the water level is being lowered, your boat will "hang." Tend

> *You should signal the lockmaster of your desire to lock through. Tying up to a dolphin and waiting is not adequate notice.*

these lines carefully. If you are singlehanding your boat, you can stand at the helm, letting out or taking in line as appropriate. There is no need for strain; a light but firm hold on the lines will keep your boat near the wall.

At many locks, you will be on your own to find a spot to stop your boat and loop a line around a post or bollard recessed into the wall. This

presents more of a challenge than when the lockmaster throws a line, but it is not at all difficult.

With a crewmember forward, bring your boat to a stop with the bow near a post or bollard. Loop a bow line around this post, then use reverse to bring the stern back to another post, where you can loop another line. Simply pass your lines around these vertical posts or bollards so the lines will ride easily along the posts as you rise or fall; *don't* tie up. Once in a while, these posts or bollards will be too far apart to use bow or stern lines. In those cases, line up with a post amidships and bring your bow and stern lines to it.

When you are totally on your own, without a lockmaster to toss you lines and without a crewmember to loop one of your own lines around a post or bollard, your best bet is to bring your boat to a stop near the ladder that most locks have recessed into the lock walls. You can reach out with your hand or boathook and grab a rung. As the water rises or falls, simply move your hand up or down the rungs. No great strength is required to keep your boat near the wall.

Special circumstances may dictate different procedures. If the lockmaster requests that you not use the ladder to hold off, and you are singlehanding your boat, you'd better ask his assistance with your lines. At other times, heavy boat traffic may require that you tie up alongside another boat. In some crowded locks, four or more boats may be rafted together.

WATCHING THE WALL

As the water in the lock chamber rises or falls, pay close attention to

Lock Locations

Thousands of miles of navigable waterways in the United States are accessible to recreational boats, thanks to more than 300 locks operated by the U.S. Army Corps of Engineers and various state and regional agencies. The waterways listed below comprise the majority of those currently in service. Pleasure boats may transit these locks at no charge.

Waterway	Location	Number of Locks
Alabama and Coosa rivers	Alabama	3
Allegheny River	Pennsylvania, New York	8
Apalachicola, Chattahootchie, and Flint rivers	Georgia, Alabama, Florida	3
Atlantic Intercoastal Waterway	Virginia, North Carolina	3
Bayou Teche	Louisiana	2
Black Rock Channel and Tonawanda Harbor	New York	1
Black Warrior, Warrior, and Tombigbee rivers	Alabama	6
Canaveral Harbor	Florida	1
Cape Fear River	North Carolina	3
Central and Southern Florida rivers	Florida	9
Champlain Canal	New York	11
Columbia River	Oregon, Washington	4
Cross-Florida Barge Canal	Florida	2
Cumberland River	Kentucky, Tennessee	4
Erie Canal	New York	35
Freshwater Bayou	Louisiana	1
Green and Barren rivers	Kentucky	2
Gulf Intracoastal Waterway	Louisiana, Texas	11
Hudson River	New York	1
Illinois Waterway	Illinois	9
Inland Route	Michigan	1
Kanawha River	West Virginia	3
Kaskasia River	Illinois	1
Kentucky River	Kentucky	14
Lake Washington Ship Canal	Washington	2
McClellan-Kerr Arkansas River Navigation System	Arkansas, Oklahoma	18
Mississippi River	Illinois, Missouri, Iowa, Wisconsin, Minnesota	30
Monongahela River	Pennsylvania, West Virginia	9
Ohio River	Illinois, Kentucky, Indiana, Ohio, West Virginia, Pennsylvania	20
Okeechobee Waterway	Florida	4
Old River	Louisiana	1
Oswego Canal	New York	7
Ouachita and Black rivers	Arkansas, Louisiana	4
Sacramento River	California	1
Snake River	Washington	4
St. Mary's River	Michigan	4
Savannah River	Georgia	1
Tennessee River	Tennessee, Alabama, Mississippi, Kentucky	13
Tennessee-Tombigbee Waterway	Alabama, Mississippi	10
Willamette River	Oregon	5

—Compiled by Charles Neuschafer
(Small Boat Journal #43)

the wall. While lock walls are designed to be free of protrusions, some of the older ones have deteriorated, and if you are not paying attention, you may find your gunwale caught under a jagged piece of overhanging concrete.

The water turbulence inside a lock is more pronounced as the chamber is being flooded. Water is usually let in through huge intake valves below the surface at both sides. Some locks also open the gates slightly at the upstream end. Seeing a 15-foot wall of water ahead of you, even though it may be only 12 inches wide, and feeling the swirl of the currents below you are part of the excitement of locking through. Relax and enjoy it, but don't forget to tend your lines and watch the wall.

It takes about 15 to 20 minutes for the water level in the lock to be raised or lowered, but the time will go by quickly. Most locks post information (how many feet of lift, how far to the next lock) and warnings (no swimming, no smoking).

At some point, the lockmaster will ask your name, home port, and destination. He may even have you fill out a form. This is a good opportunity to inquire about the conditions ahead, or to chat. Lockmasters are courteous and helpful professionals who take pride not only in the operation of their lock, but also in its appearance. A "thank you" is always appreciated; it is the only form of payment you will make. There is no charge for locking through, even though yours may be the only boat and thousands of gallons of water have to be let in or out.

When the gates reopen, just cast off or unloop your lines and motor out. When other boats are ahead of you, especially large ones whose propellers may create turbulence in the narrow confines of a lock chamber, you may want to wait at the wall until they have cleared the gates.

Whether the lock has brought your boat up or down, and whether the vertical travel has been nil, as at some tide- or flood-control locks, or substantial (at the Bay Spring Locks on the Tennessee-Tombigbee Waterway the lift is 84 feet, and 40 million gallons of water are pumped in during transit), locking through adds a new dimension to your travel and opens up wonderful new stretches of navigable water for you to cruise and enjoy.

—Charles Neuschafer
(*Small Boat Journal* #43)

Do You Really Want to Tow?

Small motorboats are not well suited for towing anything other than water-skiers. Yet, sometime in your boating career—perhaps more than once—you are going to have to help a boat in distress, drag a raft to its mooring, or pull, push, or power another floating object from one point to another. From experience, we would advise you not to take the challenge lightly. It can be dangerous work. If you have doubts about your skills, be prepared to refuse the job outright.

The problem lies in the fact that while outboard-motor boats are highly maneuverable by themselves, the minute you try to add a second vessel to the same power source, the second vessel exhibits a stubborn determination to take over. Your "simple" tow can lead you literally in circles.

Trouble starts because the towing point must be forward of the propeller for proper control. And since an outboard motor is normally mounted on the transom and small motorboats are rarely equipped with towing points amidships, about the only place to tie a towing sling is on or near the transom, right where it can do the least good. To understand what we are talking about, look at the after end of a tugboat (see photo). The towing bitts or main towing winch are located on the low deck just abaft the cabin and well forward of the transom. If the vessel were out of the water, you would see the towing gear sited considerably forward of the huge propeller(s) and rudder(s). In this way, the towing point aboard the tug serves as a pivot around which the powerful propulsion gear can push the vessel and hence remain in control. Note, too, the strong, smooth, unobstructed bulwark along the quarters and across the stern, over which the towing cable can slide while the vessel turns beneath it.

With your outboard and a transom-mounted sling, the pivot and power source are in the same place, causing most of the steering effectiveness of the motor to be lost. In addition, there is the not inconsiderable weight of the tow that has to be started, and this unwieldy mass can easily head off in the wrong direction, all the while trying to drag your relatively light-weight towing vessel with it. Even once underway, that load behind you may want to yaw all over the ocean, forcing you to constantly compensate with tiller and throttle. Knowing how to tow is knowing how to overcome

The after end of the tugboat in the foreground reveals why these vessels are so maneuverable when towing. The top of the rudderpost can be seen just inside the curve of the counter (left arrow), far to the rear of the towing bollard (right arrow), and the towing winches forward of that.

An outboard boat can tow another boat of about the same weight or less without much difficulty, provided the speed is kept moderate, preferably at or below the hull speed of the smaller of the two boats.

or at least decrease the innumerable steering problems that inevitably crop up.

An outboard-motor boat does best towing boats about its own size or smaller. Under such circumstances, the power of the motor and the bite of the hull in the water, along with judicious distancing between vessels, are enough to overcome the cussedness of the tow. We occasionally tow sea kayaks or canoes, for instance, and have found that with kayaks, the best way to tow them is to snub the bows right up to the transom—the bows *on* the transom, in some cases—while traveling at a semidisplacement or slow planing speed. If you have the room, however, the best place for them is aboard the towboat, where their only drag is wind resistance. In the case of

a canoe, take a loop of its bow line around a cleat or other towing point and then ease the canoe back so that it rides on the back of the wake just behind the towboat. If the canoe is light and the weight of any gear in it is aft of amidships, it often can be made to plane in the 10- to 12-m.p.h.

> *Your "simple" tow can lead you literally in circles.*

range. Once the right speed and distance are found, the towline can be made fast to a stern cleat with another loop or two, but we would advise against tying the line with a knot to your boat. Small lightweight outboard boats usually can be towed in the same manner.

Beyond these readily towed peanut-

shell-type boats, the laws of physics rapidly come into effect, and most attempts to tow with a line attached on or near the transom of your towboat fail as the tow takes command and tries to go its own way while you try to go yours. The tug of war can be both comical and frustrating. Now is the time for a major change in tactics and perhaps a decision not to tow at all, because towing is hazardous, particularly under rough and windy conditions. Remember again that warning we stated at the outset: Most outboard motorboats are poor towboats.

Why? Let's take another look at our would-be tugs. We determined that a towing point or points should be well forward of the propeller or, in the case of an outboard, of the engine itself. A third to halfway forward is best. It would be nice to be able to fasten a towing sling to rugged cleats on either side, but very few outboard boats have anything at all to tie to amidships. A seat or seat supports, perhaps, or oarlocks or small tie-up cleats? Maybe, but towing can exert sudden and powerful forces that could pop many of these, perhaps whipping the pieces about the boat. Add to this the fact that either sling or single towline must run smoothly over the stern and be able to slide back and forth. And what is right there in the way? Yep, the motor. And if you think that isn't a pain when you are towing, just try it. Finally, if you're running the motor using the tiller, you can add yourself to big things that are in the way of the towline or lines.

Which brings up another critical matter: that of the right kind of line for towing. Your motor is probably powerful enough to drive your boat at 30 or 40 m.p.h. That same power can break a sizable line, especially one that is old and worn. Many synthetics, and nylon in particular, can snap back like an oversize elastic band, with enough force to do damage to your boat or, more seriously, to you.

There are four kinds of line aboard most outboard boats. The most common is three-strand nylon, used almost universally as anchor line. The second is braided nylon or Dacron, often used in short to medium lengths as bow or mooring lines. The third is polypropylene, either three-strand or braided. The fourth is bits and pieces—forget them when it comes to rigging for towing, unless you have a good, rugged piece that can be used as a sling.

Since your best rope will probably be the nylon anchor line or a spare coil of the same strength, this should be your choice for towing. However, if you have a length of ⅜-inch (or more) poly in good condition, it will make a better towline, since it floats, whereas nylon will dive quickly to propeller-snarling depth at just the wrong time if given any slack. The right length for the towline will depend first on what is available and second on what works best. There are a lot of variables in this towing game when you are trying to move a heavy load with a light boat.

Another source of rope is to ask the skipper to be towed to supply the towline; after all, there's ample reason that the wear and tear should fall on his gear, not yours. We did that when we answered the hail of the skipper of a 26-foot sailboat that had lost its rudder. He dug a tangle of new ½-inch nylon anchor line out of his locker for the 3-mile tow ahead of us, and it worked just fine when tied to the towing sling I set up aboard my 18-foot aluminum skiff. The nylon sling was tied to the center seat on my boat and extended a short distance abaft the motor. Since I steer from the tiller, I was in a position to be caught by the sling in sharp turns, so I was careful not to cut too sharply. (If the sling is lower than the motor housing, the latter will prevent it from possibly sweeping you overboard.) Towing at a little less than half throttle on the 25-h.p. motor, we made reasonable time despite the fact that the rudderless sloop danced around at the end of her 75-foot tether. My steering control was adequate, thanks to the center-mounted towing sling, but it would have helped if he had dragged a pail or some of that tangled line to help hold his boat on course.

In way of interest, the towing sling was part of a 100-foot length of ⅜-inch nylon I carry as an anchor line. It was tied around the seat close to each side of the cockpit with a figure-eight loop tied at the apex to hold the towline. Since the seats are an integral part of my boat, the center seat made a good anchor for the sling ends.

Once you get your tow moving, you can quickly judge what is the best speed. Half throttle or less should be adequate for all but the heaviest loads, and will place only moderate strain on your boat and gear. We would advise against pulling anything requiring all or nearly all of your power unless your motor is very small. The risks of something breaking or going wrong are just too high. An exception would be in a matter of life and death, such as a disabled heavy motor cruiser about to drift into high surf. In that case, you may plan to tow the bigger boat out to where it can safely anchor, and then let a more powerful vessel do the tugging.

Think twice or more before taking on any tow heavier than your own rig in rough water. With all that drag back there, your ability to maneuver in and around waves will be severely limited, raising the chance of being swamped or even capsized. Waves that bother you may mean little to those in a larger boat; if the disabled craft is not in danger, let it drift or lie at anchor until help comes. If there appears any possibility of trouble, just stand by rather than risking your boat and possibly your life until it is absolutely necessary. Help should be on the way.

You will notice that we have not gone into detail on how to rig your boat for towing. That is because

> *Think twice or more before taking on any tow heavier than your own rig in rough water.*

Towing alongside is effective in close quarters since the smaller vessel has better control over the larger. Connecting lines must be taut. Note how most of the towing weight falls on the line running from the quarter of the larger craft forward to the smaller boat, in this case under the forward seat. Each boat will be different and thus require innovative setups, all the more reason to go gently and slowly. Notice that the smaller boat is as far aft as it can get so as to improve steering control.

small motorboats are not towboats, and any tow will require ingenuity and common sense more than a list of standard towing procedures more applicable to larger boats. Here are a few tips, though, that may help you decide if towing is for you:

• Be certain everyone aboard your boat has on a life jacket *before* you try anything. You are about to go in harm's way.

• Be prepared to cast off or cut the sling or towline in an emergency. Hard knots and dull knives are not wanted here.

• Do all your rigging before you start towing, and if you must make adjustments after you are underway, slow to a halt and make your corrections on slack lines. It is both safer and easier.

• Confer with the other skipper so that procedures and signals will be understood by both parties. With your small boat, you will probably be able to maneuver very close to the disabled boat or even go aboard. If both of you have radios, plan to use them. Be sure to set them at low power (one watt).

• Try to work out a mutually acceptable procedure, but if you don't like something, say so, and if the other skipper insists on doing things his way, feel free to suggest he find another source of help. This is to protect yourself from later trouble. Under the "good Samaritan" rule, you are not liable for accidents if you have acted in a "safe and prudent manner," but the latter is open to interpretation. For that reason, know what you are doing and insist that the disabled boat's skipper play by your rules or you will take your ball and go home.

• When you are satisfied that both vessels are properly rigged, apply power slowly until the rigging settles into place (if something is going to give way, this is when it is most apt to happen) and the two boats begin to move. Don't hurry things; getting the feel of the tow and then fine-tuning

your speed are critical elements in successful towing.

• It is not always necessary to tow a disabled boat behind you. If the waters are calm, you may find it easier to lash alongside, using fenders and spring lines. Your boat should tie to the other's quarter for best control.

• Be certain that the point of attachment of the towline aboard the disabled boat is strong. The mooring cleat, a rugged bitt, or a mast is best. As you look at the towing attachment, remember that if it breaks loose, you will be on the other end of the rubber band.

• With your small boat, you may be able to get close enough to hand the other skipper your towline, or vice versa, but if it is rough, a better bet is to bend a float to the end of the line and drag it across the stern of the other boat and then forward, so that the line runs around the transom of the disabled boat and can be picked up from the water by the boat's skipper or crew.

• You are morally obligated to help a boat in distress, if doing so does not place your boat and crew in danger. Payment for your services should not be asked or expected, although if your boat has been damaged while carrying out its mercy mission, the other skipper has a moral obligation to foot the repair bill.

> *If the waters are calm, you may find it easier to lash alongside, using fenders and spring lines.*

If we have made towing sound like a potentially hazardous undertaking with a small motorboat, that is our intention. Having said this, we suggest you get together with another skipper and take turns towing each other's boat. The practice will add to your seamanship skills and probably be worth a few laughs to boot.

—DRG

Defensive Boating:
When the World Is Against You

With traffic on inland and coastal waterways increasing every year, the land-bound commuter's motto is becoming increasingly applicable to small-boat skippers: Watch out for the other guy.

So without getting into a lot of nautical jargon, procedures, and equipment, the following is meant to help you steer clear of trouble. In addition to being a basic law of the sea, collision avoidance will help keep your insurance premiums down and your blood pressure steady, and it will make your day on the water more fun.

Unlike land-bound navigating, there are no apparent "roads" on the water to indicate the course of traffic. But there is a way to tell, as clearly as a stop sign at an intersec-

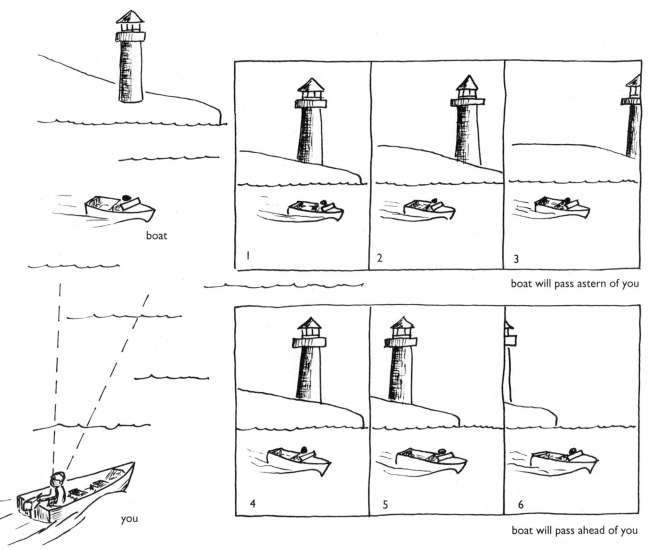

boat

boat will pass astern of you

you

boat will pass ahead of you

By sighting on a fixed object beyond an approaching boat, you can judge whether it will pass astern of you (top three frames) or ahead of you (bottom three frames). If the approaching boat's position remains unchanged, as in frames 1 and 4, then you are on a collision course, and even though you have the right of way you should be prepared to change course very soon.

tion, whether you're likely to hit another boat.

Any boat coming in your direction and in front of where you are going has the theoretical potential to run into you. To go from theory to reality, all you need to do is look carefully at that other boat and the land beyond it. Pick out a tall fixed object (a tree, a telephone pole, or a water tower) on the land beyond the boat. From one spot on your boat, watch the other boat's movement relative to that fixed object. If after a minute or two of watching, the other boat does not move relative to that fixed object, you can conclude you're on a collision course with that boat. Lacking a distant object as a point of reference, you can use a point on your boat, such as the tip of the bow. This is not as accurate as the more distant object, but it will give you a good indication as to whether your boat is closing with the other. If there appears to be no change in the positions, you can be sure you are on a crash course and should do something immediately to change things.

But don't panic. All you have to do is adjust your course to avoid the other boat. There are all sorts of rules that govern right of way in a given situation, and you should take the time to learn them; but in the real world, most newcomers to boating haven't learned these complex, extensive rules. So it's back to our maxim: Watch out for the other guy, and make only one assumption—that he will run into you if you don't change direction.

If you've determined he is closing in for a slam dunk, you can't fool around with minor adjustments to course and speed. By law, you have to make adjustments large enough to be apparent to the other vessel. Before making the adjustments to

your course, though, take a look around. Specifically, scan 360 degrees around your boat to make sure that when you change course or speed, you won't end up with another boat crawling up your transom or nailing you broadside. Again, boats coming up on you from behind are required by law to stay out of your way. But in heavy waterborne traffic, if the other skipper isn't following the rules, play it safe and take a good look around. Once you've determined it's safe to change course and speed, you can do either or both, depending on what you think the situation demands. However, it can be easiest to just change course.

Course adjustment should be at least 45 degrees away from your current collision course (90 degrees if

> *If the other boat does not move relative to a fixed object, you're on a collision course.*

possible). Make your course change quickly and obviously. This makes it clear to the other boater that you've changed course and that he should not interfere with your new course. It is safest to turn in a manner that will let you pass off the stern of the offending boat, although you're not required by law to do this. Trying to pass ahead of other boats somehow has the same effect as poking a snake with a stick. So when possible, pass off the stern.

Adjusting your course to avoid a collision isn't the end of it, though. You have to make sure you don't come too close to the other vessel. This is known as giving a dangerous situation "wide berth" or "sea room." Exactly how much room you should give the other vessel depends on how you have chosen to avoid it. If you

are still insisting on passing ahead of the other boat, you're going to have to go back to watching a fixed object beyond that vessel. You know you will pass well ahead if the fixed object appears to be moving rapidly ahead of the boat. Conversely, if the fixed object appears to be moving behind the boat, you will pass well to its stern. You already know what happens if the fixed object doesn't move at all.

In very tight situations, the body of water you are traveling may be only a couple hundred yards wide, or less. In such a case, watching a fixed object won't do you much good. There may not be enough time or room for taking a reliable relative bearing. So you will have to use good judgment and the following basic "rule of three": Try to stay at least three boat lengths away from sailboats underway, for they often must change course 90 degrees away from where they are headed. Wind conditions, rocks, shoals, and currents may force them to make these changes, sometimes without warning. So it is best to be well clear of all sailboats.

Also, maintain at least three boat lengths between your craft and powerboats that are trolling. To avoid running afoul of the fishing lines trailing well astern of the fishing boat, you should plan to pass some distance behind it (50 yards is a safe figure).

Small boats should generally keep clear of big boats by at least three of your boat's lengths. (Definition: If it looks big from your boat, it is.) Tugs with tows, seagoing ships, coastal freighters, and commercial fishing vessels at work can sweep a small boat (anything up to 35 feet) into the currents created by its propeller or equipment. Turbulence from these boats often stirs up prop-fouling debris from the bottom, especially in confined inland waters. If you still feel overly crowded as a big vessel approaches you, check your chart for depths or obstructions and then go where the large craft can't. By taking advantage of your shallow draft, you can almost always move out of the channel, slowing down until you just have steerageway, or simply stopping once you are clear of trouble, idling your engine, and waiting for the S.S. *Trouble* to pass.

Despite your best efforts, someday another boat is going to get on a collision course with you and stay there. When this happens, don't waste time trying to figure out what the other guy is up to. In the best commuter's tradition, use your horn. The correct signal is five rapid, 1-second blasts on the biggest horn you can find. The compressed-air horns found in most marine stores are very effective. Remember: You're trying to alert the other boat to the danger of a very close situation. The air horn also has many other applications. By law, it must be used in restricted visibility (fog, rain, etc.) or in certain maneuvering situations. Again, you will have to check the waterborne traffic laws for specifics.

If you follow the foregoing rules, you will already be in compliance with many of the formal Rules of the Road (see the overall introduction to this section, page 143). As the old saying goes, you have to start to be in the race.

—Ken Textor
(*Small Boat Journal* #73)

The Invaluable Nautical Chart

A nautical chart is your guide to safe travel on the water. Think of it as a water roadmap—without the roads. Instead there are numbers indicating depth in feet, and buoys, lights, day markers, beacons, and other floating or fixed devices to help tell where you are.

A chart is neither hard to understand nor difficult to follow, but it can be tricky the first few times. The biggest problem is that there are no lines of travel either on the chart or on the water. Thus, you must be able to look at the chart, locate where you are in relation to the chart and to reality, and then plot a course to your destination. Much of the time, with small boats such as ours, you can glance at the chart, note a clear passage to where you want to go, relate this information to the actual scene on the water and the surrounding land, and then go for it, with only occasional additional looks at the chart to see that you are where you are supposed to be. Naturally, this fine state of affairs assumes clear air and clear going.

More often, you will have to go around islands and other obstructions in the way of a straight-line course; hold to buoyed channels; and sort out your passage from a confusion of boats, buoys, lights, towers, and other clutter ahead of you, all the time trying to keep a close tab on where you are on that unmarked chart and where you are on the water.

To ease what sounds like a real

Charts are invaluable when boating in unfamiliar waters, but on small open boats charts should be protected from the elements even when printed on waterproof paper. A clear plastic container is most useful and can be made in an evening's work. They can also be purchased at most marine stores.

task, we have three recommendations. First, always obtain a chart of your boating area and study it carefully at home before going out on the water. You will be amazed at what you can learn by doing this, and you will admire the thought that has gone into its production. Second, always take the chart with you on the boat. Third, use it all the time you are on the water until you are familiar with its intricacies. There are scores of symbols and abbreviations that you will want to know, but it isn't necessary to learn them all at once. There are a few that you have to know right away, however, just to stay afloat.

The first, of course, is the scale of the chart, which is nothing more than the fraction denoting the length of a unit on the chart versus its length on the surface of the earth. Thus, if the scale is 1/40,000, 1 inch on the chart will depict 40,000 inches on land or water. Small-boat skippers will find charts in and around this particular scale most useful for their requirements.

Official charts for navigable ocean waters and the Great Lakes are issued by the National Ocean Survey (NOS), an agency of the National Oceanic and Atmospheric Administration (NOAA) in the Department of Commerce. These charts are available from many marinas, ship chandlers, mail-order houses, and bookstores. Charts produced by other agencies and private sources are available for many inland rivers and lakes. Since charts are quite expensive (about $15 each at this writing), you may find a book of charts is a far more economical buy if your cruising range is at all extensive.

Once you know the scale, it is equally important to know how to determine distances on the chart.

There is the usual mileage scale, but notice that it is shown in nautical miles (5,280 feet for a land mile versus approximately 6,080 feet for a nautical mile). A nautical mile is just about 2,000 yards. Distance measurements can be taken from the mileage scale shown on every chart (in yards and nautical miles), and can also be determined from the latitude marks along the vertical border of the chart. One minute (shown as "'") of latitude is equal to 1 nautical mile, while the chart is lined off in 5-minute (or 5 nautical miles) rectangles. Using a pair of dividers, one can make quite accurate measurements of distance with this scale. It's better not to use the longitude increments along the top and bottom borders of the chart.

> *Dog-eared ancients probably will be adequate in most cases, but there will come a time when the welcome sight of a buoy emerges from the fog—and its markings are not on your chart.*

Only at the equator does a minute of longitude equal 1 nautical mile. In higher latitudes, it is significantly less, diminishing to nothing at the poles.

In one or more places on the face of the chart you will see compass roses pointing to north and magnetic north. The chart is always oriented to True North, depicted on the outside scale of the rose. But if you are navigating by compass, you need only be concerned with the inner, magnetic, circle (see "Taking the Awe Out of Navigating," page 189).

Other chart information that you will want to understand immediately includes the following:

Green areas. These denote intertidal areas that are covered at high tide and exposed at *mean low water* (which is how chartmakers describe the average low water used to determine all depths marked on the chart).

Soundings. These are the numbers in the water areas and are the depths given in feet at mean low water.

Depth lines. These are the solid black lines on the water that look something like contour lines on a topographical map. Not surprisingly, they indicate underwater contours, and the depths are determined in feet (at mean low water). The first three lines out from land indicate 6 feet, 12 feet, and 18 feet (or 1, 2, and 3 fathoms), respectively. Waters between them are in different shades of blue. The next is the 60-foot (10-fathom) line. Depth lines frequently are broken by a small number indicating their depth, which is particularly helpful as one gets into deeper water. For most small-boat owners, the only concern is water depths in the blue areas.

Rocks. These are shown as asterisks in their approximate locations on the bottom. Heed them, because those marked will be close enough to the surface at times to damage small boats.

Bridges. Clearance in feet is shown for those bridges spanning navigable waters.

Lights. Fixed lights show a small red beam on the chart. Information beside them includes height above sea level, their range, and their identifying characteristics.

Buoys. Nuns—solid buoys sloping to a peak, painted red and identified by an even number. Cans—solid buoys painted green and identified by odd numbers.

Nuns and cans usually mark channel edges or hazards, with red nuns being on the right-hand side of the boat when you are returning from sea—always remembered by "Red, right, returning." When you are headed out to sea, they should be passed to your left. Other buoys of immediate interest are bells, gongs (deeper tone than bells), whistles, and lights, all of which are useful in determining one's location in poor visibility. All buoys have identifying marks that are noted on the chart.

Day markers. These may be stone pylons or monuments, iron posts embedded in a ledge, or other fixed marks that can be seen from the water. Of particular concern to us are those marking hidden ledges close to shore.

The above information should not be taken as all you need to know about charts. The charts themselves tell a lot more, much of which a conscientious skipper should be aware of, but real life shows us that a great number of small-boat owners take to the water with only a vague notion of what is involved in boating on busy tidal waters. They may have charts with them, but are hazy on understanding them. This information should at least help them get around.

A final note: Bouyage and other navigational aids change from time to time, and the only safe way to stay even with these changes is to keep your charts up to date and read the *Local Notice to Mariners,* available from the U.S. Coast Guard. Changes in navaids are noted in these publications. A lot of small-boat skippers dislike having to buy new charts, and they are willing to gamble that their wrinkled five-year-old charts will be enough. These dog-eared ancients probably will be adequate in most cases, but there will come a time when the welcome sight of a buoy emerges from the fog—and its markings are not on your chart. That may well be the day when you decide to get more serious about this chart business.

—DRG

Navaids: The Seaman's Scorecard

Navigational aids, or navaids, show an enormous variety. They can be buoys of all kinds, painted signboards on pilings, towers with wooden frameworks, towers with iron frameworks, cement lighthouses, granite block lighthouses. They range from the smallest can buoy on a remote coast to the kind of aid epitomized by Ambrose Light in the busy entrance to New York Harbor, with its four steel legs sunk hundreds of feet into the harbor bottom supporting an 80-foot-by-80-foot platform complete with helicopter landing pad, lights, and sound and electronic signaling apparatus.

Fixed and floating navaids (buoys) can differ in many ways, but they have two common denominators. Either kind can emit sound signals; either kind can emit light signals. The kinds of sound and light signals on buoys are not altogether the same as those on fixed navaids, but there is enough common ground to make it logical to first discuss these signals in general and only later specialize.

> Remember always that left and right are to be construed as "when returning from seaward."

First, sound signals. Six kinds are given in the Coast Guard's Light List (a series of publications on navaids), and I will divide them into three classes, according to the mechanism of their sound production: (1) bells and gongs; (2) whistles; and (3) horns, sirens, and diaphones.

A bell on a navaid is the same in principle as any other kind of bell—cowbell, dinner bell, church bell: A hammer or clapper strikes a concave metal casting, and a sound is produced. A gong is basically the same; the dictionary defines it as a shallow bell. A *gong buoy* is, however, different from a *bell buoy* in that the bell buoy has a single bell producing a single tone, whereas the gong buoy has two or more gongs producing tones of two or more different pitches. Bells are found on buoys and on fixed navaids. Gongs are found *only* on buoys, and they are often activated by the motion of the buoy itself, so that they may be more or less reliable, depending on how calm the waters are.

A whistle produces its sound when a blast of compressed air passes through a slot in a resonant chamber.

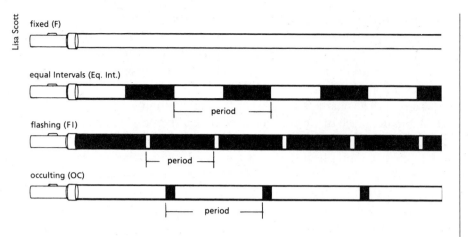

fixed (F)

equal Intervals (Eq. Int.)

period

flashing (Fl)

period

occulting (OC)

period

Basic navaid light characteristics. Fixed: Light shines continuously. Equal Intervals or Isophase: Light is on for as long as it is off. Flashing: Light is on for less time than it is off. Occulting: Light is on for more time than it is off.

The small boy who puts two fingers in his mouth and blows a blast produces sound by the same mechanism. It is hard to say in words what a whistle buoy sounds like; it is easier to say what it doesn't sound like. It doesn't sound like a policeman's whistle or a referee's whistle or a two-fingers-in-the-mouth whistle. The navaid whistle is deeper and more mournful than these. If you have ever heard the lugubrious "tooot-toooot" of a tugboat, you may well have heard a whistle of the navaid kind. The compressed air that drives the whistle is generated by a mechanism that depends on the rise and fall of the buoy in the sea, so that the duration of the whistle sound is not fixed but depends on the sea state. When it is very rough, the sounds emanating from the agitated whistle may vary from very seasick moans to desperate blats.

Sirens, horns, and diaphones have in common that their sound is produced by a moving mechanical element. In the siren, a rotor spins; the horn (also called a *diaphragm horn*) has a diaphragm that vibrates; in the diaphone is a slotted reciprocating piston. Either compressed air or electricity may move these elements. The horn sound is usually higher in pitch than is the whistle, and the blasts are of fixed duration and repeated periodically.

Sirens are scarce in my experience; I don't think I have ever heard one. When I called the local Coast Guard office to ask about them, the veteran navaids officer said that *he* had never heard one and thought they were very scarce indeed, so perhaps that is all that needs be said about sirens. A diaphone often emits a two-tone signal, with the first tone low and the second still lower—baritone, then bass.

The second common denominator of floating and fixed navaids is that both can have lights. There is a greater variation in complexity among light signals on small and large navaids than there is for sound signals. But whatever the complexity, all light systems have three features in common: color, light characteristics, and sectors.

Color needs no explanation, but light characteristics do. Some lights are steady: they are switched on, by photocells or by hand, and glow steadily for hours, days, or months. These lights are called *fixed*—a word usage not to be confused with lights on fixed structures. Other lights are on and off in a periodic pattern, one that repeats in time. For example, a light may be on for 1 second, off for 9; on for 1 second, off for 9; on for 1 second, etc. This kind of on-off pattern is called the light's *characteristic* (or its *rhythmics*); there are, of course, infinate other characteristics besides this simple illustrative example. The time needed to run through the pattern, together with the interval between pattern repetitions, is called the *period*.

There are four basic light characteristics; they are illustrated in the accompanying drawing.

A light may be "on" more than once during a period and still be called a flashing light if the total time it is on is less than the total time it is off. Example: Two flashes per period consisting of 1 second on, 1 second off, 1 second on, 7 seconds off, makes for a 10-second period, with only 2 seconds of light to 8 seconds off. Lights such as these, with multiple flashes, are called *group flashing*. The light illustrated here is *simple flashing*.

Similarly, the occulting light shown here is not the most general; it is called *simple occulting*. A light is occulting in general if, being on and off for intervals during its period, its total "on" time is greater than its total "off" time.

The standard abbreviations for light characteristics are listed completely in Section K of the National Oceanic and Atmospheric Administration (NOAA) publication called *Chart #1* (available at any chart outlet), and partially on many charts. They include: F = Fixed, Fl = Flashing, Iso = Isophase or equal intervals, Gr Fl = Group flashing. The color of the light is also abbreviated: R = Red, G = Green, W = White, etc. On a navigation chart the characteristic, color, and period are given in that order. Thus "Fl G 10s" means a

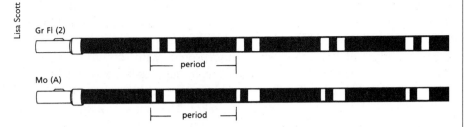

Two examples of group flashing lights.

flashing green light with a 10-second period.

A complete listing of the 16 different light characteristics in use on navaids is found in any Light List; here I will simply cite two more examples. The first is a group flashing light. In its abbreviation the number of flashes is put in parentheses, followed by the color (if it is not white), then the period. For example, "Gr Fl (2) G 15 s" is a green light that flashes twice in 15 seconds.

In a flashing light, the duration of the individual flashes need not be equal; some can be longer than others. In one important example the first flash is short and the second long, much like a dot and dash in Morse code. In fact, this short-long flash is abbreviated Mo (A) since short-long (dot-dash) is the symbol for the letter "A" in Morse code.

A final feature of lights is that they may shine in *sectors*. A sector is, in everyday terms, the shape of a piece of pie. Mathematically, it is the shape contained between two radii of a circle; it is measured by the angle between the radii. Cut a piece of pie into six equal pieces and you will have produced six 60-degree sectors. If you now imagine a light at the center of a large abstract pie, the light can have different colors, characteristics, or both in different sectors. Thus it may shine red in the 45-

degree sector between north and northeast and green between northeast and east—one example from an infinity of possibilities. As a general rule, if you are in the sector where the light is seen as red, you are in a danger zone. Sectors can be of any angular width—a few degrees wide is not uncommon.

Ordinarily only the larger lights, the seacoast or secondary lights, have sectors. On a navigation chart they are shown in plan view with the pie-shaped pieces clearly marked. The

> If you don't make an informed decision about every channel navaid, then sooner or later one will catch you out and you will be sorry.

sectors are also shown less pictorially in the Light List, where they are defined in terms of the angular bearing of the light *as seen from the two edges of the sector,* not in terms of the bearings of the edges as seen from the light. This can be confusing until you realize what is going on.

So much for sound and light signals in general. It is now time to get physical and look at the actual navaids that display these signals, and other navaids as well. Every navaid is one of two kinds: *with* lateral significance or *without* lateral significance. Typically, the first kind informs the skipper—imagined as

"returning from seaward"—that the waters are safe on one side of the navaid and unsafe on the other. Or they may tell the skipper that the waters are, for one reason or another, preferred on one side. In short, these navaids are not neutral; they take sides. They advise the navigator on how to move laterally with respect to them; hence their name. Navaids without lateral significance are, of course, ones for which there is no lateral connotation. For example: A buoy marked "Cable Crossing Limit, 5 Knots," is *without* lateral significance.

First, let's look at navaids *with* lateral significance. There are four kinds: unlighted buoys, lighted buoys, day beacons, and minor lights. Instead of trying to discuss all these simultaneously, I'll focus on unlighted buoys, partly because there are probably more of them in the system and partly because the conventions of color, shape, and numbering that apply to them are in large part applicable to other kinds of navaids. The rules that govern them are valid for day marks as well, and, with small modification, to lighted buoys and minor lights.

There are three kinds of unlighted buoys with lateral significance: channel buoys, preferred channel buoys, and mid-channel (or safe-water) buoys. The name "channel buoys" is mine; it is not an official designation in the Light List. But it is a convenient and obvious one, since I use it for the buoys that mark the port or starboard side of channels. These are described thus in the Light List: "Green buoys mark the port side of channels or the location of wrecks or obstructions which must be passed by keeping the buoys on the left hand." There is of course a similar statement with "red" in place of "green" and "starboard" in place of "port." (Remember always that

Day beacons are similar to unlighted buoys. This one would be red since it is triangular (nun) and even numbered.

left and right are to be construed as "when returning from seaward.")

Channel buoys are identified not only by their color but by their shape and numbering as well. All green buoys are can buoys and have odd numbers; all red buoys are nun buoys and have even numbers. This redundancy of means of identification is obviously a Good Thing. For example, you can often identify buoys by their shape at a distance long before you can see the number and even before you can be sure about the color. And if you see a red buoy with a "3" on it, and remember that red implies even numbers, you may be inspired to look more closely, perhaps to find that the "3" is an "8" with the left part worn away or covered with bird droppings.

Day beacons are fixed, unlighted structures with painted signs, or day marks, on them. As I remarked above, the logic of the day mark's identification is essentially the same as for unlighted buoys. They are green or red, and the colors have the same meaning as for channel buoys. The green day marks are square, since the flat top of a square recalls the flat top of a can buoy seen in silhouette; the red day marks are triangular to recall the pointy top of a nun buoy. Green day marks are odd numbered; red day marks, even numbered.

Lighted channel buoys are governed by the same conventions as unlighted buoys and channel day marks except that their shape has no navigational meaning—it may be anything. But their solid green or red color and their odd-even numbering are the same as for the other channel navaids above. The color of the light is the same as that of the buoy itself. There are a half-dozen possible light characteristics—fixed, flashing, etc.

Finally, minor channel lights—small, fixed, lighted structures that mark channels—have the same conventions of light colors and numbers as do lighted channel buoys. But neither the shape *nor* the color of the structure itself has any navigational meaning.

In the accompanying illustration, I note that the navaids must, depending on their kind, be left to port or starboard. This derives from the

Light List, which uses "must" in the same way, if in slightly different phrasing. But the "must" should be interpreted with common sense. What the supertanker drawing 30 feet requires is not the same as for a sea kayaker. The "must," then, is not an absolute prohibition to be heeded at all times and by all craft. Think of it rather as a warning, a suggestion that you interpret what the navaid is alerting you to. Then recall the state of the tide and decide whether the navaid's message applies to your craft. If you don't make this kind of informed decision about every channel navaid, then sooner or later one will catch you out and you will be sorry.

Preferred channel navaids comprise the second class of buoys with lateral significance. The Light List states: "Preferred channel buoys (navaids) mark junctions or bifurcations in the channel, or wrecks or obstructions which may be passed on either side." But one side may be preferred over the other for a variety of reasons. An example is shown here. Of the two possible passing channels shown, the one at the left will eventually peter out to 3- and 4-foot depths, whereas the channel on the right will remain relatively deep all the way. Or one side may be pre-

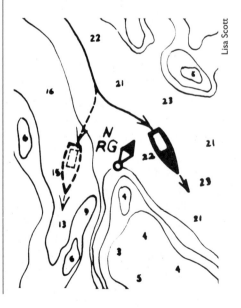

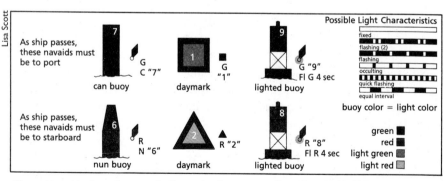

Channel navaids shown here are for "returning from seaward" on all navigable U.S. waters except western rivers and the Intracoastal Waterway.

ferred because it helps separate traffic into lanes.

There are three kinds of preferred channel navaids: unlighted buoys, day beacons, and lighted buoys. The conventions are similar to those for channel navaids; the main difference is that preferred channel aids are painted in *two* bands of different colors, with the top band defining the preferred channel. Top band red, preferred channel to port; top band green, preferred channel to starboard. The navaids are not numbered, but they may be lettered. The lighted buoy has a light the color of the top band, and the characteristic is *composite group flashing* (2 + 1, or two flashes, a short interval, a third flash, and then a longer interval before the group repeats).

Midchannel or *safe-water* navaids comprise a third category with lateral significance. There are three kinds: a spherical unlighted buoy with vertical red and white stripes; an octagonal day mark with vertical red and white stripes and a white reflective

border; and a lighted buoy also with vertical red and white stripes, possibly with sound signals, and showing a white light with the characteristic of Morse "A," abbreviated Mo (A).

These navaids do not mark dangers, but are rather meant to tell you where you are. As their name implies, they can be passed as closely as you wish. They are sometimes called *harbor buoys,* because they are often found at favorable positions for entering a harbor or in the channel leading to a harbor. In such cases they may be marked by one or two letters intended to be descriptive. For example, at the entrance to Boston Harbor's North Channel you will find RW "NC" Mo (A) GONG, with "NC" standing, of course, for North Channel. And in Monterey Bay, California, the "SC" on the red-and-white vertically striped buoy tells you that Santa

Cruz Harbor is in front of you.

Another navaid with lateral significance, but of a different kind than we have just discussed, is one called the *range.* This consists, in fact, of a *pair* of structures that act mutually to define it. The navaids discussed previously instruct you on how to move laterally with respect to them; the range instructs you not to move laterally at all with respect to it—and if you do inadvertently move laterally, to move back again immediately. I'll explain.

The range is based on the concept of the *transit.* When two objects are seen to be lined up, one behind the other, they are said to be *in transit.* The two objects together then constitute the range. If the objects are also found on the chart, the skipper who sees them line up on deck knows that his position on the chart is somewhere along the (extended) line drawn between them. This line is called the *transit line* or *transit line of position* and is highly accurate, since the eye can detect very small misalignments corresponding to very small lateral deviations from the transit.

This line of position is, in fact, so accurate that artificial ranges are set up as part of the Aids to Navigation system. For example, two marks may be placed to define an accurate midchannel line in a difficult channel through hazardous waters. These *range day marks* are standardized and consist of a large painted rectangle with a central stripe, standing on end on a supporting structure. The color of the rectangle is chosen to contrast with the background, and the color of the stripe is chosen to stand out against the rectangle. The colors used for either rectangle or stripe are green, red, white, or black. In a two-letter code in which the first letter stands for the background color, and the second for the stripe,

> *In short, these navaids are not neutral; they take sides.*

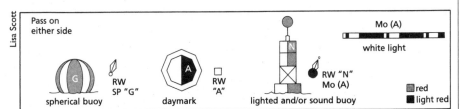

Midchannel or safe-water navaids: For navigable U.S. waters except western rivers and the Intracoastal Waterway.

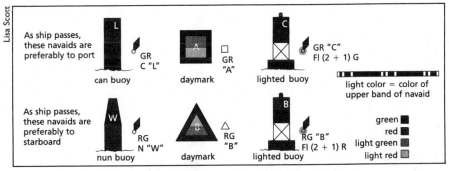

Preferred channel navaids here are for "returning from seaward" on all navigable waters except western rivers and the Intracoastal Waterway.

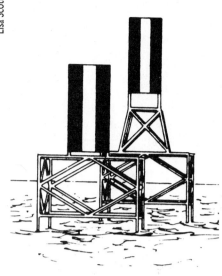

Two range day marks not quite in transit.

the 12 color combinations are: GW, WG, WB, BW, WR, RW, RB, BR, GB, BG, GR, and RG.

Navaids *without* lateral significance include beacons, lighted and unlighted buoys, and minor lights. A beacon is *any* fixed aid to navigation, usually of distinctive enough shape or structure that it can't be confused with anything else, especially if you have its detailed description from the Light List. Day beacons and minor lights are then also beacons. In fact, in scanning through a Light List one sees relatively few beacons listed, compared with the profusion of other aids. The reason is partly semantic. If what otherwise may be listed as a beacon has a day mark or light put on it, it is then entered under the listing of day beacon or minor light.

Now a look at buoys without lateral significance. The Light List divides these buoys into two categories: *information and regulatory buoys*, and *special-purpose buoys*. Information and regulatory buoys are colored white and orange, and the List quotes some of their typical uses as warnings of danger, of restricted operations, or of exclusion areas.

Special-purpose buoys are colored yellow; they may be used, among many other possibilities, to designate anchorage areas or dredging or survey sites. These examples of the uses of buoys without lateral significance don't begin to cover the large variety of uses that actually exists. Minor lights are lighted, fixed (referring to the structure, not the light frequency), relatively small navaids. They can serve as channel navaids, in which case their lights and numbering are based on the conventions for channel buoys, or they can be without lateral significance, with their lights and day marks modeled on buoys of that class. Minor lights can also be identified at a distance, at least tentatively, by their structure. This can be invaluable if you are trying to sort out some navigational dilemma and the only marks are distant ones. The information on structure is not given on the chart but *is* given in the Light List in such descriptions as "skeleton tower," "single pile," "cylindrical cement tower," etc. The Light List goes beyond the navigation chart in other ways as well. For example, it gives the characteristic—that is, the on-off pattern—of any sound signal on the navaid.

Minor lights vary greatly in struc-

ture and size, and there is no typical one.

Minor lights have weak lights on small structures, but weak and small are relative, and increasingly powerful lights and larger structures begin at some point to be called *secondary lights,* then *primary lights* (popularly, "lighthouses"). An example is given in that chapter of the tabulation in the Light List of the important features of Cape Neddick Light—range of the light, characteristics, description of the physical structure, etc. Now I want to take another lighthouse as example and show how the *chart markings* inform us about it—less completely than does the Light List, but with crucial information nonetheless.

The light is the Highland Light in Truro, Massachusetts, on the dunes of Cape Cod, and a picture of it appears here, along with a portion of the chart that describes it in an abbreviated manner. This is what the notation means: Fl 5 sec says that the light flashes once every 5 seconds; since no color is explicitly stated the light must be white. The notation 183 ft is the height, not of the structure but of the light itself, above mean high water. (The height of the structure is given in the Light List as 66 feet, so the land on which the light-

Highland Light guards the Outer Beach of Cape Cod and rates a sizable description on the chart.

house is located is 183−66 = 117 feet above MHW.) The notation 23 M signifies that the nominal range of the light, its range on a meteorologically "clear day," is 23 nautical miles. "HORN," of course, indicates that a horn is sounded; its sound characteristic is not given, but it can be found in the Light List. The notation 286 RBn signifies a radio beacon that operates on a frequency of 286 kHz. The notation -- - is the Morse code for HI, the *identifying signal* of the lighthouse. The marking &---- - means that a continuous *homing signal* is also emitted.

—Leonard Eyges
(*The Practical Pilot,*
International Marine, 1989)

Taking the Awe Out of Navigating

Our destination on Swan's Island lay 35 miles away at the end of a pinball passage through islands, reefs, thoroughfares, and coastal traffic. We stood at the launching ramp at Lincolnville Beach and could just make out the end of the ferry slip less than 100 yards to our right. The weather had all the makings of another lovely July day in Maine—if you like fog.

Pushing off, I fired up the outboard and we headed east on a course of 110 degrees, a number fixed in my mind from many misty trips across West Penobscot Bay. Ten minutes later the landing at Gilkey Harbor entrance on Islesboro ghosted into view and was gone, and we began picking up buoys as my companion called out courses for the short jumps between markers. Although Gilkey Harbor is generally less than a mile wide and about 3 miles long, we never saw land until a pier thrust out on our left near the narrow southern entrance.

A brief glimpse of Pendleton Point gave us a solid point of departure for the first leg across East Penobscot Bay, a 3-mile jump to Little Spruce Head Island. The latter is a fine target on foggy days, as it is about a half mile long and crosswise to an easterly course. I took a bearing to the center of it, and its bulk loomed out of the soup a few minutes later.

The morning passed quickly as we picked our way through a maze of islands and ledges, occasionally seeing a bit of land here, a buoy there, or a lobsterman working his pot line as nonchalantly as if it were a sunny day. We cruised along between 8 and 12 m.p.h., a safe speed for our range of vision of a hundred yards or so

In learning to deal with the fog, one soon discovers that navigating in a small, shallow-draft boat in coastal waters is not the complicated process one has been led to believe.

yet fast enough to keep my crew occupied calculating new courses and watching for marks. Busy Deer Isle Thorofare was little more than a gray tunnel of fluff, and the brick-paved waters in and around Casco Passage put some zest in the day, but still we arrived at the ferry landing on Swan's within minutes of the ETA we had set hours before at Lincolnville.

Had we been aboard a yacht, the complicated journey would have taken at least half again as long and left us exhausted from dealing safely with the many hazards in our path. As it was, the run, while certainly more than routine, was a pleasant diversion from the usual fair day and left us unconcerned by the fact that we would have to do it all over again on the return trip that afternoon. In Maine, one either learns to live with a fog mull or spends little time afloat some summers. And in learning to deal with the fog, one soon discovers that navigating in a small, shallow-draft boat in coastal waters is not the complicated process one has been led to believe. In fact, the mechanics of such navigation can be learned in a few minutes; gaining the necessary experience to use it successfully will take longer.

Before tackling the mechanics, let's make a few assumptions. We have to assume you have charts of the area you cruise in and know how to read them. They are absolutely necessary for navigation. We have to assume you have a compass aboard your boat and have used it enough to get used to its peculiarities, such as the disconcerting way it seems to "move backward" when you are underway. Another assumption is that you have checked the accuracy of your compass in its location on your boat. Lacking such adjustment, the instrument may be inaccurate because of magnetic influences such as iron or steel equipment nearby.

The key to the system we'll be describing here is the Hawkins Courser, a simple clear sheet of plastic with a series of parallel lines and a degree scale printed on it. The Courser is available in many marine supply stores and catalog houses. (In checking a pile of our marine catalogs, we found the Courser listed in the 1993 Hamilton Marine catalog for $9.19. The address is Hamilton Marine Inc., Searsport, ME 04974.) A ruler, a cheap pair of dividers, and a watch round out the necessary equipment.

If the assumptions and requirements listed above seem unusually simple and even casual, that is the intention. Put off by the apparent complexity of traditional marine navigation, some people elect to learn nothing and trust that they will be able to avoid fog or race to a safe port before it smothers the horizon. And in larger boats, they look to Loran, radar, satnav, GPS, NASA, or the NRA to help them move safely through the murk. Not so the little guy, who must learn how to navigate with nothing more than chart and compass. With the additional help of the Courser, however, coastal navigation is a piece of cake—almost.

The reason it is relatively easy lies in the very nature of the small boat. Light in weight and shoal of draft, little boats can safely go where larger vessels fear to float. Pinpoint accuracy to avoid catastrophe is rarely required (although fine piloting is possible with only a compass and should be striven for). For example, heading for the center of an island rather than a point at either end, as described in our trip to Swan's, results in a huge target that is hard to miss. This "rough" navigation leaves the

skipper with a sizable fudge factor that is better than Rolaids in keeping one's stomach quiet. Since his boat is highly maneuverable as well as of shallow draft, the skipper can approach very close to his target before bearing off on a new course, and that close-in identification may be a great help in assuring that he is where he hopes he is.

None of the above, of course, reduces the need for sharp attention to everything within the skipper's range of vision—ahead, to the sides, behind, and, critically, below. Unless the water is very dirty, one can usually see 2 or 3 feet beneath the surface, and this is normally enough to keep boats of the type we are considering out of trouble.

To find your course, you lay the Courser on the chart with one of the black lines passing through the point where you are and the point where

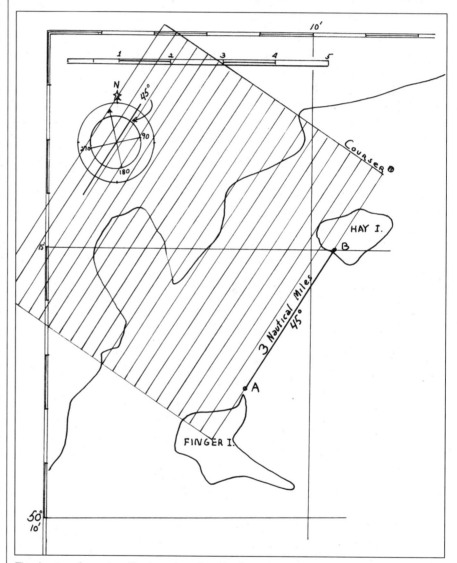

This drawing of a section of a chart shows how the Courser works. If you want a course from point A to point B, you place a line of the Courser on the two points, being sure that a compass rose on the chart is under the Courser also. If a Courser line doesn't go exactly through the center of the rose, you can slide the device until it does, or you can draw a line through the center of the rose, as shown here. Take the reading off the inner circle of the rose in the direction you want to travel. That is your course. The distance can be determined from the mileage scale or from the scale on vertical edges of the chart (each minute is 1 mile). In this case, if your safe speed is 12 m.p.h., it will take you about 15 minutes to run from A to B.

you want to go. Another of the lines must pass through one of the compass roses on the chart (you may have to move the Courser until the lines cover both your projected course and a compass rose, and then fine-tune the black line on your present position and goal again). You then look at the line passing through the center of the compass rose, follow it from the center point in the direction you want to go, and read the degrees on the *inside* circle (the magnetic reading) of the rose. That is your course. No sextant, no parallel rulers (the parallel lines of the Courser do that job), no tables, no electronic gadgets.

To find the distance between your position and your objective, you can use a ruler or dividers and calculate the distance using the chart's distance scale or the latitude minute marks on the east or west edges of the chart (don't use the top and bottom longitude scales; they are not as accurate). Each minute of latitude is a nautical mile.

If you practice finding courses in your living room, and then follow them on a bright, clear day at sea, you will soon develop adequate skill to get around in a small boat in coastal waters. Note the effect that wind and current have on your boat and learn to allow for those factors when plotting a course. Also note how long it takes you to go at a slow or moderate speed from point A to point B; that figure will be important when you are navigating in real fog and it seems you will never get where you are going.

A FEW TIPS

• Select short courses (preferably a mile or less) until you get used to navigating. Navigational buoys are excellent signposts; islands, steep headlands, and large manmade objects such as towers and high chimneys make good objectives.

• When navigating in the fog, look behind you as you leave your starting position to see what it looks like; you may have reason to return to it.

• Pay close attention to your compass. It is easy to stray from a course when everything is gray and you cannot tell water from sky. But don't fixate on the dial—it may make you seasick.

• If you are moving along the coast and must cross an unobstructed bay a few miles wide, you can set a course for the opposite shore that will give you a big cushion of land in either direction should you wander from your course a bit. When the

> *Light in weight and shoal of draft, little boats can safely go where larger vessels fear to float.*

crossing is made and land appears ahead of you, turn toward the mouth of the bay, and continue along your way with the shore in sight. Such navigation is rough, but reliable in light to moderate fog.

• If you must run several short courses to reach your goal, it will help to calculate them in advance and write them on a card, thus saving yourself the bother of stopping to plot each course when underway.

• When the fog is so thick you can only see a few feet, give serious consideration to staying right where you are. When your view is that restricted—which is rare, fortunately—the danger of collision with any number of things is increased tremendously. In most fogs, you can see at least a couple of hundred feet, and frequently a quarter mile or more, which makes navigation much less intimidating.

• When navigating from buoy to buoy, note the position of those with bells, gongs, and whistles. If you lose your way, their sounds may help you get back on course, and when one is your next target, it is comforting to hear its clanging or moaning ahead of you.

• Use your nose as well as your eyes and ears. A bird nesting island has a sharp ammonia smell, a fish plant smells like—well, fish. In fact, the odors of man are many: woodsmoke, barnyard, fresh-cut hay, refineries, diesel fumes, trash, you name it. Any of the smells mentioned, and others, are possible near the shore and may help you locate your position.

• Your foghorn can also be of help at this time, over and above keeping other vessels from running into you. Under some conditions, such as approaching a steep shore, echoes from your horn could indicate the direction and distance, a quick return meaning the shore is close by, a delayed return that it is some distance off.

• If you do get off course, refrain from dashing off in different directions. Rather, stop and consider how you may have gone wrong and then figure a new course to correct it. The best bet may be to return to your starting point and try again, which is why we suggested you look back when starting.

Remember—you are not *really* lost, just "twisted." Land is only a few miles away, at most. When all else fails, just head north, east, or west, depending on which coast you are cruising. You can't miss it!

—DRG

The Ins and Outs of Tides

Tides are the daily rise and fall of the oceans, caused by the varying gravitational pulls of the moon and the sun. As the earth turns and the moon and sun move in their paths through the heavens, their orientations with respect to any particular locale—and thus the gravitational forces they produce—change continuously. The water level at the locale rises or falls as a result.

The extent to which the water is pulled up—the *height of the tide*—varies enormously across the globe. There are 30-foot tides in the Bay of Fundy, and 10- and 15-foot tides are common off the coast of Great Britain, but the British Virgin Islands must make do with 1-foot tides; so whether or not you have to be concerned with the following depends on where you are.

Where tides are substantial, they can have an important, even profound effect on coastal piloting. If you are anchoring, you want to be sure you won't be high and dry in a few hours. If you want to take a shortcut through shallow passages, you aim to do it when there is maximum water depth. If you are hauling or launching a boat, you want to do it at that time of day when an ample depth of water makes it as easy as possible.

On the other hand, there are occasions when you want the water depth to be a minimum. If on a trip you have to pass under a bridge, and the tuna tower or other tophamper is high and the clearance dubious, you want to stack the odds in your favor by passing through at a time of min-

imum depth. But whether you want as much or as little water as possible, the problem is basically the same. How can you tell, at a given time and place, how much water there will be under the boat?

A very useful means in helping to determine a fix is a curve of constant depth. But to relate a measured depth to the chart, and thus perhaps locate yourself on such a curve, you must reduce the depth to some common denominator or standard. That is, if you have just discovered a depth of 17 feet, it may have been 15 feet a few hours earlier when the tide was out and may be 19 feet an hour from

> Although the correlation between state of the current and state of the tide may not be simple, it does exist.

now. Charted water depths are ordinarily referred to as *average low water*. It is clear, then, that without knowledge of the state of the tide, a measured depth cannot be located on the chart.

Associated with tides are tidal currents. If the water level rises locally, then water must have flowed in from somewhere else; this more or less horizontal flow is a *tidal current*. There is then a correlation between tides and tidal currents, in that if the first exists, the second must also exist. But the correlation is not simple. For example, the range of local tides is not necessarily related to the speed of the associated currents; there are areas where relatively small

tidal ranges produce large (fast) currents and areas where big tides produce small currents. And the relation between the time of maximum tidal height and the time of maximum current velocity for one locale may be entirely different from that in a spot a few miles away. Very much depends on the configuration of the sea bed and the shapes of local land masses.

Although the correlation between state of the current and state of the tide may not be simple, it does exist. In fact, if in coping with currents you want to use a tidal current chart, you must be able to predict the times of high and low water. For example, one chart applies for "two hours after slack; ebb begins" and a similar chart applies for "three hours after slack; ebb begins," etc. If you don't know the state of the tide you can't be helped by these useful charts.

There are many places, including most of the East Coast of the United States and Canada, where the tide follows the familiar *semidiurnal* pattern of two high tides and two low tides per day. The accompanying diagram (a) shows a semidiurnal tide at Boston, Massachusetts. I emphasize that this is a *typical* day; the tides in Boston are not always 8 feet high—they occasionally reach 12 feet. There is a difference of a couple of feet between the two successive highs; this is not always the case. Sometimes the difference is a little larger, sometimes it is smaller, or there may be no difference at all. But basically we see a picture of two highs and two lows of more or less

Testing the Tide (or Gambler's Choice)

Emboldened by shallow draft and light weight of the boat, the outboard skipper will be constantly tempted to cut corners around buoys, zip across shallow areas, and explore those green areas on the chart. You can safely succumb to this temptation in many instances—such is one of the many advantages of small boats—but it should be done only with care and forethought. Carelessness will eventually leave you with a pranged propeller or worse.

Taking a motorboat into unknown marine waters without a chart is always risky. All sorts of hazards may lie out of sight beneath the surface, just waiting to ruin your day. As the tide changes, so do the hazards. On a dropping tide, new hazards move upward; on a rising tide, visible obstructions such as an exposed rock or ledge disappear beneath the surface. Regardless of whether it is rising or falling, the tide can do you in.

When motoring in new waters, your safest bet is to stay in the buoyed channel, particularly so if you are trying to make time and do not want to slow down to eyeball your course. If you are in company with another boat of the same draft as yours and whose skipper has local knowledge, you can follow in the leader's wake—and we mean right in the center of the two lines of foam trailing behind the lead boat. It stands to reason that if that boat does not hit anything, neither will you. Just stay far enough behind so that you can stop if that boat *does* come to grief.

If you are going through an area at or near low tide and know you will be returning the same way, look carefully at potential shortcuts, such as broad flats and bars. If they do not show obstructions at this time, you can feel comfortable in crossing those areas when the tide is a couple of feet higher than it is now. That bit of careful observation can save you time on your return.

We like traveling close in to shore whenever time permits. There is much to see, and the navigating is usually far more interesting than counting off buoys. However, you will want to check the chart regularly, looking for marked obstructions such as old fish traps, wrecks, etc. Easy to overlook are those little asterisks that show the positions of boulders.

It pays to never forget that the near-shore marine areas marked in green drain completely at mean low water. In a period of neap tides, however, low tides can be quite "high," and a layer of water a few inches up to a couple of feet deep may cover part or all of the area. Don't be deceived by this apparently clear going; it is masked trouble.

A final note of caution: Don't be caught in these green areas on a falling tide, for they can be deceiving in more ways than one. For instance, it is not uncommon for large expanses of these areas to be nearly level (which is why they are called *flats*). Usually it is safe to pull up on a shore and stay there as long as you can still push your boat back into deeper water. On a flat, though, that deeper water may not be there when you want it, and in just a few minutes you are watching what little water there is rapidly retreating seaward, leaving you to ponder life until the tide returns.

—DRG

Hours

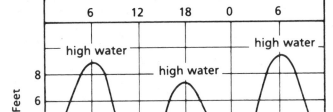

(a) Semidiurnal tide on a typical day

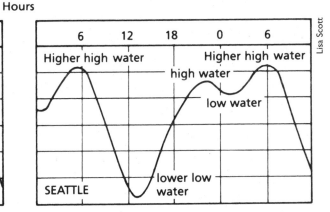

Lisa Scott

(b) Mixed tide on a typical day

Not all tides are alike. The two-stage tide is more common on the West Coast.

equal height, with about 6 hours between each high and the next low, which is what simple theory would predict.

This kind of semidiurnal tide is common but not universal. The tides on the West Coast of the United States and Canada are often a kind of modified semidiurnal—semidiurnal in that there are two highs and two lows per day, but modified in that the heights of the two successive highs are not the same; similarly for the two successive lows. This kind of tide is called a *mixed tide.*

The accompanying diagram (b) shows a typical day for the mixed tides of Seattle, Washington. In fact the two successive highs are about the same height, but the two successive lows differ appreciably. Marked differences in the sea bed configuration, among other things, cause the differences between semidiurnal and mixed tides. Since there are in a mixed tide two highs of different heights, it is often useful to identify them by name. The higher of the two is called *higher high water;* the lower is simply *high water.* Similarly, for the low tides there is a *lower low water* and a *low water.*

There are locales with *diurnal* tides—only one high and one low in 24 hours. This more drastic deviation from simple theory may be due to the fact that the underwater configuration—the tidal basin—has a natural resonance, and it may be due to above-water land masses, but since this book is not on oceanography I won't pursue the matter.

Let's look at how one deals with tides in practice. The chart gives average data on *soundings* (water depths), but says nothing about time; day by day, hour by hour the depths change, but you can't infer that from the averages on the chart. More detail is given by the Tide Tables, which (for semidiurnal and mixed tides) predict the times and heights of

the two high and the two low tides. Often that information suffices; if it doesn't there are Tables of the Rise and Fall of Tides, or a simple rule called the Rule of Twelfths (see page 195 for more detail), which enables interpolation between the times listed in the Tide Tables.

Imagine a skipper who wants to take a convenient shortcut, perhaps in a channel between islands. His boat draws 5 feet. He sees from the chart markings that the average level of water there at low tide is 17 feet, and he finds in a box on the chart called TIDAL INFORMATION that the water level has never been more than 3 feet below the average—that is, the depth in the channel has never been less than 14 feet. That is all he needs to know, so he passes through the shortcut with equanimity, indifferent to the day of the month or the time of day.

Suppose, however, that the chart showed a 7-foot sounding. Seven feet is more than 5 feet, but the sounding is only an average, and it is quite possible that the tides for any day will be lower than average. Also, a reported 7 feet may actually be 6.5 feet, since soundings are not reported in fractions of a foot. Further, the chart data may not be recent, and depths may have changed due to silting over the long term or to a special meteorological condition over the short term. All things considered, the 7-foot marking could imply 4 feet at certain times of certain days. To know whether the day of his passage is one of them, the skipper can consult the Tide Tables, which will tell him the times of the low tides for every day, and whether they are higher or lower than the *average* low tides to which the chart soundings refer. If the tides are weak that day and the lows are not as low as the average, he can pass through the channel whenever he wants; he needn't be concerned about the time of day.

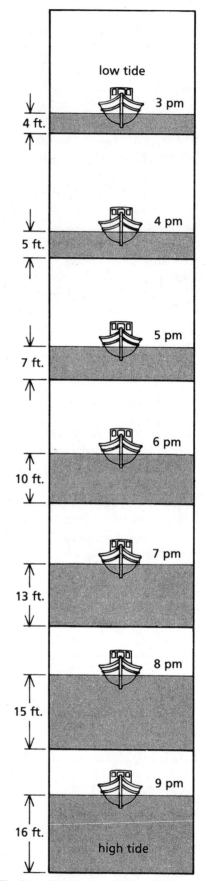

The Rule of Twelfths for a 12-foot tidal range.

<table>
<tr><td>

The tide rises or falls these fractions of its range during these successive hours:

$\frac{1}{12}$ during the 1st hour
$\frac{2}{12} = \frac{1}{6}$ during the 2nd hour
$\frac{3}{12} = \frac{1}{4}$ during the 3rd hour
$\frac{3}{12} = \frac{1}{4}$ during the 4th hour
$\frac{2}{12} = \frac{1}{6}$ during the 5th hour
$\frac{1}{12}$ during the 6th hour

</td><td>

The tide will have risen or fallen these fractions of its range after these successive hours:

$\frac{1}{12}$ after the 1st hour
$\frac{3}{12} = \frac{1}{4}$ after the 2nd hour
$\frac{6}{12} = \frac{1}{2}$ after the 3rd hour
$\frac{9}{12} = \frac{3}{4}$ after the 4th hour
$\frac{11}{12}$ after the 5th hour
$\frac{12}{12} = 1$ after the 6th hour

</td></tr>
</table>

Two forms of the Rule of Twelfths.

On the other hand, he may find from the Tables that the tides are unusually strong—the highs higher and the lows lower than average (called *spring tides*)—so that the 7-foot depth may be 4 feet at low tide. In this case he doesn't have the luxury of forgetting about time. He wants to know *precisely* the time of low tide, first so he can avoid going through at that time, and second because he wants to calculate how soon after low tide he can reasonably make it. Will it be prudent enough to wait an hour, or must he wait 2 or 3? The skipper needs the third level of tidal detail—height at various times after low tide. He may then use the Rule of Twelfths to calculate that 3 hours after low tide there will be 8 feet of water in the channel—and so the day's voyage continues without perturbation.

In extensive sets of Tide Tables the basic tables are often given for a number of centrally located places. Then auxiliary tables enable one to determine the tides at neighboring sites by applying listed differences, both in times and heights, between the central site and its neighbors.

Beyond the Tide Tables and their listings for four times during the day, one frequently wants to know the water depths at intermediate times. As mentioned earlier, these depths can be found from Tables of the Rise and Fall of Tides (available under the section "Height of Tide At Any Time" in the NOAA *Tide Tables,* and, for the East Coast, in *Reed's*

Nautical Almanac), but for the practical pilot the Rule of Twelfths is more than adequate (see illustration and table.

As an example of the first form of the rule, a tide with a 9-foot range will fall $\frac{1}{12}$ x 9 = 0.75 feet during the first hour, $\frac{2}{12}$ x 9 = 1.5 feet during the second hour, and 3.0, 3.0, 1.5, and 0.75 feet during each of the successive hours. The accompanying table and drawing illustrate the second form of the rule for a 12-foot tide in Maine.

The Rule of Twelfths is clearly an approximate formula; the tide rises continuously and not in hourly steps, and in fact it will not have risen or fallen completely in 6 hours but in 6 hours and 10 or 12 minutes. But remember also that the data on the chart and in the Tide Tables are approximate; numbers are rounded off, daily meteorological effects aren't included, etc. If you are the captain of a supertanker of 32-foot draft trying to negotiate a channel with 28 feet of water at low tide, you may want to use the Tables of Rise and Fall instead of the Rule of Twelfths, but I have always found the rule adequate for coastal piloting.

—Leonard Eyges
(*The Practical Pilot,*
International Marine, 1989)

Wind Is Weather

To the experienced small-boat skipper, the morning's weather forecast is as important as breakfast. Whether it is an official NOAA forecast, a derivation of the same over a commercial radio station, or simply a studied look out the window, the weather outlook for the day is crucial information. To the mariner at home it is the basis for deciding where to go and how best to get there, or whether to stay home and mow the lawn. For a small-boat cruiser camped on an island, the forecast may determine whether a trip around a big headland takes place, or if the day will be better spent hiking or perhaps exploring the protected backwaters of a nearby estuary.

The key factor in the forecast is the predicted weather, since *wind is weather* as far as small boats are concerned. Because it is so important, let's consider what the numbers mean:

10 m.p.h. or less: Pleasant breezes, fine boating. Small waves in open bays, but crests not breaking.
10 to 15 m.p.h.: Breezy, choppy in

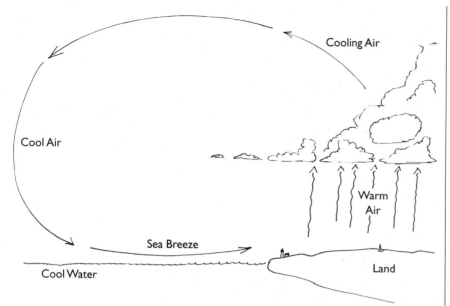

The mechanics of a sea breeze are quite simple, although other factors such as topography and prevailing winds may have a considerable effect on them. As the land is heated, warm air rises until it reaches a level where it begins to cool and form clouds. As warm air rises, cooler air over the sea is drawn toward the land (the "sea breeze"), and its place is taken by the land air that rose, was cooled, and then was drawn seaward in a great circular pattern.

the open bays, with some white-caps and streaks of foam. Rough for little boats.

15 to 20 m.p.h.: Rough in open bays for small boats under 20 feet. Frequent whitecaps and foam streaks.

20 to 25 m.p.h.: The limit of safe boating for most small boats.

25 to 30 m.p.h.: Seaworthy boat and skilled handling needed; dangerous for many small boats.

Over 30 m.p.h.: Travel at your own risk; these are powerful winds, and we are staying ashore.

If these figures sound low, they are, but like wave height, wind speed is overestimated by most of us (except at a busy dock, where it is apt to be badly underestimated or simply ignored in the rush to get on the water). Another good guide is the "small-craft advisory" issued by the U.S. Weather Service. This is a cau-

tionary warning to boatowners that the day's wind will be strong enough to make all open waters rough, and since the warning is really for boats *larger* than those we are considering here, our small-boat skipper should take them quite seriously. The small-craft advisory does not necessarily mean that all waters are unsafe for

> "Sea breezes" may sound like a gentle term, but for small boats they are often a factor of major importance.

small boats, but that caution is needed and big waters should most likely be avoided.

Another useful guide is the "lake boating advisory," the small-craft warning issued for inland lakes. Our experience indicates that the latter is information to be taken very seriously on salt water, too, since on the East Coast it is frequently issued for

strong northwesterlies, a dangerous slant of wind for saltwater boating because it is blowing toward the open ocean. Boaters in other sections of the country will find it useful to figure similar relationships between official forecasts and local conditions.

Over the years, we have made a mental note of how winds from various directions affect the weather. For example, in summer, winds on the Maine coast are reasonably predictable as to strength, direction, and duration. Easterlies and northerlies are normally mild to fresh in summer, although there are exceptions if a large storm is offshore. These same winds are stronger and of longer duration in fall, winter, and spring. Southeasterly winds can be counted on for light breezes and perhaps fog. If we are sitting under a stationary high pressure area, it will be cool with gentle westerly winds.

Often, steady conditions with crisp westerly winds will reduce or eliminate the afternoon sea breezes. "Sea breezes" may sound like a gentle term, but for small boats they are often a factor of major importance and are worth special discussion because of the key role they play wherever there are large expanses of cool water near major land areas.

Take the ocean waters off our northeast coast; they are cool in summer, with surface waters reaching, at their warmest, into the upper 60s and low 70s. During the day, the land may be heated many degrees higher than this, with 80s and even 90s not uncommon. Since warm air rises and cold air settles, the latter is drawn from the sea to the shore, its velocity determined essentially by the difference in temperature, but somewhat too by the shape of the land. The warm air rises, cools as it moves seaward to replace the cool air below moving landward, and a coastal circulation is established. Thus, if the forecast is for a hot day ashore, one can be pretty certain that a strong sea breeze will develop by early afternoon and will hold until the land cools down in the evening and the temperature differential evens out. However, if the night remains hot on the land, the sea breeze may continue well after dark before dying. If the sea surface is warm and on land the night is cool, the process may be reversed, and there will be light breezes off the land for a few hours in the early morning.

Understanding the dynamics of this process, the small-boat skipper may want to plan his day so that he heads west or south in the morning and returns in the afternoon with a following wind. For the same reason, if he heads east or north in the morning, he may find it so rough when it comes time to head home in the afternoon that it is unwise to attempt this "uphill" run.

As noted above, the sea breeze effect is common in one form or another in most coastal areas. Because of its nature, it is a local wind without the long fetch that builds great swells. That is small consolation for the small-boat skipper, because that "local" wind builds waves that are the worst size for his boat. True, in its weaker forms the sea breeze can be a blessing on a hot summer's day, but when it dusts up it means rough going. Figuring out how to reduce its wrath or how to avoid it entirely is just one more challenge for the small-boat skipper.

—DRG

Safety: Boating's Dirty Word

Water and I don't particularly get along, especially when I'm in it, so the sight of the big life jacket floating a few feet away was welcome. Swimming over to it, I carefully arranged it in front of me, punched my arm through one of the armholes, rolled over, and thrust my other arm through the second hole. The lift of the jacket under my back told me it was on, and I clipped the chest strap and tied the top and bottom strings. Snug and safe, I felt a small sense of accomplishment following the brief but tense struggle.

"Good job. Everyone out!" called the gravelly voice above. A dozen bedraggled, fully clothed persons climbed out of the swimming pool and stood dripping on the tile.

"You've proved that you can put a jacket on in the water, but it isn't easy," said our instructor, "and this was with prefitted jackets and instructions on how to do it. Imagine trying to do that in ice-cold water when you're not only scared but have never put one on before. That's a poor time to read the instructions on the package—and that's where most lifesaving gear stays in small boats—in the package it came in!"

Like most people who do a lot of boating, I had heard all this before. And had shrugged it off. Now, in example after sobering example, the truth was hitting home as I choked and gasped and struggled through a

Lifesaving gear can kill you if you don't know how to use it.

one-day Ocean Survival Course at the Maine Maritime Academy at Castine. Not only did we learn in-the-water facts about life jackets, but we also fired flares, doused flaming gasoline with fire extinguishers, donned survival suits in and out of the water, clambered aboard bobbing liferafts, learned how to swim through burning oil (fortunately, without the flames), how to escape when trapped in a sunken vehicle or overturned boat, how to recognize and treat hypothermia (which probably kills as many people in the water as drowning), and many other valuable practices we never take time to learn on our own. We also discovered that lifesaving gear can kill you if you don't know how to use it, or if you use it improperly.

The last three are so important to small-boat users that they are worth describing here, because some of the procedures go against instinct. Being trapped under a boat or in a car are good examples. During our course, there was a swivel seat and seatbelt attached to the center thwart of a dinghy. After we received instructions, we were blindfolded and strapped into the seat, and the boat was rocked and rotated a few times to disorient us, then tipped over. Our job was to get out of the seat and find our way to the surface. On going over, one took a quick breath and then, when hanging upside down in the water, unfastened the seatbelt and came up inside the hull, pausing

The Heat Escape Lessening Posture (HELP) involves holding the inner side of the arms tight against the sides of the chest, where heat loss is high. The thighs are pressed together and raised to close off the groin region, another area of high heat loss. Tests have shown this position results in a nearly 50-percent increase in predicted survival time. If more than one person is in the water, huddling so that the sides of the chests are held close together also produces a 50-percent increase in survival time.

there long enough to quiet down, get several breaths, and then grab the gunwale and slide underneath it and up into the open. A point emphasized to us was that there is always an air pocket under an overturned boat or in a sunken car. In the latter case, one waits until the car is nearly filled with water and then opens the door and swims to the surface. Another point: Stay calm, and you can locate yourself by feel even in total blackness. Finally, don't try to rush things; wait until conditions are such that you can swim free without great effort. Difficult? Yes, but everyone succeeded in escaping from the overturned boat as instructed, even though it was a bit of a trip for some!

Hypothermia is caused by a loss of heat from the body, and in cold water this can stiffen you up in a hurry. A snug-fitting life jacket will help slow heat loss from the critical trunk area, as will clothes, which trap water and let it be warmed by the body, in the same way, if not as efficiently, as a wetsuit. When operating in areas of cold water (below 40 degrees F), a float coat or other heat-holding piece of emergency clothing is recommended. When in the water, keep activity to a minimum, swimming only to the boat hull or to other persons in the water. If there is more than one person, huddling together will help preserve body heat. Keep your head out of the water; heat loss via the head is rapid (a tight-fitting wool watch cap can make a difference here).

> Whenever I am boating on cold water, and _always_ when I am alone, I wear a life jacket.

It is important to maintain a positive attitude, since the will to live is a powerful means of extending survival time. This attitude will be encouraged if you go into the water wearing a well-fitting life jacket and with a basic understanding of survival techniques. If you are up to your neck in 50-degree water wearing only swim trunks and a T-shirt, the life jackets in the cuddy are helping to keep the boat afloat—upside down—and your buddy is looking unhappy and glassy-eyed, then keeping a positive attitude is a little harder.

How can lifesaving gear possibly kill you? Don't try to put your arms through the loops of a life cushion and wear it on your back; it will force your face into the water. Don't touch off a hand flare if you or the boat are surrounded by gasoline. Don't handle a flare pistol carelessly; after all, it is a gun, and at close quarters could inflict a fatal wound.

The ocean survival course, held for the public each spring, proved to be one of the most valuable days I have spent on, and in, the water. The others in my class, including a housewife, a sailing instructor, a kayak expedition leader, and several Coast Guardsmen, agreed. It also caused me to take a fresh look at a subject shunned like the plague by boat users, namely safety.

Most of us take to the water for pleasure and to get away from the personal obligations and official restrictions that govern our daily lives ashore. Our boats are our transport to freedom, and the last thing we want to think about is injury and death. So we buy the required "lifesaving" equipment and jam it out of sight and mind in the forepeak, with the final and universal thought: It won't happen to me.

For many years, I was a charter member of this group, operating on the belief that good boat handling and healthy caution would carry me through almost any difficulty. This is the same attitude that led the skipper of the _Titantic_ and thousands of other competent boat handlers of craft big and small to wreck their vessels. Then I took up rock and ice climbing, and a more rational regard for safety began to dispel the clouds I had been walking on for so many years.

"Protection" through the use of pitons, nuts, and rope is an integral part of climbing. When you are gripping tiny holds on the face of a precipice, your protection is not something hidden in a locker and forgotten, it's right there. You *have* to know how to use it.

This realization of the importance of protection in dangerous sports began to carry over into my less hazardous but potentially lethal activities, such as driving and boating. Seatbelt use and defensive driving became standard practices in my car. And since I spend so much time alone or with one other person in my boats, many times in less than favorable conditions, I took a new look at the hazards of my favorite pastime. After nearly 40 years of active boating, participating in an ocean survival course was but another step in the process.

Now, whenever I am boating on cold water, and *always* when I am alone, I wear a life jacket. I once scoffed at such caution; I don't anymore. You can be out of a small boat and into the cold suds before you can take a breath, certainly much faster than you can grab a life jacket as you go by—given the unlikely chance it is handy in the first place.

I've also upgraded the required lifesaving equipment, and I know how to use it if ever there is an emergency. Now, in addition to the carefully located grabrail I have found so useful in my 18-footer (see "Something to Grab Onto," page 200), there is a simple safety belt I can clip to the rail with a carabiner, the aluminum snap link that is central to a mountaineer's climbing kit. This safety device may someday keep me from falling overboard, especially in rough water. Protection on the hill,

protection on the boat—they're one and the same when it comes to drawing the sharp line between life and death.

Gone is any embarrassment about what others may think, that only sissies use safety devices. I consider myself careful and competent, but honesty forces me to recall some of the close calls I have had as the result of unforeseen events or momentary carelessness. As our survival course instructor put it: "You can be macho and brag about it *after* you survive an accident because you were prepared."

Seven years and many thousands of boating miles after taking the above described course, I am more convinced than ever that a few ac-

My life jacket is not really a jacket but rather a pricey Mustang vest (Type III) that doesn't look at all like one of the bright orange "horse collars" most people associate with PFDs.

tions should become standard operating procedure aboard a small boat, actions that bear the burden of "safe" practices but that are almost unnoticed when *always* followed.

My life jacket is not really a jacket but rather a pricey Mustang vest (Type III) that is eminently comfortable to wear (particularly in the cool Maine climate where I do most of my boating) and doesn't look at all like one of the bright orange "horse collars" most people associate with PFDs. I have also paid the few extra dollars needed to buy well-fitting, comfortable life jackets that visitors aboard my boat wear without embarrassment. My advice: Buy good equipment. It is the cheapest kind of insurance, because it is accepted by those who need it.

With this good-looking gear aboard, I ask that everyone on my boat wear a PFD, especially since the skipper will be wearing his. If someone doesn't want to put one on (some persons have a mental block regarding safety equipment), I don't insist, but I do make certain that they are fitted to a jacket and that it remains handy.

Whenever I am traveling with new passengers, I make sure one of them knows how to run the motor and how to maneuver if for any reason I go over the side. Since I run the boat in a standing position, that possibility always exists. Naturally, I never expect that emergency to arise, but. . . .

On occasion when I have first-time boaters aboard, I advise my visitors before leaving the dock that if I ask them to do something, I'm telling them to do it. This is not because I suffer from a Captain Bligh syndrome, but rather because emergencies have a way of being instantaneous aboard a small boat and often fast reaction of all concerned can stave off catastrophe. A skipper has only to remember that newcomers to boating are sometimes puzzled by what is going on, and therefore it is important that they do what they are told without opening the subject to roundtable discussion and debate.

Unfortunately, safety (try thinking of it as "protection") remains a dirty word with the majority of boat users. And some of them won't change their minds until they are up to their chins in frigid water, their boats are sinking beneath them, and they are squinting at the fine print on the plastic bag holding their unsoiled life jackets.

Lotsa luck!

—DRG

Something to Grab Onto

Small boats are physically punishing in rough water, particularly so in outboards where the motor is driving the hull against the wind. Bare wood or metal seats are excruciatingly uncomfortable. Boat cushions help some; padded seats are better still. Whatever the case, one's frame is bounced and twisted incessantly. Oh, just to be able to stand up!

The single most welcome feature on my boat is a device designed to solve this problem. It is a centerline grabrail that lets skipper and passengers stand comfortably and safely in all but the roughest weather (see photo on page 201).

A grabrail can be a simple structure shaped from wood or galvanized pipe by the boatowner or a more elaborate rig custom built by a boatyard or metal shop. The possible variations in design are unlimited, but two things are important: First, the grabrail must be built of rugged materials and, second, it must be securely fastened to the boat.

I've tried four different designs on 18-foot open aluminum skiffs. The first was a chest-high, three-legged rail built of ½-inch I.D. galvanized pipe mounted on cast-iron flanges screwed to the seats. The height was dictated by the fact that the boat was being rigged for a long cruise and we needed to be able to move fore and aft at seat level or higher over gear packed in the well between the seats.

The rail was a lifesaver, but after the cruise was over, the boat was frequently used for fishing, and the high rail interfered with rod handling. The

existing pipe was easily cut, straightened, and used to assemble a waist-high, three-legged rail using the same seat flanges as the earlier model. This has worked well and is still in place eight years after the changeover.

When I took delivery of a Lund Alaskan 18 for the Maine Island Trail Association, a new design was needed. The Alaskan has a large cockpit running two-thirds the length of the boat, with narrow seat lockers along the sides. So as to permit fore-and-aft passage without having to climb over anything, I designed a sawhorse-type rail custom built of 1-inch welded aluminum pipe. Each of the four legs had a small flange on

> The rail was used by the passengers about three times more often than the seats.

the foot and was fastened to the aluminum floor frames with three thick-bodied stainless steel screws. Significantly, the rail was used by the passengers about three times more often than the seats.

Recently we took delivery of two new boats of the same model as my own 18-footer. The grabrails for these are similar in design to my cut-down rig but are made of aluminum and are therefore better looking than those made with cast-iron pipe. Other materials that would make good rails include, of course, regular stainless steel railing as used aboard yachts and larger vessels. Railing and fittings are advertised in most of the

larger marine catalogs. Thick PVC pipe from the plumbing department of the local hardware store should also serve well.

The idea for the grabrail was planted in my mind years ago by the late Pete Culler, a traditional wood-boat builder who designed a number of very successful outboard motorboats (successful designs, that is, but custom boats and therefore not widely known). Pete's boats were long and narrow, his 24-foot Blonde Bombshell being a good example. As with my 18-footers, his boats were steered at the motor rather than through forward controls, and it was assumed that the steersman would be standing. In order to secure the latter's position, Pete installed what he called a "chicken post," a well-braced wood post about belt high. Built like a bitt, with a sturdy hard-wood dowel mounted athwartships that was nice to grasp, the post let the skipper relax in standing comfort under almost any conditions.

And comfort is the key. Anyone who has tried to stand in a small boat without anything to hold on to knows the insecurity of the stance and the tremendous strain on the leg muscles. Old-time Cape Cod striper fishermen used to con their little aluminum outboard skiffs from the standing position, using the extension handle of the motor as a brace, but while this helps, it is something less than stable for the average boater. However, if we add a post or grabrail everything changes. No longer does one have to tense every muscle against

The high rail was later cut down to waist height in order to take up less room. The lanyard seen against the dark trousers is fastened to a waist belt on the person at the tiller and clipped onto the grabrail with a carabiner to prevent a fall overboard.

possibility of capsizing. Except in extreme conditions, however, the skipper can continue to stand, since the elevated position helps him in judging the oncoming seas. If I am alone in rough going, I have a clip-on safety lanyard that holds me to the grabrail (and inside the boat!) if I'm thrown off balance. Only a very few times in thousands of miles of travel have I felt the need to sit because it was too rough to stand.

The grabrail or a chicken post works best on motorboats of 16 feet or more in length. The interior layout of smaller open boats usually doesn't lend itself to installation of a rail, and in any event, if it is rough one is far safer seated. If the skipper wants to stand during smooth going, he can use the seat as a leg support and the extension handle of the tiller as an upper body prop, as did the Cape Codders mentioned earlier. A sturdy line tied to the braces on both sides of one of the forward seats and bowing back to the steersman's right hand can provide additional security.

The 18-footers, with their broader beam and added weight, handle the rails well and are considerably more comfortable if those aboard can stand. A 3-foot-long rail is adequate for skipper and crew and tends to concentrate the live weight just aft of amidships where trim is best. As a safety measure and to reduce strain on the fastenings, I advise my passengers against rocking from side to side while holding the rail. In a small way, the rail can act as a turning arm and conceivably could be an overturning lever if sufficient weight were exerted in one direction, especially on a narrower hull. This is a judgment call that needs careful consideration before installing a rail.

As always in small boats, safety factors are important. Standing people raise the center of gravity. They are also in a better position to be thrown overboard, so they should not

the moving boat; instead we can relax and sway gently, with the legs serving as shock absorbers. Most of the time this requires little more than resting one's hand on the rail; when the going gets rough, a tighter grip is needed, but this is far preferable to the body-twisting one undergoes when sitting.

There comes a point, though, when the boat is being thrown around enough to require that the passengers sit down in order to lower the center of gravity and reduce the only be advised to hang on at all times, but also to wear life jackets.

Experience has shown that even though it goes against the old adage "never stand up in a small boat," the grabrail, in practice, is an important safety device, since it concentrates weight in the right spot, keeps passengers alert to what is going on inside and outside the boat, and lets the skipper talk with them without having to constantly shout above the sound of the motor.

And if he is shrewd, the skipper can also place the largest person on the windward side of the boat where he or she will stoically break most of the flying spray. Now that's tall comfort!

—DRG

Running a Tight Ship

"I gotta take a leak."

This is a universal complaint, sometimes couched in more delicate language and other times in downright earthy lingo, but in any event it is a normal reaction to the healthy cycling of the human plumbing system. It is also one of the more deadly practices carried out aboard small boats.

Coast Guard statistics reveal the somewhat astonishing fact that among the most common causes of drownings, urinating over the side of a boat ranks at or near the top. If you find that hard to believe, take a look below at some of the other simple causes of accidents, and then think for a minute of the casual life aboard your own little packet. You may discover that you and your crew are more vulnerable than you thought.

Directly related to the problems of peeing over the side, of course, is the widespread drinking of alcoholic beverages aboard boats of all sizes. We won't pass judgment on this except to comment on its possible effect on the overall safety of the boat. It should be an accepted fact that the skipper must *always* be sober, but history shows that untold thousands of captains, in big boats and small, have acted otherwise, and the dreary record of injury and death that resulted should be enough to sober all skippers—and keep them that way.

From a purely clinical standpoint, drinking adversely affects one's sense of balance, which doesn't make things any easier for that person if he is leaning against the gunwale of a bouncing small boat and trying not to pee all over the woodwork. Alternatives to this practice are using a pail or bailer, urinating in the splash well (a quick rinsing will clean it up), or going ashore for relief (this should be standard practice on fresh water).

Another hazard often not even realized, much less corrected, is

The so-called bowrider boat style is unfortunately named. . . .

improper trim of the boat, a situation that can be worsened by persons moving around while the craft is underway. For example, the so-called *bowrider* boat style is unfortunately named, because it encourages people to ride in the comfortable cockpit forward of the windshield, a place in the very eyes of the boat where there is little bearing because of the narrowing of the bow. While the craft is under the influence of a powerful motor that lifts the bow above the surface, there is little problem. But a sudden slowing down or stopping can result in a quick drop off plane, with water quite possibly flooding in over the rail as the bow slumps under the weight of its human cargo and forward momentum. More commonly, people in the bow may hinder the forward vision of the helmsman, who may compound an already hazardous situation by sitting on the back of his seat so he can see over the crowd. A quick slowing can also throw a poorly situated person over the bow, with the boat quite likely to pass over the victim before it can be stopped.

Another trim problem sometimes occurs at the other end of the boat. If the motor stops and one or more people move aft to fix it, their weight added to that of motor and fuel tanks may submerge the stern well below its usual waterlines. The wind will then catch the lighter bow and swing it to leeward, and the following waves will wash in over the transom. Under some conditions this may well lead to swamping or capsizing.

Less hazardous but still sloppy boat management is a concentration of weight to one side of the boat while underway. This gives the craft a list that not only looks unseamanlike but also increases the chance of a capsize should a large wave, such as a boat wake, come from the side unexpectedly. Weight is best distributed evenly, with the center of the weight being just aft of center when underway.

Children can add a lot of fun and pleasure to a day on the water, but you should have an understanding with them that the skipper's word is law. A small boat is a poor place for horseplay, because it is so easy to lose things overboard—including one or more youngsters playing chicken at the rail. For this reason and the simple fact that kids will be kids, it is a good idea to teach them to accept the wearing of life jackets as part of their early boating experience. Youngsters can also clutter up a boat in a hurry if left to their druthers. This may end up with broken toys and gear, stuff to trip over, wild grabs as wind-blown items head for the drink, and other bits of unwanted excitement.

And then there are the strictly adult problems. It is bad enough to stub a bare foot on a misplaced toy, but even more memorable to kick a fishing plug with two or three treble hooks hanging from it. In little boats, fishing can be harder on the fisherman than on the fish if some sort of order is not kept. Particular care should be taken with unused rods in rod holders. The bouncing of the boat may result in a plug dropping out of its keeper and swinging about, seeking to hook close-by fishermen rather than fish.

Casters have to be particularly careful. A fisherman should avoid casting sidearm to port or starboard, because there is always the chance of a backlash or reel bail snapping shut and the lure coming around to hit the person at the wheel or tiller. Overhead casts are considerably safer. Fly fishermen are not exempt from care, either. The only really safe way to fly cast is to either side, unless you are fishing alone.

There is no one who has fished from a small boat a great deal who has not heard the vicious swish of a lure or fly close by or been slapped in the side of the head by a misdirected plug. Eventually someone gets stuck with a more serious injury than to his pride—like a hook in a finger. This can be extremely painful, if not exactly life threatening, and usually calls for some skill on the one part and stoicism on the other. If the victim is only lightly hooked and the barb has gone through the skin and come out again, the best procedure is to cut off the hook behind the barb and withdraw it back through the wound, which in turn should be washed and sterilized with alcohol. If the hook is embedded in the skin, a safer policy is to sterilize and tape the wound so that the hook is immobilized, and then get the victim to a hospital.

And while we are discussing fishing, let's not forget the fish. Some have sharp teeth, some have barbs, and all of them flap. The latter is no big deal with little fish, but a green 20- or 30-pounder can turn a cockpit into chaos if not dealt with promptly. Fencing with big fish is no job for the

A trophy fish, such as this striped bass, if not dispatched immediately can raise the rivets in a small boat. A rugged billy club is a necessity when one expects to keep the catch taken aboard a small boat. Otherwise, the fish should be released in the water, if at all possible.

shy and kindly; the fish either needs a determined and immediate clobbering or should be thrown back. Those with teeth and aggressive personalities, like bluefish, require special care and handling, since they can pare skin to the bone with a single chomp. A fish billy is as important as a fishing rod in a small boat.

Seasickness can strike with all its pain and misery, even though it is not as common on our kind of boats as on larger craft, because little boats do much of their bouncing around out of rhythmic motion that tends to bring on sickness. If you are going to be out where steady swells can be expected, it is a good idea to warn people beforehand so the susceptible can take medication far enough in advance for it to be worthwhile. Once a person becomes seasick, about the only cure is to endure it or go ashore. Fortunately, most druggists can offer a number of over-the-counter seasickness preventatives. We have found those with Dramamine most effective; others swear by skin patches.

Seasickness reminds us that cooking food—a seasick person's nemesis—is still another source of accidents aboard a boat. The problem is mainly that things are rarely still on

> Coast Guard statistics reveal the somewhat astonishing fact that among the most common causes of drownings, urinating over the side of a boat ranks at or near the top.

small craft, and it is mighty easy to spill a pot of boiling water or a pan of sizzling grease, to say nothing of having an unsecured stove upset and cause all sorts of fun and games. In the section on cruising (page 206) we advise great caution in the use of stoves aboard a small boat where gasoline is present, and we repeat the warning here because one can't have too many reminders that gasoline either explodes or burns at the touch of a spark. A smoker should keep this in mind and not lean over a portable tank to check its contents with a cigarette in his mouth.

This account of the everyday hazards that exist aboard so many small boats should encourage the thoughtful skipper to be certain that a first-aid kit is added to the don't-leave-shore-without-it list. It does not have to be elaborate, but it should contain medications and materials to deal with cuts, bruises, punctures, and burns. Most ship's chandleries and marine mail-order houses offer a variety of first-aid kits, ranging from little more than a packet of Band Aids to kits big enough to satisfy the most worrisome seagoing hypochondriac.

—DRG

Keeping Shipshape

Everyone is familiar with the word "shipshape," but evidence of this fact is lacking aboard many small boats. Dirty exteriors and messy interiors tell the viewer about careless skippers or those who consider small boats as an inconsequential means of carrying stuff and people from one place to another. Missing is a sense of respect for the boat and an awareness of just how important a well-found craft is to one's safety and the lives of crew or passengers.

To the non-boat person, shipshape is simply another word for neat, and certainly neatness is a necessary and admirable factor aboard any boat. Although neat appearance implies

> A neat boat is not automatically a shipshape one.

good organization, knowledge, and even competence, implications are not always realities, and a neat boat is not automatically a shipshape one. Rather, shipshape in its true sense is a combination of factors that, taken together, ensure that a boat is reasonably ready for most any of the surprises that life on the water can spring. In an emergency, a fumbling, bumbling skipper is something less than a pillar of trust and confidence to those depending on him.

Being shipshape is an important element of safety. All lines have their place, for example, whether they are stored in a locker or in the open, and they should be coiled in such a way that they can readily be released for use. Fancy coils and knots may look sharp, but they can be confusing to the uninitiated; simplicity should always guide your choices aboard a boat. Room for an adequate anchor is not always readily available aboard a small boat, and thus the anchor ends up in a rat's nest of twisted line, sharp corners, and candy wrappers underfoot in the bilge or stuffed into an undersize locker. It is worth the effort to find or make a place for this important device where it is available and yet out of the way. But to do so may take some finagling.

An easily overlooked (or ignored) safety aspect of a shipshape boat is where to put the life preservers. A common choice is to jam them into a locker, where they will presumably be handy while staying dry and clean. Unfortunately, PFDs are not handy when they are out of sight, and will probably collect a fine patina of mold and mildew during storage. With this attitude of out-of-sight, out-of-mind, there is a good chance that no one, including the skipper, will be able to get a PFD on quickly in an emergency. The best place to store life jackets in a small boat is in the open—ideally, hanging from the shoulders of each person aboard. On our open skiff, we store the jackets in a plastic half barrel and fit one to each passenger as they come aboard. Some of those who regularly crew with us bring their own Type III jackets right along with lunch and fishing tackle.

Other items that should be stored in the same place each time are tools, flares, and other required safety items, radio, cameras, binoculars, and boat registration papers. Finding a regular place for this gear is an important part of making your boat shipshape.

There are times when those aboard small boats wonder which is the wetter location, in the cockpit or in the water. Rain, spray, fog, and mist are all a part of real boating life you seldom see in the advertisements, and if a boat is not shipshape, just about everything and everyone are going to get soaked sooner or later. A tremendously useful piece of gear aboard any small boat is one or more small waterproof tarps that can be used to cover gear—and occasionally people—from the elements. They should be large enough to tuck under stuff or tie down so that they will not flap in the wind, but they should not be so large that they are a nuisance. Incidentally, wind is always a consideration aboard a motorboat, since the boat creates its own breeze in passage. The wind's pervasive presence cries out for ways to batten down loose gear. One thing nearly every boat manufacturer leaves out are line attachments inside the cockpit. A few eye straps screwed or pop-riveted into the seats, sides, or cockpit deck will pay their way in usefulness and permit you to corral a lot of flapping and flying material (see sketch on page 41).

Boats of 16 feet and over usually have some, if not a lot of, covered storage space; shorter craft may have a small hinged locker or two, but most of the space is used for human cargo. In either case, *watertight* space is at a premium, so containers of some sort are needed for food, clothing, and other stuff that doesn't like water. Solid containers such as coolers make excellent storage boxes for dry goods as well as wet, and nowadays the better ones can also serve as seats. These usually are heavy enough to stay in place without tie-downs, and if they are not fastened in place they can be moved around to trim the boat. Since weight mounts quickly in a small boat, we have found that PVC-coated canoe bags are great for storing clothing, sleeping bags, and other things that must be kept dry. In addition, they are much easier to store and handle than solid containers, fitting into nooks and corners to save precious space.

Anyone who has lived in a single room for an extended time or who has cruised in a small boat for several days knows the difficulties of keeping track of things and keeping them in order. They also soon learn how necessary it is to live by the ancient adage, "A place for everything, and everything in its place." Good seamen know there is more to being shipshape than sweeping the deck. It has to be a way of life on the water.
—DRG

> *PVC-coated canoe bags are great for storing clothing, sleeping bags, and other things that must be kept dry.*

CRUISING

Introduction

Far-fetched ideas have a way of sticking in one's mind. Years ago an acquaintance named Bill Warren, on one of his pass-through visits to the Maine coast, stopped by the office and dropped the following gem on me.

"I've got the answer to dirt-cheap cruising," said the peripatetic Rhode Islander. "I'm going to build me a big skiff—straight sides, flat, cross-planked bottom, pointy bow—and build a little house on it. The boat will be about 24 feet long, 8 or 9 feet wide, and I'll strap a 25-horse outboard on the transom for power. Simple, solid, cheap. Great boat to cruise down the Inland Waterway in. She'll draw so little, I'll be able to overnight in backwaters so small they never see a boat."

To the best of my knowledge, Bill's cruiser was never built, except in my mind. Dozens of times I've put her together with pine planks, two-by-fours, and plywood from the local lumberyard. In her, I've felt the pull of the Cape Cod Canal's swift current as I headed south, the acrid smell of wood smoke drifting back from the little cabin chimney. I've tided her out on the flats behind the Outer Banks and explored the winding creeks of Georgia's islands. And she hasn't cost me anything, for, to paraphrase an old adage, "The Lord does not subtract from one's life the hours spent daydreaming about boats."

On a more practical note, this "dirt-cheap" cruiser is not so far-fetched as it might sound. Thousands of successful boats have been built from ordinary lumber, especially the eminently versatile Rhode Island quahog skiff, the Florida gillnet skiff, and the semi-dory and its relatives (see page 35). Any of these common workboats and others of their breed could be used as the hull of a simple coastal or river cruiser, boats both cheap to build and cheap to run by today's high-priced standards.

Unfortunately, the tendency today is to think of small boats in terms of glamour and speed, both of which cost a lot of money. In addition, glamour is a transient thing, today's glitter being tomorrow's tarnish. As for speed, our whole culture seems to be keyed to its apparent charms, with little time spent to consider where we are going. Very wisely was it said, "All travel is dull exactly in proportion to its rapidity."

Five miles of river or bay is 5 miles of flashing-by nothingness at 30 m.p.h. Poking along the same shoreline in a small boat at 3 m.p.h. is to spend the better part of a day in constant discovery. Speed and glamour have their place, but we should not be cowed into believing there is no other way.

Small-boat adventurers early in the century were little concerned by what others might think about their peregrinations. A pup tent ashore, a simple canvas shelter aboard, either was sufficient to house their simple needs, for theirs was the thrill of the chase and not a fashionable stroll on the boardwalk. We can do well to mirror that attitude today, using our little cruiser as a means of transport to new ports of call rather than as a status symbol to elicit the envy or scorn of persons less fortunate than ourselves.

The canvas dodger drawn tight over a frame of wood or metal still

> To paraphrase an old adage, "The Lord does not subtract from one's life the hours spent daydreaming about boats."

Cruising can take one in directions other than to wild coasts and exotic seas. An unusual and thrilling way to see New York City and its magnificent harbor is in a small boat. Several marinas and some interesting gunkholes offer plenty of opportunity for overnighting.

makes a useful and inexpensive "cabin" for the small open boat. A more permanent house resistant to the rain, bugs, and cold can be fashioned from a light spruce frame covered with plywood or pine. Inside, folding pipe berths, a tiny sink, a wood-burning pot stove, and simple storage lockers or bins can be installed to make one's craft ready for truly serious cruising.

How does one go about bringing this daydream craft into being? The options are several. One can build new, buy a new or used hull, restore a wrecked or neglected hull, or have one custom built. All but the latter can be accomplished at quite low cost, although innovation, imagination, and ingenuity will be required to contain expenses.

For those who have never built a boat but feel that a basic skiff-type hull might be within their skill range, books on boatbuilding and simple boat designs are available in libraries, bookstores, and by mail order. Need inspiration, instruction, and design in one place? Then try to find a copy of Sam Rabl's classic *Boatbuilding in Your Own Backyard,* or order a copy of John Gardner's mini-masterpiece, *The Dory Book* (available from Mystic Seaport Museum, Inc., 75 Greenmanville Avenue, Mystic, CT 06355-0990).

Prefer to start with an existing hull? Try finding a used workboat. It will probably be beat-up and ugly at first sight, but look beneath the grime and chafe to see if it is sound enough to restore. Two of the best boats I

> "All travel is dull exactly in proportion to its rapidity."

have owned were cast-off fishing dories that were cheap to buy, cheap to fix up, and a pleasure to use. And don't overlook the possibilities of rebuilding a fiberglass hull. The material is tough and long lasting, and can often be repaired and reinforced to make a perfectly safe and sound boat, particularly so if it will be used as a low-speed craft.

A fine cruiser for protected waters can be built on one of the big jonboat hulls. Most of these are aluminum and tough—dented perhaps, with a few weeping rivets, but all this can be fixed with the magic materials available today.

Of course, always keep in mind that the goal is to have a safe boat when you are finished turning your dream into a reality. Hulls must be strong enough to do the job, but in a slow cruiser weight is not the problem it would be in a speedboat, so one need not stint when beefing up where needed. Fuel must be separated under all conditions from heating or cooking fires elsewhere on the boat. Handling should be reasonably good. And electrical and fuel systems should be up to marine standards. In all circumstances, simplicity cannot be overemphasized: Complexity costs.

For your labors, you will have acquired two joys that are endless in their rewards: You will own a boat you have customized to meet your personal needs, and you will never need to take a thousand-mile voyage to derive the profound pleasure of cruising in a small boat.

—DRG

Cruising in Small Powerboats

Cruising in small motorboats is a sport that awaits discovery. Cruising on the water is almost always associated with larger craft, with their comfortable cabins and many of the facilities of a land-based home. True, cruising in a few specialized craft such as canoes and kayaks has a long history, but we usually think of long-distance travel in these boats as sport for the young and hardy. All but missing from this mix is that wonderfully versatile cruiser—the small motorboat.

Overnighting in small powerboats is certainly not unknown, and in some regions—the southern rivers, some of the big northern lakes, and a few coastal areas with large, protected bays—the sport has built a tolerable following. But the average boater, from the owner of a small aluminum skiff to the metalflake bassboat skipper, is blissfully unaware that he may be piloting a wave-riding magic carpet. Much of North America, including most of our western desert regions, has a bountiful supply of good to spectacular small-boat cruising waters; yet all too often the range of possibilities for using our boats is unknown and thus unappreciated.

The reason for our ignorance is not difficult to find: most of us simply don't know what we have. We buy a small boat for a specific use such as fishing, water-skiing, commuting, daytripping, or sightseeing. We are told that our boat is designed just for that purpose, and in most cases it looks the part. Fishing boats have rod lockers, bait wells, rod holders, swivel seats, and graphics to match. Sport boats have racy lines, comfortable fore-and-aft-facing seats, sometimes a tow bar, and invariably a powerful motor. And then there are thousands of boaters like the one who says: "All I own is a little light-weight cartopper, just big enough for me, a friend, my dog, and a six-pack. Cruise in that dinky thing? Do I look like a fruitcake?"

Let's just respond by pointing out that some of the more famous cruises in boating literature have been made in craft smaller than that little cartopper. In fact, the latter has great potential as a long-distance river cruiser—it is tough, maneuverable, light in weight for dragging over shallows, and can also be poled or rowed when the going gets thin. Two persons with minimum gear could spend days exploring one of the hundreds of navigable rivers available to American boaters, and if the skipper were the adventuresome type with time to spare, he and his dog could cruise our river systems for an entire season in "that dinky thing."

You don't want to travel alone, you say? Try finding a companion to go along with you in his or her boat. Cruising with others, each in a minimum boat of this type, is exciting and satisfying. Alone, you find that a 10- or 12-foot open skiff has adequate room for you and your gear. If you want to go first-class on river, lake, or coastal bay, move up to one of the roomy and remarkably seaworthy 14-foot aluminum boats of a type carried in one brand or another by just about every boat dealer in the country. Most of these make dandy cruisers, but we recommend them only with this warning: Know your boat, yourself, and the limitations of both. Little boats and inexperience are a recipe for trouble.

DETERMINING A SUITABLE BOAT

We start this discussion with words of praise for these unpretentious craft, not because we think they are the best cruisers, but rather to make the point that most boat types, large and small, have cruising potential. Where and how they are used, however, are the keys to their *suitability*. And that is something else entirely.

Evaluating the suitability of your boat or one you might buy for the purpose of cruising requires the weighing of many factors. Most important is where your boat will be used. Will your cruising ground be the sunny sounds of Texas or North

Small-boat cruising takes many forms—and sharp contrast is the norm. In the photo at the top a group of Georgians are pictured on one of their occasional cruises down the Ocmulgee and Altamaha rivers from Hawkinsville to St. Simons Island on the coast. The photo at the bottom was taken at Rockland in 1987 midway on the first official cruise of the 325-mile-long Maine Island Trail.

Hugh Lawson

CRUISING

Carolina, or the cold, windswept waters of the Maine coast or British Columbia? That dinky 10-footer might be entirely suitable for cruising a river but would be way out of its league on a rambunctious saltwater bay. In the latter case, a 14-foot skiff is adequate for a lone cruiser who knows his stuff, but a boat 16 or 17 feet in length with a corresponding increase in beam and weight will offer more in the way of comfort, safety, and carrying capacity. If all of your cruising will be on big waters, then a heavy hull may be a benefit by providing a softer, smoother ride. But greater weight means you will get less speed with the same power or you will need a larger motor to retain a desired speed. Complicated? To a degree, yes, but don't be intimidated; there are some fairly safe generalities you can use in determining the suitability of your boat for the type of cruising you want to do.

Tiny boats (9 feet in length or under): Some are OK for cruising in protected waters such as small to medium rivers or protected fresh- or

Probably the most popular outboard type of all, and a craft readily converted to cruising, is the runabout, a sleek example being this Bayliner 1800 Capri. Standard features include adjustable sleeper seats and convenient storage compartments. Add a screened fabric top, grub, and sleeping bags, and you make a long-ranging cruiser out of what most people think of as a dash-about day boat.

saltwater river systems. However, the boats are only safe for one person and a minimum amount of gear. Considerable skill and sound judgment are required for safe use. In practical terms, these boats are really too small for pleasant cruising and

can quickly be dangerously overloaded. They are easily overpowered.

Little boats (9 to 12 feet in length): Many are suitable for protected waters, the more burdensome ones capable of carrying two persons and minimum gear. Generally they are a chancy choice for big water; safety margins match the size of the boat—small. Skill and sound judgment are required for safe use. And as with the tiny boats, they are easily overloaded and overpowered.

Medium boats (12 to 15 feet in length): Some of the better models in this range are very capable and amazingly economical cruisers, yet few of them are comfortable for more than two adults and a couple of small children, at best. If several models of a brand are available, choose the "seagoing" model for cruising. Try to keep weight of gear as low as possible, even sacrificing some of the more frivolous items to save a few pounds. That is because these boats are at their safest and most effective when loaded to two-thirds or less of their rated maximum

This 12-foot Sea Nymph cartopper would appear to be a poor choice as a cruiser, yet it would make an economical and capable riverboat for a lone traveler.

capacity. The same two-thirds factor holds true for motor horsepower also. For example, a 14-foot aluminum boat rated for a maximum of 35 h.p. will give excellent service with 15 to 20 h.p. if the boat is loaded at or below its two-thirds-rated-load capacity. As you can see, there are considerable savings to be realized both in cost and weight by choosing the smaller-horsepower motor.

Of interest to those seeking maximum *low* figures: For years we cruised two adults and their food, and camping gear, in a 14-foot Starcraft Seafarer aluminum skiff with a 7.5-h.p. Mercury outboard. This little mill would get the loaded boat up on plane at a top speed somewhere between 12 and 15 m.p.h., an acceptable pace (to us) under the circumstances.

Larger boats (15 to 20 feet in length): Many boats in this range make good to excellent cruisers, thanks to cockpits big enough to store ample gear and supplies for three or four persons, with a bit of legroom to spare. However, even the largest of them is really too small to sleep four comfortably. But if the plan is to sleep ashore, boats in the mid- to upper part of this size-range will accommodate two couples or a family with two or three children. As a rule, the boats can handle a fair amount of rough water. (What's a "fair amount?" It is what *you* consider ordinarily rough; your ratings will change as you gain experience.)

WHAT KIND OF POWER?

Once you have some idea as to the suitability of your cruising hull, the next consideration is the engine. If you are adapting an existing boat for cruising, you may choose to stick with the motor it has now, either for economic reasons or because it seems well suited to the hull. But if

you own more than one motor, or if you are buying a new one, there are interesting options to think about. Some of the more important points to ponder are mainly subjective: What is the purpose of your cruise? What do you expect to gain from it? Are you doing it mainly for the boating, or do you have a destination or main purpose (fishing, for instance) in mind? Are you planning to explore, or do you want to cover as much water as you can in the course of a day? Realistic answers to these questions can help you make your decision about power choice.

If your purpose is relaxed cruising with no definite goal, much of it at the displacement or semidisplacement speed of your boat, a relatively small motor may be all you need. If your boat has a planing hull, we

Many boats in the 18- to 20-foot class sport hardtop shelters or fabric dodgers that turn them into miniature yachts. The Eastern 19 is a traditional northeast hull with 7-foot, 5-inch beam. The 20-foot Privateer Roamer has 6-foot, 4-inch headroom and bunks forward. It gains cockpit room by mounting the outboard motor on a bracket.

would advise you to supply enough power to be able to take advantage of that useful feature when you want it. Ordinarily, about one-third of the maximum rated horsepower of your boat will be adequate. What this means for boats under 20 feet in length is that all but the heaviest of them can use one of the so-called *fishing* outboards in the 7- to 30-h.p. range. Today, quite a few of these motors have extremely efficient sound insulation and can hardly be heard when throttled down to walking speeds, the ideal pace for poking along an interesting shoreline.

Since some people like to cruise with destinations in mind, which may be points quite a distance apart, the ability to move along at a solid planing speed is required. The best powering bet here is to move to the other end of the scale and look at motors in the horsepower range in the top third of your boat's rating. If you find that your big motor doesn't idle along smoothly, you might try what many fishermen do to eliminate the coughing and wheezing of the big mills: clamp a fishing motor on the transom or an outboard motor mount. A 10- or 15-h.p. motor will push almost any boat 20 feet or under in length, and will do it all day on a few gallons of fuel.

We are strong advocates of carrying a second outboard rather than a large stock of parts and tools to match. Murphy's Law will almost certainly be in force, assuring that the part that breaks is not in your inventory of spares. This will happen in a spot or in conditions that make working on the motor a misery. How much easier to be able to lift a small outboard onto the transom or simply tilt down one that is already there and buzz off at a reasonable pace, if not in style.

We would offer one comment on cruising at high speed: You don't see much, and though it may be exhilarating for a while, your passengers, who don't have the pleasure of conning the boat, may soon find it both boring and uncomfortable. Unless you are dead set on covering as much water as you can, a better way is to build-in a diversion or two, slowing down to coast the shoreline for a while or exploring a cove or river mouth.

Our experience is that what one sees on a cruise is in direct proportion to the rate of speed; the faster you go, the less you see. This fact was brought home to us as far from the sea as you can get. My wife and I were bicycling across country and were about to enter the vast high desert country of northern Colorado.

> The two-fer system is based on the theory that an item that does two jobs is better than an item that does only one.

We steeled ourselves to enduring several days of heat and boredom as we pedaled past nothing but sagebrush and sand hills. What a joy it was to discover how wrong we were! At our quiet 10 m.p.h., the desert began to reveal its secrets: prairie dogs were caught by surprise at the edges of their holes; antelope watched us curiously until we were almost upon them and then departed in stiff-legged bounds, white rumps bouncing high; flowering cacti added splotches of brilliant color to the fragrant sage; and birds flitted and soared as the desert displayed a marvelous world of life and action. The dreaded desert soon became our favorite ride. Meanwhile, an occasional car zipped by at a mile a minute, its passengers encased in steel, glass, and boredom. A similar "other world" is also seen by the person in an open boat quietly following a wooded shore or idling under great sea cliffs: smells, sounds, and sights known only to the slow traveler seeking communion rather than dominance.

RIGGING YOUR BOAT

Suitability is more than having the right kind of hull under you. And it is here that cruisers sail off on their personal courses with regard to how they set up their craft for overnight journeys afloat. Some want as many comforts and conveniences built into their boats as ingenuity and money can provide. Everything comes aboard, and everything has its place, from a special locker for the charts to neat side pockets for hand-held radio and binoculars to a sleep-in cuddy with fully equipped galley. Rigging such a craft is great fun, and in many circumstances the boat will be a pleasure to cruise in. But in setting up this boat, especially if it will be cruising big waters, always consider the weather: rain will fall, spray will come aboard, the sun will beat down, the wind will snort and search. The elements will work you and your gear over from stem to stern. So go forearmed and forewarned.

Other cruisers, particularly those planning to camp ashore, rig their boats as simply and lightly as possible. If conditions are right, they can beach their boats for the night, and if not, they can moor them off on special anchoring rigs. Their gear is designed to be removed from the boat quickly, being stored in canoe bags, boxes, and milk crates. There is nothing more frustrating than to anchor off, set up camp, stretch out for a leisurely meal, and then find there is something absolutely needed that was left aboard in some drawer or cupboard where it was overlooked.

Cruisers of a third type walk a conservative line between the rig-em-up-Scout school and the minimalists, modifying their boats with such things as dodgers and perhaps a galley-in-a-box that can be used both aboard and ashore. Usually, they use their boat for more than one purpose and therefore don't want to compromise its basic utility with too many fixed additions. They also know that simplicity in gear is just plain common sense aboard a small boat.

TRIP PLANNING

One of the great pleasures of winter is planning a summer cruise aboard your boat. This is a wonderful time to sit back and ponder where and how you want to go, to study charts and maps and travel information, and to read the marine and outdoor catalogs for fresh ideas on gear and equipment. The temptation is to plan to the last little detail, both as to rigging for your boat and timing of your travel. It is also a good time to back off and raise your cruising to a level above that of your daily routine. Most of us must live by the clock on land; but we do not have to do so at sea.

In fact, if there is one piece of advice we can offer, one seed we can plant in your mind, one bit of reality that can in a single stroke of the brush eliminate most of the stress on a vacation cruise, it is to caution against living by the clock when you are on the water. If you turn instead to Nature's clock—the rise and fall of the tides, the coming of the wind, the

sweep of fog, the simple passage of the sun—and let that guide the decisions of the day, you will know the peace of mind that comes with the acceptance of Nature's guidance. You cannot control the elements, and attempting to go on in the face of adverse conditions in order to meet a preset schedule is folly of the first order, and almost always unnecessary for those on vacation. People who work daily in the open, such as commercial fishermen, woodsmen, and farmers, accept the weather as a fact of life and adjust as the day requires. The small-boat cruiser will profit mightily by doing the same.

Most of us with small motorboats

We have turned to carrying virtually everything on and off in heavy canvas bags, waterproof canoe bags, milk crates, and just plain wood boxes. The most useful "storage" items we have are a couple of lightweight waterproof tarps. . . .

also have trailers with which to move them around, an advantage that gives us far longer "legs" than all but the globe-trotting yachtsman—who must spend weeks getting a boat to a place we can reach day after tomorrow, a place he may not be able to get to at all. We, by contrast, have the ability to move from sea to lake to river to pond and then back to one or the other as often as we wish. We have motored up streams hardly wider than our boat, across bays so wide the land was a distant blue blur, and through lake systems one could explore for weeks, all within a day's drive of home. Every state has its own set of water courses just waiting for the modern explorer, and today

there is as much information on those waterways as you could want to know. State highway maps are a super source of initial guidance, and beyond them is the finer detail found in tourist guides, waterway guides, large-scale maps and charts, and the superb detailed state-by-state map books offered by such companies as DeLorme Publishing Company of Freeport, Maine. Tracking down this sort of material, taking it all in, and digesting and sorting the information to fit your own needs is the finest kind of winter work.

SELECTING YOUR ROUTE

The waters of the sea are level, but the sea is not a level playing field. Not only is the apparently obvious course not always the best one, it may well be the worst. We have read how mariners avoid many of the great capes of the world because of their concentration of storms, currents, and gales, but what we may not realize is that an apparent route close to shore, perhaps one used regularly by larger boats, can be just as hazardous to us in our small boats as the more notorious regions are to big vessels.

A good example is the Petit Manan Bar between Petit Manan Point and Green Island, about 2 miles offshore of eastern Maine's rugged coast. The obvious route across the bar is the buoyed channel used by most of the coastal traffic that chooses to go inside of the low islands anchoring the seaward end of the bar. However, the big tides of this region flow over the bar with significant force, directly into the face of the prevailing summer southwesterlies. In a short time, Petit Manan

CRUISING

x

Bar can become a mess of steep, short waves where no self-respecting small-boat skipper wants to be. But a careful study of the chart shows a narrow band of deep water cutting into the bar only a short distance off the mainland point, a channel that slips quickly across the bar itself and then returns to deep water again. This channel is marked on the chart as the "Inner Bar," but an unknowing skipper might look at the ledges dotting the chart and decide the outer route was still the better one. Seeing the Inner Bar from the water only reinforces this decision. Waves break almost constantly over Bar Ledge and the Old Bull, which form the outside edge of the Inner Bar channel, while on the inner edge great swells hump and shatter on the low rocky point at the tip of 'Tit Manan, as it is called by Mainers. The Inner Bar is menacing to look at from the low level of a small boat, but almost always it is the best route to take because it is somewhat protected by those menacing wave-washed ledges and offers a short passage through a precarious area. Such information is called *local knowledge,* and it can be of great value to the cruising skipper. But seeking out such crucial information can take time, which is another reason why holding to a tight schedule that does not allow for deviation can be dangerous.

A handy tool to have at hand when you are studying charts and maps for possible routes is a magnifying glass, the main purpose of which is to read the fine print and other marks that are easily overlooked. Much can be told about freshwater lakes and rivers by contour lines and heights above sea level, the latter usually a single number in blue placed roughly in the center of the body of water. Dams, bridges, and similar possible barriers or drops may also be shown, although not infrequently they are faintly marked or must be deduced by detective work (look, for example, for town names with "Falls," "Portage," "Rapids," or "Mills" in them). Similar problems hold true on marine charts. For instance, Blue Hill Falls is a village on the Maine coast, but someone unfamiliar with the area would never know by looking at the chart where the community got its name, or why. The truth is that there is an impressive reversing falls at the entrance to the Salt Pond, a lovely inlet just south of the village, one that is exciting enough to lure whitewater kayakers there on favorable tides. At first glance there is no telling what tidbits of value a chart may hide, but if you are planning a cruise it pays to give more than a cursory glance.

OUTFITTING YOUR BOAT

The cruiser, like the backpacker, takes his or her house along on the trip. Kitchen, clothing, food, tools, water, bed, and a roof over the head are among the necessities one must always have, but fitting this outfit to one's pack or boat can be like trying to cram 5 pounds of candy into a 4-pound bag. We fought this battle of the bulge for years before we switched to the two-fer system, a method of gear selection that works the best of the many we have tried—though we still have our days when too much seems not enough.

The two-fer system is simple in concept but demanding in practice. It is based on the theory that an item that does two jobs is better than an item that does only one. The latter stays home. Used rigorously, the system will eliminate an amazing amount of needless gear that is brought along "just in case I need it." As the one-use stuff is set aside, you will discover that there are very few absolutely necessary items in the discard pile and that the two-fer pile is smaller than you would have imagined. Sure, a few things go back in the lineup, but the discipline of having to choose makes a big difference in how much gear you really have to take with you. Let's take a look at how the two-fer system works.

Veteran small-boat cruisers frequently combine kitchen equipment into a box of some kind (perhaps with shelves and drawers) that can be moved about in the boat or carried ashore. A steel or iron frying pan (we like those with a folding handle) seems to season better than an aluminum one. We avoid pans with nonstick linings since scorching is common when cooking over camping stoves or open fires and nonsticks don't like being overheated. In addition to the usual cooking, the frying pan makes a good toaster over a hot, concentrated flame like a camping stove. A deep pot is as important as the frying pan and can be used for regular cooking, heating water, and storage. Incidentally, if fresh water is scarce, as it sometimes is on coastal islands, cooking water often makes perfectly acceptable coffee or tea water (two-fer with *water?*) and almost always can be used for personal washing. Also, seawater can be

> The average boater, from the owner of a small aluminum skiff to the metalflake bassboat skipper, is unaware that he may be piloting a wave-riding magic carpet.

used in many ways for cooking, a good way to save on your drinking supply. A long cooking fork (which can be used for toasting, too) and a small spatula that can be used for stirring as well as flipping are about all that is needed for basic food preparation. We also carry a couple of tin pie plates that serve as both warming dishes (they don't burn or melt) and extra eating dishes.

Each person has a medium-depth bowl that serves as dish or bowl; a spoon that stirs, forks, and spoons; and presumably his own sheath knife or jackknife. An insulated cup is good for hot and cold drinks and soups. We've added a couple of stainless steel Sierra cups to our kit to serve as backup cups and bowls.

The above is an admittedly minimal kitchen, but it works. You can add as you see fit. The missing item, of course, is the stove, and for most trips a backpacking stove with a self-contained fuel supply is adequate (for more on the subject, see "Camping, or Backpacking by Boat," page 216).

For sleeping aboard or ashore, our choice around water is a three-season sleeping bag with synthetic filling rather than down. On small boats, everything seems to get wet sooner or later, and down-filled bags lose most of their insulating qualities when soaked, while synthetic bags retain a fair amount of loft and hence their warming feature. A sleeping bag in its stuff-sack makes a good backrest if you are sitting on the ground, but they really are pretty much a one-use item—though not one you want to leave behind.

When outfitting our boats, we place a star on the list beside the word "Water." Potable drinking water is not as plentiful as it once was, even on freshwater lakes and rivers. Pollution by both man and animals is common, and although it can usually be tolerated to some degree by the body's immune system, we are better off taking good drinking water with us or treating questionable water in the field. One-liter soda bottles or 2-quart milk bottles make good containers for carrying water aboard; water stored in several containers is easier to use and less apt to be lost through contamination or leakage. A built-in water supply on a small boat is not advisable for reasons of weight, leakage, spoilage, and space.

If you enjoy building-in at least a few special storage places, making a place for accessories such as cameras, binoculars, hand-held radios, other portable electronic equipment, and the like is a useful exercise. Relatively expensive and subject to damage by being dropped, wetted, or lost overboard, these items warrant

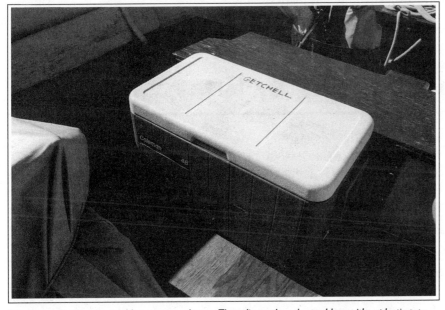

Dry storage is always a problem on open boats. The editor solves the problem with a plastic tote box and one or more plastic coolers, the latter equally good for clothing and other things one wants to keep dry. The waterproof diver's box atop the tote box can be used to protect the compass, cameras, binoculars, and other valuable gear.

special care and a place where they always end up—other than in the bilge. Using the forward cuddy and other storage areas in the forward half of the boat is not advisable, because they may be subjected to pounding whenever you hit rough water. Better to build a watertight locker in the after half of the boat and then make sure the electronic machines are well padded. Even though modern electronics are solid-state and housed in hard plastic or metal, a steady battering isn't going to do the dials, antennas, and other mechanical devices any good; better to baby them and thus be confident they will operate when needed.

Other important items you will want quick access to are tools and spare parts. Our choice for this is a plastic fishing-tackle box that can be carried on and off the boat or to anyplace where it is needed. The main storage area in the box is large enough for the few tools we need—pliers, wrenches, screwdrivers, electrician's tape, galvanized wire, and a few other items—and the trays serve well to hold a variety of fastenings, new spark plugs, and other small stuff. The tools are kept in a plastic pouch and are regularly sprayed with WD-40, as are the rest of the contents of the toolbox. Since a good deal of our cruising is in wilder areas where we can camp ashore, we always carry a light ax, small bow saw, and, occasionally, a set of long-handled pruning shears, the latter handy in clearing a campsite. These items will stand up to the wet surroundings only if they are kept well oiled. This is particularly true of the saw blade.

Allotted space is needed for anchor and lines (don't stint on rope, because you rarely have enough) and required safety gear such as life jackets and signaling equipment. And then there are the usual perishable papers, such as charts, maps, books, owner's manual for the motors, etc.

This is just basic gear—where in the world does it all go?

Over the years, we have tried building-in storage with the addition of lockers and shelves, and while some is helpful, the fact is that built-ins usually require more room than carry-ons, and the damp environment in the drawers or compartments is brutal on anything left there for any length of time. So we have turned to carrying virtually everything on and off in heavy canvas bags, waterproof canoe bags, milk crates, and just plain wood boxes. The nice thing about this system is that the containers are readily moved about the boat so that trim can be fine-tuned, depending on the size of the crew and the amount of gear everyone has brought aboard. As a result, the most useful "storage" items we have are a couple of lightweight waterproof tarps, plenty of light nylon line, and many tie-down points.

All of this may appear to be pretty confusing to first-time cruisers, but some of the gear is required whenever you use the boat. You'll soon get used to where it is kept aboard—ideally, always in the same place. With much of the balance, the easiest way is to start with minimums and then work up, slowly. If your boat is small, think small. If you have more room, think small anyway. And if you are planning to take along a half-dozen friends on your cruise, think smaller still, and bring in another boat or two. It will be a lot more fun.

—DRG

Camping, or Backpacking by Boat

Boat camping, whether you are aboard or ashore, can be great fun or raw misery, but rarely is it boring. To newcomers with high levels of expectation, staying aboard overnight reveals just how small a small boat is and proves that needle-nose saltwater mosquitoes are no more deterred by water between boat and land than a squadron of F-15's would be. The hoped-for joys of living aboard are slow to materialize. To veterans of the sport, whose expectations have been leavened by many lessons in reality, boat camping is a time to enjoy

Times have changed, and so have the manner and methods of camping.

the simple pleasures, one of the more important of these being the ability to move ashore, lock, stock, and wine bottle, where there is room to stretch and where the underpinning is not quite so jiggly.

Experience has shown us that the best approach to boat camping is to think of it as "backpacking by boat." Sea kayakers, limited in what they can take along by the piddling size of the cargo area of their little boats, can accept this counsel without argument. The motorboat skipper may be tempted to load aboard everything up to and

Boat camping is with backpacking gear, since the equipment can be compacted into a small space. And space is at a premium on all boats under 20 feet.

including cots and a portable TV. When it becomes obvious that there is no room aboard to *use* all this paraphernalia, and the decision is made to move ashore, the time and effort needed to transfer the van-load of stuff from boat to land will quickly convince said skipper that the backpacking level is a more reasonable place to start.

All of which assumes you can go boat camping in the first place.

The thought of going to sea in a well-equipped boat, cruising during the day and camping on an uninhabited island or wild shore by night, is considered by many of us to be the ultimate adventure in small-boat travel. Not too long ago, one could land on almost any unsettled shore and feel reasonably certain no one would complain about a brief visit. That is no longer the case. Shore property is now so valuable that a lot of owners don't want any uninvited visitors, even if only for a stroll or a picnic, because of a desire for privacy and concerns about fire, rubbish, and liability. As a result, that dream of camping in a waterside wilderness has the more realistic possibility of turning into an unwanted and embarrassing confrontation.

Think of it as "backpacking by boat."

Fortunately, there are exceptions to this trend, particularly for the skipper willing to do some advance study. For instance, many states have river- and lakeside parks, and a few even have oceanside facilities where those traveling by water can actually pull the boat up the beach or anchor it in a quiet cove and pitch a tent within sound of the waves lapping the shore. Some water-blessed states—Maine, for instance—have established primitive lakeside and oceanside campsites in hundreds of places, many of which are available free on a first-come basis.

The important thing the camper should note here is that times have changed, and so have the manner and methods of camping. Whether you are at an organized campground or are fortunate enough to be in a place where no one has been before, low impact is the goal, with the sign of an experienced modern camper being virtually no sign at all.

The first big step toward accomplishing the goal of leaving no mark

CRUISING

is to eliminate the most flamboyant signature of camping, the fire ring or fireplace. For instance, there is a standing rule among experienced island campers: Never build a fire on the upland. If you feel the need for a cooking or warming fire (and if it is legal; most states require a permit for recreational fires), it should always be placed below the storm tide line, or better still, below the daily tide line and in a location out of the wind. These two practices alone reduce the danger to acceptable limits and, if properly done, assure that all signs of the fire will disappear within one or two cycles of the tide. On fresh water, try to build a fire on the bank or better still on a sandbar rather than in the woods, using the techniques described below.

When building a fireplace below the tide line, avoid placing the fire against a ledge or large boulders, as the scar will last for years. Instead, use sand and small rocks to contain the fire itself and set the windbreak of larger stones or logs back away from the flames. A shallow hole serves as a good fire pit on a gravel beach or sandbar. Building your fire in a metal pan, such as a rubbish-can lid, will all but eliminate any chance of scars. The fire should be kept small, not only as a safety precaution but also to save firewood, which is scarce

> *The amount of debris can be reduced remarkably before you leave home if you take food out of its packaging and store it in weightless plastic bags or containers.*

around many sites and on islands. When leaving the campsite for good, you can throw the small fire rocks into the water and redistribute the larger rocks along the shore. Partially burned firewood can also be thrown into the water. Unburned sticks should be scattered along the beach above the tide line so that others can use them. Wherever the fire is built, the fire site should be built in such a way that it can be dismantled and all signs eliminated before you leave.

Of course, the way to solve the fire hassle is to use a camping stove with its self-contained fuel supply. Such stoves are convenient and safe, and their use eliminates the need to gather firewood, which can be a major chore.

Pounding feet have a direct impact on the upland, and because islands and many headlands are frequently capped with only a thin layer of duff and mineral soil over solid rock, it is important to tread lightly once you leave the shoreline. One way to reduce the concentration of foot traffic is to locate the kitchen area on the beach, where sand, gravel, or rock will absorb any amount of beating. This will leave the tenting area only for sleeping. Another advantage of this is that you can pitch your tent some distance from the boat without having to carry all your kitchen gear to the sleeping site. Try to select a ledge or rocky place where you can go onto the upland from the beach without having to scramble up a grass or gravel bank that is apt to break down and erode if a footpath is made on it.

By the way, if you plan to stay on the island for a couple of days, you'll probably find it a good idea to take down your kitchen daily before you leave camp and store it neatly and securely in a shaded portion of the upland. Crows, gulls, and small animals have a great fondness for human foods, and these pint-size marauders can do a number on your stuff. In some remote northern areas, bears are also a potential nuisance, a strong reason for cleaning up the kitchen area after every meal, hanging food from a tree out of the reach

In tidewater areas, fires should be confined to the beach below the high-tide mark. Note the two-fer system, described in the previous article, in action here. A boat cushion has become a comfortable shoreside seat while the cover of the big plastic tote box is being used as a table.

One-burner stoves are adequate for camp cooking for one to four persons. This MSR XGK II will burn a variety of flammable liquids, including outboard oil/gas mix. Probably the hottest-burning of the backpacking stoves, it is great on the beach but flares up too much during priming to use on board. The folding aluminum wind screen at the top looks flimsy but has lasted for years.

of the big animals, and locating your sleeping area elsewhere. Another equally powerful and far more common force that can damage or wreck your food supply is the sun. Don't be misled by a cool breeze, because the sun's heat is little affected by it and an ice cooler cover can get hot enough to spoil the contents if it is left in the sun all day.

Tents should be located on grass, if available, which makes a tougher base than the needle cover under evergreen trees. Matted grass will

The little Svea 123R burns white gas but it, too, flares during priming and thus should not be used on board. All of the stoves pictured here are well-used working models, which accounts for their less-than-new look.

usually rejuvenate itself in a couple of days. If poles are needed for a fly, use driftwood instead of cutting green poles, or use a long line strung between two trees as a ridgepole. A more subtle and aesthetic point to consider is how your campsite is seen from the water. Brightly colored tents and gear clash with the softer natural colors of the island or mainland shore, so you may want to pitch your camp in a sheltered or inconspicuous spot where it begins to blend with the countryside. Both the kitchen area and the tent site should be restored as close as possible to their natural state when you are through with them.

To this point we have talked mainly about camping ashore, and in truth this is usually a far more comfortable way to spend the night than trying to find sleeping room aboard a 16- or 18-foot boat. But there are times when there is little choice—it is anchor and sleep aboard or keep going in the dark. Unless you are tied to a tight schedule, which we advise against, prepare for an adventure and throw out the hook. Living aboard is possible and even comfortable if you have given the matter some forethought. If you still have doubts, look at it pragmatically: you can survive *one* night of almost anything.

The real secret here is to keep the amount of gear you travel with to a conservative amount. Consider the backpacking concept. Listen to the birds and not the TV; sleep on the deck or bench and not on a cot; precook your food or go simply in this regard to save an inordinate amount of clutter and frustration.

And be sensible. Open flame aboard a small boat carrying a lot of gasoline is dangerous. If you must cook aboard, make sure your stove is well isolated from your gas supply, and check to make sure the spare gasoline tanks have not overflowed during the heat of the day. That event

The Coleman Apex burns white gas but does not require priming. Pump and fuel bottle detach for separate storage away from food. In use on the stove is an MSR Alpine stainless steel cook kit with heat exchanger, which captures heat normally lost up the sides of the pot. It is said to save its own weight in fuel, cooking four to five meals for two persons.

could be a bomb just waiting to go off. Be certain your stove is reliable, that it is located someplace where it will not be tipped over, and that it is filled with fuel. Having to refuel it halfway through the cooking cycle is always hazardous; aboard a little boat it is just plain crazy.

When we were cruising the coast of Labrador in our 18-foot skiff, we often cooked aboard, using an Optimus 111B fired by gasoline mix taken from one of the outboard motor portable tanks we carried. The Optimus was about as stable as small stoves come and was as reliable as gasoline stoves can be, which, unfortunately, is not completely so. One evening, there was a mild flooding problem with the stove and almost before you could wink, flames were licking against gear stored between us and the gasoline tanks. Quick response with a handy jacket doused the flames, but it was probably the most frightening moment of our entire trip. Twenty-odd gallons of gasoline would make quite an impression if they were to explode 6

feet away from where you were frying fresh cod.

We were carrying several week's worth of food, camping gear, climbing gear, and extra fuel on this northern trip, which didn't leave a lot of room to stretch out on the cockpit floor. So we packed our soft stuff be-

tween the seats and slept quite comfortably on top of that. Some small-boat cruisers carry a sheet of plywood that serves the same purpose, but the big sheets are awkward to handle and take up valuable room. Worth considering is building a movable storage box that just fits between the seats on one side, in effect making a cot, which serves two purposes whereas the plywood serves only one.

It is only slightly more of a bother to take your rubbish with you than it is to leave it scattered behind for others to clean up. The amount of debris can be reduced remarkably before you leave home if you take food out of its packaging and store it in weightless plastic bags or containers. It will be much easier to handle on the boat and at the campsite, and the containers will go back into the pack with room to spare. (You may want to tear off the cooking instructions and place them in the bag along with the food.) It is useful to carry a few tough plastic trash bags in large and small sizes; their uses are legion. A good gesture to the environment is to pick up any rubbish you may find

Simplicity itself is this Sterno solid-fuel stove costing about $7. Refined from earlier Sterno stoves, this one will boil water quite quickly. A 7-ounce can of fuel will usually cook two to three meals.

washed up on the beach or left by previous visitors and take it with you for proper disposal.

Next to fire, dealing with human waste is the biggest problem a camper faces. The natural tendency is to find a sheltered spot, dig a shallow hole, deposit the waste, and cover it up. This may work on large islands or on the mainland in places where use is very light, but on most of the small, rocky islands it often means toilet paper scattered on the ground or hanging from bushes, and piles of smelly excrement. Strangely enough, on a marine island, a better way in an emergency is to relieve yourself well below the tide line, where bacteriological action is higher than on the upland, and let the tide flush away the waste. You may be able to burn toilet paper, although if it is wet and soiled it probably won't ignite. Baby diapers, sanitary napkins, tampons, and similar absorbent materials will not burn and should be carefully packed and taken home—along with the used toilet paper.

A commendable practice becoming more common on the islands and along some of the more heavily used rivers such as the Colorado, especially among environmentally concerned commercial outfitters who take kayaking groups on multiday

Propane/butane-burning stoves are safer than liquid-fuel stoves aboard a boat because their flame is easily controlled. This Epigas Backpacker burns a propane/butane mixture from a detachable container and operates well down to about 20 degrees F. The Gaz Globetrotter, not pictured, operates on a similar fuel, simmers exceptionally well, and burns cleanly.

trips, is to carry out all solid human waste. Their clients are given personal plastic bags with kitty litter, wood ashes, or sawdust in them; these are used as toilets, and the bags are then sealed and placed in a waterproof container to be taken out with them. If your boat is large enough to carry one, a portable toilet such as the Porta-Potti eliminates the elimination problem nicely. If for nothing else than the sake of the outdoors, get one. You will quickly find that its comfort and convenience alone are worth the money.

If you would like to know more about low-impact camping, the National Outdoor Leadership School has published an excellent little book by Bruce Hampton and David Cole entitled *Soft Paths* (available from Stackpole Books, Cameron & Keller Streets, P.O. Box 1831, Harrisburg, PA 17105).

—DRG

REPAIR AND MAINTENANCE

Introduction

Today's boats, whether they are plastic, metal, or rubber, tend to be tough and durable (although there are always exceptions!) and require only routine care to stay that way. But tough and durable also means well put together of materials that may not be easy to repair in your backyard. So there are trade-offs, and in this section we weigh the gains and losses of trying to do everything yourself. There is an essay on the care of your outboard motor or sterndrive in the section on outboard motors (page 95), but we hold off on instructions on repairing this machinery because of the variations in motor design, their complexity, and the not uncommon need for special tools.

You will be amazed at how much money you can save by following a schedule of simple maintenance for your boat, motor, and trailer. Most big problems start small and grow; routine care not only slows such unwanted development, it also nips a lot of it before it starts. Regular inspection of your rig will turn up little things that can be fixed with a quick adjustment, and will reveal potential problems that are well within your skills range to fix now—so you won't have to pay later.

To cut down time and maintenance costs even further, you may want to take a few minutes to consider how you *use* your rig. A little TLC (tender loving care) works wonders with human relationships, and it does the

> You will be amazed at how much money you can save by following a schedule of simple maintenance.

same with things mechanical. Ignoring potholes, misjudging curbs, barreling over railroad crossings, and in general expecting your loaded trailer to ride as easily as your softly sprung car will stress your equipment, causing it to reach its breaking point far sooner than if you give it the same sort of consideration you would to friends—few of whom you depend on to keep you safe, comfortable, and

alive, as you do your boat. The same holds true for boat handling on the water. Rough water is just that, and while your boat presumably is designed to take a reasonable hammering, there is a limit beyond which things begin to bend and break. Ways to deal with rough going are described in detail in "Rough-Water Handling," page 146.

Fortunately, you don't have to be a mechanic to maintain your boat, motor, and trailer. Anyone can work a grease gun or press the squirter on a can of WD-40. In addition to lubricating the usual fittings, adding a dab of grease on trailer-wheel bolts, trailer nuts, and the propeller-hub nut may save having to strip or break the fastenings after they are frozen with rust. As for WD-40 and similar lightweight lubricants, their uses are unlimited. For instance, three or four times each season we remove the engine hood and spray the entire power unit with WD-40. This isn't what you would call major maintenance, but we also check over the exposed

MAINTENANCE

mechanisms, perhaps put a heavier lubricant on some of the moving parts, and wipe off any dirt or rust specks that show. As for the engine block, it looks like new despite its dozen-plus years of steady use.

If you plan to work on boats built of products other than wood, it will be a lot more fruitful if you know something about the properties of the materials and how to work with them without doing damage to the boat and your peace of mind. Some instruction is necessary before you can successfully work with fiberglass cloth and resin, and we begin this section with essays that will go a long way toward reducing the frustration factor. However, virtually everything involved with fiberglass, whether it is preparation, application, or cleanup, involves the use of chemicals—and some of these are not just hazardous to your health, they may be deadly. Thus, before tackling a fiberglassing project, it is important to read up on the subject, particularly so if you will be working with epoxies. An excellent place to start is with the books by Paul and Marya Butler and Allan Vaitses, from which the pieces on epoxy fillets and fiberglass repairs are excerpted.

The chemical mix reaches well be-

> *Read the small print on a boat-paint can before it is hidden behind super-hardened drips—you may be in for a shock.*

yond simple boatbuilding and repair. For instance, if you are used to slapping a coat of latex paint on the kitchen walls and believe that that is all there is to painting, you might be in for a shock if you happen to read the small print on the paint can before it is hidden behind super-hardened drips. The reason many modern boat paints are so effective is that they are special coatings rather than just plain paint. If you don't do things exactly right, you can ruin a can of very expensive stuff and perhaps harm yourself in the process, since there are frequently some pretty potent chemicals in the mixtures that have to be handled with respect. Don Casey's interesting piece on painting a boat is worth reading if for no other reason than staying up with the changing times.

We have also included a short piece on repairing aluminum, but as you will see, there is not a lot the backyard repair artist can do to fix an aluminum hull that a professional metalworker cannot do more quickly, and probably a lot better.

But don't be put off by these caveats; there remain scores of tasks you can do yourself. In fact, becoming a handyman is part and parcel of become a boatowner—the very essence of "messing about in boats."

—DRG

Fiberglass Repairs

If, at some time in the best-forgotten past, you have barged right into a fiberglassing project without really knowing what you were doing, and literally stuck to it until you were finished (never again!), you were doing it the hard way. Some people even work with fiberglass for a living and get along quite nicely. Here, Allan Vaitses, one of the best custom fiberglassers around, points out some of the pitfalls and hazards, and shows us how to 'glass without tears.—DRG

Laying up a fiberglass repair can be messy and frustrating, or it can go along as smoothly as a squirrel on a rail fence. Practice helps, for it teaches (the hard way) neatness and planning ahead. Even if you are a complete novice, however, you can avoid a number of pitfalls as well as the massive cleanup that unsuspecting workers often make for themselves. Just keep in mind the following simple but important points:

1. Protect the areas not involved in the repair from spills, drips, and runs of resin. The surest way to do this is to cover adjacent areas with newspaper and masking tape. You can also wax nearby fiberglass and other nonporous materials such as metal or glass, which will keep resin from getting a grip.

2. Your setup should include:
- A convenient table for cutting the glass-fiber fabrics. A plywood or corrugated pasteboard top is best to withstand the marking by mat knife and shears.
- A place to dispense, catalyze, and stir resin. A piece of disposable corrugated pasteboard makes a good mat on which to place the containers and do the mixing. NOTE! *Have clean water, at least a gallon jug if not a hose; an eye*

cup with eye wash; cotton swabs; and a mirror nearby this station and near the job in general in the event that anyone splashes resin or, worse, catalyst in his eyes.

- A place to wash one's hands and clean tools (see "New Materials for Cleanup," page 227), and a 5-gallon bucket with cover in which to store tools temporarily.

3. Cut the fiberglass materials first—all of them—and have them piled neatly in the order in which they will be used before you catalyze any resin for the job. Cut the pieces from 38-inch-wide rolls. This width is the easiest to handle.

4. Small pieces are best. Use pieces that can be easily handled, completely wet out, and neatly rolled down before rolling is rushed or stopped by incipient gelling. Until you become adept at hanging them (it is a little like wallpapering), pieces for vertical or near-vertical surfaces should be no larger than 2 square yards for one worker or 4 square yards for two. Slightly larger pieces are permissible on horizontal surfaces; pieces for overhead surfaces should be much smaller.

5. Butt all pieces laid up on the outside of the part, lest you build up ridges in the laminate where edges overlap. Any such ridges would have to be faired out before finishing.

> It *is* a little like wallpapering. . . .

6. Overlap those pieces laid up against a mold or backing; overlaps make the layer stronger, and ridges on the interior surface of the part are of little consequence.

7. When the thickness of a laminate is to be tapered to nothing at its outer edges, always put on the shortest pieces first, so that each succeeding piece will cover the edge of the one under it and each will get a new grip on the underlying surface along its outer edge. By so doing, you hedge the bond of the new laminate to the surface beneath it, whereas laying down the biggest piece first leaves the entire laminate dependent on the first layer's bond. To compound the problem, as the shorter pieces shrink, they tug at the bond of that one piece.

8. Always use mat for the first layer against any other material to ensure best adhesion; mat between layers of roving materials to minimize peeling and shattering; and mat at the outside face of the part to best seal it against water penetration. How many layers should you apply? There are too many variables to permit a hard-and-fast formula, even one that takes into account the size of the boat and the location and function of the part you're laying up. As a starting point, however, look at the lami-

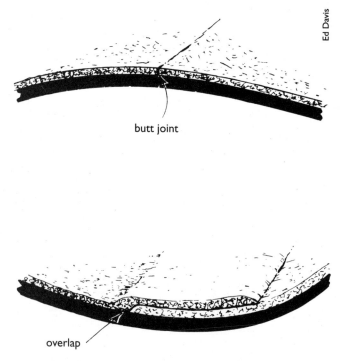

butt joint

overlap

Butt all laminate pieces laid up on the outside of the part. Overlap those pieces laid up against a mold or backing.

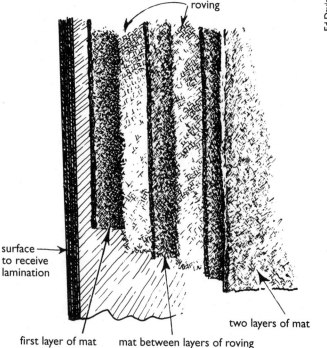

roving

surface to receive lamination

first layer of mat   mat between layers of roving   two layers of mat

A typical laminate, laid up against a core material such as plywood. Two layers of mat provide an effective seal against water.

MAINTENANCE

nate thickness in the part you're repairing, and give your repair that many layers or, if the part was too weak to begin with, a few more.

9. Never laminate over fiberglass or gelcoat that hasn't been sanded recently, unless it was laid up within the preceding 24 hours.

10. Always paint a surface with resin before putting the glass materials on it, unless it is already quite wet with resin from the previous layers.

11. Catalyze only small quantities of resin at a time; use 2½-quart non-waxed paper containers. This allows you to take your time without losing too much resin due to gelling in the pot. Small batches also facilitate more frequent adjustment of the amount of catalyst as the work proceeds; you can use more catalyst if cure is too slow, or less if cure is too fast.

12. Use throwaway tools for applying resin: cheap bristle brushes for small jobs, and fluffy paint rollers for wetting out large areas.

13. Use hard, knubbly paint rollers, or grooved aluminum ones, for rolling down the material. Rolling compacts the laminate, works the resin through it, and wrings the air bubbles and excess resin out of it, all at the same time.

14. Presaturate small pieces or strips of material by laying them on a disposable piece of pasteboard and wetting them with a few quick, gentle passes of the brush. Then, when they are saturated and softened by the resin, you can fit and form them easily to the job without tearing them to pieces or balling them up by trying to "wet them out" in place.

15. Two layers at a time are usually laid up on large areas. This results in a more efficient use of labor, and because the second layer sponges up some of the first layer's excess resin, there is an overall reduction in the amount of resin needed. Furthermore, under adverse conditions a single layer may be agonizingly slow to cure, whereas two layers curing together have sufficient thickness to permit a buildup of exothermic heat, which accelerates the reaction.

Conversely, too many layers carried together over a large area build up too much heat, which, especially in hot weather or bright sunlight, will "cook" the resin, rendering it weak and brittle. Even if the reaction does not become too hot, there will be a very fast cure with excessive shrinkage of the laminate, which tends to distort its shape.

16. More layers can be laid up simultaneously in cool conditions, on small areas, or in narrow strips—in other words, whenever the concentrated mass of the laminate is slight or the heat it gives off can be expected to dissipate into the surroundings. For instance, you

Ed Davis

grooved aluminum roller

textured roller (may be hard or fluffy)

2-inch radius roller

squeegee

Grooved aluminum or hard, knubbly rollers (having the texture of a short-nap industrial rug) are used for rolling down wetted reinforcing materials to get out the air bubbles and compact the laminate. Seven-inch rollers are the workhorses, 9-inch rollers may be used for big jobs, and very short rollers (1- to 3-inch) work well in corners and concavities. Thick, fluffy rollers are used for applying resin. In Vaitses's opinion, a squeegee is no better at compacting a laminate and working out excess resin than a roller or a brush, dragged toward its heel. There are many times, incidentally, when the best way to use a brush, particularly to avoid pulling or tearing out mat strands, is to jab or "stipple" rather than drag through the work.

MAINTENANCE

might well pack 8 or 10 layers simultaneously into a small hole, or build up a smashed toerail with 4 to 6 layers, or wet out as many as 4 layers in a backed hole the size of a dessert plate, but under the same ambient conditions you would be likely to warp the top of a hatch cover if you tried to lay up more than 2 layers at once.

17. Wash your tools regularly; wash your hands, too, unless they are protected by gloves, which also ought to be washed (see "New Materials for Cleanup," page 227). Do not leave resin-covered tools lying around, for if anything distracts or delays you from cleaning them, they will inexorably turn to stone and become worthless. Get into the habit of washing the tools every time you break from work for any reason. Keep a 5-gallon bucket with a reasonably tight cover and a half-gallon to a gallon of acetone or lacquer thinner in it (depending on the size of the job or number of tools) in which to store your tools during breaks, lunch, or overnight. Always change the acetone before a weekend or longer downtime. To be safe for extended periods, wash tools thoroughly and store them dry; given time enough, any resin left in them or settled to the bottom will harden even under acetone.

Alternative cleaners and problems associated with acetone are discussed under "New Materials for Cleanup," page 227.

18. *CAUTION!!! Acetone and MEKP (catalyst) are very volatile and flammable, and polyester resin is also flammable.* Read the labels and take precautions to keep flame away from them.

19. Water ruins green fiberglass. Don't fiberglass in the rain or on a wet surface, and do cover uncured fiberglass from rain and dew with a polyethylene or Mylar sheet.

20. Don't try to fiberglass over a leak dripping out of the boat. It won't work. The water will simply ooze through the uncured resin, leaving a path that will not heal. Either dry out the boat or staunch the flow of water with hydraulic cement, which goes by such brand names as Water Plug and Water Stop. Then your patch will work.

21. Work on many-faceted or detailed parts separately from laying up large uncluttered surfaces. If you try to cover toerails, hatch coamings, guardrails, or skegs while you are laying up large pieces you will be too rushed to do a good job on the fussy work, too preoccupied to keep ahead of the curing of the big pieces, or both.

22. If a detailed part contains sharp corners, you will find it easier to form with an all-mat schedule, or by turning unidirectional roving to run along the corners. You certainly will not want to try to bend the roving in an adjacent plane surface over or into corners, for it will persist in bridging them, will take the crispness right out of them, and will frustrate you no end.

   Even when a detailed part calls for the great strength of roving, as

> *More layers can be laid up simultaneously in cool conditions, on small areas, or in narrow strips.*

Allan Vaitses

A hand-layup laminator's tool kit: catalyst measuring pump, paper pot (wax-free) and stirrer, brushes, roller, and shears.

MAINTENANCE

undirectional roving *will* lie down lengthwise ... but will bridge corners that cross it

Unidirectional roving will readily conform to sharp curves or corners along the line of the strands, but turning corners will stop any roving configuration cold. Use mat to cover complex shapes.

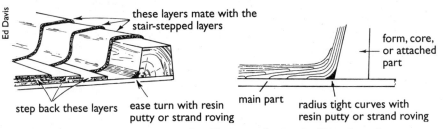

these layers mate with the stair-stepped layers

step back these layers

ease turn with resin putty or strand roving

main part

form, core, or attached part

radius tight curves with resin putty or strand roving

Bonding an attached part to a plane surface: The layers of roving should interleave for greatest strength, and to provide a smooth surface. The laminate of the attached part may be laid up over (left) or under (right) the main part's laminate.

where a skeg attaches to a hull, you are better off to cut and fit the roving in pieces, applying them so that they taper out onto the plane surface. Blend the corresponding pieces of the plane surface into these small pieces with, at worst, some of the plane surface laminate lapping a short way onto the base of the detailed part.

23. Don't forget, when fiberglassing inside a boat, to blow out the fumes and bring in fresh air with a good, big fan. A portable space fan in a rectangular case lying flat over the forward hatch does a great job, exhausting fumes and the dust of grinding up through the hatch and dragging fresh air through the boat.

SAFETY

Fiberglass repair tools and materials are capable of great things, but they are also hazardous. Be circumspect. Treat them with the care they deserve.

- When grinding fiberglass, wear goggles and a toxic-dust mask, if not a respirator. Direct the debris stream away from you.
- When grinding or laminating, consider using disposable Tyvek suits. These can be difficult to find, but disposable clothing is usually no farther away than a Salvation Army or Goodwill store, or the back of your closet.
- Wear disposable gloves at all times. Gloves don't get dermatitis. Use drip guards (such as half of a hollow rubber ball) on tools. Barrier creams provide an extra layer of protection.
- Styrene, which comprises 40 percent of polyester resin by weight, is a strong irritant to skin and mucous membrane and has resulted in long-term neurotoxicity among fiberglass workers, leading to premature senility. Compared with epoxies, polyester resins are relatively benign, but don't take chances. Wear a respirator when laminating.
- Acetone, the solvent most commonly used by fiberglass workers to clean hands and tools, causes severe dermatitis and, in large quantities, causes nervous system dysfunction. In addition, the vapors are explosive. Do not smoke; tolerate no open flames; and do not use electric tools around acetone.
- Catalysts, such as MEKP, can splash when poured. Keep them away from your eyes, preferably with goggles. If you're unsuccessful, flush eyes immediately with cold water.
- Accelerators have no place in an amateur boat shop. Buy a resin with the correct formulation, and adjust cure times with catalyst.
- Although epoxy smells less formidable than polyester resin, it is actually more toxic, causing skin irritation, headaches, and nausea. In addition, the side effects are cumulative. The more you use it, the worse the effect.
- Keep fire extinguishers handy; use big fans to ventilate; closely follow manufacturers' safety recommendations.

NEW MATERIALS FOR CLEANUP

Until recently, acetone, lacquer thinner, and other solvents, but particularly acetone, have been the accepted agents for removing resin from hands and tools. But they have problems: they cause severe dermatitis; because the dissolved resins are held in solution, they present hazardous waste disposal problems; and they are extremely flammable. More than 3,000 boatshop fires have been directly attributed to acetone.

Fortunately, one is no longer

MAINTENANCE

solely dependent on acetone and its precarious ilk. There are other cleaners. Unfortunately, many of the less hazardous cleaners are available only in large quantities to commercial users, a situation that will change as the hazards of acetone become better known, and demand for more benign products opens the consumer market.

Water-based emulsifiers are probably the most promising cleaners for the small user. Readily available in quantities as small as 16 ounces ($6) is Product 855, a biodegradable 1:1 concentrate from Gougeon Brothers, Inc., P.O. Box 908, Bay City, MI 48707-9918; (517) 684-7286. This is basically a tool cleaner. A spokesman from Gougeon said he has found waterless skin cleansers, such as those used by auto mechanics, do a good job of cleaning resin off exposed skin. Some are better than others, he said, the best he has used being SBS #3, a cream. He also recommended keeping on hand a supply of alcohol pads of the sort found in most any drugstore. These will quickly remove drips of epoxy or polyester resin from skin or tools. A second cleaning product is Noraclean, which is called a "water-based alternative" to acetone by its producer, Norac Co., Inc., 405 South Motor Avenue, Azusa, CA 91702; (800) 786-6722. Presently, this is available only in quantities of 5 gallons or more as a 15:1 concentrate, but a spokesman said distributors would probably offer it in smaller amounts if demand were strong enough.

Noraclean works like soap and requires agitation to remove resin from brushes and tools. The residue is allowed to settle, and a drop or two of catalyst is then added, causing the resin to harden so that it can be removed in a single piece. The clear liquid can be used again and again until it is eventually spent, at which time it can be drained safely into most sewer systems.

—Allan H. Vaitses
(*The Fiberglass Boat Repair Manual*, International Marine, 1988)

The Adaptable Epoxy Fillet

The epoxy fillet is so useful, it is worth consideration all by itself. The strength of epoxy resin is well known, and when combined with a filler and shaped to a curve it becomes both a powerful reinforcement and a tenacious fastening that can be used in an almost endless number of ways in fiberglass or plywood construction. Fillets can make a lightweight bulkhead an integral part of the boat, can beef up places subject to heavy stress such as the transom, can ensure solid adherence of fiberglass where the edges of sharp angles join, and provide strength and good looks to equipment mountings and other additions (from live wells to seats, consoles, and lockers) to your fiberglass boat. Here, boatbuilding expert Paul Butler tells how to make and use this simple device.—DRG

A fillet is a concave or shaped fairing applied in corners, such as where a bulkhead meets a side of the hull, or where the deck meets a sheer clamp. Epoxy fillets are structural, forming a web that will increase hull stiffness. They are also watertight. They have a very pleasing appearance when painted over, and they complement good shapes to make a structure look "organic," as though it had been

> Epoxy fillets may be used on fiberglass, wood, and aluminum hulls.

formed from a single piece.

Epoxy fillets are so abundantly useful when building and finishing a boat that it's hard to imagine how we got along without them. Mostly what we did was to spend a lot of time messing around with fiddly little moldings, caulkings, and sealants, trying to reinforce and make watertight all those angles where components and cabinetry meet.

It's not that fillets are radically new; we used them years ago with polyester resins. Back then they were usually a mixture of sawdust, sand, asbestos, and various other floor sweepings. The idea was sound; the fly in the ointment was the polyester resin, which swelled, shrank, cracked, and wasn't really a very good bonding resin in the first place. Epoxy changed all that. It is a tenacious glue and does not absorb moisture. With the readily available variety of fillers, you can now engineer a fillet to match almost any requirement.

Epoxy fillets may be used on fiberglass, wood, and aluminum hulls. Wood surfaces must be dry, unpainted, and unoiled: in other words, bare, clean wood. Fiberglass gelcoat should be removed if there's any doubt about its condition.

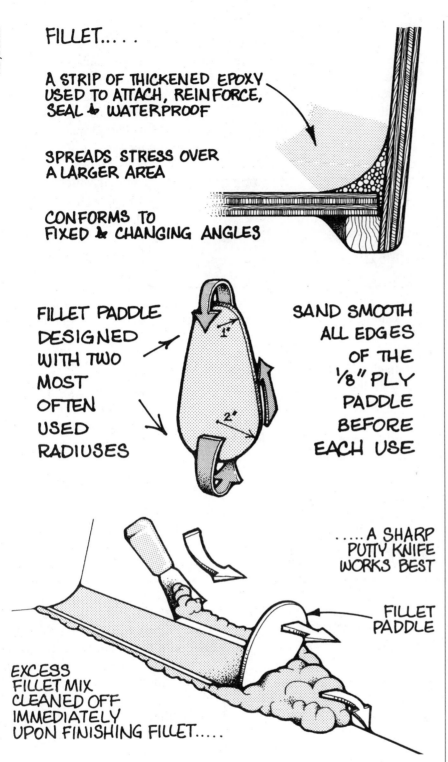

FILLET.....

A STRIP OF THICKENED EPOXY USED TO ATTACH, REINFORCE, SEAL & WATERPROOF

SPREADS STRESS OVER A LARGER AREA

CONFORMS TO FIXED & CHANGING ANGLES

FILLET PADDLE DESIGNED WITH TWO MOST OFTEN USED RADIUSES

1"

2"

SAND SMOOTH ALL EDGES OF THE 1/8" PLY PADDLE BEFORE EACH USE

.....A SHARP PUTTY KNIFE WORKS BEST

FILLET PADDLE

EXCESS FILLET MIX CLEANED OFF IMMEDIATELY UPON FINISHING FILLET.....

Marya Butler

balloon, filling it with the mix, and using it like a cake decorator to squeeze the mix into the groove, to be followed immediately with the fillet paddle. You may also just dab the mix in place and follow with the paddle, working short sections at a time and pulling, not pushing, the fillet paddle along in contact with both sides of the joint. If you've mixed the ingredients in the right proportion and consistency, the fillet will be smooth. Once applied to satisfaction it should be left alone. Add extra material *later,* if needed in low spots, by sliding the paddle over the surface again. You can also vary the thickness and profile of the fillet by tilting the paddle slightly, a necessary technique if the angles are not constant where the paddle meets both sides. When the fillet is the way you want it, clean the excess from the edges by scraping with a sharp putty knife. Then leave it alone to kick.

Although a number of fillers are available for specific functions, we use red microballoons and colloidal silica, almost exclusively, for epoxy fillets. Both are available from any number of mail-order and boatbuilding supply houses and also from many epoxy suppliers.

Because it's very dense and heavy, silica is used for a high-strength mixture where weight is of little consequence. Silica fillets are also nearly impossible to sand—almost like trying to sand a pane of glass.

Red microballoons form a lighter filleting mixture that is still strong enough for most applications. It's best as a cosmetic and can be sanded and painted. Even when making low-density microballoon fillets, it's a good idea to use a small amount of silica to promote a smooth-spreading slick consistency that helps in applying the fillet.

We vary the ratio of silica to microballoons according to the

Aluminum must be well sanded, grease-free, and dry. For critical applications on aluminum, an acid etch is recommended.

The fillet is applied with a paddle made to the appropriate radius; a gloved finger may work best for small sizes and tight places. The fillet

conforms to almost any fixed or changing angle, and may be applied overhead as well as on vertical or horizontal surfaces. We normally apply the fillet mixture straight from the mixing bowl with a putty knife or fillet paddle. For long, small fillets, try cutting the top third from a application. For our whitewater river dories, which take a lot of abuse and are held together exclusively by epoxy fillets reinforced with fiberglass cloth and tape, we use the following mix: 10 pumps of epoxy from a standard pump mixer, 3 scoops of microballoons, and 7 scoops of silica. Our scoop is equal to 2 rounded tablespoons. It always seems to take some experimentation to arrive at the best ratio for each job, and the temperature of the resin also will affect the filler-to-resin ratio.

Larger fillets will sometimes have to be formed in two or even three stages. They require a lot of material, and once the epoxy starts to catalyze, it gathers momentum rapidly. For this reason, small batches are more manageable, and in hot weather they're necessary to provide the time to apply, spread, and clean up the epoxy properly.

For critical applications, such as on our river dories where the fillets hold everything together, we sometimes start with a silica-enriched mixture and then reduce the percentage of silica in subsequent layers, ending up with a microballoon-rich mixture that sands easily.

> *Epoxy fillets are so abundantly useful that it's hard to imagine how we got along without them.*

For sanding fillets you can sometimes find or make a dowel of the proper size. For larger sizes you can often attach a handle to the sanding form by gluing on a short piece of plywood. Wrap a piece, or half a piece, of sandpaper around the form and hold the edges under your fingers where the sandpaper can easily

be rotated slightly as sections of the sandpaper dull. Finish by hand sanding on edges and corners; the fillet is then ready for undercoat and paint or fiberglass tape.

We sometimes use a radius as large as 4 inches, and possibly slightly larger for certain applications. Depending on the angle at which the two pieces meet, you can put in a large or a small amount of filler. Large fillets look great but must be properly applied and finished. They provide a surprising amount of structural support to a joint, and waterproof it, too.

—Paul and Marya Butler
(*Fine Boat Finishes,*
International Marine, 1991)

Tools for Working Fiberglass

For the most part, working on fiberglass boats draws on familiar carpentry skills: cutting, fitting, fastening, finishing. If you own a small glass production boat, the unfamiliar element may lie in how to transpose these traditional woodworking skills to the realm of fiberglass and epoxy. Healthy fiberglass is a tough material. With a strong, well-maintained gelcoat, it has excellent abrasion resistance and substantial puncture resistance—which you will quickly realize the first time you try to drill or cut into it. Fiberglass carpentry is not all that difficult, but it does take some getting used to, and some specialized tools and techniques.

CUTTING AND DRILLING FIBERGLASS

Drills and Bits

Drilling accurate, clean holes into the laminate requires sharp drill bits, and it may be necessary to center-punch lightly or score the gelcoat surface to get an accurate start. Metal- and wood-cutting drill bits both work, but sharp metal-cutting bits may do slightly better when drilling through laminates ½ inch and thicker. Butterfly wood-cutting bits, also known as spade bits, do not work well on fiberglass laminate even when they are sharp, and we usually

resort to conventional metal- or wood-cutting bits. Drilling through fiberglass tends to dull even good laminated steel bits in a short time, so prepare to sharpen periodically. A hand-powered rotary drill is handy for drilling small holes in tight places, and a larger brace-type drill provides additional leverage for bigger holes. It's nice to be able to crawl around in the bilge without dragging an electrical cord behind you, and manual tools are safer when water is nearby, as when you drill up into the damp bilge of a boat on a cradle.

Scoring a line on the gelcoat as a guide for drilling or cutting is best accomplished by holding a straight-

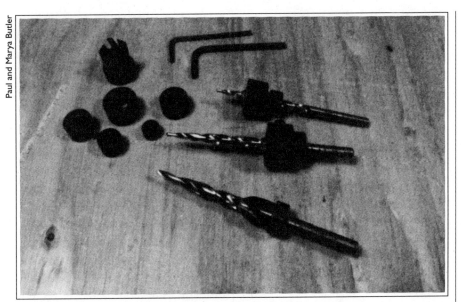

Tapered wood bits, countersinks, and stop collars, with Allen wrenches for adjustment.

edge or wood template against the gelcoat surface and pulling a sharp tool along the edge. An ideal tool for marking or scoring gelcoat is a sharp carbide tooth on a handle, such as is normally used for scoring plastic laminates, but an awl or even a sharp nail will do the job. An ink marker is sometimes handy for drawing guide patterns on gelcoat or cured laminate, as long as the mark is removed by cutting away.

If you are making a cutout for an oval, round, or oddly shaped portlight or other piece of hardware, it may be easier to drill holes at corners, at intervals along the perimeter, or both, and then cut between the holes with a jigsaw, much like a connect-the-dots drawing. When cutting small-diameter holes for transducers and through-hull fittings, try to do as much of the cutting as possible with a small-diameter drill bit; then knock out the center plug and finish the job to precise fit with an oval or round rasp.

Saws

Professional-quality hole saws with mandrels are an alternative way of making clean, small-diameter holes (up to 3 or 4 inches) for through

hulls. But unless the hole saw has carbide teeth, it will last for only a few cuts—maybe only one cut in thick glass—before it becomes uselessly dull and you find yourself burning slowly through the laminate instead of cutting a clean hole. If you do a lot of small-hole cutting in glass hulls, carbide teeth are a wise investment. Not only do they last much longer than high-speed steel teeth, they also do a better job.

Jigsaws are the old standby for cutting fiberglass laminate, and a hand-held jigsaw with a scrolling head is a particular blessing, because

Marya Butler

2" DIA. HOLE SAW WITH CARBIDE TEETH

it allows you to cut arcs and circles while hanging upside down in the bilge, standing under the boat with the saw extended overhead, or working in tight corners. If you can afford to double up on your power tools, it is a smart idea to keep one jigsaw exclusively for fiberglass work, to avoid wear and tear on your good wood-cutting tools. The abrasive glass dust is hard on quality tools.

It helps to have a large assortment of extra blades on hand, from fine-tooth metal-cutting blades to rough- and fine-tooth wood-cutting blades, and including a few wider, flush-cutting blades for working up against coamings and decks. A blade usually will last for only a few feet of cutting in thick, cured fiberglass anyway; once it is dull it will either start to burn without cutting, or else it will break. Forcing the blade will only break it sooner, and it will overheat your saw motor as well. Stopping every few inches or so to let the blade cool will make it last longer, but few people seem to have the patience for this. (If you cut a lot of fiberglass with a jigsaw, you will probably learn where you can buy blades in bulk packaging.) If the blade bends sideways, stop and let it cool, then bend it back straight; otherwise you will be spending a lot of time with a rasp, trying to clean up the sides of the cut.

Some types of jigsaws seem to have more success cutting glass than others, and it pays to experiment. Some have a slight rotary action instead of a straight-up-and-down blade movement, and many saws have adjustable power settings or blade speeds. This latter feature can be a real advantage, for slower speeds seem to preserve the blade slightly longer than fast speeds, and also make a cleaner cut. We have a heavy old Sears roller-bearing jigsaw with blade speeds that graduate from 1 to 12; at a medium or slow speed

MAINTENANCE

with plenty of sharp blades it does a quite satisfactory job. By all rights it should have been retired with honors, but it continues to plug along, and I now use it exclusively for cutting fiberglass. Our new Porter-Cable jigsaw has all the adjustments, and its thick, stiff blades seem to last longer than other jigsaw blades when cutting tough materials.

Panel saws and circular saws (Skilsaw is a popular brand) can be used for making relatively straight, fast cuts in flatter sections of fiberglass. Carbide blades are again a necessity if you expect to cut more than a few inches before the blade overheats and gets uselessly dull. Circular saws also generate considerable fiberglass dust, which not only ruins bearings in power tools but can pose a significant health threat. Respirators for dust and goggles for eye protection are a necessity; ear protection is also advisable.

Routers

Routers with carbide bits make the cleanest possible cuts in fiberglass, and with a minimum of dust. Routers turn at very high speeds, and it takes some experience to get the best out of them, but they are the tool of choice when cutting in relatively flat areas of the hull and deck—as, for example, when installing hatches. There is a variety of cutter bits available for ¼-inch-shaft routers (the standard home handyman model), and an even wider variety of specialized bits for larger professional routers with ½-inch-diameter shafts. Half-inch bits are quieter, cut easier, and are a lot safer than ¼-inch bits, but they also cost more and require slightly heavier-duty motors to turn them.

A router bit normally turns clockwise, and the cut has to be made

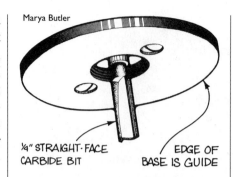

Marya Butler

¼" STRAIGHT-FACE CARBIDE BIT — EDGE OF BASE IS GUIDE

SLEEVE SCREWS IN UNTIL FLUSH WITH ROUTER BASE FOR USE AS TEMPLATE GUIDE

A typical ¼-inch-shaft router with a small carbide V-groove bit.

against that clockwise rotation to prevent dangerous skipping. It becomes evident very soon if you are moving the bit in the wrong direction. An edge guide or template is required to control the bit; freehanding a router is not only dangerous, but usually results in sloppy work and possibly disaster. The only

Keep your best tools for finish woodworking and accumulate a group of second-string tools for glass work.

exception is when you have to remove a lot of material from a given area to a specific depth. In that case, it usually works well to crisscross the area with the router and use the resulting cuts as a depth guide for removing the balance of the material with a chisel or sander.

The cutting and trimming bits we use most often are ¼-inch-wide

straightface bits with two carbide flutes (cutting edges). Depending on the project, we use them either with or without a sleeve. A sleeve is an attachment, available for various types of routers, that screws into the base of the router to act as a permanent edge guide for the bit. It allows somewhat more precise control than using the base of the router aligned against a batten or straightedge for the same purpose. The sleeve fits to within less than an inch of the cutting bit, whereas the base of the router is usually some 3 inches away from the cutting bit edge. Another type of carbide bit, not commonly seen but available from specialty tool shops, has a roller bearing on top of the cutter flutes. The edge of the bearing is aligned flush with the surface of the cutters. The advantage—and it is a substantial advantage—is that it allows a template (pattern) to be made to the exact size as the hole to be cut, which enables a visual inspection before cutting. You can also make plunge cuts (cuts started without a pilot hole) with this type of router bit.

Templates and Edge Guides Long battens or wood straightedges can be screwed temporarily to the deck or hull of a glass boat to serve as an edge guide for the router; after the cutting is done, they are removed and the holes filled with dabs of epoxy. Duct tape will sometimes hold a guide batten in place securely enough to allow you to make the cut; if not, you can position a helper on either end of the batten to hold it in place. On curved surfaces, where control seems difficult no matter what you do, it may be best to resort to a jigsaw, although the router is faster and neater.

Templates for standard-size portholes, hatch cutouts, through-hull fittings, deck irons, and other such

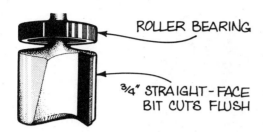

ROLLER BEARING

3/4" STRAIGHT-FACE BIT CUTS FLUSH

SAVE FACTORY EDGE OF PLYWOOD FOR A STRAIGHTEDGE

4"-6" WIDE PIECE CUT ON TABLE SAW FOR PERFECT PARALLEL

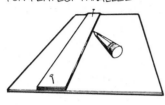

1/2" PLYWOOD (STIFF) GOOD FOR FLAT SURFACES.....

THINNER PLY LIKE 1/8" (FLEXIBLE) BEST FOR CURVED SURFACES LIKE CABIN SIDES

items can be made from solid-core plywood and used over and over again—a helpful shortcut if you do a lot of retrofit work. But avoid poor-quality plywood, which tends to have voids in the inner plies; if your roller bit or sleeve falls into a small void, it will take a tiny bite out of your cut.

Templates for small items such as portholes or through-hull fittings are often made doughnut-hole fashion: first cut out the desired pattern on the plywood; then use the "doughnut" (the plywood with the hole in the middle) rather than the "hole" (the cutout piece itself) as your guide. Depending on whether you are using a sleeve or the edge of the router base as a cutting guide, the template must be made exactly that much larger

Four carbide-tipped router bits, all 1/4-inch shaft size. From left: 1/2-inch bullnose or rounding bit, cove, ogee, and 3/8-inch rabbet bit.

than the hole to be cut. For best control, it may be necessary to make the final 1/2 inch of the cut with a section of hacksaw blade held in a pair of Vise-Grips.

SANDING AND FINISHING

Serious sanding of fiberglass is most easily accomplished with a large disc sander and a fresh, dry, aggressive grit pad with stiff backing. If you have to smooth the inside surface of a hull for laminating-on more glass, or if there are drips and hairs left over from a sloppy laminating job when the hull was built, a two-speed disc sander with a relatively small-diameter, 6-inch disc is about as useful a tool as you will find for this dirty job. An even smaller-diameter disc (4- or 5-inch) will allow you to cover concave areas of the hull and to reach down into the bilge and up under sheer-clamp structures. It's a dirty job at best. Orbital sanders and other types of vibrating sanders provide good control and are easy to use, but their effectiveness is limited mostly to cosmetic sanding, because they remove very small amounts of glass or gelcoat and tend to ride over bumps instead of removing them.

Often it is possible to avoid sanding altogether. Vigorous scraping with a sharp steel cabinet scraper may do the job faster and much more cleanly. If the surface is relatively flat, a sharp block plane usually works well for shaving off small hairs and drips. Save sanding for a last resort, and be particularly cautious when using power equipment. Aside from the ever-present health risks from fiberglass dust, and the considerable skin irritation, there is also the danger of noise damage to the ears. OSHA-approved ear protectors are necessary even for small jobs—especially in small hulls, where noise is the worst.

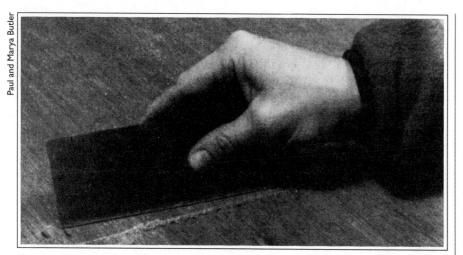

Vigorous scraping with a steel cabinet scraper will usually remove drips and hairs faster and more cleanly than sanding. The scraper is normally held at a slight angle, which allows one corner to cut at each pass.

Standard woodworking hand tools such as block planes, rasps, files, spokeshaves, and chisels can be used for light fiberglass work, but the blade edges will be quickly dulled and you will spend a lot of your time sharpening. Keep your best tools for finish woodworking and accumulate a group of second-string tools for glass work.

FASTENING

A good epoxy glue bond is almost always superior to mechanical fastenings such as screws and bolts. Over time the metal in fastenings may corrode and leach into the surrounding glass; it may also condense water into the hole. If gluing is not practical, stainless steel self-tapping screws, or bolts of stainless steel, brass, silicone bronze, or Monel, depending on the application, are the best of the mechanical fastenings for attaching hardware and decking to single-skin fiberglass hulls and decks. Caulking or epoxy is always recommended to maintain a good seal.

A short screw inserted into fiberglass requires a drilled pilot hole of exactly the right size—too small and the glass may crack; too large and the threads will not bite in. It pays to experiment first on a piece of scrap glass or wood. (Set a positive stop collar on the bit when the correct depth and diameter are achieved.) A drop of epoxy in the pilot hole seals and strengthens the fastening and will help to avoid trouble later. This is particularly important for critical applications such as winches, cleats,

> *A good epoxy glue bond is almost always superior to mechanical fastenings such as screws and bolts.*

chainplates, and other hardware that will be under considerable stress.

For these critical applications, it is a sound procedure whenever possible to further reinforce the fastenings through the use of backing blocks (also commonly but inaccurately known as *butt blocks*). A backing block is a piece of wood (generally a single layer or multiple laminations of high-quality marine-grade plywood) that is glued to the back side of the laminate (or embedded within the laminate) to receive and spread the stress of the fastening.

PATTERNING

The interior of a small hull is not the easiest place to work. Unlike a square room in a square house, nothing in a boat is necessarily level, square, flat, or straight-sided, and the angles can get confusing. When building or modifying small boats, the process of patterning and fitting is repeated dozens of times and often requires considerable creativity and ingenuity.

For smaller-size projects, patterning with sheets of stiff cardboard works well. Cardboard is good patterning material for partial bulkheads, modular cabinetry, and galley build-ins—particularly countertops and other flat surfaces—but it is usually too flimsy for accurate patterning of larger items. A better solution for bunk bottoms, cabin soles, and other large, awkward shapes is to make a pattern of scrap plywood strips, which are shaped individually and then fastened together with screws or clamps.

Patterning large pieces of plywood is not easy, and despite your best efforts at accuracy you will probably find that further fine-tuning is sometimes necessary. When modifying small boats, it seems that you're always wrestling with yet another piece of plywood—shaping, cutting a little more here and there, taking yet another shaving off the edge with a block plane to help the pieces fit properly. Patience is a large part of the job.

—Paul and Marya Butler
(*Upgrading Your Small Sailboat for Cruising*, International Marine, 1988)

Repairing Aluminum Boats

Other than dents, scratches, and loose fastenings, aluminum boats rarely need fixing. But occasionally people do run their boats into things above or below the surface, or constant hard scraping on a chine or edge between the transom and bottom will wear through the tough metal and start a leak. Temporary repair may be easy, but lasting repair will probably require the work of an expert.

An obvious repair over a worn place would seem to be fiberglass and epoxy, and while this may keep out water for a season or two, the patch will either wear through or peel off the metal. The best long-term answer is to weld the worn place, and since the thin metal requires an experienced touch and a TIG welding machine, take your craft to a boat doctor and forget home remedies.

As for dents, if they are smooth sided, you can work them out using a lead hammer and a leather-covered mallet. But be careful of sharp dents; the metal may break in the course of pounding. Hammering, by the way, hardens the metal, causing it to lose some of its resiliency.

Weeping rivets should be replaced, providing you can find the right size rivets. Aluminum pop rivets carried at your local hardware store have just one thing wrong with them—a hole in the middle. You could probably seal this with careful use of a ballpeen hammer inside and out, but a better choice would be a conventional aluminum rivet—which is not sold at most hardware stores. A metalshop might be able to help you, but they usually weld instead of rivet when joining metal. An aluminum-worker told us that anyone looking for such rivets could probably find them in the McMaster-Carr catalog, a 2,200-page book about twice as thick as a *World Almanac*, which appears to list everything a person would need to build a skiff or a freighter. The catalog is published by McMaster-Carr, P.O. Box 440, New Brunswick, NJ 08903-0440; (908) 329-3200.

Punctures in aluminum hulls are infrequent, to say the least, because the metal is so tough, which is the main reason some boat manufacturers guarantee their hulls against puncture. But it can happen. A small hole can be sealed by flattening out its ragged edges and drawing pieces of plywood—one inside and one outside—together with a stainless steel bolt, or bolts with a sealing compound in between. If the hole is small and you are jury-rigging, duct tape may be all you need for a temporary repair. In any case, a hole in an aluminum hull is serious and should get professional attention as soon as possible.

If the repair is to a part other than the hull, aluminum is quite easy to work with since it cuts with tin snips or hacksaw and can be fastened with pop rivets or stainless steel screws and bolts. Sheet aluminum can be bought at most metalshops, along with various sizes of bar, rod, and pipe. Many hardware stores carry a few sizes of bar and angle stock. We have found that both stainless and bronze fastenings can be used to fasten wood to the hull as long as they are above the waterline.

—DRG

The Fine Art of Painting

The difference between refinishing a fiberglass yacht and a fiberglass outboard boat is mainly one of size, time, and expense—the methods are very much the same. With today's wonder materials and a willingness to take the time to do the job correctly, a motorboat owner can give his old glass boat a look as bright and sparkling as that of her newer and larger sisters. The following essay describes the basic techniques, and though it is condensed from Don Casey's book on restoring larger craft, the owner of an 18-foot fiberglass runabout in dire need of a new look will find that the text applies equally to his little craft.—DRG

Some years ago, I shared a seawall with an old Pearson with a chalky blue hull. The gloss had long since disappeared from the hull of my own boat, but next to this partly cloudy Pearson my boat still looked good. Then one weekend I arrived to find the Pearson in a cradle on shore, her owner sanding away on the hull. The next time I saw the boat, the hull looked as though it was coated with blue mercury. The paint was a new product, something called Awlgrip, and never had I seen such a beautiful finish. In a week, this old boat had been transformed from scratched glass to polished diamond. I never looked at my own hull through the same eyes again.

Nothing has a more immediate impact on the way a boat looks than putting a mirror finish on the hull. Thanks to space-age technology, doing just that is within the capability of almost any boatowner.

BRUSH BASICS

I have heard the virtues of synthetic brushes extolled, but I have never used a synthetic brush that I liked. Conversely, I have rarely been disappointed with the performance of a natural-bristle brush, even the cheap, throwaway variety. Most natural-bristle brushes are made from hog bristle and are called *China* (or *Chinese*) *bristle*, because China is the principle hog bristle supplier. Ox and camel hair are also used in better-quality brushes, and the finest brushes are made of badger bristle.

> *I have yet to see a paint job worth dying for.*

What makes natural brushes superior is split ends. This splitting or "flagging" on the ends of the bristle works like the split tip of a drawing pen, allowing the bristle—and the brush—to hold more paint and to give it up more uniformly. The natural taper of the bristle also serves to give the brush a lighter touch at the tip. Toward this end, better brushes are also trimmed to a point—called a *chisel trim*. Less-expensive brushes are cut flush at the tip, or only slightly rounded.

SANDPAPER SAVVY

You are likely to encounter six or eight different kinds of sandpaper in a dozen different grits. To prepare almost any surface for painting, you are only interested in two kinds of paper and three or four grits. The type and grit will be printed on the back of each sheet.

Most of your sanding will be done with dry (or production) paper, and the kind of production paper you want is aluminum oxide. Aluminum oxide is a tough, long-lasting abrasive, and aluminum oxide paper is brown in color. Avoid lighter-colored

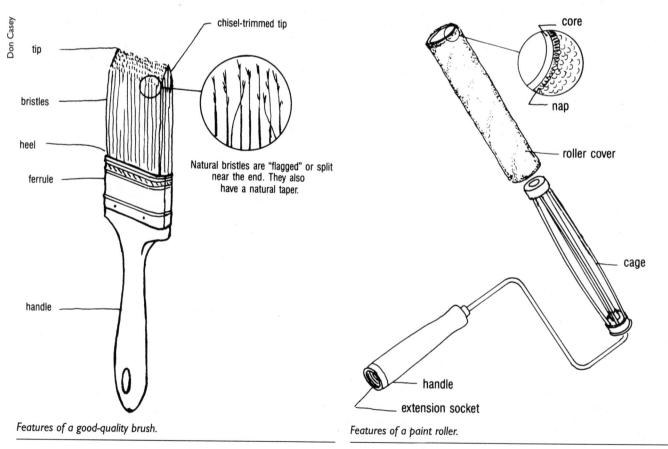

Don Casey

Natural bristles are "flagged" or split near the end. They also have a natural taper.

Features of a good-quality brush.

Features of a paint roller.

flint paper or red garnet paper; both are too soft to last on fiberglass. You will usually need 80-grit and 120-grit for initial preparation, and 220-grit for sanding between coats.

The other type of sandpaper you are likely to use during a painting project is silicon carbide. This is the charcoal-colored paper you may know as wet-or-dry, or by the trademark Carborundum. Wet-or-dry sandpaper is used to sand between coats of paint or varnish when a very fine finish is desired. For this use, 340- or 400-grit should be selected. You might also use coarser grits wet as a substitute for production paper to minimize dust—when sanding toxic bottom paint, for example.

ROLLING AND BRUSHING

Slip a new cover onto the cage of the roller handle and roll the cover into the paint. Lift it out and roll it over the sloped part of the tray several times, dipping the roller into the paint again as necessary to get paint evenly on all sides of the cover. After initially loading the roller, the process to reload the roller is to dip it into the paint, then lift it and roll it two or three times *down* the slope, but not back into the paint.

Applying paint with a roller usually begins by painting the surface with a big W or M with the freshly loaded roller, then continuing to roll the area until it is fully covered. The size of the area covered will typically be about a 3-foot square. The direction of the stroke is not important, and you may want to roll a rough surface in two directions to ensure total coverage. If the roller fails to cover the uneven surface of the interior of the hull, you may need a roller cover with a longer nap.

Rolling usually leaves the paint with a slight texture. On paints like alkyd enamels that tend to flow out smoothly, the surface will dry to the texture of an orange peel. This is perfectly acceptable in some instances, but to eliminate this orange-peel texture on more visible painted surfaces, tip the paint with a brush. Immediately after you have rolled on the paint, lightly drag the tip of a dry (meaning not dipped in paint) brush in long, uniform strokes across the

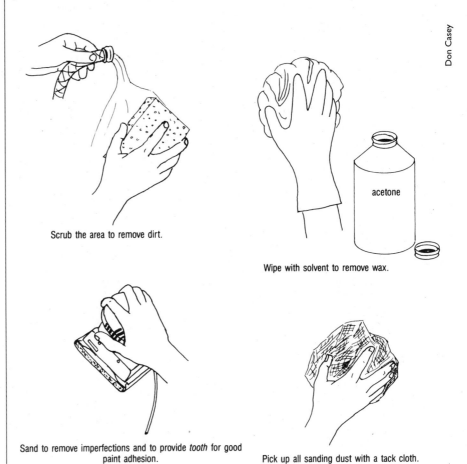

Don Casey

Scrub the area to remove dirt.

acetone

Wipe with solvent to remove wax.

Sand to remove imperfections and to provide *tooth* for good paint adhesion.

Pick up all sanding dust with a tack cloth.

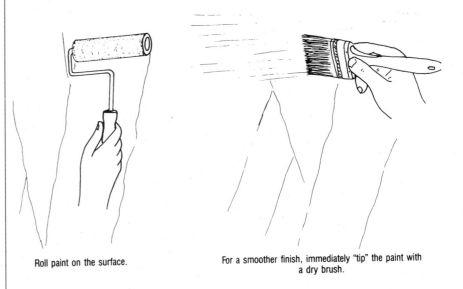

Roll paint on the surface.

For a smoother finish, immediately "tip" the paint with a dry brush.

Six basic painting steps.

MAINTENANCE

painted surface. Do not drag the brush across the same area more than twice. Roll the next area, then tip it, dragging the brush back into the previously tipped area. Do not stop the brush, but lift it to minimize brush marks.

On a small area, it may be preferable to use a brush only to apply the paint, and even when the area is large enough to justify the use of a roller, a brush will be required to trim the paint into the corners or around hardware. Never paint right out of the can the paint came in. Aside from expos-ing the paint to the air, causing it to begin to thicken, you also expose it to contamination from bristles and old paint. Pour as much paint as you need into a clean tin can or plastic container, then clean and close the paint can.

Dip only the tip—never more than a third of the length of the bristles—of the brush into the paint, then draw the brush across the edge of the container to unload the paint from one side. If the job is large, I punch two holes near the top of the container (before pouring paint into it) and run a piece of coathanger wire through them. The wire gives me a straight edge rather than a curved one to drag the loaded brush across, and the paint is less likely to find its way to the outside of the container.

When you apply paint with a brush, you want to do it quickly and with as few strokes as possible. Use only the tip of the brush, angling the handle in the direction of travel—like leaning into a strong wind. You want to spread the brushload of paint into a uniform, thin coat, then stop. If the paint is not covering, don't try to put it on thicker; you are going to need a second coat. Skill with a brush comes with practice. When you get it right, you'll know it.

THE ART OF THINNING

Thus far I have failed to mention thinning. As long as you have ideal weather conditions, you should be able to use the enamel as it comes from the can—which is to say you had better learn how to thin paint. Almost everyone has trouble when first mixing in thinner. When the paint is too thick, the brush (or roller) drags, the paint does not flow out, and every brushstroke shows. But if you thin it too much, it runs and drips, and the gloss is destroyed.

You don't have to be smart to get the proportion of thinner just right. You just have to be *patient*. The trick is to creep up on the correct viscosity by adding the thinner in very small, measured portions. Add just a few drops; too much thinner and you will render the paint useless—unless you have some unthinned paint left to save it. For this reason, thin only the paint you are using, not the entire can.

A vertical scrap of window glass is the ideal surface to test the paint on before you start painting. If the brushstrokes fail to disappear, add a

Don Casey

Prepare a clean container with a piece of stiff wire across the open end near the top.

Stir the paint thoroughly.

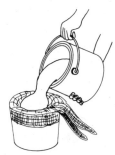

Pour up a small quantity of paint. For best finish, filter the paint through a mesh filter or discarded pantyhose.

Dip the tip of the brush—no more than 1/3 of the bristles—into the paint.

Unload *one* side by dragging the brush over the wire.

Test the flow of the paint on a test surface. A scrap piece of glass is ideal because it can easily be wiped or scraped clean for reuse.

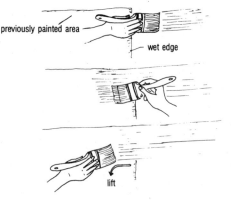

previously painted area

wet edge

lift

Begin brushing with the loaded side of the brush to the surface. Brush back toward the previously painted portion. Flow out the paint with as few strokes as possible. Finish with a stroke into the previously painted area, lifting the brush while the stroke is still in motion.

If the brush drags, add a *small* amount of thinner. If the paint runs or sags, you have added too much thinner.

Brushing technique.

MAINTENANCE

few drops of thinner, mix thoroughly, and try again. Continue to add thinner a few drops at a time until the paint flows out the way you want it to. If the paint develops a tendency to run, you have gone too far. You will need to add more paint, but keep in mind that it will take a cupful of paint to offset the effect of a capful of thinner.

What do you do when nature calls or you suffer a Big Mac attack? The answer is to wrap the paint roller and the brush in plastic kitchen wrap. Also pat a layer of plastic onto the surface of the paint in the tray, including the wet paint on the slope. Protect the paint in the container you are using with your brush the same way—by covering the surface of the paint with plastic. When you are ready to start painting again, just peel away the plastic, and your roller, brush, and paint will be as fresh as when you left.

When storing half a can of paint or less, you can extend the life of the paint by covering its surface with plastic before sealing the can. The plastic will protect the paint from the air in the can and keep the top from forming a skin. To use the paint, remove the plastic and mix the paint, thinning if necessary.

REFINISHING THE EXTERIOR

Two-part polyurethane paint is today the only sensible choice for restoring the gloss to an old fiberglass hull. Two coats of properly applied polyurethane should still have most of its gloss after five years and may last twice that long. And, as with varnish, if the first application has been done with care, when the time finally does arrive to repaint, it is basically a matter of sanding the surface and laying on a fresh coat.

Perhaps you have heard that polyurethane is expensive, dangerous, and finicky. All true, but don't be put off. Take expensive, for example. Polyurethane costs two to three times the price of the most expensive enamels, and it requires special primers and pricey solvents. But expensive is relative. Compared to the cost of enamel, the life of the polyurethane is the cheapest option in the long run—not to mention the savings in labor.

The reputation for danger is not exaggerated; polyurethane can kill you. However, when the paint is applied outside with a brush or a roller, protecting yourself from risk involves no more than wearing gloves and eye protection. The most serious hazards are associated exclusively with spray applications. The solution is simple: NEVER spray polyurethane. (Professional refinishers who do spray it wear protective suits and use positive-pressure respirators.) I have yet to see a paint job that would have been worth dying for. And the flow characteristics of polyurethane are so good that I defy you to tell the difference between a sprayed coating and one carefully applied with a roller and tipped with a brush.

What about finicky? Polyurethanes don't like high humidity, and they should be applied when the temperature is between 50 degrees and 85 degrees F. They prefer shade to direct sun, and any significant wind, aside from blowing trash into the finish, will actually set up tiny wave patterns in the free-flowing

> *Keep in mind that it will take a cupful of paint to offset the effect of a capful of thinner.*

paint. You can do most of the preparation in any weather, but you need a couple of dry, moderate, still days, preferably with a high overcast. Applying polyurethane in less than ideal conditions is almost certain to yield less than ideal results.

Should you take on this project at all? If you are willing to devote the time and have the patience, there is little reason why you should not attempt it. It is, after all, painting, not cutting holes in the hull. If you don't like the way it comes out, you can sand it down and do it again.

The question of *who* does the job may be academic anyway. Professionals in my part of the country (Florida) charge about $100 per foot to refinish a hull and $200 per foot for the deck. Not everyone can afford those prices; most smallboat owners can't even think in those terms.

Preparation

The first step is to select the *brand* of paint you are going to use. Optimum results are assured only if you follow the instructions of the specific manufacturer, including using the proprietary preparatory products (say that backward, three times!) that they recommend. Differences in chemical composition may make one manufacturer's primer less compatible with another manufacturer's finish coat. There is really no way of knowing if a different brand is compatible, so play it safe and buy fillers, primers, paint, and thinner from the same manufacturer.

If the hull of your old boat has been previously painted with anything other than a polyurethane, the aggressive solvents in the urethane are likely to affect the old coating like paint remover. If the surface is in good shape, a "conversion" coating can be applied to protect the old finish from the urethane, but if the old paint shows any signs of poor adhesion, it should be removed. Stripping a painted hull back to the gelcoat is never a bad idea unless the old coating is polyurethane.

Wash the hull (and/or deck) thoroughly to get it as clean as possible, then wipe it down with the specified solvent to remove all traces of wax. Fill all scratches and gouges in the gelcoat with the epoxy filler the paint manufacturer recommends and allow the epoxy to cure. Block-sand the repairs with 80-grit production paper, then sand the entire surface with 120-grit paper. A finishing sander is ideal for this step. Not long ago, when I stopped to talk with a couple refinishing their hull, I was astonished that they both had finishing sanders. The best ideas always seem to be so obvious!

If your gelcoat is in perfect shape, you need only wipe down the hull with solvent and lay on the polyurethane, but the gelcoat of few old boats is in such shape. Keep in mind that polyurethane, unlike alkyd enamel, goes on very thin and will not cover any flaws. In addition, the extreme gloss of polyurethane will actually highlight imperfections. To achieve a beautiful finish, the surface must be flawless, but the gelcoat of a neglected old boat is likely to be porous and perhaps crazed. The solution is epoxy primer.

After the gelcoat has been sanded and thoroughly wiped down with solvent, apply a coat of epoxy primer—the specific primer called for by the manufacturer—with a brush or a foam roller. Sand the cured primer with 120-grit paper, then inspect the surface closely. If all crazing and porosity is not filled, apply a second coat of primer. Once the prime coat has been sanded perfectly smooth and all traces of sanding dust have

been wiped away with solvent, you are ready to apply the urethane.

Painting the Hull

Follow the manufacturer's instructions for mixing and thinning the paint, using cups or spoons for accurate measurement of smaller quantities. More than any other single aspect of the process, thinning the paint with the *perfect* amount of solvent will lead to the perfect finish, but because of varying conditions, you cannot just add a specified amount of solvent. Some experimentation is required to get the paint thinned properly. When I painted my own hull, I painted the hull of my hard dinghy at the same time (including all the preparatory steps), making most of

> *Nothing has a more immediate impact on the way a boat looks than putting a mirror finish on the hull.*

the mistakes on the dinghy before I touched a bristle to the hull of the boat. One of the great characteristics of two-part polyurethane is that you will know almost immediately if you have it right. If the paint runs, it is too thin; if it fails to level out, you need to add solvent. The coating also needs to stay "wet" long enough for overlapping sections to flow together; if the paint sets too quickly, the temperature or the humidity may be too high. Pinholes or little craters in the paint indicate that the surface is still porous and you need additional primer. "Fish-eyes" indicate wax or other contaminants on the surface.

If you don't have a hard dinghy, maybe someone you know would accept a free paint job on theirs. If not, do your experimentation on the

transom where the motor will be or on the bottom of the boat, where it will be hidden on the trailer. Keep your testing area small, and if problems do show up you can remove the paint immediately with a solvent-soaked rag.

Two-part polyurethane has a pot life of about eight hours, but it remains stable for only about two hours before you have to start adding solvent to maintain the viscosity. You can mix enough paint in the morning to last the day, but pour up only what you will use in two hours and refrigerate the rest; refrigeration will extend the time it remains stable and minimize the amount of additional thinning that will be necessary. Determine the amount of paint to mix by measuring the surface you intend to paint.

Before you begin painting, wet down the ground around the boat thoroughly to hold down the dust. Tape off the rail and the bootstripe or the bottom paint with Fine-Line masking tape. Try to paint when the hull is in the shade.

Pour the paint into a paint tray and roll the coating on thinly with a special foam roller intended for use with polyurethane paints. (The solvents in polyurethane will dissolve standard foam rollers, leaving you with a flocked hull.) Immediately tip out the paint with a dry badger-hair (or other high-quality) brush; one or two even strokes back into the previous section will be sufficient. With two people painting—one rolling the paint onto the hull and the second following behind and leveling the paint with the tip of the brush—the side of a hull can be coated in a matter of minutes. And the results are stunning.

Two-part polyurethanes are always applied in at least two coats. The second coat, if applied within 48 hours, can be applied over the first coat without sanding, *but don't do it.* Allow the first coat to dry overnight, then wet-sand the entire surface with 340-grit wet-or-dry sandpaper. Flush away the resulting scum with plenty of fresh water. When the surface is totally dry, wipe it down with solvent and apply the final coat of polyurethane. Now look at your reflection in the hull with that stupid grin on your face. Try not to be too smug. Anybody can paint the flat expanse of a hull. When you can put the same flawless finish on the multifaceted surface of a deck, then you are entitled to brag.

Restoring the Deck

Preparing and painting the deck is the same as for the hull, with two important distinctions. The deck surface may be interrupted by handrails and hardware, not to mention windshield and hatches. And the integrity of the nonskid surface that covers much of the deck must be protected.

For the best refinishing job, remove as much of the deck hardware as you can. Removal has several benefits. First, it makes sanding and painting easier. Because it simplifies flowing out the paint, removal also tends to reduce lap marks and breaks in the finish that may result from painting around a cleat or handrail. It allows more of the surface to be initially coated by rolling, which yields a more uniform coating and a better finish than brush application. And it reduces the number of exposed edges; the reinstalled hardware sits *on* the new coating. Any deck hardware or features that will not be removed must be masked.

How you treat nonskid surfaces will depend upon the condition of the original texture. While some later molded-in patterns had sufficient definition not to be compromised by a

coat or two of polyurethane, most early nonskid was only marginally effective to begin with. Two coats of high-gloss paint added to two decades of wear yields a surface more suitable for ice skates than for deck shoes. You may also want the nonskid to be a different color from the rest of the deck.

Assuming that the nonskid requires special treatment—either to enhance the nonskid characteristics or to provide a contrasting color—the smooth portions and the nonskid portions of the deck will have to be painted separately. No such segregation is required for surface preparation. Once the entire deck has been de-waxed, filled, primed, and sanded as required, carefully mask the nonskid areas and apply two coats of polyurethane to the smooth areas.

There are two reasons for painting the smooth surfaces first. Typically the smooth areas are white, while the nonskid has color; color covers white better than the other way around. The second reason is that if the final masking is done on the nonskid rather than the smooth surface, a sharp line between the two will be difficult to achieve.

After coating the smooth surface, mask it and paint the nonskid panels. The nonskid properties of a painted surface are enhanced by adding grit to the paint in one of two ways. Paint manufacturers usually offer a nonskid additive—typically polymer beads—that is mixed into the paint, providing a rough surface as the paint is rolled on. (There is no reason to tip nonskid paint.) This method is effective, but because the beads tend to settle almost immediately to the bot-

tom of the paint tray, the resulting texture is usually irregular.

Shaking the grit onto the paint-coated surface provides a more uniform grit pattern. Sand, pumice, or ground walnut shells are the traditional grits, but the plastic spheres and beads of nonskid additives can also be applied this way. Apply a coat of epoxy primer and, while it is still wet, cover the surface entirely with grit sifted from your fingers or a large shaker. When the epoxy kicks, use a soft brush to gently sweep up the grit that did not adhere (it can be reused on another nonskid area). Roll on two coats of polyurethane, encapsulating the grit.

Painting the Bottom

If you have just put a mirror finish on the topsides, how much of a challenge can painting the bottom be? Not much. Sand the old coating smooth and roll on a couple of new coats.

—Don Casey
(*This Old Boat*,
International Marine, 1991)

> *How much of a challenge can painting the bottom be? Not much.*

NOTE: *Bottom paint is not required for boats kept on a trailer or in fresh water, which constitute the majority of craft under discussion in this book. If you do keep your boat in salt water and want greater detail on applying bottom paint and other finishes, Casey offers much additional information in* This Old Boat.—*DRG*

Freeing Frozen Parts

Problems with frozen fasteners are inevitable on boats. One or more of the following techniques may free things up.

LUBRICATION

Clean everything with a wire brush (preferably one with brass bristles), douse liberally with penetrating oil, and wait. Find something else to do for an hour or two—overnight if possible—before having another go. Be patient.

Clevis pins: After lubricating and waiting, grip the large end of the pin with Vise-Grips (mole wrench) and turn the pin in its socket to free it. If the pin is the type with a cotter pin (also known as a *cotter key* or *split pin*) in both ends, remove one of the cotter pins, grip the clevis pin, and turn. Since the Vise-Grips will probably mar the surface of the pin, it should be knocked out from the other end.

SHOCK TREATMENT

An impact wrench is a handy tool to have around. These take a variety of end fittings (screwdriver bits, sockets) to match different fasteners. The wrench is hit hard with a hammer and hopefully jars the fastener loose. If an impact wrench is not available or does not work, other forms of shock must be applied, with an acute sense of the breaking point of the fastener and adjacent engine castings, etc. Unfortunately this sense is generally acquired only after a lifetime of breaking things. Depending on the problem, shock treatment may take different forms:

For a bolt stuck in an engine block: Put a sizable punch squarely on the head of the bolt and give it a good knock into the block. Now try undoing it.

For a pulley on a tapered shaft, a propeller, or an outboard motor flywheel: Back out the retaining nut *until its face is flush with the end of the shaft* (this is important to avoid damage to the threads on the nut or shaft). Put pressure behind the pulley, propeller, or flywheel as if trying to pull it off, and hit the end of the retaining nut or shaft smartly. The shock will frequently break things loose without the need for a specialized puller.

For a large nut with limited room around it, or one on a shaft that wants to turn (for example, a crankshaft pulley nut): Put a short-handled wrench on the nut, hold the wrench to prevent it from jumping off, and hit it hard.

If all else fails, use a cold chisel to cut a slot in the side of the offending nut or the head of the bolt, place a punch in the slot at a tangential angle to the nut or bolt, and hit it smartly.

LEVERAGE

Screws: With a square-bladed screwdriver, put a crescent (adjustable) wrench on the blade, bear down hard on the screw, and turn the screwdriver with the wrench. If the screwdriver has a round blade, clamp a pair of Vise-Grips to the base of the handle and do the same thing.

Nuts and bolts: If using wrenches with one box end and one open end, put the box end of the appropriate wrench on the fastener and hook the box end of the next size up into the free open end of the wrench to double the length of the handle and thus the leverage.

Cheater pipe: Slip a length of pipe over the handle of the wrench to increase its leverage.

HEAT

Heat expands metal, but for this treatment to be effective, frozen fasteners must frequently be raised to cherry-red temperatures. These temperatures will upset tempering in hardened steel, while uneven heating of surrounding castings may cause them to crack. Heat must be applied with circumspection.

Heat applied to a frozen nut will expand it outward, and it can then be broken loose. But equally, heat applied to the bolt will expand it within the nut, generating all kinds of pressure that helps to break the grip of rust, etc. When the fixture cools, it will frequently come apart quite easily. [I've had luck using a Makita heat gun to loosen a frozen through hull. It didn't heat the metal to cherry-red, but it worked.—Ed.]

BROKEN FASTENERS

Rounded-off heads: Sometimes there is not enough head left on a fastener to grip with Vise-Grips or pipe (Stillson) wrenches, but there is enough to accept a slot made by a hacksaw. A screwdriver can then be inserted and turned as above.

If a head breaks off, it is often possible to remove whatever it was holding, thus exposing part of the shaft of the fastener, which can be lubricated, gripped with Vise-Grips, and backed out.

Drilling out: It is very important to drill down the center of a broken fastener. Use a center punch and take some time putting an accurate "dimple" at this point before attempting to drill. Next use a small drill to make a pilot hole to the desired depth. If Ezy-Outs or "screw extractors" (hardened, tapered steel screws with reversed threads, available from tool supply houses) are on hand, drill the correct-size hole for the appropriate Ezy-Out and try extracting the stud. Otherwise, drill out the stud *up to the insides of its threads, but no farther,* or you'll do irreparable damage to the threads in the casting. The remaining bits of fastener thread in the casting can be picked out with judicious use of a small screwdriver or some pointed instrument. If a tap is available to clean up the threads, so much the better.

Pipe fittings: If a hacksaw blade can be gotten inside the relevant fittings (which can often be done using duct tape to make a handle on the blade), cut a slit in the fitting along its length, and then place a punch on the outside alongside the cut, hit it, and collapse it inward. Do the same on the other side of the cut. The fitting should now come out easily.

MISCELLANEOUS

Stainless steel: Stainless-to-stainless fasteners (many turnbuckles, for example) have a bad habit of "galling" when being done up or undone, especially if there is any dirt in the threads to cause friction. Galling (otherwise known as *cold welding*) is a process in which molecules on the surface of one part of the fastener transfer to the other part. Everything seizes up for good. Galled stainless fastenings cannot be salvaged—they almost always end up shearing off. When doing up or undoing a stainless fastener, if any sudden or unusual friction develops, stop immediately, let it cool off, lubricate thoroughly, work the fastener backward and

forward to spread the lubricant around, go back the other way, clean the threads, and start again.

Aluminum: Aluminum oxidizes to form a dense white powder. Aluminum oxide is more voluminous than the original aluminum and so generates a lot of pressure around any fasteners passing through aluminum fixtures—sometimes enough pressure to shear off the heads of fasteners. Once oxidation around a stainless or bronze fastener has reached a certain point it is virtually impossible to remove the fastener without breaking it.

Damaged threads: If all else fails and a fastener has to be drilled out, the threads in the casting may be damaged. There are two options: to drill and tap for the next larger fastener; or to install a Heli-Coil insert. A Heli-Coil is a new thread. An oversized hole is drilled and tapped with a special tap, and the Heli-Coil insert (the new thread) is screwed into the hole with a special tool. You end up with the original-size hole and threads. Any good machine shop will have the relevant tools and inserts.

—Nigel Calder
(*Repairs at Sea,*
International Marine, 1988)

Inflatable Care and Repair

The toughness of inflatable boats means that they tend to lead a life of neglect, but like any boat, an inflatable needs a bit of care and maintenance if it is going to have a long and active life. Unless the boat is very heavily used, a check-through once a year is probably adequate to identify any problems.

For the smaller, yacht-tender type of inflatable, this check entails care-

fully looking over the whole boat for any areas where the woven fabric is showing through the coating and checking the seams to make sure that the covering tape is still glued down well. The valves should be cleaned out with fresh water and their metal parts examined for corrosion. If a boat is going to be stowed away for any length of time, washing and drying it thoroughly is a good practice.

For the larger inflatables with floorboards, the most likely area of wear is at the bottom of the transom and along the inside of the boat where the four corners of the floorboards are designed to live together in reasonable harmony with the fabric; when sand gets into the bottom of the boat, the continual movement of the inflatable causes abrasion.

Howard Shure of The Air Works,

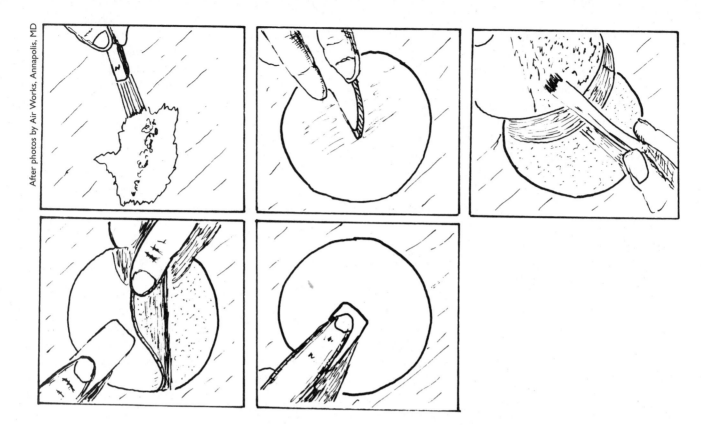

Leak Repair (left to right): To locate a leak, brush a detergent-and-water mixture on the tube and watch for the tell-tale bubbles. Mark the area and roughen both the tube and patch. For a tidy job, cut the patch to match the repair area, apply at least two coats of glue to both surfaces, and allow to become tacky dry. Then roll the patch onto the tube starting at one side and working toward the other. Pressing a blunt knife over the patch forces out any trapped air.

an inflatable-boat repair center in Annapolis, Maryland, recommends periodically disassembling the boat and rinsing out any sand and dirt. Maintaining proper inflation levels will also help keep the hull from working and abrading itself.

The floorboards themselves may need a coat of paint or varnish, and so may the transom. Otherwise, the maintenance is much the same as that for the smaller inflatables. Also, inspect the attachment point of any lines, particularly if the boat is fitted with outside lifelines, which inevitably seem to wear every time you go alongside.

If you find areas of wear and tear on the boat or if you have a leaking tube, then it is time to get out the boat repair kit. (Inflatable-boat repair kits are available from manufacturers, dealers, and repair centers.) It doesn't require a lot of skill to put a patch on, but it does require very careful preparation and attention to detail if you are going to get the patch to stick properly. The repair kit contains pieces of the same fabric from which the boat is made, and some special glue. The one-part glues that are simply squeezed onto the surface and the patch are generally not successful over the long haul, but will serve for emergency repairs that will get you back to the dock.

In the original construction of the boat, most manufacturers use a two-part glue in which ingredients are mixed before applying. These glues are much stronger and more durable than one-part systems, though more demanding in the way they are applied.

> Dampness and high humidity are the enemies of good repair work.

LEAKS

If you have a leaking air tube, first find the leak. A hole may be very obvious if the boat has been damaged, but you can also get small pinprick leaks. The way to find these is to mix up some detergent and water, then brush this over the surface of the tube. The leak will soon reveal itself by the collection of bubbles.

Ideally, inflatable repairs should be

carried out in a warm, dry atmosphere, but if you have to do them in the field, then some form of localized heating will help the process along. Dampness and high humidity are the enemies of good repair work, as are wind and direct sunlight.

For proper adhesion, surface preparation is extremely important. If your inflatable is made of Hypalon, first thoroughly clean the fabric around the area with fresh water. Then rub it down with coarse sandpaper or a pumice stone to create a fresh, rough surface for the glue. Cut out the patch with a generous overlap (2 inches minimum) and give the patch surface the same treatment as the tube. For a really tidy patch, you should draw around the patch on the tube before you start so that you know the precise area on which to apply glue.

Finally, clean both surfaces with a solvent such as toluene or acetone. (These are potent chemicals; wear rubber gloves and work in a well-ventilated area.) When this is dry, apply a thin coat of glue to the tube and the patch. Do not touch the surface of the fabric with your fingers. Allow these to dry (about 10 minutes) and then apply a second or third coat, according to the manufacturer's directions. When this coat is tacky, apply the patch to the tube, starting at one side and rolling it on. Then press a small metal roller or blunt knife over the patch to make sure any trapped air is excluded and that the edges are firmly glued down. After a couple of hours, it should be possible to inflate the boat, and you are back in business.

For inflatables manufactured with a Strongan fabric (such as Zodiac or Bombard) the process is similar; however, the preparation of the surface is different. No sanding or

> *It does require very careful preparation and attention to detail if you are going to get the patch to stick properly.*

roughing up of the surface is necessary, and the cleaning/prepping is done with MEK (methyl ethyl ketone). In addition, a different glue, which is available from the manufacturer, is required for this material.

The same procedure applies if you are applying a patch over an area of badly chafed fabric or repairing any partly unstuck patches or fittings. In the latter case, you need to lift the existing fabric back to a soundly glued area. This can be done by carefully applying hot air from a heat gun and gradually easing the pieces apart.

TEARS

Once you have mastered the technique of gluing, it is possible to tackle fairly major repairs, but for these you must plan very carefully. For a major split in an air tube, you have to patch inside and out, and it is tricky to get the inside patch on, because you are closing up the hole while you are doing so. The final gluing down of this inside patch can be achieved by very gentle inflation of the air tube. For a professional-looking repair, go to a professional repair shop.

Finally, if you have an older inflatable boat, it is possible to paint it. Special Hypalon-based paints are available for this purpose, but if these are to be used successfully, very careful surface preparation over the whole of the boat is essential. Don't expect wonders with these paints. They will never restore the boat to its former glory.

A final note of caution: A painted inflatable boat can be much more difficult to repair than one in its original form.

—Dag Pike
(*Small Boat Journal* #52)

The Marine Supermarket: Finishing Touches

If it's marine, it costs twice as much.

I believed this old saw for many years, cursing the ripoff artists gouging us poor boatowners and often doing without rather than paying what appeared to be outrageous prices for the things I wanted. Time— and a good deal of comparison shopping—has mellowed my attitude. You can pay exorbitant prices for just as many "civilian" goods as you can for marine stuff. And most of the high prices in both markets are on the fancy goods, where they ought to be.

Many of your everyday marine items can be bought at reasonable cost, although, as with your ordinary goods, you may have to shop for any real bargains. In determining what is an acceptable price, it is only fair to remember that if some marine products seem more costly, there is often a perfectly logical reason—they have to be made to stand up to a hostile environment. To meet that requirement costs the manufacturer—and you—money. Doubt it? Just compare ordinary latex house paint and two-part polyurethane boat paint. Both are designed to cover an exterior surface and last for several years. But you would probably be losing money if you used the much cheaper latex for your boat hull. It would look lousy and be gone in no time. The only thing the two products have in common is the name "paint."

Which is not to say there are no good substitutes at cheaper prices for some marine products. There are, but to find the worthwhile ones you have to know the characteristics of the product in order to judge if it will survive in the marine world. For instance, most stainless steel products will thrive in almost any environment. But some of the cheap stainless will rust if exposed to salt water, and a lot of good stainless will corrode in a closed, wet, salty environment, such as a stainless steel retaining band on a boat fuel tank. The exterior will look fine, but the side pressed against the tank metal may be being eaten away.

A person coming fresh into boating is certain to be baffled by many of the aspects and requirements of the game. Boating has its own language and a perplexing array of specialized products, some of which are absolutely necessary and many of which are not. It is possible to muddle through, especially if your boating will be limited to fair days on quiet waters. But if you are serious, you will need knowledge about generic marine items—what they are for, where you can get them, and how much they cost. Fortunately, there are a number of excellent sources of

information, some of which are close at hand even if you live in the middle of the desert.

Four of them we will consider here. They are marine stores and chandleries; catalogs, both regional and national; department stores; and hardware stores. The last two sources are also good places to find less-expensive alternatives to certain marine products, although one must be careful here, because a marine version of the product may actually be available at a cheaper price. *All* retailers use sales to keep their inventories turning over.

MARINE STORES AND CHANDLERIES

A visit to a marine store or chandlery

> A visit to a marine store or chandlery is time well spent even if you do not plan to buy anything.

is time well spent even if you do not plan to buy anything. There is no substitute for seeing an item firsthand, asking about its use, feeling it, and evaluating it for your specific needs. You will also see related equipment, some of which may do a better job than the item you had originally considered. If you are the handy type, you will see some things that can be built just as well in the home shop and be customized to your boat at the same time.

And always watch for goods on sale. If you know beforehand what a particular item might normally cost (and that is not necessarily the "list" price used to make the sale price look better), *and if you need it,* this may be a good chance to save money. Of course, if you buy it only because it's

such a bargain, the item will probably join the clutter of other super deals that gather dust in the garage or rust in the bilge.

In coastal areas where commercial fishing is active, local or regional marine suppliers usually stock gear and equipment for both commercial mariners and recreational boaters. Frequently, these products are excellent choices for the small-boat skipper whose equipment may get just as hard use as that aboard a fishing boat. We have received first-rate service from Hamilton Marine, Inc. (East Maine Street, Searsport, ME 04974; 207-548-6302), a supplier to the boatbuilding and fishing industries, and you may find a similar business in your area. They are worth looking for.

Many retail stores, including Hamilton Marine, also publish catalogs. The next section lists some of the better ones.

CATALOGS

For sheer variety, product description, good prices, and quite often excellent generic information on such necessary gear as rope, anchors, and the like, a good marine catalog can't be topped. Two excellent ones are the Boat/U.S. Equipment Catalog and M & E Marine Supply Co. Boating Supply Catalog. They are singled out only to show two different approaches to selling marine gear. Both guarantee no-hassle returns and refunds, an important consideration when buying by mail.

The Boat/U.S. catalog is published by the Boat Owners Association of the United States, a membership organization that works like a cooperative. With a membership of nearly one-half million, Boat/U.S. provides its members with "savings, service and representation." Its "Price Guard" program guarantees the lowest "everyday" prices available and vows to match any proved lower. In comparing its prices against similar products in other catalogs, we found Boat/U.S. prices consistently among the lowest, but not always *the* lowest. The association also offers a number of services, ranging from towing to travel to insurance to charters. A consumer protection bureau and a product information phone line are useful services when a member feels puzzled by claims or put down by a warranty hassle. Boat/U.S. membership is $17 from Boat/U.S., 880 South Pickett Street, Alexandria, VA 22304-4606. The Boat/U.S. catalog, by the way, has more generic information on marine products than any other we have seen.

The M & E catalog (M & E Marine Supply Co., Inc., P.O. Box 601, Camden, NJ 08101) is a more traditional sales publication, printed on good-quality newsprint and listing thousands of items, many of which are described in detail. Of particular note are its wide variety of marine hardware and its several pages of boat-trailer parts and accessories.

Other marine catalogs we have seen on the same level as those above include Overton's (111 Red Banks Road, P.O. Box 8228, Greenville, NC 27835; 1-800-334-6541). Claiming to be "The World's Largest Water Sports Dealer," Overton's also carries an impressive line of electronics and trailer parts. Its full-color catalog is particularly well laid out. On the West Coast, West Marine (Catalog Sales Division, P.O. Box 50050, Watsonville, CA 95077-5050; 1-800-538-0775) also publishes an easily read color catalog. While there is much here for the yachtsman, there is also a good se-

lection of small-boat equipment.

One of the best outboard-boat suppliers is E & B Discount Marine (201 Meadow Road, P.O. Box 3138, Edison, NJ 08818-3138; 1-800-533-5007). Strong on electronics, accessories, and gear for small boats, E & B has impressively low prices. All three of these suppliers pride themselves on their no-hassle guarantees.

Specialty catalogs can be of great use to small-boat owners looking for specific gear. An exceptional catalog for the fisherman is Cabela's Fishing, Hunting and Outdoor Gear Catalog (Cabela's, 812 13th Avenue, Sidney, NE 69160). In addition to a breathtaking amount of fishing gear (mostly, but not exclusively, for fresh water), there is an excellent boating section, highlighted by several pages

> *Boating has its own language and a perplexing array of specialized products, some of which are absolutely necessary and many of which are not.*

on electric outboard motors and electronic depthsounders/fish finders. And for the small-boat skipper looking to outfit for camp cruising, there are few places with a greater selection of camping gear at good prices than the Campmor Catalog (810 Route 17 North, P.O. Box 997-H, Paramus, NJ 07653-0997; 1-800-526-4784).

DEPARTMENT STORES

Another source of gear for your small boat is local department stores, especially some of the big chains that can buy goods in large quantities and sell at low margins. If you know what you are looking for, this can be

a big advantage, and you may find some items at true discount prices; if not, you can end up with gear and gadgets that just won't stand up to hard use, especially a saltwater environment that can test the best of equipment. Be wary of anything made of metal, particularly so if it will be used around salt water. Coatings of paint, thin chrome, cadmium plating, and the like will quickly deteriorate in these harsh conditions. By contrast, rugged plastics like polyethylene are usually safe choices, welcome aboard small boats because of their ability to stand up to the bashing they are almost certain to receive.

The department store is also a great place to find real bargains in storage containers, including coolers of all sorts and sizes. We have found coolers make fine storage compartments for things other than food, because they are waterproof and their hinged covers make them readily accessible. If food storage will be the primary use, then good insulation is critical. Thin sides will provide more space if straight storage is planned. In any event, the coolers should be strong enough to sit on (they will be, in any event!). Avoid metal models or coolers with metal handles or hinges, because they corrode and because they break.

HARDWARE STORES

A fourth source of boat equipment, although it rarely is considered as such, is the hardware store. Well-stocked stores have good selections of galvanized, stainless, and other rust-resistant fastenings, and, as would be expected, a vast choice of tools. However, our experience shows that a few basic tools (blade and Phillips screwdrivers, pliers, hammer, crescent wrench, plug wrench [that fits your spark plugs], and an assortment of stainless steel fastenings) will cover one's needs aboard. The places to mine for potential treasure are the other departments. In the plumbing section you will find several kinds of plastic and metal pipe with every fitting imaginable. Here we found a perfect tip for our boat's push pole, a reducer fitting for copper pipe—the soft metal "grips" well on rock and shrugs off salt water with nothing more than a thin film of green. In the building department are such useful things as acrylic sheets (Plexiglas), wood rods and dowels of all sizes, a variety of aluminum stock, and both exterior and marine plywood. When you have an hour or so, just go looking. You won't be wasting your time.

—DRG

MAINTENANCE

INDEX

Note: Numbers in **boldface** refer to illustrations.

If you enjoyed *Outboard Boater's Handbook,* you may be interested in the following books from the International Marine library.

Northeast Guide to Saltwater Fishing & Boating (Maine to Virginia, including Delaware & Chesapeake bays)

edited by Vin Sparano

Where can you get to the water? What fish can you expect to find and when? What's the best rig? What about licenses? Records? Launch ramps? It's all here, plus advice on techniques, baits, and much more from 15 experts who collectively have spent close to 300 years fishing the waters of the Northeast. Heading farther south? Pick up a copy of *Southeast Guide to Saltwater Fishing & Boating* (Virginia to Florida, including The Keys and Gulf Coast).

Northeast Guide: Paperbound, 384 pages, 260 illustrations, $24.95. Item No. 158023-9

Southeast Guide: Paperbound, 384 pages, 260 illustrations, $24.95. Item No. 047979-8

Boatowner's Guide to Marine Electronics, Third Edition

Gordon West and Freeman Pittman

Takes you from purchasing to installing, integrating, using, and optimizing equipment such as radar, Loran, satnav, GPS, and cellular telephones.

"Well worth its cover price. No matter what kind of boat you own, this guide will help take the mystery out of marine electronic equipment and how to use it to its full potential." —*The Ensign*

Paperbound, 272 pages, 168 illustrations, $19.95. Item No. 069549-0

The Old Outboard Book,
Revised and Expanded Edition

Peter Hunn

Now that you've got your outboard running, why not try your hand at finding an older kicker and starting a collection? Peter Hunn—a lifetime collector of outboard motors—details their history and provides practical advice. The new edition features rarity ratings, the first-ever price guide, and a chapter on miniature outboards.

"Love old outboard motors? Check out *The Old Outboard Book*."
—Motor Boating & Sailing

Paperbound, 288 pages, 255 illustrations, $19.95. Item No. 031281-8

Fine Boat Finishes

Paul and Marya Butler

Lays out simply and clearly how to achieve a professional finish on wooden or fiberglass boats—everything from varnishing brightwork to cosmetic hull repairs and painting.

"Not only packed with information, it's also fun to read. Just about all types of finishes are investigated, on both wood and fiberglass boats. This is an excellent book."
—Better Boat

Paperbound, 160 pages, 112 illustrations, $15.95. Item No. 009403-9

Fiberglass Boat Repair Manual

Allan H. Vaitses

Covers not just cosmetic dings and scratches, but also major repairs of structural damage to hull and decks, delamination, refinishing, blistering, and more. Invaluable for anyone seeking to buy an old and perhaps damaged boat.

"Represents the distillation of half a lifetime of experience. . . . Filled with excellent drawings that serve as almost infallible guides. . . ."*—SAIL*

Hardbound, 192 pages, 200 illustrations, $29.95. Item No. 156914-9

The Complete Canvasworker's Guide: How to Outfit Your Boat with Fabric, Second Edition

Jim Grant

A thorough, step-by-step guide to making all common items of fabric boat gear, including boat covers, bags, sail covers, bosun's chairs, cushions, dodgers, bimini tops, flags, hatch covers, and much more. This new edition is larger by half than the universally praised first edition.

Paperbound, 192 pages, 230 illustrations, $19.95. Item No. 024080-9

Boatbuilding with Aluminum

Stephen F. Pollard

Compared with building with wood, far fewer skills and specialized tools are needed to build aluminum boats, and high-quality materials are more easily found. Only a lack of information has kept aluminum from becoming a popular material for backyard boatbuilders and small-scale professionals. Here, for the first time, is everything builders need to know to successfully build aluminum boats of almost any size or type.

Hardbound, 288 pages, 174 illustrations, $29.95. Item No. 050426-1

Look for These
and Other International Marine Books
at Your Local Bookstore

**To Order, Call Toll Free, day or night: 1-800-822-8158; or Fax 614-759-3644;
or Write to International Marine, c/o McGraw-Hill, Inc., P.O. Box 182067,
Columbus, OH 43218-2607**

Title	Item No.	Quantity	Amount

| | | Subtotal: | $ _____ |

Shipping and Handling Charges		
Order Amount	Within U.S.	Outside U.S.
Less than $15	$3.50	$5.50
$15.00–$24.99	$4.00	$6.00
$25.00–$49.99	$5.00	$7.00
$50.00–$74.99	$6.00	$8.00
$75.00–and up	$7.00	$9.00

Subtotal: $ _____

Shipping and Handling
(charge from chart at left): $ _____

Add applicable state and local sales tax: $ _____

TOTAL: $ _____

❏ Check or money order made payable to McGraw-Hill

Charge my   ❏ VISA   ❏ MasterCard   ❏ American Express

Acct. No.: _____ Exp.: _____

Signature: _____

Name: _____

Address: _____

City: _____

State: _____ Zip: _____

Daytime Telephone No.: _____